Civil Society, Constitution, and Legitimacy

Civil Society, Constitution, and Legitimacy

Andrew Arato

ROWMAN & LITTLEFIELD PUBLISHERS, INC.
Lanham · Boulder · New York · Oxford

ROWMAN & LITTLEFIELD PUBLISHERS, INC.

Published in the United States of America
by Rowman & Littlefield Publishers, Inc.
4720 Boston Way, Lanham, Maryland 20706
http://www.rowmanlittlefield.com

12 Hid's Copse Road
Cumnor Hill, Oxford OX2 9JJ, England

British Cataloging in Publication Information Available

Library of Congress Cataloging-in-Publication Data

Arato, Andrew.
    Civil society, constitution, and legitimacy / Andrew Arato
        p.   cm.
    Includes bibliographical references and index.
    ISBN 0-8476-8771-6 (cloth : alk.paper)—ISBN 0-8476-8772-4 (pbk. : alk. paper)
    1. Europe, Eastern—Politics and government—1989–   . 2. Post-communism—Europe,
Eastern.   3. Civil society—Europe, Eastern.   4. Constitutional history—Europe, Eastern.
5. Democracy—Europe, Eastern.   I. Title.
    JN96.A58 A68   2000
    321.09'094—dc2   99-055368

Printed in the United States of America

♾™ The paper used in this publication meets the minimum requirements of American
National Standard for Information Sciences—Permanence of Paper for Printed Library
Materials, ANSI/NISO Z.39.48–1992.

To My Hungarian Friends

Contents

Preface

The studies in this volume are products of almost ten years of reflections on the meaning and consequences of the democratic eruptions of 1989. They are not products of value-free social research. The author takes his stand on the side of those seeking to introduce liberal and democratic institutions in Central and East Europe, and specifically those friends and colleagues in Hungary who have contributed so much to the almost miraculous outcome: a more or less consolidated, on the whole well-functioning parliamentary democratic regime. The book is dedicated to these friends, above all to János Kis, the leader of the Hungarian Democratic Opposition in the 1980s.

Written at a time of great change, the chapters, and even more the book as a whole, have a developmental character. Most noticeably they document a shift in interest from the problem of civil society to that of constitutional politics. My abiding interest in the concept of civil society is expressed in chapters 1 and 2. In the first of these, dealing with Western interpretations, I focus on the absence of the concept of civil society or its particular use as the most important clue to the inadequacy of the analyses I criticize. My critique of the so-called theories of transition requires going beyond such a limited framework of criticism, owing to the unusually ambitious nature of the relevant conceptions. In the second chapter, I reconstruct the career of the politics of civil society in Hungary and Poland from about 1976 on, squarely facing the issue of implosion stressed by many theorists of transition, but avoiding the diagnosis that demobilization must mean obliteration or even "normalization." Recognizing the empirical phenomena of the depolitization of civic initiatives and social movements at the time of the Round Tables and the first competitive elections, I was nevertheless deeply concerned about the neglect of autonomous associations and publics in the emerging political designs and in the policy-making process. I came to the conclusion, however, based on my differentiation between civil society as movement and as institution,[1] that civil society had to be securely institutionalized before becoming a key terrain of participatory politics in the long term. Thus while I now admit that a weakly institutionalized civil society of movements could seriously interfere with the emergence of a workable party system, without which modern democracy is impossible, I call for the institutionalization rather than the atomization of civil society. As A. Stepan and J. Linz have shown, such institutionalization is especially important for the stage of the consolidation of democracy.[2]

I have always stressed fundamental civil and political rights as the necessary conditions for the institutionalization of a modern civil society. These rights, however, could be established only in a setting that satisfies the demands of liberal constitutionalism. This is how I can explain my shift in interest to the study of constitution making, constitutional adjudication, and constitutional politics. Liberal constitutionalism today can be established only by designing, gaining the acceptance for, and legally enforcing modern constitutional documents. Such is especially the case where formerly legal nihilism and paper constitutions were the rule.

As the third chapter, "Revolution, Restoration, and Legitimation," demonstrates, I was greatly concerned about the dangers to the establishment and survival of constitutionalism in the midst of radical democratic transformations in the countries of the former Soviet imperium. Nevertheless, I believed that in Hungary at least (and in several other countries too), the overall trend of institutional change would adhere to a constitutionalist pattern, because of the experience with the self-limiting politics of civil society that went under names like "the new evolutionism" and the "self-limiting revolution," to the fully negotiated character of the regime change, to the adherence to the rule of law at all stages, and to the emergence of a strong constitutional court. The resistance of the political culture, shaped through evolutionary processes away from Communist rule, to populist and revolutionary enticements and rhetoric may have been even more important. The positive outcome was nevertheless hardly predetermined. In potential crisis situations the new democracies especially have to rely on the always scarce resource of political legitimacy if they are to defend their new institutions. Several of the studies (chapters 4 and 5, and on a more empirical level, chapter 6) are therefore concerned with the problem of how the existing constitutionalist pattern could be reinforced through democratic legitimacy.

Negotiated transitions on the pattern pioneered in Spain around 1977, later accomplished in some Latin American countries as well as in Poland, Hungary, and Bulgaria, and most recently in South Africa, have great advantages from the point of view of liberal democratic institution building. The maintenance of the rule of law at all stages especially helps avoiding the revolutionary hiatus when all new institutions seem to be "built on sand."[3] But negotiated transitions do have important liabilities as well. That absence of political legitimacy, which, in the analysis of János Kis, is characteristic of regime change through Round Table compromise,[4] is difficult to make up for even during subsequent political change. Free elections, for example, organized under negotiated formulae obviously help legitimate the emerging governments, but cannot, logically at least, do the same for the constitutional formulae (i.e., the regime structure) under which they take place. This legitimation deficit is the reason why I took the danger of a "second revolution" as seriously as I did, even in a country like Hungary where the mood of the immense majority remained decidedly nonrevolutionary.

The legitimation of constitutional regimes has now occurred in several countries. The mechanisms or models followed have been different in almost all of the cases. Here I can mention the cases I have stressed in the chapters themselves. In Romania revolutionary constitution making through a constituent assembly and provisional government was initially denounced by very small opposition forces as an imposition by an organized minority. The charge was certainly correct, even if the overthrow of Nicolae Ceausescu and his allies earned a great deal of credit for the National Revolutionary Front in the eyes of the population. When the resulting constitution, in part modeled on the French Fifth Republic, came to be used as the framework of effective political opposition and alternation in power, the document came to acquire general authority. In Bulgaria the rather exemplary procedure that produced a well-drafted constitution has always been illegitimate in the eyes of the main anti-Communist grouping because of the control of the process of drafting by forces from the old regime. As late as 1996 the opposition demonstrated against the Round Table and its constitutional heritage. But when, for the second time, these forces of the opposition relying on constitutional means were able to replace the restored Communist Party, their attitude to the inherited basic law fundamentally changed. Even its overrigidity was no longer considered a potential hindrance to constitutional learning. Of this, however, I am unconvinced.

Constitutions produced by full-fledged constituent assemblies can rely on relatively strong revolutionary and/or democratic legitimacy. In Romania the credentials of the "revolutionaries" were earned above all by getting rid of the hated ruling clique, while in Bulgaria the democratic procedural legitimacy of the constituent assembly was difficult to challenge, in spite of the great dissatisfaction of the non-Communist forces with the substantive meaning of the process.

A strong claim of initial constitutional legitimacy was asserted in both cases by the difficult amendment rules enacted from the beginning. These rules, as chapter 4 maintains, may be well conceived and even innovative in themselves. They would be excellent rules to establish *after* a period of constitutional learning. As Steven Holmes and Cass Sunstein have argued, however, when introduced too early rules may interfere with learning processes necessary in countries without traditions of democracy and constitutionalism.[5]

Thus when problems of design inevitably emerge, a system that is consolidated too early may not be able to respond. In 1996, for example, Bulgarians discovered that the popular election of a president can delegitimate a previously elected parliament controlled by another party. Without a limited presidential right of dissolution of Parliament as in the French Fifth Republic, the issue could be resolved only by large-scale collective action bordering on violence. Clearly the constitution should now be amended to provide for a right of dissolution at least in this specific situation. The existing amendment rule, however, interferes with institutionalizing what has been learned.

Evidently, piecemeal parliamentary constitution making as in Poland and Hungary is advantageous from the point of view of initial learning. Moreover, such an approach does not inevitably mean that the period of constitution creation will remain open indefinitely, with all the negative consequences rightly stressed by Bruce Ackerman.[6] In Poland a constitutional learning process did lead by 1997 to the drafting, enactment, and ratification of a modern liberal democratic constitution. Aside from the issue of constitutional legitimacy, the Polish framers successfully dealt with the deep systemic problem of their interim constitution caused by the incoherent relationship of parliament and presidency. Today Poland is unambiguously a parliamentary republic. To be sure, an analogous but less grave systemic problem of the separation of powers in the supposedly temporary Hungarian constitution did not sufficiently motivate constitution makers in Budapest. Admittedly, the conflict of two protoconstituent powers, Parliament and Constitutional Court, does not deform ordinary day-to-day politics to the same extent as jurisdictional struggles between a president like Lech Walesa and the legislature. Yet this relationship is nevertheless a potentially troubling one. Unfortunately, the parties that were to lead the constitution-making effort between 1994 and 1996 in Hungary were not blessed, as were their Polish colleagues, with the absence from the legislature of right-wing formations that wished for constitutions very different in structure than the parliamentary republic promoted by the liberal forces that led the regime change. Finally, the leadership of the Hungarian post-Communists around Gyula Horn turned out to be far less loyal to the new liberal democratic order than the analogous forces around President Aleksander Kwasniewski. For all these reasons the attempt of Hungarian constitution makers to rationalize and relegitimate the public law regime that emerged in the regime change could be sabotaged by an unlikely combination of forces, the only time (fortunately) when a red-black coalition reared its ugly head in that country.

To be sure, even in Hungary the constitution of the regime change that was created primarily between 1989 and 1990 does remain in place. In future moments of challenge, this serviceable constitution will at best have to rely on a species of traditional legitimacy, one administered and cultivated by the justices of the Constitutional Court, the elders of the republic. If this is the future,[7] the Achilles' heel of the regime will remain the built-in contradiction (unique in the world) between the extraordinary powers of this very same Constitutional Court and the quasi-constituent powers of a parliament in which, because of the given electoral rule I have repeatedly criticized,[8] it is not too difficult for ruling coalitions to attain a constitution-amending super majority.

I cannot prove with any rigor that democratic and liberal forms of constitutional legitimacy are necessary conditions of democratic consolidation. Nevertheless, I strongly believe that this is the case, even if functional substitutes are always imaginable. The point can be made plausible in light of the challenges faced by the relevant countries. Even radical economic deprivation and dislocation; the emergence of second revolutionary, counterrevolutionary, and nationalist rhetoric; and, in two of the cases—Bulgaria and Romania—total international disinterest, have not led to the weakening of democratic institutions in the four countries I mentioned. The same could also be said about the Czech Republic and Slovakia. Compared with a similar group of other countries in any other region having gone through democratic transitions in the face of even less severe systemic problems, this is a fantastically good record. Not only do I believe that effective constitutionalism and the political stability it provided played an important role in all this, but in any future similar situation, with the new learning experiences at our disposal, I would recommend paying even greater attention to constitutional politics.

I am convinced that the spectacular success of the South African parties to manage the explosive potentialities of their own great transformation could not have been possible without appropriating the lessons in constitutionalism of at least some of the Central European countries. The South African constitution makers learned both the importance of interim arrangements for constitutional learning and the importance of setting up a timetable within which the interim constitution would have to be replaced by a genuinely democratic final synthesis.[9] It was this attention to learning and time that guaranteed the conclusion of the process in a noncontingent way without damage to democratic legitimacy. The institutionalization of a learning period also allowed South Africans the use of crucial, but in the long term dangerous, consociational structures within a manageable time frame and their timely replacement with constitutionalist and federalist safeguards.[10]

The experience of constitution making in the new democracies has put constitutional politics on the international agenda. The challenges of the end of the Cold War and new forms of regional and global integration certainly seem to imply that it is not only the former authoritarian regimes that should consider the redesign of their constitutional structures. My last chapter, "Forms of Constitution Making and Theories of Democracy," seeks to present what I have learned from the experience of the new democracies about constitutional politics. Note that I continue to accept Ackerman's key contribution to the contemporary discussion: a conception of constitutional (as against ordinary) politics that focuses around the related problems of making, amending, and adjudicating constitutions. I too think that the traditional American emphasis on judicial review has to be corrected by reference to democratic constitutional politics. Unlike Ackerman, I do not think that the supposedly original moment of constitution creation outside of legality represents the best understanding of constitutional politics within constitutions. Maintaining the parallel between creating and amending, I instead wish to argue that it is the democratic amending process, "always under law,"[11] that should be the model for a dedramatized understanding of constitution making. My proposal of regulating constitutional legislation by pragmatic combination of normative principles applies equally to amending and creating.

Of course I do recognize that the maintenance of legality within change may not be strictly possible in the case of authoritarian regimes or even democratic ones with extremely rigid constitutions like the U.S. Articles of Confederation of 1781 and the French Constitution of 1791. Accordingly, I consider the efforts of Central European constitution makers, especially the architects of the Round Tables, to postulate the fiction of legal continuity with a past without legality, one equivalent to the fiction of operating within a legally binding constitution, highly innovative and worthy of imitation. From a point of view informed by their efforts the past too will look different. We will be impressed, not by the extralegal actions of James Madison and the Federalists, of the makers of the 14th Amendment, and of the proponents and judicial opponents of the New Deal, but by their various and different efforts to repair a legality threatened by their own actions. As Hannah Arendt recognized in her critique of the Abbé Sieyès (in reality Carl Schmitt!), the idea that the constituent power is in the state of nature cannot be the foundation of viable constitutional democracy. Unfortunately she could point only to the single and unique experience of the American revolutionaries who were able to build something entirely new on institutional continuity. It is the great contribution of the Central and East European struggle for legality in the midst of radical transformation that, even without inherited republican institutions, the new can be built without total rupture with the past. This past can be changed more radically and in a more desirable normative direction when its formal and, originally, entirely fictional capacity for change is exploited rather than totally denied.

Chapter 1

Interpreting 1989

One can sympathize with Karl Marx in 1843; it is not easy to interpret the revolutions of others. Theirs is the golden field of action, while we are left with the gray realm of theory. In the late 1970s and early 1980s the role Marx assigned to the practical French belonged to the Poles, while the one that he half-ironically reserved for the theoretical Germans fell to Hungarians.[1] But fortunately, by 1988 at the latest, the action came to Hungary too, and, along with Poles, Hungarians were to lead the great transformation that spread to the western, the eastern, and the southern peripheries of the Soviet imperium. With the best East European intellectuals involved in politics and other practical tasks, the task of global interpretation seems to have fallen to Westerners, at least for a while.

Of course Marx's formula was not actually right for the epoch of the French Revolution; it represented either a mere joke, or incredible theoretical hubris. Evidently the greatest of all revolutions had distinguished interpreters in many European countries, including France itself: counterrevolutionaries like Joseph de Maistre, conservatives like Edmund Burke, liberals like Benjamin Constant, Jules Michelet, François Guizot, and Alexis de Tocqueville, radical socialists like Marx himself as well as Pyotr Kropotkin.

Today too there is a geographical spread of interpretations. It is nevertheless striking that the most significant comprehensive efforts so far have come from the West, from outside the space of action. Once again, the old roles seem to be occupied, if sometimes in paradoxical ways. This is so because it is difficult to decide whether the East European overthrow of the heritage of not only authoritarian socialism but of the whole tradition of the October Revolution can still be seen as itself a *revolution* in the modern sense of the term. Now the counterrevolutionaries are the few remaining Leninists who denounce the events as "counterrevolution." Interestingly, there are still some on the extreme right, in Europe at least, who agree with their definition, to be

1

sure with reverse evaluation. Thus, the old counterrevolutionaries become in effect malgré eux revolutionaries. The conservative position, at the same time, is largely occupied by those independent leftists, remaining market socialists, and Social Democrats who would like to see preserved some existing institutions and practices like a part of large-scale state ownership and existing forms of social redistribution, and who are very critical of actual trends to the contrary. Unconsciously taking their cue from Burke, they denounce the abstract formalistic utopias of the "Bolsheviks of the market-place." Only in East Europe do some locally based conservatives of the old paternalistic type, partisans of usually vague and at times somewhat ominous "third" or "national" roads agree with them. The places of the liberals alone are still occupied by liberals of different stripes. Only they are able to play the same role as did their counterparts in the nineteenth century, denouncing both despotism and socialism, promoting the freedom of both the market and the individual. Marx's own role finally falls at the moment to Jürgen Habermas, for whom the fall of Communism is a revolution that does not, and cannot, go far enough, like the bourgeois revolutions of old.[2]

There are, however, some new intellectual roles as well. In an influential 1990 article, "Die nachholende Revolution," Habermas distinguishes six positions altogether.[3] From his somewhat arbitrary and overly typological list that (perhaps for the sake of symmetry) sees more "leftist" and fewer "rightist" positions than actually relevant, two interesting new roles need to be added to the survey here. They are occupied by the heirs of the old conservatives in the West, the anti-Communists, whom he mistakenly identifies with the explicit counterrevolutionary position, along with the brand-new protagonist of postmodernism, whom he strangely enough insists on labeling as on the right— perhaps to maintain the symmetry of his typology. Both of these support today's "revolution" while being opposed to the memory and the consequences of the revolutions of the past. This apparent paradox is best understood if we are willing to recognize, unlike Habermas, the historical novelty of "revolutions" that reject the tradition of modern revolutions.

As against Habermas, I wish to distinguish between counterrevolutionary and conservative revolutionary positions on the right. The distinction was already anticipated by Maistre, who juxtaposed "the contrary of revolution" to "contrary revolution." Evidently, we have already met advocates of the second: both in the version of the last Marxist-Leninists totally opposed to the changes and impotently hoping that they would be reversed by whatever means and in the version of the right who make a virtue of the supposedly counterrevolutionary character of the events. It is easy to agree with Habermas that neither position is at all tenable, because the processes of 1989–91 owe little (except occasionally in rhetoric) to the classical instrumentarium of counterrevolution and white terror, still so evident in the Latin America of only ten years ago. The leftist version of this diagnosis, along with the left conservative position held by independents and some Social Democrats, is obviously embarrassed furthermore by the popular and democratic character of radical change in East Europe. It is not surprising, therefore, that no important interpretation has emerged from these three points of view, at least in their pure form.

The same cannot be said about the remaining positions. While Habermas's argument, unfortunately breaking with the tradition of immanent criticism, sees only error in the conservative revolutionary and postmodernist positions and no more than trivial truth in that of the liberals, it would be better to recognize the presence of important insights in each case. My own criticisms of all of them is formally similar: Since each contains important elements of truth, as exclusive interpretations they are all necessarily partial. I am not suggesting, however, that they should be simply added up or somehow synthesized. Indeed such an effort too would miss the nature of the various options (for example liberal democracy and restoration) as alternatives around which there is and will be much conflict in the actual theater of political affairs.

Each option moreover faces structural constraints. These limitations are not in the main those faced by the revolutions of the past. Most ideologically motivated Western analyses, adhering to the old dichotomy of reform and revolution, go wrong by taking seriously the journalistic slogan of "the revolutions of 1989." Since the Central European changes go beyond all possible meanings of reform, they must accordingly signify revolutions whose "logic" is known from the experience of the "great revolutions" of the past. Many social scientists, however, especially those expert in Southern European and Latin American politics, know better. Using what has been learned in the recent "transitions from authoritarian rule," they have a better chance to understand the nonrevolutionary radical changes that occurred after 1989. But they too run into difficulties, not only because historical analogies can never be strict, but because, unlike Southern Europe and Latin America, in all East and Central European settings not only the change of political regime but also that of the economic model is on the agenda. And, simultaneous change in these two domains creates entirely new historical challenges and, though rarely seen as such, opportunities.

Problems of simultaneous political and economic change have been analyzed mainly by rational choice analysts, concentrating in particular on the conflict between the roads to political democracy and market economy. For reasons difficult to fathom, the analyses are uniformly committed to the view that the East and Central European transformations face almost insoluble paradoxes. Since Latin America has produced weak democracies and poor market economies, and since the East and Central Europeans must confront more domains of change, the Latin Americanization of Eastern Europe may be the best possible outcome that can be admitted by these approaches. Under much less favorable circumstances, the new democracies cannot, in other words, repeat the "miracles" of Spain or West Germany.

None of the interpretations, from Habermas to Offe, really grasp the meaning of what is potentially new in the transformation of the East, the option of a self-democratizing civil society. This dimension is not only crucial if we are to understand the self-limiting radicalism of the transitions but gives us one of the keys to how the burdens of the "double transformation" to liberal democracy and market economy could be managed. In what follows, I put special emphasis on this missing dimension of analysis that will form one of the major themes of my own interpretation of the prospects of post-Communism.

CONSERVATIVE REVOLUTION?

It is a mistake to fully conflate the views of an Ernst Nolte with right wing counterrevolutionary doctrine, even if in the end Nolte finds it hard to avoid convergence with such a position. For me his intentions, well expressed in the article "Die unvollständige Revolution," are as important as the ambiguous outcome of his analysis. To be sure, from the outset of his argument Nolte does view the "incomplete revolution" of 1989 to be the completion of the European civil war that began with the Russian Revolution in 1917.[4] While this reference seems to place the events on the same side as the White counterrevolutions, he quite explicitly stresses that the "incomplete" character of the revolutions of 1989 is linked to their peaceful and nonviolent character. Accordingly, even their nationalism is said to be defensive rather than aggressive. It seems to be, moreover, his implication, though he makes the point only in the case of National Socialism, that the bloody counterrevolutions of the twentieth century imitated the methods at least of the complete revolution par excellence, that of the Bolsheviks. Thus the events of 1989 are in effect seen and applauded as Maistre's contraries of revolution, rather than contrary revolutions.

To be sure Nolte's argument is not consistent. Since all "European" revolutions, including 1789, 1848, and 1918 in Germany, are also said to be incomplete, nonviolence cannot be an essential feature of the incompleteness of a revolution. Actually, the distinction of complete-incomplete is derived from the young Marx, astonishingly enough. Accordingly, incomplete revolutions preserve an existing class structure, while the complete ones, that is, the Marxian revolutions of the twentieth century, involve a "clean sweep" and allegedly establish the classless society of Marx's dreams. To improve on this argument, based in any case on extremely doubtful sociology, we might add therefore that while a complete revolution necessarily involves violence, given the need to eliminate whole classes, an incomplete revolution may or may not do so, depending on the circumstances. Thus it could still be said that nonviolence remains a sure sign, whenever present, of an incomplete revolution.

It is important nevertheless not to confuse Nolte's "incomplete revolution" with the East Central European concept of a "self-limiting" revolution. The second has to do with a project of radical transformation that would practice self-limitation for strategic and, more fundamentally also for normative, reasons and stop short in the face of some institutions or practices of the established system, hoping for their evolutionary transformation.[5] Nolte's idea of a "conservative revolution" has nothing to do with any compromise with some existing structures. Rather, the revolutions of 1989 are said to be incomplete because like all "European" revolutions, but unlike the Communist ones, they stop at the threshold of the bourgeois and the nation, seeking presumably to preserve rather than to eliminate them.

I write "presumably," because here a silence on Nolte's part covers yet another and more important weakness in his argumentation. In his conception, taken from Marx, the incomplete revolutions could remain incomplete because they could confine themselves to changing the political system while confirming already existing (bourgeois) class relations.[6] In Eastern Europe, however, precisely this possibility does not exist; after all it is also Nolte's own thesis that all class relations, and especially the bourgeois class, have been abolished in the violence of the Communist regimes. If we add the obvious that Nolte somehow leaves out, namely that new institutions, a new structure of power, and a new social hierarchy did emerge in these regimes, his formula of stopping short of the bourgeois inevitably means restoring relations that have not existed for at least forty years and eliminating rather than conserving another set of relations. The new stress on civil society [*Zivilgesellschaft*] that he identifies in East Europe cannot help him in this context, because he uses this category not to focus on elements of self-organization emerging under declining Communist regimes and has in mind simply the concept of bourgeois society [*bürgerliche Gesellschaft*]. Thus in this context too Nolte cannot avoid the necessity of a new, postrevolutionary creation, cannot make clear how the preservation of anything is supposed to work, and cannot make sense of the idea of stopping at some threshold in analogy with the incomplete revolutions of the past.

The problems are similar with the supposed stopping at the limits of the nation, given Nolte's (in many cases false) insistence that Communist regimes have eliminated all its symbols and institutions. Again stopping short actually can mean nothing other than restoration. To be sure, in this analysis made conspicuous by its silences, it is not at all clear which (often quite different) institutions and which (often opposed) symbols of the nation repressed by Communism and which historical period represented by them need to be restored or returned to. Neither is it clear whether in any of the countries the two thresholds of bourgeois and nation can be made in fact incompatible. Nolte astonishingly disregards this last very real line of fissure in much of contemporary East European politics. Moreover, since it does not follow from any part of his argument that incompleteness requires any caution when eliminating the structures proper of the Communist old regimes, we are left wondering how the revolutions that are supposed to be incomplete can after all avoid a "clean sweep" with respect to all present institutions. As a result it is no longer clear how the nonviolence of the process could have been maintained in most of the countries. With all that must be restored (rather than simply preserved), with all that must be abolished to make room for the old, we may have the right to question whether Nolte's version of the contrary of the revolution, any more than Maistre's if it were realized, could actually stop before turning into counterrevolution.[7]

Unfortunately, however, the ambiguities and dangers of Nolte's analysis do not allow us simply to dismiss him. His specific thesis of the conservative revolution points to the very real restorationist tendencies present in all of the relevant countries. Moreover, the dynamics of his argument point to an internal link between national conservatism and right wing populism. Significantly, Nolte's ambiguities are identical to those of many of the actors themselves, suspended between backward- and present-oriented conservatisms, between bourgeois and nation, between liberal and authoritarian national traditions, and between conservation and nationalist revolution. If his argument is in many respects fallacious and evasive, it is nevertheless still clearer and more explicit than most similar ones in the theater of action. One dismisses it out of hand only at one's own peril.

THE LIBERAL REVOLUTION

It is hardly trivial to insist on the world historical importance of the fall of Communism, representing the last of the "totalitarian" regimes in Europe.[8] Liberals, and not only they, have good reason to celebrate this event. It is unfair, moreover, to maintain in a blanket fashion as does Habermas that the liberal interpretation covers up "the beam in its own eye," in other words, that it uses the idea of a liberal revolution in the East, as did Francis Fukuyama, to apologize for all the existing institutions and practices of Western liberal democracies. There are to be sure liberal interpretations that support this charge. Leaving aside the triumphalism of journalists and politicians, rather diminished in the last year or so, there are serious scholars like Daniel Chirot who speak in an undifferentiated way of the "triumph of liberalism," even if not the final one.[9] Chirot's conception of liberalism is primarily the economic,[10] even if he considers it routinely part of a package with representative government and individual rights. He finds the victory of this package secure only in the capitalist West; elsewhere, including in East and Central Europe, he details the possibility of strong challenges to it from varieties of fundamental-

ism, populism, fascist corporatism, and antienlightenment environmentalism. But, and this is the crucial point, he believes that these challenges, unlike
that of the socialism that failed, would all be on behalf of pre- or antimodern
ideologies. Not only will systems based on them fail in the modern world, but
when the failures do occur the only modern answer can and will be again liberal capitalism.

To be sure Chirot does see some of "the beams in the eye" of liberal capitalism that expose it to radical challenge over and over again. Yet he is nevertheless entirely convinced that liberal capitalism, linked to a social and economic
system that works despite its flaws, remains the only alternative among modern ideologies.[11] He does not see that precisely such insistence, even in the
terms of his own analysis, opens the way in many countries (some evidently
in Eastern Europe) to a hopeless oscillation between a liberalism that fails
politically and forms of authoritarianism that fail economically.[12] If, however,
the only lesson of the East European revolutions were that only a few fortunate countries can ever hope to escape this cycle, this would be slim ground
for any feelings of triumph.

Ralf Dahrendorf's thesis of the "liberal revolution" is made of different
cloth.[13] His point is hardly to pronounce the triumph of the specific established institutions of the West. Rather, drawing on a distinction between constitutional and normal politics, he affirms "only" the victory of an open society over the closed one in East Central Europe. Invented by the Abbé Sieyès
(*pouvoir constituant* and *pouvoir constitué*), and repeatedly revived by students
of revolutions,[14] this distinction easily allows Dahrendorf to escape any
charge of liberal apologetics: He is a constitutional liberal who in normal politics is a radical reformist, one deeply concerned with the social entitlements
of citizenship.[15]

It is extremely important for Dahrendorf's position that while in normal
politics there are many choices and always a third, a fourth, and a fifth way, in
constitutional politics there can be only a single choice, that between open
and liberal, and closed and illiberal, society, and any thought of a "third way"
between the West and the East, capitalism and socialism, should be banished.[16] In his view the constitutional decision for an open society, made by
the Round Tables of 1989 in Poland, Hungary, and Czechoslovakia, as well as
subsequently by the ministers of finance, L. Balczerowicz and V. Klaus, is our
key to the significance of the events. For constitutional politics can establish
the open society only if it secures, aside from fundamental rights and legitimate governments, the basic principles of a free market economy: the freedoms of private property, contract, enterprise, and (in the face of monopolies)
competition.[17] Here again he sees only two options, and no room for any
negotiation, dialogue, or compromise. For this reason, Dahrendorf, consistently enough, supports the economically most extreme liberal policies of
transition in spite of his own admittedly social liberal inclinations. A free mar-

ket economy must first be established before there can be any thought of new ways of compensating for its negative effects.[18]

Even in Dahrendorf's version, the liberal interpretation remains, however, doctrinaire, at times consciously so. This feature of his thinking is most pronounced when he discusses the politics of constitution making. Does it make sense, outside of the stark contrast with a totalitarianism that must be abolished, to consider the option on the constitutional level to be that between open and closed societies alone? Is there nothing essential to negotiate on this level, so that once we have decided for a free society the actual task of constitution making can be left simply to lawyers, even if the most creative ones? In fact, the history of constitution making in East Central Europe does not support Dahrendorf's contention that this is merely "the hour of the lawyers."[19] Should our table of rights include or exclude social rights? Should one simply copy the legal protections of existing constitutions, or also establish new ones? What electoral frameworks are the most democratic? Should a presidential or parliamentary regime be created? Should there be a constitutional court, and with what kind of powers of judicial review? Should an economic framework based on private property be developed through privatization or reprivatization, and who should be in charge of the process? Should the openness of the new system of property be preserved by establishing safeguards for a plurality of forms of property? These and similar questions dominated the discussions. They are not initially legal, but political and even philosophical. Moreover, the Round Tables and Constituent Assemblies forced to face them could not be guided here by the simple choice of freedom and unfreedom. Yet normal politics could not fully commence until such issues were decided at least provisionally, for a time.[20] Indeed, more and renewed constitutional politics cannot and should not be excluded from the political futures of the new any more than the older democracies; even from the point of view of their stability it is best to leave constitutions open and revisable. But there are better, normative reasons for not considering the process of constitutional politics ever completely closed.[21] This too shows that there is a plurality of choice in constitutional politics.

Dahrendorf is right against Hayek: Constitutional politics should be not so inflated that normal politics disappears entirely and every political issue is posed in terms of the fundamental choice of freedom and bondage. But he errs on the other side, by accepting Hayek's definition of constitutional politics and by constricting this terrain in such a way as to exclude from it anything but the same choice. Thus he is forced to reduce foundational politics to a single decision, already made in the West of course, and to exclude the possibility of any innovation on this level. According to him, therefore, the fact that the Revolutions of 1989 supposedly involved no new ideas, no historical creation, is a virtue rather than a deficiency.[22] The rediscovery of civil society too is said to represent only a return to an old European idea.[23]

Thus it seems to me that Dahrendorf's important mistake lies in identifying the issue of open versus closed society, with the totality of the stakes in constitutional politics. He is right in treating the idea of the open society, stressing fallibilism and a plurality of possible forms of life, as the crucial discovery of modernity; indeed it is a key determination of modernity, if not its *differentia specifica*. He is also right in stressing both the fundamental link of this idea with liberalism in the broadest sense. Thus the obliteration of all elements of liberalism, and in particular the establishment of the cultural monopoly of a ritualized, repressively enforced body of dogma, is a proof of the only partial modernity of Soviet type societies, despite their (incomplete) modernization. I would even concede that it is possible and generally necessary to anchor modernity on the constitutional level; such is above all the role of fundamental rights.[24] But while Dahrendorf would never dream of claiming that the establishment of the open society can be simply the task of constitution making, he does not also see that constitutional politics should not be simply reduced to the dimension of the liberation of society.[25] He seems to recognize this gap in his own analysis when he stresses the need for innovation in the contemporary system of parties. But when speaking about the tasks of constitutional politics, he stresses only the establishment of a sufficiently strong but not really that of a sufficiently democratic government. He does not tell us or attempt to justify why the ground rules of democracy are any less important from a normative point of view than those of liberalism.

It seems to me that Dahrendorf makes the highly debatable choice of many versions of liberalism, namely, of establishing liberal values as fundamental and reducing democratic forms and procedures to merely instrumental significance. Be that as it may, at the very least an instrumentally significant level of democratization is needed, at least under contemporary conditions of mass politics, to secure if not to establish the open society. Somewhat inconsistently, Dahrendorf fervently wishes the growth of a sturdy civil society and democratic political culture in the East, even if for no other reason than to provide the sociological underpinnings of the open society. But having overly restricted the role of constitutional politics, he can only say that these will require longer-term, more organic processes. Yet it is not at all convincing that there is nothing that can be done on the level of constitutional politics to establish political patterns of participation that would contribute to a more active civil society and a more participatory civic culture. In this context any reference to the English and American experiences, where such constitutional provisions were neglected, would be misleading because these were in different ways based on genuinely organic developments of older forms of civil society into more modern ones. After the devastation, if not obliteration, of all independent social life, in today's East Central Europe, as to some extent after the fall of other dictatorships, the institutionalization of civil society (if not its origins and later development) especially in democratic versions, are foundational tasks. This is true as we now see even in the two or three countries where some kind of civil society (in the forms of movements and initiatives) has participated in its own liberation.[26] Dahrendorf's all-too-narrow model of constitutional politics, to be sure corresponding to the ideals of many liberal politicians and intellectuals in the region, cannot help in this project despite his homage to the ideals of civil society.

THE IMITATIVE REVOLUTION[27]

Habermas's central concept of modernity, even more than Dahrendorf's, should have provided for an ideal vantage point to view the events of 1989.[28] Indeed, because Habermas insists on modernity as a not yet completed project rather than an already old and well-tried condition of humanity, he is in a better position to judge both the achievement and the not yet fulfilled promise of this new phase in the history of democracy. In fact, however, he too sees nothing new, no innovation, no bases for any learning from the events and the accomplishments. In this he echoes François Furet, for whom such a state of affairs implies that we should not speak at all of revolutions in the modern sense,[29] as well as Nolte and Dahrendorf, for whom novelty would be a demerit rather than a virtue. Evidently, for Habermas, since democratic innovation is the road for the completion of modernity, its supposed absence is cause for a rather patronizing if not critical attitude. In East Central Europe we see, according to him, only the extension of the boundaries of the existing version of modernity. Nevertheless, he insists (if not quite consistently) that we should see 1989 as a revolution in its modern sense. According to Habermas, both the normative claims (human rights and popular sovereignty) and the action repertoire (large masses mobilized in streets and squares) of the transformations belong to the armory of modern revolutions.[30]

Unfortunately Habermas does not notice that the second of his criteria, the one dealing with forms of action, does not apply to the two countries that played the pioneering roles, where the changes were most authentically internal, Poland and Hungary! More importantly, even the reference to normative models is incomplete. All modern revolutions after the French adopted its semantics and established a positive set of references to its tradition. Neither this relationship nor, on the whole, the corresponding revolutionary experience were present in most of the countries. Habermas himself, like Furet, notes only one aspect of this: the complete absence of future-oriented ideas. It is for this reason of course that Furet insists on a "raging passion of restoration," rather than a revolution. And indeed this dimension appears in Habermas's essay as well. The revolutions are depicted as both seeking to overtake *(nachholen)* and join the liberal West, and attempting "under the sign of a return to old, national symbols" to reattach themselves "to the political traditions and party organizations of the interwar years."[31] Habermas does not notice that this linkage, involving a synthesis of liberal and conservative interpretations, does not actually work. What is wrong with it is not primarily factual inaccuracy, even if the statement about party revival is simply wrong. On the whole it is new parties, with foundations in the preceding epoch of dissidence, and not "nostalgia" or "historical" parties that dominate the scene. But Habermas is right to refer to both imitative and restorationist trends and is wrong only because of overlooking the deep conflict between them. In most countries going back to interwar traditions is not compatible with imitation of Western liberal institutions, even in the sense of a time sequence that would put a "*rückspulende* Revolution" first, and a "*nachholende* Revolution" second. The institutions of the interwar years cannot serve as the bases of liberal political and even economic reform.

Furet's way out of this difficulty is purely verbal: Where a return to anything actual will not be possible, imitation will be merely masked as restoration. But the rage to restore will not be so easy to contain, even where the possible objects of this passion are quite unattractive, and hardly modern. This state of affairs is not easily made compatible with the linear temporal dimension of modern revolutions on which Habermas insists. And indeed in one context he makes a fatal concession, noting the reappearance of the premodern semantics of "revolution" as "the return of political regimes following one another in continuous cycle like that of the heavens."[32]

Given this ambiguous interpretation, it is not surprising that Habermas finds little to learn from the transformation of the East, aside from an insistence on the necessity of markets for any modern economy, a point already made in *Theory of Communicative Action* ten years before. The democratic completion of modernity in general, and the reflexive, nonstatist and radical democratic continuation of the welfare state in particular, are projects apparently suitable only for the more fortunate countries of the West. Only after being in our situation can East German intellectuals, according to Habermas, be expected to develop radical reformist critiques of capitalist society.[33] It is revealing of course that he chooses to single out East Germans here, because the others (including the Poles and the Hungarians who are actually far more advanced in reflection concerning the past and the present) will obviously have rather longer to wait by the same criterion. The imitative revolution, not to speak of the restorationist one, cannot be expected to leap over historical stages, to learn from the errors of others, or to respond to the challenges of the twenty-first century. This being so, we are not told how this revolution can escape its own contradictions, not only between conservatism and liberalism, but as we will see, also between economic liberalism and democracy, an issue that Habermas curiously enough neglects altogether.

THE POSTMODERN REVOLUTION

It is a definite virtue of the postmodern interpretation of 1989 and its consequences that it insists on the novelty, and I daresay universal significance, of
the events. Obviously this position should not be identified in terms of the
categories of left and right.[34] Such identification ultimately depends on self-
identification, or at least the appropriate labeling of the adversary. But the
postmoderns, usually of leftist background, refuse to engage in this traditional
battle of political labels: To them the distinction between right and left and the
old struggle between socialism and liberalism have now become largely irrelevant. Habermas's counterarguments against such position or positions,
moreover, are weak. Since he identifies the key postmodern thesis as one that
posits a revolution, but refuses the modern tradition of revolution, it makes
little sense to counter this by insisting on the utilization in 1989 of the classical instruments of revolutions. For the postmoderns, if these instruments
were in fact used in some countries (and in several they were not), then it was
for the very purpose of ending the epoch of revolutions. To be sure it is true
enough that the end of this epoch cannot be identified with the end of
modernity in Habermas's sense, and certainly nothing in 1989 indicates such
a project. But had Habermas himself not needlessly accepted just this identification of the epoch of the great revolutions with modernity, he could have
remained more open to what remains valid in the thesis. Certainly the widespread rejection of the tradition and of the semantics of modern revolutions
and the almost general adoption of unusual qualifiers of the term—gentle,
velvet, peaceful, constitutional, and legal—support the insight that the revolutions of 1989 seek to break with the revolutionary model that emerged in
1789, and in particular with its perceived logic from a liberal to a radical
phase, one leading toward civil war, terror, and dictatorship. Instead of criti-
cizing this insight as somehow linked to irrationalism, we should recognize in
it a more self-reflective model of reason able to build its own history into its
model of action.

With this said the contents of the postmodern position remain rather
underdetermined. To my knowledge only Agnes Heller and Ferenc Feher
sought to give it determinate content. But their interpretation suffers from
many ambiguities; in particular their use (as just about everyone else's) of the
term *postmodern* covers several different, and in part incompatible, intellectual strategies. I will not quarrel with their (inconsistent) definition of political revolutions as changes of (the form or the possessors of?) sovereignty, one
that would include many events no one ever thought of calling a revolution,
like military coups, for example, or the end of authoritarian regimes as in
Greece and Spain.[35] According to Heller and Feher, the events of 1989 are
*post*modern revolutions, because they, unlike the classical European "modern"
revolutions, overthrow modern rather than premodern regimes; bring East

Central Europe into the processes of genesis of an expanding postmodern cosmopolis (which does not transcend modernity but seeks only to make it livable); reconcile, or allow the coexistence, of processes that recall the premodern meaning of revolution as a return to a previous state of affairs, with scenarios drawn from the modern history of revolutions; and build into their politics reflection on the negative experiences of previous revolutions, bringing the epoch of revolutions and the grand narratives of modernity to an end.

The first of these claims depends on our acceptance of Soviet-type societies as fully modern. As we have seen, they could not be so regarded from Dahrendorf's or Habermas's points of view. At stake of course is our definition of modernity. But even if we were inclined to regard the Soviet path of industrialization, urbanization, extension of education, and so forth simply an alternative path of modernization, rather than as a dead end to modernization, we would do well to pay some attention to the much lower level of differentiation between politics and the rest of society, and in particular the absence of a civil society, before we spoke about "modernity" rather than "modernization." Even more importantly, in the sphere of culture, we should ask if the absence of differentiated cultural spheres, of a decentered view of the world, and the existence of a canonical and ritualized official culture qualify as modern. Finally, to maintain this argument, we would have to close our eyes to the turn of many of the countries toward conservative old regimes, as well as the deep freezer effect of many of the structures of the societies involved for old cultural patterns, symbols, and aspirations that seem now to come to the surface. If my counterargument is right, we will discover just those analogies between 1989 and modern revolutions stressed by Feher. But in this case we also cannot use this first definition of postmodernity as Heller does to explain the supposed absence of innovation in 1989.

There is little to be said on the second point. It is quite right to argue that the countries of East Central Europe can now participate in common European projects. But it is not exactly clear why these should be called postmodern, especially if their only task is to make modernity livable. It is certainly not right to claim, as Heller did in an interview in Népszabadság, that East Europeans are ahead in postmodern political development because they have broken with the class bases of politics and with ideological class parties.[36] These changes can be dated to the nineteenth century in the United States, and at the latest to the 1960s and 1970s in all European countries. There is no reason to call them postmodern.

The third point, involving an entirely different definition of postmodernism, is all the more important to examine in detail. Heller's primary thesis here is that of a restorationist revolution, one that restores the premodern meaning of revolution as return, as well as, in intention at least, modern conditions, representing states of affairs before the Communist regimes disrupted each nation's genuine history. The category of postmodernism allows her to treat the premodern and modern conceptions of revolution as fully compatible, a trick that we used to refer to as dialectical.

Heller's depiction of the trend of restoration is quite original. Instead of focusing on dubious interwar arrangements as did Habermas, Heller proposes instead 1956, 1968, and 1981 as dates when the authentic national histories were interrupted. According to Heller, these are the dates to which Hungarians, Czechs, Slovaks, and Poles sought in 1989 to return, at least symbolically, since she excludes any such possibility in the literal sense. This ingenious and attractive thesis is unfortunately based on wishful thinking. Starting with the Poles, their proper history was not at all broken in 1981; many then-formed actors (of course quite changed in the process, but never eliminated) fought through the extremely historical and certainly not (as Heller implies) totalitarian period of the 1980s, in which a dualistic organization of society inherited from 1980–81 survived if in a cultural version. The struggle in 1988 was to relegalize solidarity, not to reinvent it. The Round Table that accomplished this was moreover a new institutional innovation; its compromise solutions, however, embodied a strategic conception invented as early as 1976 and kept alive through the 1980s. Even more emphatically, the Hungarians of 1988–89 were not returning to the model of 1956 in spite of the symbolic role of Imre Nagy's reburial and the party's earlier redefinition of the revolution as a national uprising. The really important parties (as Heller admits) as well as the key institutional innovation, the Round Table of the Opposition, were new inventions with respect to 1956. The National Round Table was adopted from the Poles. There was no question of the opposition accepting the leadership of reform Communists, many of whom were undoubtedly far more radical than Nagy ever was. Neither the idea of radical democracy in general nor the movement of workers councils was seriously revived, and when the latter did emerge, it did so only in the form of a type of unionism. Even on the level of intention and ideology 1956 was never really central for the majority of the major actors. I am more struck by the absence of a renewed influence of Istvan Bibó, the major political philosopher of 1956, than by the repeated (but less and less frequent) references to his name.[37] Finally, the Czech and Slovak oppositions that took power were most explicitly not 1968ist despite Alexander Dubček's uneasy role among them: Their inspiration came from post-'68 dissidence as well as from the interwar republic.

To be sure Heller is not wrong about the desire to return to previous states of affairs, but she is wrong to try to affix a date to this aspiration. From the details of her own analysis, and even more from subsequent events, it is clear that it is "the raging passion to restore" that is common; the actual targets vary greatly. In Hungary, for example, with a grain of salt one might say that the key dates are 1987 for the state administration, 1956 for its old militants, 1947 for the Small Holders Party fighting for reprivatization, 1937 for defenders of church prerogatives and real estate, 1917 for the enemies of Trianon, and so on. All restorations suffer from just this kind of ambiguity, because of the variety of available traditions in each national history, all open to interpretation. Here the category of postmodern (along with the loose usage of the term *deconstruction*) simply helps to paper over contradictions that, in actual politics, unfortunately often tend to be resolved by the thirst of power of different restorationists as well as the revolutionary search for enemies common to them all.

Heller's task is all the more difficult, however, because she seeks to reconcile restoration and the symbolic return to previous historical moments with a determined movement forward to liberal democracy. Thus, inconsistently, we are told that the model of reconstruction is not based on any actual 1956, 1968, or 1981, but on those of existing Western societies. Here Heller runs into the same contradiction as Furet and Habermas, and like them is not aware of its full significance, even if she is more conscious of the dangers of various fundamentalisms. The concept of postmodernism stops her from noticing that one cannot make modern politics around concepts of return to the past, that restoration as an ideal is incompatible with liberal democracy.

Interestingly, the problem for Ferenc Feher is not at all to make restoration or revolution in the premodern sense compatible with modernity.[38] His dilemma rather is to see the events as both a part of the history of genuinely modern revolutions (1789, 1848, 1917 being its first three waves; 1989 the fourth) and as a revolution that ends the epoch of revolutions. He therefore stresses the identity of only some of the instruments of 1989 with classical revolutions. He also notes the difference introduced by other important features of the gentle revolutions, like limitations on violence, the concern for civil society, and especially a new leisurely rather than accelerated consciousness of time. It is somewhat unclear why this complex is referred to as the purest form of revolution; indeed the idea of using minimum violence to bring about domination-free communication, quite different than Heller's definition of revolution, comes closer to that of civil disobedience. What is clear, however, is how Feher uses this insight to flesh out the notion of ending the epoch of revolutions. Evidently, a shift in the instruments and strategies was needed to break the hold of the old revolutionary logic on the actors. Whether or not this will in the end be successful, Feher is entirely right that actors like Václav Havel, Adam Michnik, and György Konrad were trying at all times to promote a revolution without a revolution. But even more important is the stress on the rejection of utopian narratives and the hubris of making history, after an absolute break from a unified, self-conscious point of view. It is far more convincing to trace the rejection of ideological and institutional innovation to this attitude, rather than to a stage model where postmodern follows modern (Heller) or to a recognition of liberalism as the single constitutional option if we want freedom (Dahrendorf). The contemporary revolution can end the age of revolutions only if it refuses to be so like the modern revolutions as to repeat their logic, but to be enough like them to be able to accomplish a full transformation of existing regimes. In my view the recognition of this apparent paradox is the beginning of the way out of the Tocquevillian dilemma, according to which the most radical revolutions can involve the greatest continuity on the level of the structure of the state.

Nevertheless, the paradox does not disappear just because we can show the conservative side of radical revolutions; conservative revolutions do not thereby become radical. This is just the problem with Feher's version of the postmodern thesis, the most defensible one. How is the "postmodern" revolution to be distinguished from a partially modern, partially conservative one? In any case the term is a misnomer, given the idea of postmodernity as the completion of modernity Feher shares with Heller, the term *self-reflective* or *self-limiting* modern revolution would be better. But this terminological shift would also not resolve the problem, unless we and especially the actors recall that the normative (versus the strategic) dimension of the idea of a self-limiting revolution was always linked to a project organized around the self-emancipation and self-institutionalization of civil society. Feher in fact discusses this key, innovative idea coming from East Central Europe, but without ever assigning it full significance. Thus he too is forced to remain extremely cautious, like Agnes Heller, concerning the possible role of innovation, intellectual and institutional.

In the face of current oscillation between imitation and restoration the caution is well warranted. But we cannot give the postmodern position anything more than a purely negative (ending an epoch) and formal (self-reflection, self-limitation) content unless we explicitly raise the question of what could, at least in principle, be the bases of political innovation that would not only end the epoch of revolutions but help usher in a new one, within modernity.

TRANSITIONS TO DEMOCRACY I:
THE MODEL OF LIBERAL OLIGARCHIES

The postmodern interpretation of 1989 and its aftermath is torn between two alternatives: Do the events add up to an entirely new type of revolution, or does postmodernity imply that the very concept of revolution and the old contrast with reform has become obsolete? The sloganeering of Western journalists referring to the "revolutions of 1989" promotes the first option, but the testimony and the language of most of the key actors lends support to the second.[39] No semantic effort like Timothy Garton-Ash's ironic term *refolution* can resolve the issue. If reform means (as it must) significant change while identity is maintained, and revolution means (as it also must) change of identity, the two concepts cannot be somehow combined in relation to the same object of analysis. Moreover, in order to understand the present we have to rely on what we learn from the historiography of the past. The actors themselves, as the author of the *18th of Brumaire* once pointed out, cannot do without historical analogies when they seek to orient and justify themselves. The same is true for hard-nosed social scientists to whom the present can give only insufficient data (always too few cases and too many differences) for systematic investigation.

It may be possible of course to develop a concept of revolution that involves no military confrontation, physical violence, or bloodshed, but it remains true nonetheless that the historiography of revolutions knows no such cases. At the same time, however, we do know of a large number of cases involving radical political change in the context of legal continuity and negotiated settlement that are nevertheless different from top-down reform, implying the preservation of the original regime identity.[40] The rather colorless and overly broad term *transition* has become extremely popular recently among social scientists to describe such cases, but of course the phenomenon referred to hardly starts in 1989 or even 1977, the time of the regime change in Spain. Given the obvious objection that everything in politics is transitional, the term is very much improved by adding the adjective *regime.* Finally, the notion of *regime transition* seems more useful to help us understand the end of Communism when we add: transition *to* democracy, or, less ambitiously, *from* authoritarian rule. Political democracy is the undeniable goal of the transformations in question, and it is even less in doubt that the terminus ad quem of the process is in most current cases a type of dictatorship that cannot be easily subsumed under any available theory of totalitarianism. To understand the transitions from either of these two points of view, the "to" and the "from," social scientists have at their disposal not only cases but also relevant theories and models of comparative analysis. However, like all such models based on incomplete analogies, these can be used but also abused.

As far as the actors are concerned, they have no other choice but to take analogies like the Spanish model seriously unless, stressing the complete uniqueness of their experience, they wish to rely on will and normative considerations alone. The former is in fact what important participants like Adam Michnik and János Kis did in the late 1980s. In my view political analysts do have the advantage of being able to use large-scale analogies more systematically, and they have a better chance to control for significant differences. But they cannot easily match the prudential tests of relevance available to actors with political experience, unless they too, like the actors, come to know some cases (at the very least one) very thoroughly and more or less from within.[41] Successful interpretation presupposes a participant's perspective. But since the analysts cannot be fully participants, they can make up for their relative lack of experience only through critical relations with the analogical models they are forced to use.

There are two major interpretive lines, based on historical analogies that seem especially plausible in light of the ongoing processes of transformation in the new democracies. The first has to do with transitions in North Europe from liberal oligarchy to mass democracy; the second, with recent transitions from authoritarian rule in Southern Europe and Latin America.

The analogy between Northern Europe then and East and Central Europe now relies on the supposed identity of the terminus ad quem. As all the original examples (including the partially deviant case: Great Britain) were in fact successful transitions to mass democracy, these offer potentially useful lessons concerning the preconditions of a design capable of producing stable democratic institutions.

In order to apply the lessons of the North European cases to current transitions from dictatorships, analysts had to neglect Robert Dahl's warning that democratization of inclusive hegemonies (i.e., populist dictatorships) is a different and much more difficult matter than was the introduction of mass democracy under competitive (i.e., liberal) oligarchies.[42] They do so because they have not only cases but also an interesting theory, that of Stein Rokkan, that they hope to use to interpret "a theory-starved subject matter." Undoubtedly Arend Lijphart, Friedbert Rübb, and at times even the more complex framework of Jon Elster are inspired by Rokkan's method, namely, protorational choice analysis of the origins of universal suffrage and proportional representation, and by the fact that to the casual observer the East and Central European institutions resemble the outcomes in Northern Europe.[43] According to Rokkan's persuasive argument, when universal suffrage was introduced in Northern Europe, reigning bourgeois parties faced the likelihood that one or more of them could be eliminated under two-party systems if majoritarian electoral systems were retained. Thus many of these parties accepted proportional representation, favored for some time by the rising working-class parties, who were long dissatisfied with winner-take-all plurality elections, and who, even in the beginning of mass democracy, were too weak or too pessimistic (or, most likely, too ideological!) to take their chances with plurality or majority elections.[44] That the application of this analysis is not hopeless seems to be indicated by the large number of new democracies that have wound up with variants of proportional representation (PR). Most recently in South Africa, the sudden conversion of the National Party to PR seems to fully indicate the relevance of the analogy. While under apartheid the party could gain quasi-dictatorial powers through plurality voting; with black suffrage only the proportional representation it successfully sought during comprehensive negotiations could save it from complete devastation.[45]

Several contemporary analysts seem so enchanted with the cogent but modest idea behind the Rokkan thesis, that they wish to greatly extend it to institutional domains with which the original author was not concerned. To an extent they are right to try to do so, because even a theory that is difficult to apply is a better guide to comparative analysis than no theory at all. Accordingly, it is argued that wherever democratization takes the path of negotiated transitions between Communist parties and organized oppositions, both sides hedge their bets and agree to "power-sharing" formulae involving guarantees of future participation consisting of proportional representation, presidential government, and bicameralism.[46] This claim is maintained in spite of the fact that the analysts are repeatedly forced to concede that the outcomes in the countries under consideration support the "Rokkan hypothesis" at best only partially.[47] Interestingly this relatively inadaquate fit between the hypothesis and the actual cases occurs even though the focus is restricted to cases where genuinely two-sided negotiations actually took place. "The logic of power sharing only operates," according to Lijphart, "if the new institutional structures are the outcome of a genuinely negotiated agreement."[48] In this case, the applicability of the model would have to be modest from the very outset, since in the majority of the new states emerging from Communism formal negotiations did not, in fact, take place.

More serious is the state of affairs that Rokkan's own historical cases, all constitutional monarchies moving toward parliamentary sovereignty, did not at the relevant time adopt either presidential or judicial limits on the powers of the legislature. This alone should have made his recent followers, who are certainly aware of the issue, think twice about overextending his model; after all, it is not clear why old parties seeking to maintain themselves in parliamentary elections and to participate in future parliamentary coalitions (something achievable by PR alone) should seek to limit the powers of parliament when the chances of the new parties to achieve absolute parliamentary majority through PR would be small.[49] If the old bourgeois parties sought only the guarantee of PR, it was probably because this was sufficient for them both under the given conditions and given the goals they were trying to achieve.

The point is not only the truism that conditions were different after 1989. Even more importantly, the analogy between declining bourgeois parties and state parties facing the collapse of the party-state cannot be sustained.[50] Here is where Dahl's early distinction between the problems of democratization under exclusionary representative systems—that is, the competitive oligarchies of Northern Europe and inclusive hegemonies, of which the Soviet type systems were the main examples (along with Mexico and other populist forms of authoritarian rule)—retains its importance. In the present context this difference means several things:

1. Inclusionary regimes have different types of dominant parties than do exclusionary regimes. A Communist Party, of which each relevant country has only one, and which has extensive social networks penetrating also the "popular" strata, need not fear electoral collapse under majoritarian or even plurality voting to the same extent as did the turn-of-the-twentieth-century bourgeois parties, of which there were several in each

country, without, however, social ties to mass electorates. This was especially true given the positional advantage (in labor unions for example)
of the Communist parties to become the Social Democratic Party of
their country. The facts sustain this analysis: Without exception the state
parties initially advocated plurality electoral systems where (i.e., everywhere except the Soviet Union and Poland) they could not impose
schemes that involved guaranteed seats for themselves.

2. Thus with respect to electoral arrangements (which are, strictly speaking,
   the only domain to which Rokkan applied his analysis), the options of formerly dominant parties of liberal oligarchies and the dominant party of
   Communist regimes were the opposite. It does not matter in this context
   that the latter were mistaken, and, as the results of the Polish Senate and
   Hungarian mixed system clearly show, the former Communist parties
   would have performed better under a pure PR system and much worse in
   the case of a pure plurality or majority system. It is true enough that even
   a specifically self-tailored, at least three-contestant formula for the second
   round (à la Hungary) did not help its intended beneficiaries. But for the
   model, only the actual calculation matters and not what would have been
   rational, given hindsight. To the extent that proportional electoral systems
   emerged in many of the cases in East and Central Europe as well as in the
   supposed forerunners in Northern Europe, the processes leading to such
   an outcome had to be quite different in the two historical contexts.

3. The hegemonic parties of dictatorships conceived operation under the
   democracies to come quite differently than parties accustomed to operate in competitive liberal frameworks. The latter were ready to take their
   chances under new political rules and in general tended to accept formal
   rules as more or less the actual framework of the operation of regimes.
   The former were not accustomed to open competition and, having little
   experience of operating under binding formal rules, were used to relying
   on informal arrangements and personal loyalties. Thus the Communist
   parties sought not just political *guarantees* for future operation as did the
   bourgeois parties, but if at all possible a *conversion* of former dominant
   powers under new formal rules. They understood presidentialism or
   semipresidentialism therefore not as a formally constrained component
   of a system of the separation of powers in the American style, as the analysts influenced by Rokkan seem to assume, and as some (but certainly
   not all) of the *formal* constitutional patterns that have emerged seem to
   suggest. Instead they aimed at presidentialism as an *informally* powerful,
   quasi-authoritarian vantage point from which old hegemonic powers
   could be transformed into new ones. Indeed their choice of plurality
   electoral rules, which could (and did in Serbia and Croatia) transform a
   substantial minority vote into an impressive majority of seats, can be
   seen as a conversion strategy as well.[51]

4. The more institutions there are that can be used for the strategy of conversion as against power sharing, the better the chance that this strategy would succeed. This is the reason why the Communist parties negotiated hard to achieve several new institutional arrangements deemed desirable, and not just one as did the bourgeois parties in Rokkan's model. Moreover, institutions of conversion as presidentialism and plurality voting have a zero-sum logic: They provide advantages to one side while depriving the other side. They must be distinguished from institutions as proportional representation and bicameralism that can provide political guarantees to one side only when doing so for the other side as well. Characteristically, the Communist parties sought in the initial negotiations the type of democratic political institutions that would allow the conversion of their power, and it was their opponents who pushed for institutions that would guarantee political participation to all sides.[52]

5. To the extent that the former dominant parties of Communist regimes needed guarantees, these were not only or even primarily relevant to political participation. Many of the regimes and their leading officials have been guilty of dramatic human rights violations and unjust expropriation, and those who have participated in repression and benefited from large-scale property transfer both during the first and the last phases of the old regimes did not necessarily feel protected by the continued political role of their party, increasingly dominated by new politicians. Thus many of the Communist parties supported for the first time strong judicial institutions, including a constitutional court capable of preserving the continuity of the rule of law (and of property) in the midst of great social and political transformation. In other words, like the bourgeois parties of Rokkan's analysis, they did hedge their bets in spite of their conversion attempts and did seek guarantees, but, let us firmly note, in an entirely different institutional area.

Thus it seems inevitable that an analogy between two processes based only on the supposed (actually rather incomplete) identity of political outcomes had to fail because of starting points that should have been systematically differentiated. But what if both the termini ad quem and ad quo resembled one another to a much greater extent?

TRANSITIONS TO DEMOCRACY II:
THE MODEL OF THE SOUTHERN DICTATORSHIPS

The application of the experience of the more recent "transitions from authoritarian rule" to East and Central Europe during and after 1989 seems to be far more promising than the historical analogy of the shift to proportional representation under declining liberal oligarchies. The southern regimes in question, unlike the liberal oligarchies, were dictatorships. Moreover, even though not themselves populist in their most recent incarnation, they operated in countries that have gone through populist and even mass democratic processes of political incorporation. Equally important, almost all the cases analyzed by the "transition literature" involved democratization after 1975 and thus belong to more or less the same world of cultural assumptions, vocabulary, and discourse about democracy as do the somewhat later East and Central European cases.

Finally, the transitions in Southern Europe and Latin America involved a variety of types of paths of change and were not restricted to the negotiated path like Rokkan's cases. In Portugal, for example, a military insurrection ended the authoritarian regime. Elsewhere the changes were peaceful. In other places, in particular in Argentina and Greece, the military regimes collapsed and were unable to impose conditions on the recovering democratic forces. In these countries, the institutional transformation, when it finally began, was extremely rapid. In Spain, Brazil, and Chile, on the other hand, the institutional change was slower, involving more stages, and the authoritarian actors were capable of imposing conditions or obtaining guarantees. Such conditions could involve formal and procedural limitations on democracy, as in Chile, or only protection for some traditional institutions like the monarchy and the church, as in Spain. This variability of paths, leading to interpretive typologies rather than a single model of transition, is particularly relevant to the East and Central European cases where the changes also took place according to different paths and producing different outcomes. Note also that the two sets of paths are strikingly alike in their overall structure: Change of regime is achieved in the greatest number of cases within legal continuity, though there are two cases of insurrectionary (revolutionary) change as well: Portugal and Romania.

Nevertheless, like all historical analogies, the one between South and East has serious difficulties. When not based on claims of historical uniqueness and the supposed incomparability of Leninist political culture, the most serious objections stress the greater complexity of the "triple" transition in East and Central Europe as compared with the primarily political transitions of the South, which did not involve problems of change of the fundamental economic model (as all of the East European cases), or of state formation (as did some of these cases).[53] These objections cannot be answered by a flight to abstraction,[54] and even less by arguments that pretend that contemporary economic problems are more or less similar among the regions.[55] I believe, however, that the very same objections can be met when (as already recommended) we turn from causal-explanatory to analogical-interpretive approaches that stress a participant's perspective, and, at the same time, assume the relative autonomy of the political subsystem.

Admittedly, there are problems with the comparison even on the strictly political level. In short, with the exception of Mexico (which is largely neglected by the transition literature) and Spain (which is often considered a miracle), the southern dictatorships were not ruled by elites that could transform themselves into effective and genuinely competitive parties under electoral democracy. Military leaderships could not become parliamentary parties, and when the traditional parties and party systems reemerged they were rarely, if ever, successful in sponsoring effective new parties of their creation. The Communist parties were politically and sociologically different formations than the bourgeois oligarchic parties of Northern Europe and the groups running the military regimes of Latin America. Some of the Communist parties have an electoral past, even if a distant one, and they have sister parties with an electoral present. With all of them disposing over the requisite networks and organizational skills, they rightly judged themselves to be capable of transformation into modern electoral parties, capable of mass support.[56] This expectation produced a different logic of negotiations and different outcomes in East Europe than in most countries of Latin America and (as we will see) makes predictions on the bases of the experience of the latter hazardous. Nevertheless, the specific differences owing to military regimes (indeed different types of military regimes as in Stepan's works: hierarchically led rule of military as an institution vs. nonhierachically led) can be fortunately accounted for in the literature on the transitions, since there have been at least three southern dictatorships (Portugal, Spain, and Mexico) that were not (or no longer) military at the time of the beginning of the transitions.[57]

With this said, the East European transformations, many of them significantly different than classical reforms or revolutions, clearly belong to the new world of political change that was pioneered by the Spanish transition, practiced by many Latin American countries, and to which the changes in South Africa still belong.[58] The literature on the transitions remains the best attempt to deal with this new world comparatively, and especially with its preeminently political path of transformation.[59] In its more recent versions, moreover, this literature has attempted to apply the lessons of the South to the East, yielding more or less general conceptions of contemporary processes of democratization.[60]

Unfortunately, the initial results were not sufficiently convincing. I would like to explore the difficulties through the work of Adam Przeworski, who was the first to make a comprehensive attempt to directly apply to the East what has been learned in the South.[61] I see three serious problems with his approach that indicate the difficulties faced by many other analysts who share his assumptions. First, he operates with a rather reductionist model of types; second, he misapplies the supposed lessons of negotiated transitions; and, third, he misses the relevance of the civil society problem (along with the issue of legitimacy) to political consolidation and even the economic transitions. Przeworski's weaknesses are important, because they characterize the intellectual trajectory of the mainstream of transition studies. Only the most recent effort by Juan Linz and Alfred Stepan begins to free the South and East comparison from its schematic character, and from the specific liabilities I have in mind.[62] Yet even their rich comparative survey does not in all respects overcome the *theoretical* limits of the "transition literature" as previously established.

In the early analysis of Guillermo O'Donnell and Phillipe Schmitter, transitions from authoritarian rule tended to be conceptualized under three types: collapse of authoritarian governments in no position to negotiate, pacted transitions, and transitions "initiated from above by authoritarian incumbents with sufficient cohesion and resources to dictate the emerging rules of the game."[63] The apparently (but only apparently) corresponding outcomes (minus a full authoritarian reversion) were seen as three: democracy, restricted democracy *(democradura),* and soft dictatorship *(dictablanda).* In my view, one admittedly colored by East and Central European developments (and logical considerations too), these two sets of types of paths and outcomes are just about the right ones to stress, even if the causal linkage of collapse with genuine democracy, and that of the negotiated path with democradura, seems to be fallacious.

Interestingly, however, the subsequent development of the transition literature on the whole did not pay much attention to the third, top-down type (in spite of the potential availability of the Mexican case), and the dominant view by default reduced the variety of transitions to the collapse of authoritarian regimes and to extrication through some kind of negotiation in which regime soft-liners and oppositional moderates play the leading role.[64] Note that O'Donnell and Schmitter, too, considered the outcome of "liberalization," namely, soft dictatorship, the result of openings from above or of pacts with the military or both, to be extremely vulnerable to the resurgence of civil society.[65] It may very well be this otherwise convincing train of thought that allows the reduction of possible types.[66]

Historically, the eventual passing of Brazilian "liberalization" into "democratization," and the super long-term stalling of the Mexican transition, may of course have had more to do with the streamlining of typologies. A Mexican road seemed to be, after all, impossible for the military regimes, and Mexico's own road could be seen (I believe falsely) as mere restructuring of a rather soft form of authoritarian rule, rather than genuine liberalization and especially gradual, if slow, democratization.[67]

It is still a big step from here to assert as a logically necessary proposition that liberalization, that is, top-down reform that stops short of full democratization, cannot "succeed" and that attempting mere reform through liberalization must on formal grounds lead to either full democratization or to a reassertion of authoritarian controls.[68] Only if this argument were foolproof, both empirically and logically, would the two-term typology of transition paths attain theoretical sufficiency. There are of course plenty of historical cases that seem to demonstrate, especially to a retrospective point of view, the difficulties of stabilizing liberal reforms that already go too far for some important constituencies and do not go far enough for mobilized oppositions. But if we look further back and elsewhere, plenty of examples will demonstrate the contrary, especially if by "success" we do not mean "forever." Only if we forget the case of Mexico, can the long-term stabilization of a liberalizing regime be more or less plausibly represented as an empty set even for the recent southern cases. The case of Mexico, moreover, gives us the institutional domain entirely absent from Przeworski's formal considerations, the domain of electoral reform as a terrain of liberalization.[69]

Here the overly sharp dichotomy between stages of liberalization and democratization shared by most analysts of the transition literature helps to mislead.[70] Democratization cannot be reduced to the establishment of the formal institutional conditions of liberal democracy. The recovery of civil society and the public sphere, though based on liberal assumptions, already establishes key elements of a democratic regime. These developments, though liberal, should not be identified with mere "liberalization." But in fact the period of liberalization almost everywhere involves some kind electoral reform as well, which of course has to do with a partial democratization of state institutions (even if electoral institutions are not in themselves sufficient conditions for democracy),[71] and this may in general be a key part of the arsenal of top down reformers.[72]

The East and Central European dictatorships, including even the Polish case, were not military regimes, and the closest resemblance to their ruling parties among the southern forms of authoritarian rule is to be found in fact in Mexico. The analogy becomes even stronger, as Jorge Castañeda has pointed out, if we focus on those Communist regimes that are legitimated through the tradition of indigenous revolutions: Russia, Yugoslavia, China, and Cuba. Unlike Castañeda, who draws a different conclusion,[73] and in spite of the Cuban example that seems resistant to top-down reform and the Slovenian regime that was rapidly democratized, I believe that the common resource of revolutionary legitimation these regimes could draw on made them all plausible candidates for a type of transformation that stays for a sufficiently long period within a model of soft or liberalized dictatorship or one of hard or merely partially democratized democracy. In fact the Mexican case can be best understood in terms of a long-term historical process from the original authoritarian regime consolidated in the 1940s through various stages of *dictablanda* and *democradura* that even today have not yet yielded all the minimum criteria of a polyarchy. And that is certainly a type of success, from the point of view of the architects. There is reason to believe that the number of countries in East Europe that are today implicated in a Mexican type of trajectory is no smaller than the number of those to which the model of collapse and that of negotiated transition (taken together) are applicable.

In summary, in its simplest, dichotomous yet most influential form, the theory of "transition" gives us only two transition paths: extrication and collapse. This approach works for too few of the East European cases and probably cannot fully do the job for all of the southern ones either. It is not entirely surprising, therefore, that the attempt to anticipate institutional consequences on the bases of such foreshortened typology of paths can even lead to the consequence (probably already assumed on the ground of a method stressing interests and power constellations instead) that transition paths may not matter all.[74] If that were true, the role of the southern transitions in helping to interpret the paths from Communism would have to be rather modest. But the pessimistic conclusion is based on the wrong typology, fortunately.[75]

A second difficulty with Przeworski's influential conception has to do with the comparative evaluation of the two types that are in fact taken seriously. He assumes, and others follow him, that the Polish case[76] in East Europe proves that "transitions by extrication leave institutional traces" and are "more problematic and longer in countries where they result from negotiated agreements with the old regime."[77] This time it is the case of Spain that is unfortunately forgotten, or pronounced as a miracle from which accordingly nothing could be learned.[78] The cases of Chile and Poland, close to each other in time, seemed to fully confirm the logically plausible assumption that agreements with authoritarians produce results that will be burdens for a future democracy. Even before these dramatic cases, O'Donnell and Schmitter, who from the point of view of the stability of transitions seemed to have preferred negotiation to imposition from either side, considered various versions of limited democracy *(democradura)* to be the typical result of negotiated pacts interpreted largely on the model of corporatist, exclusionary bargaining.[79] Subsequently, however, Round Table negotiations in Hungary, the GDR (which had its free elections on the bases of the Round Table agreements before unification), Czechoslovakia (arguably), Bulgaria, and finally, and most dramatically, in South Africa confirmed that the Spanish model could be followed in a variety of contexts, without formally undemocratic institutional concessions and with better overall results than other contemporary transition paths. And this conclusion is in fact drawn by Linz and Stepan who uniquely in the literature consider Spain the desirable model for imitation, rather than an extremely fortunate exception.

Linz and Stepan make clear that military dictatorships (especially dictatorships based on the existing structure of command, the "hierarchical military") are both less likely to move toward fully negotiated transitions than civilian-led dictatorships, and, when they do accept such a process, military elites are much more likely to insist on formal, nondemocratic "reserve domains" in the political package that is negotiated.[80] Because these authors too neglect Mexico and, what is most striking about this case, the strong legitimation resources of its rulers, they do overestimate, in my view, the likelihood that civilian-led regimes will opt for negotiated transition. But their case studies of Chile and Spain do demonstrate the key differentiation they seek to make with respect to nondemocratic concessions extorted by military power holders.[81] Both countries had versions of negotiated transitions, with rather favorable economic environments as their contexts. Yet their processes of institutional design and the respective outcomes do not resemble one another: In Spain a newly and freely elected parliament produced a constitution that satisfies liberal democratic criteria on a high level. Chileans, however, in spite of their success in other respects, still labor under the authoritarian dimensions of a difficult to change constitution designed at the height of the military dictatorship. To understand which of these two patterns was likely to prove relevant to negotiated transitions elsewhere, the difference between the two cases must be stressed. It makes a great deal of difference that one had a military regime whose great human rights violations were in the recent past and the other a civilian dictatorship whose major links to violence were attenuated by time. It is this difference that is the most important clue to the Communist cases.

Linz and Stepan rightly warn those who would attempt to treat ruling Communist parties as if they were military juntas. In their view, only the experience of civilian-led authoritarian regimes is really applicable to the "post-totalitarian" versions of Communist rule. Evidently, Przeworski considered at least Poland to be similar to the "bureaucratic authoritarian" military regimes, and the nondemocratic concessions conceded to the authoritarians in Chile do seem to parallel the spirit (certainly not the letter) of the negotiated formula in Poland. This juxtaposition, however, badly misunderstands the nature of the admittedly nonclassical party political regime inaugurated by martial law on December 13, 1981.

What actually produced the undemocratic concessions of the Polish pact of 1989 was timing. Poland was the first transition in the given geopolitical context, one with a highly uncertain international environment. The key is not the process of negotiations with the power holders who in any case resembled those of Chile only superficially. Note that while Poland was the very first Central European transition, Chile was the last of the Latin American cases of the southern cone. In light of all subsequent negotiated cases we can now be fairly certain: Results similar in the short term were produced not by what was similar between the two cases (negotiations and compromise) but by two different circumstances: timing in the case of Poland and an intact military regime in the case of Chile. Significantly, the outcomes in the somewhat longer term were to be highly different as well: It was comparatively easy to get rid of authoritarian concessions in Poland, but not in Chile.[82] This is true because after the other countries had their transitions, and the Soviet Union stood quietly by, it became impossible to justify the structural concessions given to the regime at the Round Table. In Chile, however, the reason for the concessions, the force of an intact military organization, remained in place.

Of course it might be said that the political economy of repression (the term is Linz and Stepan's) lay at the concessions granted in both cases. At the time of the first negotiated end of a Communist regime, it was the still uncertain response of repressive forces (but Soviet and not indigenous) that improved the bargaining position of the government in place. But outside of the rarest instances, indigenous militaries stay, while imperial powers can and do leave the scene. Already when the other Central European transitions became possible, it was clear, precisely because of the Polish experience, that the Soviet Union would not insist on a semidemocratic rather than a fully democratic formula. These countries did not even have the trappings of military dictatorships, and this prima facie implied the greater relevance of Spain as long as the balance of powers or the self-limitation of the actors implied that the transitions would be negotiated. The point was well understood by key participants who considered the Spanish model (and certainly not the Chilean countermodel) significant for their strategies.

It may be generally the case that in negotiations, the government side seeks restrictions of the future democracy. Even in Spain this was initially true. But where the forces of repression have no direct stake in such restrictions, or no longer have one, the opposition side cannot easily concede them. What is equally important, the government side in these civilian cases is much more able to give in to the demands of the opposition than are military governments. The reason is that a party political or civilian bureaucratic old regime has a far better chance to directly represent its political interests in a formally unrestricted democracy than do military power holders. The organizational experience, the linkages to front organizations like unions, and the potential social bases of Communist parties are all important resources for future electoral activity in a fully competitive democratic system. More important even than this state of affairs was the correspondingly optimistic judgment of the negotiators of the ruling parties. At the time of the first free elections many of us scoffed at their hopes, but these have been fulfilled at many subsequent elections by the performance of most of the ex-Communist successor parties in the countries of the negotiated transitions.

Beyond formal restrictions on democracy, what does matter for a ruling Communist Party is the type of competitive democracy. As we have seen, some institutional options they prefer, like presidential government and plurality elections, may have to do with the conversion of power and are therefore, politically speaking, zero-sum solutions. For this reason negotiated transitions produce a higher quality democracy when the bargaining position of the ex-ruling party is not too strong. Even when its weakening bargaining position remains strong, the adverse results can still be corrected in the short term by popular mobilization, which again is easier under a formerly civilian authoritarian regime like Hungary than a military regime like Chile. At the same time, the government side in negotiations will be interested in avoiding later personal retributions against their members and adherents. But here the relevant institutional devices, like strong constitutional courts, have a positive-sum character: All participants in negotiations may benefit from them. Thus it is paradoxically also important for the quality of the outcome that the government side not be too weak. When the latter is the case, only self-limitation by the new forces (as in Czechoslovakia) can produce the type of positive-sum solutions that ordinarily require a balanced relationship of the negotiating sides.[83]

Note that the strength of the opposition in negotiations and its ability to limit itself presupposes some organizational experience, and this in turn is difficult to attain under Communist regimes. This brings us to the civil society problem. In almost all southern dictatorships, to an extent even Spain, the oldest southern authoritarian regime, historical political parties, intact or renewed, could play the required role. Under the more extreme repressive conditions of Soviet-type regimes this option was foreclosed even in the few places where there was a history of democratic politics. The so-called bloc parties that survived Communist rule as its window dressing, were too discredited to play a significant role. Only new forces arising from below, organized in a historical phase of relatively advanced detotalization, could be creditable actors in negotiated transitions. Yet a third problem with the argument of most of the transition literature is that the role of civil society is restricted to the phase of liberalization, while democratization becomes the hour of "political society." This assumption, anticipated by O'Donnell and Schmitter, generalized by Stepan, is built in to Przeworski's model, in which the two- or three-actor model of the liberalization phase is superseded by the four-actor phase of democratization in which all the protagonists are strategic political actors.[84]

But the assumption turns out to be a very pessimistic one if we admit what Linz and Stepan have now come to accept, namely, that civil society is one of the key arenas of democratization. In that case liberalization implies the rebuilding of one dimension of democracy, hence (partial) democratization. At the same time the implosion of civil society during the transition would seriously endanger not just the quality but even the consolidation of the future democracy.

All the same, wherever there are more or less intact political parties of the opposition, the thesis of the implosion of civil society seems nevertheless empirically justified for several reasons. It is difficult to negotiate with a large plurality of movements or with a great social movement that draws its energy from identity politics. Moreover, authoritarian societies have a shortage of cadre ready to engage in democratic politics, and when the action shifts to negotiation these go where the action is: to the parties.

And yet, one should, however, notice the important point that it is not yet genuine parties that participate in the Round Tables on the democratic side in Central Europe. Even in Hungary, the partial exception, the degree to which the fledgling new parties retained their link to civil society and to their movement identity is all important. Given the history of self-limiting politics, how-ever, the movement parties of the opposition not only did not interfere with the strategic context of the bargaining, they were the very conditions of its success. Even where some of them turned against the Round Table compromise, as in Hungary, we should note the highly restrained and limited manner in which they challenged through popular mobilization only specific portions of the agreement, and refrained from using their formal veto power with respect to the package as a whole.[85]

Undoubtedly, even in the Central European cases, the implosion of civil society to an extent did take place with the development of party politics. But we should not underestimate the results of the heavy involvement of human rights activism in the development of constitutions that without exception sought to establish the conditions of a future civil society as a fully institutionalized dimension of social life. In this respect the political transitions proper can be seen not as the final disempowerment of civil society but as its transformation from movement to institution. Of course, as in all constitutional areas, the success of the actual institutionalization of civil society varies among the East and Central European countries. But Linz and Stepan are right to insist on the key role of this dimension in the consolidation of democracy. Especially the legitimation problems of the new regimes cannot be solved unless they can draw on symbolic resources generated by past, present, and future forms of self-organization from below.[86] This issue is central if we are to understand how political transition can be made compatible with the emergence of capitalist market economies.

DEMOCRACY AND CAPITALISM: RATIONAL CHOICE MODELS

The application of the Latin American cases to East and Central Europe has yet another dimension. When interpreters like Przeworski speak about the Latin Americanization of East Europe, they have in mind the unstable coexistence of poor capitalist economies with unconsolidated democracies. Their model of democracy is based in other words on the recurring Latin American experience of an apparently unresolvable conflict between populist, redistributive pressures from below and technocratic or neoliberal attempts to rationalize economies suffering under the burden of heavy state intervention as well as politically sustained clientelistic practices. In the back of their minds, moreover, are a few Latin American cases, especially that of the Chilean dictatorship where economic measures in line with neoliberal ideology were successfully carried out, but under an authoritarian rather than a democratic regime. According to this cast of mind, democracy in East and Central Europe will be incompatible with radical, market-oriented economic transformation. Thus the experiment associated with 1989 is bound to fail.

Even some analysts, who contest the analogy between Latin America and Central Europe see only a "tunnel at the end of the light."[87] If it is difficult to make democracy and capitalism compatible in Latin American countries even though they are already capitalist, have viable states, and have some important democratic traditions, it will be much more difficult to simultaneously establish political democratic, state, and free market institutions where none of them has existed before. Or, the ever-present tension between democracy and capitalism is more likely to become an insoluble paradox under a double or triple transition than where transformation is merely a question of a change of political regime.

It is evidently assumed that the starting point for all the separate transitional tasks is zero. But of course many of the countries have viable states. Hungary and Poland have widely experimented with market forms and private ownership, and democratization too has taken place on the microlevels of civil society and publics in several of the countries (Poland, Hungary, and the Soviet Union especially). This of course does not mean that the dismantling of a Communist system does not involve grave tasks in all three areas of state, market, and regime formation, but that is hardly the same as starting from scratch.

Finally, it is hazardous to automatically assume that the greater the task and the number and types of tasks, the smaller the likelihood of success. This deceptively persuasive idea, around which all of Offe's arguments turn,[88] becomes specifically wrong when we explore the consequences of economic challenge for democratic institutions. When the consciousness of the structural tasks is greater, the amount of breathing room given to governments is greater as well, especially in societies relying on crumbling state redistribution where economic populism is widely discredited.

Let us for the moment (counterfactually) concede that the simultaneous transitions to democracy and markets begin from point zero. Without focusing on any specific context, Jon Elster lays down the fundamental challenge.[89] His remarks rightly focus on two historically unprecedented tasks: the creation of a market economy in the context of dismantling an already industrialized command system and the establishment of liberal institutions in strongly democratizing settings. According to Elster there are four absolutely necessary requirements for such a change: the establishment of genuine market prices and of private ownership, as well as of political democracy and constitutionalism. This vastly oversimplified analysis, which neglects altogether such tasks as change of the material structure of production, demonopolization, and even the ending of most of the components of soft budgetary constraints, is quite convincing in showing two necessary linkages: price reform with privatization, on the one hand, and economic reform taken as a whole with constitutionalism. The brunt of the thesis, however, lies in the relationship of democracy to the other terms: Constitutionalism is said to be impossible without political democracy, while each of the terms of economic reform (privatization enriching some lucky few, price reform impoverishing—if for a time—the unlucky many) is presented as incompatible with democracy, expressed in particular through the preferences of voters and union members. Thus democracy turns out to be both incompatible with and indispensable for economic liberalism. This paradox is made even stronger by Offe.[90] Whereas for Elster the necessity of democracy for marketization is indirect, via the variable of constitutionalism, Offe argues that the fact that the transformation will have to be politically instituted directly requires democratic legitimation. Yet to work, the transition to markets will require drastic limitations on democratic participation.[91] Note that neither author really tells us what kind of democracy they have in mind, with what institutions, and if their arguments are meant to apply to any democracy that meets the threshold of a polyarchy.

There indeed were some East European liberals who at one time agreed about the blockages democratic politics could mean for economic reform and who as a result tried to weaken the linkage between constitutionalism and democracy.[92] While Elster's thesis against the viability of a reform dictatorship, and other arguments like it in the region itself are cogent,[93] this cannot mean that there won't be experimentation with this alternative. Nevertheless, the real option of the economic liberals lay elsewhere, one apparently entirely unanticipated by him and Offe. The concept of elite democracy, often turned by East European politicians from a mere description of fact into a norm, evidently indicates that "constitutional dictatorship" and "political democracy" are not the only alternatives. There was in other words a widespread expectation of using electoral mechanisms, party politics, and parliamentary decision making to vastly narrow the channels of participation, to reduce, that is, the role of the population in politics in time (once every four years), in space (the ballot box), as well as socially, by promoting the atomization of citizens. This procedure was to work, as in the West supposedly, by producing democratic legitimacy without democratic participation. Accordingly the difficult economic decisions could then be undertaken by governments supported by parliamentary majorities, without consultations with anyone else. If the measures were successful, the electorates would reward those responsible for them.

To be sure success was never by any means certain, especially within a single electoral time frame. Przeworski is right to point out that radical strategies of marketization, if they are to work, inevitably have very negative short-run consequences for both prices and employment. The population as a whole, and not only the unemployed, take a significant loss in real wages. It is this short-run economic decline that is the basis for the prediction that democratic political activity of voters (and in another version: unions) will turn against the reformers. This argument, however, leaves political parties out of consideration. The reformers will be turned out of office, if at all, by rival political parties. Even if these promise to halt or moderate the reforms, nothing can bind parties to their precise electoral promises. Not only do the winners in second and subsequent elections still face the constraints of international organizations and friendly Western governments, they are also getting closer to the period when the positive results of hard measures finally begin to manifest themselves. Why should they not continue on the path of reformist rigor? At the very least there are now also many beneficiaries of the reforms, and in a proportional system of representation and especially in Hungary's mixed system it does not take the support of half the voters to be capable to form government.

The elite democratic option is to be sure not an attractive one from the normative point of view. Przeworski is right to counter that if parties violate their electoral promises routinely the prestige of democracy itself suffers.[94] However, it is striking that the winners of free elections after 1990 in Poland, Hungary, and the Czech Republic managed to refrain from promising a reversal in neoliberal economic policies (until 1998 at least!) and could win anyway. We are forced to conclude that in light of the general public understanding of the magnitude of the economic task, even many in economic pain tended to accept the necessity of price stability, privatization, and the structural change of the whole system of production. Those parties on the extreme right and extreme left that claimed otherwise tended to be generally distrusted. The East European disadvantages with respect to other democratizing experiments turned out in some of the countries at least to be advantages. With respect to Latin America, it should also be noted that inequality is widely rejected in East and Central European electorates as well. Nevertheless, the previously largely egalitarian structure of society continues to keep the new inequalities within much narrower limits than those involved in similar economic changes in most Latin American countries.

To be sure empirical reality in the beginning did indicate in some countries various combinations of repeated elections, weak governments, populist response, slowdowns in ownership reform, all seemingly vindicating Elster's thesis in the face of the elite democratic escape valve.[95] None of the governments emerging in 1990 seemed to be initially strong enough to continue radical economic reforms for a sufficiently long period if these were in fact commenced upon. As it turned out, however, some did continue, while others did not. The variable seems to have been political legitimacy, polemically neglected by Przeworski. József Antall's government, having eschewed the significant legitimating advantages of a great coalition of all the civil society-based new forces (MDF [Hungarian Democratic Forum], SZDSZ [Alliance of Free Democrats], and FIDESZ [Alliance of Young Democrats]) lost its courage to ask for popular economic sacrifice after the taxi drivers' and truckers' strike of 1990. On the other hand, as the Mazowiecki government's tenure in office shows, a government can be strong and difficult decisions can be undertaken on the basis of accumulated reserves of legitimacy acquired not through elections primarily, but through a history of involvement of political-intellectuals in social movements and grassroots organizing, in keeping open rather than narrowing social channels of communication. Elster in effect admits this point (giving up thereby some of the narrow assumptions of rational choice theory) but replies that such a legitimacy so laboriously built up can be dissipated in a mere year or less if new governments cannot deliver the goods, if they impoverish the many and enrich the few through their early economic policies. The Polish case seemed to bear out this argument, since in the first free election for president, Mazowiecki was in fact repudiated in favor of candidates who played the populist card (Walesa and Tyminski). It is another matter that Walesa subsequently appointed a new prime minister, who was himself an economic liberal, and was ready to continue radical reform.

I should, however, add that during the first year of the Solidarity government in Poland not only did a great many people feel the economic strain, but also, with a certain oligarchic closure of the elite around the government many channels of earlier or potential communication even with organized society were closed down. Not having been elected in a genuinely free election, and not being able to maintain its ties with organized society, the Mazowiecki government was at least partially responsible for its legitimation crisis. This outcome was not, however, inevitable. What we do not have is credible evidence that it was the pain of economic reform, and not its lack of initial electoral legitimacy and loss of societal support, that was primarily responsible for electoral defeat. Note that the Antall-led coalition in Hungary was freely elected and avoided shock therapy. Nevertheless its loss of support, as measured by local elections, by-elections, polls, and the elections of 1994, was far greater than that of any Polish governing coalition. The reasons, in my view, have to do with the authoritarian political style of this government. Such style, however, was also not unavoidable.

Admittedly, we have not yet seen in any country the successful combination of two senses of legitimacy, the legal procedural one that today can be achieved only by democratic elections, and the sociological one that requires the keeping open of social channels of communication between rulers and ruled. But what if the ruled were as disorganized as Offe thinks, and incapable of anything other than passivity or populist, redistributionist pressure? That there is nothing beyond this choice is inherent in the concept of democracy presupposed by Elster's argument. It seems to me that his notion reduces to this: The masses use their instruments of participation in the electoral system in order to attain the goods they want. While quoting Tocqueville ("those who prize freedom only for the material benefits it offers never kept it long") against such an instrumental view, in fact Elster does not derive from him or from anywhere else an alternative conception. He brackets the question of democracy and constitutionalism as an end in itself, and he, unlike Tocqueville, is silent about participation on the microlevel in intermediate institutions. But democracy understood as a set of "ends" (mechanisms and institutions) beyond participation in the national electoral system potentially provides an opening toward liberalism, while it is democracy as a means to achieve (especially short term) material satisfaction that closes the doors to price reform and privatization.

The East Central European concept of civil society indicates both a wider concept of democracy than one referring to state institutions and one that can be more easily understood as an end and not only a means. Let me recall the origins of Solidarity, when the workers at the various strike sites were willing to forgo wage increases for the right to unionize and for other civil rights. An example from 1989 shows a complementary phenomenon: The negotiators for Solidarity again considered the legalization of the union their main goal and were willing to agree to political representation in Parliament only reluctantly. The point is not that material gains or national political participation can be simply neglected, but only that actors in the process of self-organization are willing to agree to trade-offs involving the delay of other political and economic benefits for the institutionalization of those dimensions of civil society where they can more directly participate. This would be even truer if institutions were established where the new bodies of interest representation would be repeatedly and seriously consulted before difficult decisions were taken. Here lies the opportunity for continually refurbishing democratic legitimacy in the sociological sense that is easily used up if dependent only on prior political events and relationships, including general elections. The existence of relevant bodies and associations, and serious consultation and compromise with them, would help underwrite democratic legitimacy at times when difficult decisions are undertaken. But of course a political democracy with open channels to a more organized civil society would not be elite democracy, either in norm or in fact.[96]

Even if one insists on the instrumental interpretation of democracy, it could be said that it is worthwhile to trade in unattainable present benefits for organizational possibilities that will make participation in future and genuinely attainable benefits more plausible. Such considerations could justify a strategy of waiting and postponing immediate struggle for material satisfaction. In any case, the civilized self-restraint and self-limitation entertained by Offe as the only way to solve Elster's paradox is certainly not going to be achieved through economic miracles, extensive Western help, or lavish social policy. The last, moreover, would also require Western subsidies, and if linked to full employment policies, would retard the dismantling of the existing paternalist systems.[97] It seems to me that Offe, while on the right track, also misses the point when he throws some doubt on the feasibility of the fourth, a civil society-oriented alternative.[98] The point is not whether the relevant associations or intermediary bodies already exist in great numbers (though they do exist and are numerically growing), but whether constituencies otherwise open to populist appeals would be attracted by the possibility, legally guaranteed, of institution building on this level, and would be willing to forego other benefits in return. In this context nothing demonstrates the supposed fundamentalism, inability to enter into negotiation and compromise that he ascribes to East European civic movements, in contradistinction to Western actors. In my experience the opposite has been true. After all the strategy of self-limiting revolutionary change has been invented and brilliantly practiced by East European intellectuals and activists. Indeed, the spirit of this strategy can be shown to have been present in most of the great transformations of 1989. The question, however, is whether it could be embodied in lasting institutions.

LIBERALISM AND DEMOCRACY: CONSTITUTION MAKING AND CIVIL SOCIETY

My critical review of Western interpretations of 1989 thus converges in the concept of civil society from two directions. This concept, I have tried to argue, is the key to the possibility of innovation in the East Central European transitions and also points to the possible locus of reconciliation between economic liberalism and political democracy, both evidently necessary and yet in conflict in the difficult processes of transition at hand. Nevertheless I cannot simply dismiss the fact that this concept is entirely missing in Habermas, Furet, and Elster; is de-emphasized, with respect to the literature of the 1980s for example, by Heller, Feher, and Offe; is again identified with bourgeois society by Nolte; is considered capable of realization only through a relatively long, organic process of development by Dahrendorf, or finally, is held to be relevant only to the phase of liberalization by the bulk of the transition literature. These positions, corresponding to the judgments of many social scientists and philosophers in the region (e.g., Jadwiga Staniszkis and Lena Kolarska-Bobinska in Poland, Miklós Szabó and János Kis in Hungary), indicate a period in which the new states and political societies have the initiative, while civil society, demobilized in its earlier movement forms, has not yet generally found the new forms for its institutionalized existence. If civil society was the "hero" of dissidence, political society became the major protagonist of the transitions.[99] It is just this shift that lends credence to Elster's challenge, which can be answered only if we can show not only that in spite of demobilization, civil society had a role in the transitions, but, even more importantly, that the processes of establishing new regimes point in some important respects to the possibilities of its wider institutionalization.

Ulrich Preuss is one of the very few Western interpreters who has attempted to respond to this challenge. Indeed he has most strikingly placed civil society into the center of his understanding of the significance of 1989. As a West German constitutional lawyer observing the "revolution" in East Germany, Preuss was struck by a number of characteristics shared by most of the East European transitions that differentiate them from the modern tradition of revolution. At issue is not so much the nonviolent character of the events in most countries, though the desire to avoid violence was an important motivation of most leading participants. Preuss stresses in particular the general absence of particular forms of violence entailed by political trials of adversaries, including the previous rulers, the destruction of their organizations (here: parties, unions, front organizations), or at least their exclusion from the political process, and their personal and institutional expropriation on the basis of merely political decision. It is these features of the great revolutions that associate their very concept not only with civil violence but with civil war.[100]

To be sure some rather moderate, but clearly revolutionary, breaks like the 1918 overthrow of the German imperial state and the establishment of the Weimar Republic also dispensed with the forms of violence Preuss listed (if not with revolutionary semantics *tout court*). But Preuss manages to use this very example to his advantage.[101] In the German Revolution of 1918 one can precisely date the end of the old constitutional legality as well as the beginning of the new one. This revolution produced a provisional government as well as a constituent assembly, the latter clearly asserting its revolutionary legitimacy by appealing to the will of the German people as a whole, the *pouvoir constituant*. This constituent assembly, as the "sovereign dictator," was bound by no previous rules and exercised decree powers for the duration of its existence.

It was otherwise with the transitions from Communist rule in 1989. Focusing on the GDR, Preuss notes the continuity of the process that allows no dating of the fundamental break, the maintenance of the framework of the old constitution whose own rules of amendment and for the recall of deputies are utilized for all constitutional change, and most fundamentally the renunciation of the status of a constituent assembly rooted in a unified constituent power by the main instance of constitution making, the Round Table. This agency claimed neither revolutionary nor any other form of strictly political legitimacy; it passed no decrees or otherwise formally exercised political power. The new elites relied instead on their power of persuasion in the reconstructed public sphere, a "power" rooted in the superiority of a powerless morality over an immoral power.[102]

Can such a process still be depicted as a revolution?[103] Drawing on a distinction rooted in the work of Carl Schmitt, Preuss claims that neither the term *constitutional* revolution *(Verfassungsrevolution)* nor the term *social revolution* adequately describes the events.[104] The East European transitions involve dramatic changes not only in the system of government but also on the levels of social and economic organization; thus they are more than constitutional revolutions limited to the making of a new political constitution, whose model is supposed to be that of the American Revolution. But unlike social revolutions on the French and Russian model, here the classical nexus between a unified constituent power and friend and enemy relations defined in class (and in most countries also national) terms is missing. No instance has claimed sovereign dictatorship for the duration of the transition legitimated by its supposed identity with a homogenous class or national grouping or both under the heading of "the people." To show this has been the burden of the whole argumentation.

With the two major models of modern revolution excluded it is not surprising that many of the major actors refuse to speak of revolution at all.[105] Indeed a revolution within the framework of the inherited constitutional legality seems to be a contradiction in terms. And yet Preuss insists that we should speak of revolution as long as the fundamental rules of the game, its constituent principles, are changed. Whatever has replaced it, a principle of sovereignty based on "the working people in the city and the country" or on "the working class in firm alliance with other strata" is no more.

This last idea seems to bring us back to Agnes Heller's definition of revolution as a fundamental change in sovereignty. For her the transitions of 1989 are revolutions because they involved the replacement of party sovereignty by popular sovereignty, similar apparently to the replacement of monarchical by popular sovereignty. Preuss certainly does not take over this theory; that would amount to one consistent Schmittian reading of the meaning events.[106] Unfortunately, not quite correctly, he at times seems to suggest that in any case, in modern revolutions it is not so much a change of sovereigns at stake as a change in who manages to identify with the sovereign successfully.[107] I believe, however, that the dynamic of many of the great modern revolutions involved both types of change, indissolubly linked. The transition from monarchical sovereignty, which requires no duality of identifier and identified, except in relation to the same physical body, to a unitary popular sovereignty does involve an empirical doubling of the new sovereign, initially as constituent power and constituent assembly.[108] According to Schmitt, who described this model in a convincing way, the link between the two can only be that of "identification" based ultimately on emotional or affective motivations. If successful, this means that the enemies of the signifier (of the assembly) are successfully claimed to be, and thus indeed become, the enemies of the signified, of the people. The ability of any constitution to successfully maintain the burden of such identification is, however, always in doubt, as we have seen most dramatically in the history of the Weimar constitution, but also throughout modern French history. Identification and its possible alteration are functions of politics; they are by their nature unstable and cannot be regulated by the constitutional system itself. Permanent revolution is in effect built into the model.

In Preuss's analysis, one can detect two interrelated devices by which the East European revolutions sought to avoid the logic of permanent revolution, one leading to dictatorship. First, the protagonists acted as if there was no need to abolish an existing form of sovereignty. And while in effect they did abolish it even formally by eliminating references to the leading role of the party in those constitutions where this was present, doing so within the framework of existing constitutions and by the inherited rules of constitutional revision or amendment nevertheless promoted the idea of continuous constitutional legality, and this was incompatible with a break in the structure of sovereignty.[109] Thus in effect the regimes were treated as if their claim to represent a particular version of popular sovereignty was somehow valid.[110] In the process, however, this very version of unitary sovereignty became highly questionable. Thus the second, and more important, device[111] was to renounce, at least implicitly, the model of unitary sovereignty, and the corresponding idea of its undivided representation by a constituent assembly bound by no rules, a sovereign dictator possessing revolutionary legitimacy. Arendt has detected just such a renunciation in the United States: "The great and in the long run greatest American innovation in politics was the abolition of sovereignty within the body politic of the republic, the insight that in the realm of human affairs sovereignty and tyranny are the same."[112] This innovation was possible according to Arendt, because the American *pouvoir constituant* was not in the state of nature, as in Sieyès's theory (according to Arendt closely followed by French reality), but, on all levels was rooted in already politically constituted bodies rather than the totality of atomized individuals ruled by no valid laws.[113]

To be sure the principle of free federation appealed to by Arendt is on the whole inapplicable to the countries of Eastern Europe, which are compulsory federations or unitary nation states. But in Preuss's presentation, Sieyès's dilemma, the inevitable circularity of a constituent power that is unable to generate sufficient legitimacy outside itself, is solved in two ways in East Europe. The process of constitution making is not in the state of nature for two fundamental reasons: It assumes the constitutional rules of the previous system and refers back not to the unified but unstructured people, but to the organized groups, bodies, and institutions of civil society.[114] The interpretation is favored both by the existence of written constitutions in Soviet-type societies, the homage as it were of a hypocritical prerogative state to political modernity,[115] and the decade-long struggle in three countries at least for the self-organization of civil society. In Preuss's depiction, civil society becomes the stand-in for the *pouvoir constituant* and the alternative framework to a unitary sovereignty. To be successful, of course, given the relatively underdeveloped state of institutionalized civil society in the East, the argument presupposes that the new constitutions will be those of civil society as well as the state, promoting the development of civil society through the establishment of both its powers and limits.[116] Thus the old quest articulated by Schmitt, and reformulated on the basis of a very different conception of politics by Arendt, namely, to go beyond the alternative of permanent revolution and conservative constitutionalism by preserving something of the spirit of the revolutionary constituent power in constitutional politics, now reappears in Eastern Europe in the form of the relationship of civil society to both constitution making and settled constitutionalism.[117]

In a more recent article, written only a year after the works I have analyzed, Ulrich Preuss has become rather pessimistic about the chances of a civil society–based "reflexive" constitutionalism anywhere in Eastern Europe.[118] Undoubtedly the outcome of the German process of transition played a role in this. Now operating in a framework adopted from Elster and Offe, he expresses doubt concerning the simultaneous solution of the two problems of transition, to a market economy and to a democratic polity. He doubts in particular the chances of democratization through "self-imposition" (whatever could this mean?), in other words, through imitation of the West. Thus he argues that either presidentialist semidemocracy or state corporatism will be the most likely solutions of the puzzle Elster himself did not try to resolve. In other words, in line with Elster's other argument, namely, the impossibility of a transition to markets without (as well as with) democracy, Preuss proposes semidemocracy in two versions that complement the version analyzed here, namely, elite democracy. Without wishing to de-emphasize the "heroism" of the struggles in East Europe, he now seems to believe that only a democratic-liberal minimum has been attained, one compatible with restricted as well as self-expanding democracies.

It seems to me that Preuss is throwing in the towel a little early. So far all experimentation with all three forms of restricted democracy mentioned have shown them each to be extremely open to further democratic pressures. Indeed, because of their formal and procedural deficiencies, presidential democracy and corporatism are more vulnerable than elite party political rule. Yet as a whole series of conflicts and electoral outcomes in Hungary and Poland have shown, even elite democracy and trends toward parliamentary absolutism do not go without serious external challenge. All the more, we repeatedly see all semisecret arrangements immediately denounced and opposed. Finally, even traces of presidential authoritarianism, as in the case of Walesa at one point, have also run into determined opposition and tended to involve decreasing popularity for the figure of the leader. For this reason I would still maintain that shifting the locus of democratization to civil society, involving both organizational and symbolic trade-offs for economic goods, is a better way of solving the problem of the relationship of the two transitions.

The strengthening of civil society does not imply one of two possible zero-sum games with the democratic state and the liberal market.[119] Indeed, any of these three spheres can become genuinely stronger, rather than in appearance merely, only if the others are strengthened. It is this solution that Preuss now refers to as excessively utopian. But the excessive realism of his later considerations is in fact less realistic for at least the three Central European countries than the supposedly utopian solution. Here the choice seems to be not between semi- and full democracy, but between civil society and forms of left and right populism that would make any consolidation illusory. Finally, given the fact that the civil society-based project emerged spontaneously in Eastern Europe and has been now widely disseminated in the region shows that only this approach escapes both the charge of insufficient democracy and that of imposition or imitation.

Of course my considerations imply only that a civil society-based political project is possible in East and especially Central Europe, and that it should be of interest to liberals and democrats. I do not underestimate the forces opposed to such a project symbolized by the figures of the radical revolutionary, the bourgeois, the proletarian, the party politician, and the nationalist, these former allies of a self-forming civil society who have become its opponents or at least its competitors, and who often see their various conflicts with civil actors in zero-sum terms. I claim only that weakening civil society, interfering with its institutionalization, can only weaken the state, the market as well as the nation.

Chapter 2

Civil Society, Transition, and the Problem of Institutionalization

INTRODUCTION

The concept of civil society was revived about twenty years ago among neo-Marxist critics of socialist authoritarianism, who along with this conceptual move reversed one of Marx's most fundamental assumptions and thus became "post-Marxist." Evidently the concept could have been, but was not, in fact, first revived in a neo- or post-Montesqueuian, Burkian, Tocquevillian, or even Laskian, Parsonian, or many other intellectual traditions. Remarkably enough, the pioneering works of this revival, those of Leszek Kolakowski, Zdenek Mlynar, Mihály Vajda, and Adam Michnik in the East, of Jürgen Habermas, Claude Lefort, and Norberto Bobbio in the West, of Francisco Weffort, Fernando Henrique Cardoso, and Guillermo O'Donnell in the South, were rooted in the same or analogous traditions of Western or neo-Marxist discourse. For them a knowledge of G. W. F. Hegel, the young Karl Marx, and Antonio Gramsci represented living links to the usage of the concept of civil society and the state-society dichotomy that were in different ways nearly universal in the nineteenth century, but which nearly disappeared in twentieth-century social and political science and philosophy. At an earlier stage, the task of Western Marxism was to deepen Marxian social philosophy by a return to philosophical roots and to reveal the connections of a re-Hegelianized Marx to some very specific works in non-Marxist philosophy and social theory: to Max Weber, Georg Simmel, Benedetto Croce, and Sigmund Freud among others. At that time concepts like alienation, fetishism, reification, rationalization, repression, and praxis were in the center stage. Reviving the concept of civil society was apparently an analogous move, since its presence in the young Marx justified a critical reexamination and appropriation of ideas of yet another series of non-Marxist thinkers from Alexis de Tocqueville to Hannah Arendt. And yet this time instead of using the best of Marx against the worst, the conceptual strategy focusing on civil society everywhere used Gramsci to turn even the young Marx on his head in order to redevelop a concept that was able to, self-critically, pinpoint the earliest origin of the authoritarian turn in their own tradition that provided a link ab ovo with state socialism with "Communist" politics. In short, the young Marx's demand that the separation and differentiation of state and civil society be overcome was now understood as the origin and justification of the Marxist statization of all aspects of social reality.

Initially only a new, but hardly unanticipated, conceptualization of totalitarianism was the fruit of the enterprise in France and most notably in Poland and Hungary, which were certainly not totalitarian. This was an inauspicious beginning that would have yielded little more than a new, critical, and polemical concept. The remarkable historical success of the revival of the concept of civil society was due to its anticipation of, convergence with, and intellectualization of a new radical reformist or evolutionary, dualistic strategy for the transformation of dictatorships, first in the East and soon after in Latin America, based on the idea of the self-organization of society, the rebuilding of social ties outside the authoritarian state, and the appeal to an independent public sphere outside of all official, state- or party-controlled communication. Used along these lines, the concept of civil society became a focal point of orientation, first in Poland, for a period in France, then (perhaps with the mediation of French intellectuals) in Brazil, followed by more general East European and Latin American discussion after the early successes of Solidarity and the abertura. At the very least in Hungary, Czechoslovakia, Yugoslavia (especially in Slovenia), Russia, Chile, Argentina, Mexico, and finally South Africa, further conceptual development and the formation of political strategies went hand in hand through the 1980s. In the process earlier transitions (those of Spain and Greece notably) as well as successfully stabilized authoritarian systems (above all China) were increasingly interpreted both by participants and outsiders by using various versions of the concept of civil society. In some places like Hungary, where the transition was successful and where the intellectual strategy actually had a political role, the concept of civil society now turned into a journalistic commonplace. Finally, there is now a vastly expanded discussion in many Western countries with established civil societies where the focus is different, depending on the ideological proclivities of the various discussants. For some, including myself, the goal is finding new loci of the potential democratization of really existing democracies, new ways to revitalize the public space of these societies. Others, however, are interested in agendas as diverse as the reconstruction of the supposedly communal presuppositions of society and the radical liberation of market rationality from political regulation and social constraint. The concept of civil society has been used to justify all of these potentially incompatible strategies. But it cannot be denied that all the perspectives mentioned can find their progenitors during the course of the initial revival in Central Europe.

THE RISE AND DECLINE OF CIVIL SOCIETY

It is now almost beyond dispute that the concept of civil society has played a major role in recent transitions to democracy, both in the formulation of strategies of democratization and in the journalistic, historical, and social scientific analyses of the relevant processes.[1] At the very least in the leading countries of Poland and Hungary the civil society strategy was the historical precondition for the successful turn to political society, for the successful achievement of radical regime change through political negotiations. But even in the Soviet Union, *glasnost* is best interpreted as an attempt to stimulate the reconstruction of the public sphere and of civil actors, who were to be allies in a project of reform carried out from above *(perestroika)*. Mikhail Gorbachev's project was indeed based on the incoherent hope that independent civil society could be somehow controlled from above, and it had to fail.[2] But, contributing to the transformation of Soviet foreign policy and even the end of the Communist regime, the role of glasnost in the transitions in East and Central Europe was considerable to say the very least.

Whether the pressure for an opening to civil society originally came from below as in Poland, from above as in the Soviet Union, or involved both openings from above and autonomous activities from below as in Hungary, it is now more or less accepted wisdom that the self-organization of society against the state cannot represent the central process of the transition to democracy. Civil pressure is supposed to lead either to repression as in Poland in 1981 and later China, or to a process of extrication in which political actors, displacing civic initiatives and social movements will play the major role.[3] As I have shown in the previous chapter, this argument is connected to the general thesis that *liberalization cannot succeed* and as such is not universally true. Let me note that Polish developments played a large role in the formulation of this thesis, which retains its relevance for the interpretation of that country's politics in the late 1970s and 1980s.[4] Nevertheless, under conditions of a Soviet-type society, it would be extremely misleading to describe the politics of the reconstruction of civil society that was the hegemonic form under which oppositional activity was organized in Poland from 1976 to 1988 as unsuccessful.[5]

The Birth of a Project

Though not without earlier anticipations,[6] the East European project for the reconstruction for civil society was born in Poland in the mid- and late 1970s. In the writings of Adam Michnik,[7] the new strategy was based on negative and positive learning experiences. According to Michnik, in the given geopolitical constellation dominated by an intact imperial system under Soviet hegemony, complete social transformation on the patterns of the Hungarian revolution from below (1956) and the Czechoslovak reform from above (1968) were still impossible. This was the case not only because of almost absolutely certain Soviet military response often stylized as "the Brezhnev doctrine," but also because the ruling elites in each country and even their more pragmatic elements have learned that all serious reformism from above leads to internal splits in the ruling parties, social mobilization, and loss of control by the reformers. Nevertheless, Polish experience, in particular the workers' protests in 1956, 1970, and 1976, have shown that within limits significant change can be achieved in at least some of the societies of the Soviet type.

For Michnik, an opposition interested in such a change must formulate a program of radical reform from below, addressed to independent "society" or "public opinion," which through its pressure should be able to achieve some significant concessions as long as these stay well within the limits of the geopolitical interests of the Soviet Union, and the control by the existing ruling party of the central positions, within the sphere of the state. In such a struggle, Michnik argued, party moderates or pragmatists might become reluctant reformers, ad hoc partners though never genuine allies. The actual force for reform must come from below. But from where exactly?

Interestingly Michnik's argument, in an apparently contradictory manner, both appealed to an independent society and postulated the formation of such a society as the goal of a dualistic program that would radically transform the social sphere and leave that of the party-state intact. The last phrase reveals a second potential contradiction, the obverse of the first. In the totalitarianism theory assumed by Michnik, the party-state penetrates and controls all of society, and thus any carving out of an independent social sphere could not leave the rule of the party in the state intact.

Michnik's own answer to these contradictions, and that of the new organization KOR (Committee in Defense of Workers) he helped to found, was first of all political-existential. We should act as if we already had several significant rights enshrined in our paper constitutions—the freedoms of association, assembly, and communication (the central rights of civil society!)—and so acting, we can contribute to the genuine institutionalization of just these rights. Under such an assumption KOR not only organized itself but proceeded to facilitate the self-organization of select constituencies of workers to whom they provided legal, journalistic, economic, and organizational support. This program amounted to the self-organization and defense of civil society in the form of a movement or protomovement, of which KOR was only one important organ, one that was to play a dramatically important role in the strike movement of the summer of 1980 that led on August 31 and in the subsequent days to the apparent legal institutionalization of some of the key rights of civil society—first and foremost the right to form free unions.

The first successes of the new strategy did not of course depend on only intellectual elaboration complemented by a political-existential stance. Civil society as a movement did not emerge ex nihilo. Michnik himself stressed the successive learning experiences of Polish workers who historically could become conscious both of their power and its limits. Similarly, as he showed in a famous book, the history of the Polish church demonstrated that important freedoms could be attained and defended by an independent institution as long as its formal limits remained well defined.[8] These examples, however, along with the survival of private agriculture, seemed to indicate that the theory of totalitarianism, even if a useful polemical tool, did not really apply to Polish society. As Kolakowski already argued in 1971,[9] while there was a totalitarian project built into the structure of rule in Soviet-type societies, this project was only incompletely successful in the face of largely unconscious and disorganized spontaneous social resistance. This resistance, only a residual category for Kolakowski, was thoroughly elaborated by Polish sociologists of the 1970s who stressed the survival and growth of independent circles and networks of social relations (friends, colleagues, informal working collectives, networks of informal support and assistance, economic reciprocal ties, and so on), especially as the regime's pressure on the private sphere was vastly reduced following the explosions of 1956.[10]

Thus in Poland, a self-organizing society could rely on microstructures, learning experiences, as well as institutional models. It was the unique combination of these givens that distinguished this country from all other contexts in the Soviet imperium. Even if civil society in the sense of stabilized institutions existed at best in the case of the Catholic Church, elements of independent social life existed throughout the whole society, some of which (in particular workers and intellectuals) were already tested in political and social conflicts. The project of organizing civil society in the form of a movement aiming at its institutionalization presupposed these levels and appealed to individuals who were already associating and communicating and were quite different than the atomized, entirely state-dependent individuals stylized by the totalitarian theory. The Communist regimes indeed tried to create such individuals, but in the long run unsuccessfully.

Thus KOR's strategy initially sought "only" the transformation of de facto existing forms of social independence that could be organized in the form of a movement for reform into legally institutionalized structures.[11] Purely theoretically at least, it was possible to postulate without self-contradiction that such a transformation would not reduce the actual framework of authority of the party state but only transform the status of the societal sphere that this ruling structure already did not control. What was not yet clearly realized, however, (or was realized but tactfully suppressed) was that this could not happen unless the status of the party-state sphere itself was transformed.[12] Even the formal granting of some of the rights constitutive of civil society was legally (though not politically, as long as the movement was very strong) meaningless as long as the structure of the state was based on the prerogative power of the ruling party rather than constitutionalism, at the very least in the form of an authoritarian *Rechtsstaat*.[13]

The program of the reconstitution of civil society was not, strictly speaking, a revolutionary one, even if ideas like "the new evolutionism" and "radical reformism" express their strategic content only imperfectly. The program was radical in that it appealed to actors "from below" and aimed at structural transformation of the existing Soviet-type society. Yet like all reform it involved a built-in "self limitation" with respect to certain institutional givens (the one party political system) and geopolitical relations (Poland's place in the Soviet bloc). All the same, there was a revolutionary element in the program as well, because even the institutional frameworks that would not be challenged were to be relocated, as it were, from a monolithic system where political prerogative alone regulated the relations of state and society to a dualistic society where these relations would be coordinated by some (vaguely understood) combination of legal guarantees and institutions of negotiation and compromise. Thus, in my view the term *self-limiting revolution,* invented by Jacek Kuron and popularized by Jadwiga Staniszkis,[14] best characterized the kind of change required by the new strategy. As Michnik and Kuron often repeated, the "revolution" they aimed at ought to be self-limiting not only because of the obvious geopolitical constraints for the countries of the imperial periphery but also because of the very negative experiences of all unlimited social revolutions of the Jacobin-Bolshevik type. In order to avoid the unintended emergence of a new, authoritarian state, once again incompatible with the building of a democratic civil society, the classical instruments of social revolutions, their elitism, their violence, their semantics, all linked to the desire of an impossible total rupture with the past, should be consistently avoided. Such learning from the history of revolutions was an essential dimension of the new orientation to civil society.

Civil Society under Solidarity

While the term *new evolutionism* reflected a period (1976–79) in which the small democratic opposition in Poland was on the defensive, the idea of "the self-limiting revolution" presupposed an offensive strategy based on the existence of a rapidly growing, remarkably united social movement, Solidarity. Evidently this movement was not simply the product of the new strategy, or of the organizing activities of intellectuals. It took the dramatic decline of Poland's economic situation in the late 1970s and the opportunity presented by the government's administratively ordained price rises in 1980 to produce a vast, initially spontaneous industrial strike movement, most of whose participants were entirely new to politics. Nevertheless, groups of intellectuals and workers actively involved in the development of political networks and forms of communication on the pattern of the new strategy played a decisive role in the organization of the movement, in the formulation of the central demands, in the negotiations with the authorities, and in leadership and expert-advisory roles. It was because of their influence that Solidarity, the first independent and self-managing union in the whole Soviet imperium, came to be understood and to understand itself as the first, but only the first, legally secured institution of an independent civil society. Never a revolutionary movement or merely a social movement alone on behalf of its own worker constituency, Solidarity was above all a "movement for the liberation of society."[15] In effect this meant that the organization would struggle to promote the self-organization of all important spheres of society, rather than seek to represent these spheres as some kind of new avant-garde. In victory as well as defeat, from the fight for rural solidarity and an independent student association in early 1981 to the failure to establish an organization of fire cadets in November of that year, this program, making Solidarity in one of its dimensions into a vastly expanded and more powerful version of KOR, was never abandoned. And yet Solidarity could not simply stay within the original program for the reconstitution of civil society.

To begin with the vast strata mobilized had in large part no experience in earlier protests and dissident activity. While in the beginning it was easy enough to accept the strategy of self-limitation, this did not in all likelihood apply to its principled, normative postrevolutionary dimension. Very soon, the simultaneous growth of the organization and the deepening of the economic crisis without an end in sight was to produce a fundamentalist movement within the movement and, to some extent, a split between a pragmatic leadership and many rank and file groups. The latter in turn were divided: As the research of the Touraine group has shown, different worker constituencies were oriented to democratic, national, and ouvrierist aspirations. Each of these orientations could be developed in fundamentalist directions, targeting not only the ruling system but their own organization as well. As a result the Solidarity leadership was alternatively (and I believe inconsistently) criticized as insufficiently democratic or radical.

Equally important, the growth and the central role of the organization for all social conflict brought the adherence of new groups of intellectuals with different programs than the civil society orientation of the most important early experts and advisors.[16] In particular the national revolutionary orientation of the groups such as KPN (Confederation for an Independent Poland) was to find some response from rank-and-file groups impatient with the leadership. While the organization managed to find some ways of accommodating radical ouvrierist demands in its programs of industrial self-management, there was no way to organically integrate nationalist fundamentalism within any program of self-limitation. Yet, given the decentralized organization of Solidarity, all fundamentalist strains stayed within the single movement, producing the illusion of power within increasing weakness. The vocal role of these fundamentalists, moreover, helped to produce an atmosphere in which a final collision with the authorities seemed inevitable. Of course the major role in this was played by the authorities themselves who did all they could to avoid serious negotiations. This avoidance in turn strengthened the hand of the fundamentalists.[17]

The program of the reconstruction of civil society through the vehicle of the one great movement, within a framework of dualistic self-limitation, had serious internal weaknesses. First, there was an obvious conflict between the goal to establish a pluralistic civil society and the formula of the one unified movement. While new islands of independence were indeed continually created, politically, in the face of a unified and intact enemy, these were continually reabsorbed in the workers movement that represented nevertheless a specific constellation of identities and interests. Not a political party, Solidarity was on the same plane of interest articulation and identity formation as all the other protomovements, associations, and initiatives, but on this plane there could be no competition between the giant movement and its tiny offspring and allies. Any social proposal, any economic initiative could become serious in this context only if it was first adopted by Solidarity. I believe it was this structural situation and not the supposed authoritarianism of the Solidarity leadership that led many intellectuals, especially after the defeat of December 13, 1981, to remember the movement as monolithic, authoritarian, or even neo-Bolshevik and "totalitarian."

Second, the project of a dualistic reconstruction of society reluctantly leaving the sphere of the state intact and in the hands of the ruling party, perhaps impossible in itself, was all the more untenable in context of a vast, largely unified, increasingly politicized movement of society.[18] In such a context dualism produced extreme polarization and, for a while, a political stalemate that was all the more disastrous given the economic situation. Vast democratic mobilization from below but within definite limits led to a situation where one side continued to possess administrative power but without legitimacy and the other side came to have significant democratic legitimacy but without administrative power. As a result neither could generate policy. There was, as a result, no social actor capable of undertaking a radical reform of the economy, a project that would inevitably involve new austerity. A regime without legitimacy could no more institute economic changes involving sacrifices in 1981 than in 1980 when the strike movement first challenged the price rises. But without power in the state, Solidarity also could not initiate economic reforms or even accept the responsibility for programs arrived at without its participation. And yet, the actual economic ideas of the two sides, or at least of regime reformers and Solidarity experts, were probably not too far apart. Negotiated compromise was, however, impossible in spite of the desperate attempts of the Solidarity leadership around Lech Walesa and Jacek Kuron, as well as third parties connected to the church. Any arrangement that would have made Solidarity a junior partner would have meant only participation in the responsibility for new hardships without any genuine authority, without a chance to guarantee trade-offs to its constituency. Yet any arrangement that would have involved equal participation in decision making threatened to absorb the regime in the vastly more popular Solidarity.

This situation led not only to impasse but, in my view, to tacit support for the only one violent solution geopolitically possible. On the one side, organized society remained potentially powerful but increasingly also fearful of its own power and its consequences: political stalemate and unresolved economic crisis.[19] This power could only be a negative one; it could block solutions without being able to generate alternative ones. Solidarity remained popular, yet its negative power left society in the midst of economic collapse without any perspectives. Anyone with a plausible scenario of extrication had to have some support, and no one outside of General Wojciech Jaruzelski had such a scenario, however unattractive it was and however implausible it now appears in retrospect. Moreover, in spite of the claims of the fundamentalists, a revolutionary option was feared all the more when the logic of the situation began to point to it. There was still widespread agreement among groups as diverse as the moderate leadership of Solidarity, the episcopate of the Catholic Church, and the military leadership that revolution was equal to the worst evil, namely, Soviet intervention, which was in any case continually threatened. Finally, the regime, given the growth of Solidarity, increasingly had no other resource than military violence, and even this resource, exposed to the potential discontent of enlisted men and junior officers, could be lost if not used quickly.

The defeat of Solidarity by the martial law regime of December 13 demonstrated that the sustenance of civil society in the form of a highly mobilized movement and in the absence of adequate institutionalization was highly unstable. It became clear, moreover, that institutionalization relying on a single isolated legal act, the legalization of the union, was entirely insufficient in the context of an intact prerogative party-state capable of reversing without due process any and all legal guarantees. In a society without constitutionalism, the written constitution offered no protection for the central rights of civil society: association and assembly. And a social movement, even the strongest, could be a functional equivalent for constitutionalism at best only through the upward phase of its life cycle.

And yet, one cannot, in the manner of Michnik's early thesis, group the civil society-oriented program of 1980–81 along with revolution (1956) and reform from above (1968) as yet another merely negative learning experience.[20] Polish society was not normalized as the result of martial law repression; there was no return to any pre-Solidarity status quo ante. In particular, the existence of a second sphere of public opinion, based on countless illegal publications and forms of assembly, could not be suppressed by the authorities that only made halfhearted attempts to do so. Equally important, the civil society-oriented strategy was successfully introduced in the 1980s in several other countries: Hungary, parts of Yugoslavia, and, significantly, the Soviet Union itself. The contrast with the normalizations following 1956 and 1968 could not have been more impressive.

Civil Society in Hungary: Intellectual Origins

Hungary too represents an excellent test case for theories seeking to understand the role and the limits of civil society in the transitions to democracy. First and foremost, the story of the concept in this second country, and of the activities oriented to it, demonstrates that we are not dealing with mere Polish exceptionalism when we insist on its importance.

Indeed, in the 1980s, the strategy of the reconstruction of civil society was imported or reinvented in other East European countries. In Hungary, the pride of place belongs to the "post-Marxist" democratic opposition, organized around the early samizdat projects of the late 1970s and 1980s. The dualistic Polish project was in particular first adopted by János Kis and György Bence, who were, however, clear that the model had both internal problems and special difficulties when applied to Hungary. They saw in particular from the outset, and before the experience of 1980–81 in Poland, that the combination of a fully self-organized society and an intact party-state was logically and politically self-contradictory. More immediately relevant was the fact that Hungary had no ongoing history of a working class or any other social movement to which a democratic opposition could refer and respond.

Today the point can be put more generally. In Hungary neither did a model for independent civil society like the Polish church exist, nor were a series of learning experiences like 1956, 1970, and 1976 in Poland available, when a movement could learn that radical action within limits could make significant gains. Indeed, the key learning experiences of Hungarians were 1956, which seemed to teach that radical, collective action leads to disaster, and the Kádárist reform of 1968, implying that only individual pursuit of self-interest can lead to relative success. It was this whole nonpolitical trend in Hungarian learning, ingrained in the population, that the small opposition sought to counteract by example, by exhortation, and by the proposal of programs.

Fortunately, because of the partial modernization of Hungarian society by the economic reform of 1968 and the related relaxation of the private sphere, in Hungary, as well as in Poland, independent groupings, networks, practices, and forms of communication existed around which an alternative or second public sphere could be organized. Increasingly dependent on Western goodwill and wishing to avoid a climate that would endanger independent economic activities, the regime found it difficult to use sufficient force to entirely suppress this support system. As a result "the second public sphere" was not only not suppressed despite some administrative sanctions against its organizers, but its interaction with parts of the official framework of communication, especially in the social sciences and the humanities, could not be prevented.[21]

The plans and proposals of the early samizdat, in particular Kis's editorials in *Beszélő* in the early 1980s, consciously operated with a dualistic Polish model, in spite of the defeat of Solidarity. Kis in particular insisted already in 1982 that the defeat of the Polish democratic opposition was not like the defeats of 1956 and 1968—that in particular the Soviet Union did not have the economic strength to normalize Poland.[22] This analysis was connected to the contemporary one of T. Bauer, an economist close to Kis and *Beszélő*, who was the first to systematically outline the reasons for what he called the beginning of the "general economic crisis" of the whole Soviet-centered CMEA bloc.[23] To be sure, the devastatingly accurate economic projections of this long-range diagnosis only very partially corresponded to popular experience in Hungary at that time at least. In the absence of a social movement, Kis was forced to decisively modify the Polish model. In Hungary the much smaller democratic opposition could not hope to directly support the self-organization of an already active society against the party-state, and aside from creating a few islands of independent activity (the samizdat, the "independent university," and a group dedicated to helping the poor, SZETA) it was forced to address, according to Kis, semi-independent groups and networks *between* itself and the regime.[24] Kis had in mind primarily social scientific intellectuals, tolerated and even used by the regime as independent experts, as well as "populist" writers and their followings at uneasy peace with the regime whose ideology and insufficient "national" character they rejected. These groups were, each in its own way, critical of the regime, but on the whole still accepted the Kádárist assumption that any overt political action or pressure is impossible and counterproductive. To counter their fears, Kis insisted in a debate that the mere existence of the samizdat, establishing an alternative public sphere, was not enough, and that in the new situation political programs for change were needed, programs both significant enough yet plausible under Hungarian conditions.

Accordingly, *Beszélő*'s first formulations of a new program were certainly minimalist. Let us merely fight, Kis argued, for the conversion of our existing spaces of autonomy and our privileges into rights. Of course, this formula already contained the assumption that the regime can hope to legitimate itself under conditions of economic difficulty only by taking some steps toward the rule of law. Subsequently this notion was generalized in a new version of dualism: Hungarians should aim at the establishment of rights in the sphere of private law, a sphere understood somewhat more narrowly than the Poles understood civil society, and the rule of law in the state sphere.[25] Addressed to a 1985 meeting in Monor Forest of the democratic opposition with the social scientists and the populist writers, this model clearly sought to overcome the rigid dualism of the older Polish formula. It counted among other things on the revival of reformism within the ruling party. Finally in 1987, in the pamphlet *Social Contract*,[26] Kis and the editors of *Beszélö* made a wide-ranging proposal whose main features involved a comprehensive constitutional regulation of a society increasingly autonomous and self-organized, a state divided into a genuine parliamentary sphere, a sector (itself bound by rules) reserved for the ruling party, and an economy whose main pillars were private property and industrial democracy. This proposal, to be sure, surpassing all earlier versions of the Polish model in its radicalism, came at a time when the decline of the Hungarian economic model was clearly visible, when social initiatives had begun to mushroom, when, in response to the requests of a part of the ruling party, radical economists had already (1986) produced their own comprehensive proposal for economic reform.[27] The extended discussion in 1987–88 of *Social Contract, Fordulat és reform* and several other proposals presupposed and expressed the existence of a dynamic new public sphere as the central organ of a self-emancipating civil society.[28]

Civil Society in Hungary: Movements and Initiatives

In Hungary, the new civil society whose highest point of development was reached in 1988, while open to the discussions and proposals of the democratic opposition and of critical social scientists who themselves enriched associational life, was the result of largely spontaneous forms of self-organization. Of course, these efforts took advantage of the opportunities presented by ongoing processes of economic reform and modernization, as well as the relative social relaxation that characterized János Kádár's regime after 1968. In this country, no single organization like KOR, Charter 77, or Solidarity ever played the preeminent role in the organization of other groups. The colorful picture of associational life and civic initiatives in existence in 1988 can be summed up only under a variety of headings.[29]

Clubs, Circles, "Colleges"

In the first half the 1980s ("the era of circles"), there was a mushrooming of intellectual, primarily university-based, circles and clubs dedicated to the study, discussion, and debate of a variety of issues, including the economic, social, and political problems of the day. By 1985 the need for coordination was felt and the first council of clubs included representatives of almost twenty clubs.[30]

Professional "colleges," anticipated by a forerunner in the 1970s, were organizations combining university training with the life of small academic communities of intellectuals dedicated to both intellectual pursuits and ideals of public service.[31] It was the colleges that first organized teaching activities for members of the democratic opposition entirely excluded from professional life. Both clubs and colleges were to organize summer "camps," and in 1988 their members were to meet together at a national summer camp, that is, conference, in which a thousand people participated.[32] Initially eschewing direct political participation, the clubs, circles, and colleges came to see themselves by the second half of the 1980s in terms of the program of reconstructing civil society from below.[33] Down to this day, many of those who participated take seriously the program of a self-organizing democratic society, rich in movements and civic initiatives.

New Social Movements

The relative modernity and openness of Kádárist Hungary to the West made it a likely place for the emergence and proliferation of the most modern social movements, especially ecological and youth movements, and, to a lesser extent, pacifism as well. Significantly, all three tended to emerge from the organizational matrix of circles and colleges; thus the self-organizing forums of youth had a catalyzing role for social movements.[34] Both peace movements and ecology movements initially eschewed, however unconvincingly, any general political intentions.[35] The youth movement, with the creation of FIDESZ (Alliance of Young Democrats) in 1988 by members of the college movement, followed by a new national umbrella organization of youth, was the first to deliberately pass through the political threshold.[36]

Given the politicization of the youth movement at the same time it became comprehensive, and the general weakness of pacifism, the ecology or environmental movement was the Hungarian new social movement par excellence, not a remarkable fact, given the ecological disaster in the wake of state socialism. Politically, this movement was a great success story, absorbing for a time the energy and some of the best people of other movements, including not only those of youth but also the democratic and populist oppositions. Organized by members of the club "movement" from 1984 around one national movement battling against a potentially disastrous dam project on the Danube (Bös [Gabcikovo]—Nagymaros Dam)[37] and a variety of locally based single-issue movements, ecology and environmentalism generated a variety of organizations (clubs, foundations, action committees), and activities (forums of discussion, demonstrations, petition campaigns, campaign for a referendum, campaigns for the recall of deputies). Even before the government and Parliament were forced to finally suspend the Danube dam project in 1989, the battle for and in an independent public sphere was won by the ecologists and their supporters. Their movement, consciously oriented to a program of the self-organization of civil society, became an important training ground for many of the militants of later movements and parties.

Interest Representations and Professional Associations

Unlike Poland, in Hungary, very likely because of the individualistic consequences of the second economy, independent interest representations came into being relatively late. Almost too late to the extent that the dramatic expansion of self-organization and its politicization seemed to storm over the arena of interest representation, according to one participant.[38] Nevertheless, in 1988 an independent organization of entrepreneurs (VOSZ) and several small, eventually affiliated unions of intellectuals workers did emerge, playing an important role not only in exploring the legal and constitutional possibilities of association and coalition building but also in such social movements as ecology. Of the latter, TDDSZ (Union of Scientific Workers) was the first and most important, playing a role in organizing new, independent unions of filmmakers and teachers, and a new umbrella organization, the Liga (or FSZDL: League of Independent Trade Unions). This organization was followed by two others, Workers Solidarity and Alliance of Workers Councils. All these organizations of the defense of worker interests, influenced by different aspects of the model of Polish Solidarity, understood themselves as promoting a fabric of thick social self-organization from below, as building and fighting for a civil society with important elements of participation in economic and political life.[39]

Two professional associations, founded in 1988, were especially important, not only because by their existence they expanded the space of civil society, but because they were dedicated to the institutional protection of dimensions of civil society presupposed by all other movements. The Publicity Club was organized by journalists, lawyers, and scholars (who included a member of the democratic opposition, an ecologist, and two reform social scientists) to promote the full freedom of speech, information, communication, and press, in order to provide all the requisite forums for independent opinion and criticism, a life necessity for the new movements and initiatives to which the founders of the club explicitly referred.[40] The Independent Forum of Jurists was founded by 135 lawyers in order to help inform society about the legislative projects of the authorities and to propose legal and constitutional alternatives capable of securing rights, expanding democratic participation, and promoting the establishment of a sturdy civil society, along with the controlling function of the public sphere.[41] Both of these organizations were to play a crucial role in the legal and political changes of the next year, with the Publicity Club continuing its activism in 1990–91 as well.[42]

Political Umbrella Movements for Reform

While it is true that in Hungary no comprehensive movement for reform ever emerged, many of the hopes of those who formulated reform proposals were tied to such a possibility. To be sure, the various social movements were interlocked through common memberships, networks, and events like the important meetings, debates, and discussions at the Jurta Theater in Budapest.[43] Yet this fact indicated also that the overall membership was rather small both in context of the whole society and compared with Solidarity in its ascending phase. There was a need not only for the coordination of many diverse activities but also for their politicization, if the population at large, not able to identify with the existing movements, were to be given any realistic alternative outside of the illusory one of a reform carried out entirely from above. Politicization was also necessary to avoid a polarization of society in the style of Poland in 1980–81.

The one and only major attempt to create an overarching political movement to include the democratic opposition, the social scientific intellectuals, and the populist writers and their following at Monor in 1985 did not succeed in bridging historically inherited differences or differences in the degree of radicalism. After the populist intellectuals formed their own movement (Hungarian Democratic Forum or MDF) in 1987 at the conference of Lakitelek, to which representatives of the democratic opposition (with three cosmetic exceptions) were not invited, political umbrella organizations became inevitably more partial. Such was the caucus of primarily democratic-liberal, social democratic, and alternative organization the Network of Free Initiatives, in which the intellectuals of the democratic opposition played a leading role, and from which the social liberal Alliance of Free Democrats (SZDSZ) was to emerge within less than a year. Of lesser importance was the reform-Communist New March Front that was unable to make the full step to politics, but which was to help nevertheless to activate the reformers within the ruling party. Evidently MDF and SZDSZ were protopolitical organizations able to become political parties, even if this was not the inclination of some members (especially of the Network, but the same was true of many of the populist literati). The same was true of FIDESZ emerging from the youth college movement, eventually unwilling to integrate itself into a nonpolitical umbrella organization of youth. Nevertheless, all of these three organizations were originally part of the ferment of movements in and for civil society, and never completely lost their movement character.[44] For the early FIDESZ for example, the Polish model of Solidarity was decisive.[45] Indeed, FIDESZ was to play a Solidarity-like central role in promoting the freedom of self-organization in the context of existing constitutional and legal loopholes, a move that was to encourage other organizations as well as an unsuccessful attempt by the authorities to produce in 1988 a more restrictive, formally correct legal regulation of the right of association. The eventual outcome after a long struggle for public opinion, the entirely modern liberal and democratic laws of association and assembly of January 1989, represented a victory for civil society analogous to (though far more comprehensive than) the legalization of Solidarity in 1980.[46]

The victory over the Law of Association testified to the success, within limits, of the strategy, or rather strategies, oriented to the reconstruction of civil society in Hungary. Above all, the new organizations and movements, armed with a variety of reform proposals and supported by a variety of popular

actions came to dominate the public sphere, first the realm of scientific publications, eventually penetrating some journals like HVG *(Weekly World Economy)* and dailies like *Magyar Nemzet.* In such a context, as the struggle for the
law of association showed, the regime was unable to build legal legitimacy by
tightening legal restrictions that for the first time would be honored. The
defeat in the public sphere meant not only that the regime lost instead of gaining legitimacy but also appeared vulnerable as well. The public discussion of
the draft of the law of association, perhaps intended as sham or controlled
democracy, turned out to be the first democratic political discussion of legislation in Hungary in more than forty years.[47] And yet in spite its successes, the
method oriented to public discussion alone could not be relied on in an ongoing fashion, even from the point of view of the organizations of civil society.
First it was too time consuming: A whole constitution (which was increasingly
recognized as necessary) could not be created by a method that took six or
more months with respect to merely two fundamental rights (association and
assembly). Second, the ruling party could and did try, after its defeat, to
manipulate the time and procedure of "societal debate," depriving the process
of all participatory character. Third, Hungarian society and its organizations
were already too plural to speak with one voice on issues other than the few
fundamental rights all parts of civil society required. Fourth, even after a few
signal victories for the groups of civil society, it was very risky to allow the old
parliament, under Communist control, to remain in the position to legisla-
tively establish the parameters of a new political system. As it became clear in
the draft for a new electoral law proposed in 1988 (but received with total
antipathy by society),[48] it was possible to come up with a formally democratic
procedure and timetable that would allow the ruling party to convert its
monopolistic power in one system into a hegemony in the next. Here the civil
society-based strategy was ultimately defenseless.

Yet the regime was also in a poor position to merely impose new semidemocratic rules, since its own formal instance of legislation and constitution
making, the undemocratically elected Parliament, was now highly unpopular
because of its well-publicized and criticized role in the conflict over the
Danube dam and certainly did not have the legitimacy to act on its own. The
existence of organized civil society, moreover, with important victories behind
it, implied that the failure of reform could lead to a type of polarization that
only violent acts on one side could resolve. But in the context of the transformation of Soviet foreign policy, the hard-liners of the government could not
count on repression being successful, as it still was in Poland in 1981. Once the
Round Table was created in Poland, and especially as a comprehensive agreement was successfully concluded by the government and Solidarity early in
1989, it became more or less unavoidable that in Hungary too, a new forum
of negotiation and compromise would have to be established as a way out of
potential stalemate and as a quasi-legitimate road to democratic system.

From Civil to Political Society: Poland

In spite of the defeat of the movement in 1981, the organization of Polish society in the first Solidarity epoch was not in vain. The martial law regime and even its Soviet backers never could feel themselves powerful enough to terrorize society into submission. Moreover, the unprecedented involvement in the movement of large parts of society, as well as its decentralization, made the job of normalization all the more difficult. Throughout the 1980s, the earlier program of organizing an alternative sphere of public communication was not only resumed but was vastly expanded.[49] Gradually, new groups, organizations, and forums appeared, concerned with ecology, peace, draft resistance, defense of consumer interests, economic and educational projects, and above all free and independent publishing efforts.[50] Solidarity as an organization also survived, first as a largely decentralized underground led by a few important national leaders. Later, after the 1986 amnesty of its imprisoned leaders, it was to move from a double existence, both underground and semiopen to a largely open, though not yet legal, operation. Attempts on the part of the government to work out a bargain with the episcopate alone never really succeeded, despite some initial willingness on the part of some bishops, and the Church soon resumed a role of collaborating with independent social and cultural activities on the local level and a potentially mediating posture on the national one.

The civil society in formation in the 1980s was both more extensive than that of the 1970s, and far less oriented to an organizational center than in 1980–81. Not only the organizations but even more the ideologies of this period became much more pluralistic; there were attempts to formulate different versions of liberal, nationalist, and social democratic ideologies, many of which were explicitly critical of the earlier Solidarity.[51] In this context the remnants of Solidarity, its underground activists, intellectuals as well as its undisputed leader, Walesa, had a privileged position only in that the regime attempted to exclude (through 1987) this group more emphatically than all others from any possible political negotiations.[52] This negative privilege, the memory of the earlier Solidarity, as well as the unrivalled political experience of the still-cohesive leadership group, made it into a kind of democratic counterelite that alone had the aspiration for comprehensive political action in independent society. Thus the self-organizing society of the second half of 1980s was not only more pluralized in the horizontal sense than its predecessor in 1980–81, but now began to exhibit vertical differentiation between the civil and the political. When in 1988 regime reformers led by Generals Czeslaw Kiszczak and Wojciech Jaruzelski, facing a continued economic and legitimacy crisis, the revival of working-class discontent, and the probable loss of their ultimate Soviet guarantee, sought partners for undertaking radical economic reform, it was to this political counterelite, born of civil society, that they were to turn.[53]

Thus emerged the great institutional innovation of the Round Table. Designed to achieve a relatively narrow political compromise, like many distinguished predecessors, the Polish Round Table became a runaway institution. The negotiating sides could, as it turned out, achieve their narrow aims only by conceding new political mechanisms that were previously hardly even entertained as possibilities and were in fact generated from within the new institution with its peculiar logic. The party gained a powerfully strengthened presidency in this process, while Solidarity received an entirely freely elected assembly with genuine if subordinate powers, the Senate, and, as an inevitable byproduct, guarantees that the elections for both chambers would take place in an atmosphere of free and public contestation. The two sides were willing to swallow the bitter pills of the complete reversal of the martial law regime on the one hand, and, on the other, the organization of unfree elections for the lower, dominant chamber, the Sejm, that were to guarantee the ruling party its constitution-making two-thirds majority. Most important: Operating on the ground of legal continuity, the Round Table produced expectations that this continuity would remain unbroken in the future and that the sides could thus count on the legal enforcement of what they were agreeing to. Almost equally important: The Round Table was almost completely monitored by the electronic media, producing expectations for future openness and guaranteeing that inevitable private deals, like the famous Magdalenka arrangements, would produce only results that could be publically defended and justified.[54]

In its new political reincarnation Solidarity was socially much weaker, yet more capable of strategic action than its great predecessor in 1980–81. It was both less threatening to the authorities and more capable of bargaining and negotiation. But, most importantly, after almost a decade of struggling for an independent civil society, it was the only political organization in Poland with the important resource of legitimation, which the regime reformers—deluding themselves as it turned out—hoped to be able to draw on. The legitimacy was real enough, but it was to become the support of a different government than the Round Table tried to make almost inevitable through its prearranged electoral formula. The unexpected electoral defeat for almost every freely contested seat (100 percent for the Senate, 33 percent for the Sejm) and the initial rejection of the so-called national list, which were technically uncontested, made the projected role of the party reformers as senior partners irrelevant. Indeed, Solidarity had to agree to retrospectively modify the electoral law, to give the party its agreed upon parliamentary super-majority. Similarly, Walesa and his colleagues in the new Parliament had to tacitly support the election of Jaruzelski to the presidency, in order to fulfill the Round Table agreements.

Significantly, Solidarity was also mistaken about the limits of its possibilities at the negotiating table and indeed about its very identity. As to the first of these mistakes, it was, to be sure, unavoidable, because during this first case of transition from Communist rule the limits of Soviet tolerance could not be known. All other subsequent cases benefited from the example of the Polish exploration of the entirely unexpectedly wide limits of the possible. The mixed, only in part democratic, formula that emerged from the Polish nego- tiations and the several structural and nondemocratic concessions given to the outgoing regime followed from the great political uncertainty faced by all the negotiating partners. Understandable and rationally justifiable these con- cessions may have been, irrelevant as some of them turned out to be politi- cally, they nevertheless led to an erosion of the legitimation reserves upon which the Solidarity leadership could initially draw. The Round Table formula and the constitutional arrangements resting on it were open to radical politi- cal challenge from the moment that the concessions granted to the regime could be clearly seen as after all unnecessary.

The second mistake, regarding the self-identity of Solidarity, flowed from the first. Since no complete political transition initially seemed conceivable, the leaders of the democratic side could not yet see themselves as primarily politi- cal actors. Thus an organization that was in the process of being reconstituted as a political one in the narrow sense continued to see itself as intimately con- nected to a program oriented to civil society. Thus the relegalization of the union was its primary demand, and participation in the political system was at first only a reluctant concession. It was only unexpected strength in negotia- tions, subsequent elections, and in the business of government formation that confirmed the shift of Solidarity to the level of political society, using for the purpose its new electoral organization that was appropriately named Citizen Committee. The subsequent difficulties of generating a plurality of political parties from this body, of overcoming its double origins as a union and as a protoparty, and even the eventual fragmentation of the parliamentary party political landscape, indicate the difficulties inherent in the glorious heritage of the one great movement for the reconstruction of civil society.

From Civil to Political Society: Hungary

In Hungary, 1988 has been widely considered the year of civil society, during which a whole series of movements and civil initiatives, from ecology to youth, and from the democratic opposition to the populist semiopposition, put the weakening party-state under decisive pressure. Even before, during the 1980s, there was continuing experimentation with various Hungarian ver- sions of the Polish strategy of new evolutionism, one that resulted in the solid achievement of an alternative public sphere as well as some valuable political experience of a small, but expanding circle of activists. Moreover, in 1987 a whole series of reform proposals, most importantly the *Social Contract* of János Kis and his collaborators in the democratic opposition, offered both government and society radical programs of reconstruction around the dual- istic idea of the full emancipation of civil society in the context of a more partial reform of state institutions. Thus, all attempts on the part of the party-state to consolidate a reformed version of authoritarian rule, or more likely to carry out a program of reform merely from above, ran into the determined opposition of organized groups and publics that possessed their own alternative models of change.[55]

Nevertheless, because of the acceleration of the process (owing to international factors) and the unexpectedly quick crumbling of the old regime, compounded by the internal weaknesses of the civil society strategy, the model of transition was not ultimately steered from below, from the grass roots, by the social movements, networks, and initiatives. Instead, the process of transition was, as is well known, negotiated on the mezo-level of political society, where political parties emerging from both civil society (MDF, SZDSZ, and FIDESZ) and from the party-state (the MSZMP in the process of becoming the MSZP) played the central role. Remarkably enough, since in Hungary the independent forces were weaker, the outcome was not a dualistic program such as the one proposed by the *Social Contract* of the democratic opposition in 1987, a mixed, partially democratic, electoral arrangement as agreed upon by the Polish Round Table, or even the Polish formula of the summer of 1989, which the reform Communists and their conservative partners among the opposition sought to in part imitate (Michnik's "your president, our prime minister"). It was a complete institutional transformation, a veritable change of political regimes without any undemocratic guarantees.

The institution that accomplished this change was here too a national Round Table. But in Hungary there was no partner with political legitimation that the government could select. The oppositional groups in existence, three groups emerging from civil society (MDF, SZDSZ, and FIDESZ), and four political parties, organizationally barely in existence but nostalgic claimants to famous party names from the past,[56] had to constitute their own organization, the famous EKA (the Oppositional Round Table), and to agree not to negotiate separately or without any of its members before the NKA (the National Round Table) could be formed. These organizations did not have the prior national reputation or the political power to agree to any formula that would not be self-legitimating, that is, a fully democratic arrangement without undemocratic reservations. A fully democratic arrangement, however, involved increasingly more institutional presuppositions, and in the end the actors had to accept the task (against the stated views of their liberal members) of creating more or less a new written constitution. In this respect they went beyond their Polish colleagues, who in any case could not have constitutionalized the semidemocratic arrangement they agreed to. Without the requisite legitimacy, however, the political actors of the Hungarian Round Table too were careful to insist on the merely temporary character of their constitutional product. They too insisted on the framework of nonrevolutionary legal continuity and therefore the formal utilization of the existing undemocratic parliament and the existing rule of constitutional revision to ratify their constitutional inno-vations. Unlike the Poles, however, and evidently troubled by the internal divi-sions within the oppositional groups, the publicity of the negotiations was only perfunctory. This last aspect helped to create an atmosphere of a deal among political elites.

Finally, the deal that did emerge, unlike in Poland, did not go unchallenged. Under the leadership of the SZDSZ, four parties dissatisfied with the mechanism that involved the apparent concession of a directly elected presidency to the ex-ruling party, organized a successful petition campaign and referendum to reverse this result. The Hungarian arrangement could not support undemocratic con-cessions, even of the informal variety. But the campaign around the referendum opened up fissures among the parties of the opposition that were never to heal.

That victory used campaigning methods developed in the earlier struggles of the various civil initiatives, establishing a presidency elected by the first demo-cratic parliament. It seemed to have been the last hurrah of the politics of civil society. Hungary entered the democratic period with politics dominated by seven new parties (six from the opposition and the reconstituted and renamed ex-rul-ing party, the MSZP), of which six were to survive the first two free elections and five the third. The formation of a stable party system was far less difficult here than in Poland, even if the three dominant parties of the opposition's long-pre-served aspects of their movement character and not only their names were rooted in the initiatives of civil society. In each of these formations there was a signifi-cant debate concerning the very adoption of the party form (if not the name, until FIDESZ added in 1995 MPP—Hungarian Civic Party—to its acronym). The two major parties rooted in civil society, moreover, adopted a movement style that entailed uncompromising hostility toward the other. Many of the fail-ures of an otherwise quite modern party system and governments based on it could be traced to this incomplete transition from the civil to the political.

The Implosion of Civil Society?

According to the reigning hypothesis of the literature on transitions, the con-cept of civil society generally loses (and in most versions should lose) its rele-vance in the actual negotiations that lead to transitional pacts. A system of mutual guarantees can be worked out only among actors capable of divorcing themselves from the maximalist pressures that are likely to emanate from their original constituencies or allies (the radicals in the population and the hard-liners of the old regime). Because of the turn to "political society," moreover, and the corresponding demobilization of the civil sphere, it is further implied (though rarely argued) that the politics of civil society has little to do with the consolidation of democracy.[57]

The transition literature[58] does recognize the important role of civil society in the historical phase before the actual process of negotiated extrication from authoritarian rule. But the interpretation of this phase merely as liberalization as against democratization misrepresents the state of affairs that on a microlevel it is democratic institutions and culture that are being built.[59] A result of this conception, and of intellectual strategies concerned only with rational, purely strategic actors, is that the phase of "liberalization" has only the role of provoking the choice of either repression and the end of the period of the abertura, or a political bargaining process leading to democratization. Civil society accordingly would be either repressed by the authoritarians or must be demobilized by its earlier supporters and beneficiaries. In the latter case, demobilization is necessary if a bargaining process is to be successful. Political radicals or maximalists can be brought under the control of the moderates and continue to play a role in the negotiations, but the difficult-to-control movements of civil society must be demobilized and reatomized.

To understand why the above thesis does not do full justice to the role of civil society in the preparation of democratic transitions, it is worthwhile to again recall Robert Dahl's early argument concerning democratic transitions. According to him transition to polyarchies would be most difficult in the case of "inclusive hegemonies" where democratic institutions would have to be created all at once for a complex society, with potentially sharp and multidimensional lines of cleavage.[60] The contrast here is with "competitive oligarchic" or "exclusionary liberal" regimes where the institutions of representation and rule of law can be consolidated well before the main groups of modern society would have full access to them. The stress in this argument is winning time for institution building and possibly for the building of the requisite political culture. Leaving to the side the important issue that the creation or long-term stabilization of polyarchies or near-polyarchies where there were originally liberal oligarchies has also not proven easy in Latin America for example, Dahl's argument presents an important challenge for East and Central Europe. How then can we explain that the "transitions to democracy" and indeed the "consolidation" of the new democracies occurred relatively smoothly in so many East and Central European settings whose starting point fully corresponds to the type of "inclusive hegemonies"?

It would be tempting to find the answer alone in processes of negotiation leading to pacts of transition and in the institutional innovation of formalized Round Tables. This transitional institution evidently allowed elites to set up the major institutional framework of representative democracy, which subsequently can be assumed as a framework within which the conflicts of the larger society can be processed.[61] Beyond the formal arguments of Adam Przeworski and others it needs to be added that successful pacts presuppose radical change within a model of legal continuity, the noneconomic element of the contract as it were. Even with this addition, however, I do not find the line of reasoning fully adequate. What is missing from it is precisely the element of time (stressed by Dahl) needed to establish a culture of interaction binding the elites themselves to their agreement concerning institutional structures, leading to a politics of self-limitation even when, as is very likely the result of democratic elections, the balance of forces dramatically changes. Even law to which the actors cannot yet have an "internal" relation in the sense of H. L. A. Hart cannot supply what is missing. I believe the needed time and pattern of self-limitation are desiderata that are won by the emergence of a civil society (however narrow its scope) well before the transitions. I believe, moreover, that the first Round Tables in Poland and Hungary—which were subsequently imitated elsewhere—were themselves possible because of a long period of civil society-based politics in the two countries. Where such a prehistory is absent, pacts and roundtables played either no role (being displaced by top-down electoral strategies) or a merely formal one. This is not to say that a prehistory of civil society-based movements was the sufficient condition for genuine negotiated transitions; a rough balance of forces was equally important. But in any case, all the countries that had successfully negotiated transitions had prior experiences with the organization of parallel publics and associations, with the debatable exception of Bulgaria, where the ruling party remained very much in control of the negotiations.

Accordingly, I maintain that the self-limiting politics of civil society, originally developed for primarily geopolitical reasons, is a crucial prerequisite for successful transitions of the negotiated type, the type that in my view offers the best prospects for the consolidation of democracy. Under weakening but intact Communist regimes only this politics allowed for democratic institution building outside of the framework of state power, training above all future elites and molding elements of a democratic political culture based on discussion, negotiation, and compromise. The viability of both processes of formalized negotiations and of its operative legal assumptions presupposes such a learning experience.[62] Equally important, the longer-term acceptance of the pacted institutional framework or its replacement fully within the framework that was established, relies to an even greater extent on the self-limitation of actors capable of treating former enemies as legitimate political opponents. This was especially important in Poland where the Round Table pact involved authoritarian reserves and the abolition of these might have involved, but did not, severe social conflicts.

With this said, I cannot entirely reject the demobilization thesis on both theoretical and empirical grounds. I do think it underestimates the diffuse cultural pressure of ongoing public discussion and the continued potential of new forms of grassroots mobilization that remain the counterweights to the old regime's repressive capabilities. But I also believe that the negotiated option (as against top-down, manipulated electoral models and bottom-up models of insurrection) does require the prior building of a new type of narrowly *political* institution, where actors, wherever they came from, must act in more strategic ways than can the movements and initiatives of civil society.

The new institution was, of course, the famous Round Table, and the new actors were political parties or protoparties. When the action shifts to Round Tables and parties, so do the activists and resources, and in the short run at least the organizations of civil society tend to withdraw from politics and even decompose. While all the demands emanating from civil society are hardly fundamentalist or especially radical, genuine roundtable bargains do presuppose that the politically relevant actors can be formally committed to them. This must mean that actors inevitably left outside the Round Table must be demobilized.

To be sure empirically the full demobilization of civil society did not always occur during negotiation processes in the countries with Round Tables.[63] In many countries it was the actual pressure of the streets that established the predominance of the opposition in the negotiations (Czechoslovakia), maintained the equality of the two sides (GDR), or made a very immature and fledgling opposition at least a viable partner (Bulgaria). But even in Hungary the formally permitted demonstration during the Imre Nagy reburial in June 1989 indicated that the opposition could bring already organized sectors of the population into the streets. And this omnipresent option contributed to the negotiating success of political groups that had little membership, meager resources, and even doubtful legitimacy. With this general point made, when the democratic side at the roundtable does not seek external demobilization, as in Czechoslovakia, the GDR, or Bulgaria, this is a clue to the political weakness and lack of self-assurance of the new elites engaged in bargaining. Mass collective action becomes the only means to shore up their bargaining position, and the results are not likely to be genuine pacts, even if the formal character of the "pact" (and especially the legal continuity that may be uneasily maintained) will influence many outcomes. As to the main transitional political framework, if the existing government collapses under the pressure of external collective action, the opposition will dictate the terms that will be agreed to (Czechoslovakia). If no collapse occurs, the old ruling group will (Bulgaria).

As against these three examples, the classic type of negotiated transition does imply demobilization of civil actors, and the Polish and Hungarian developments indeed confirm this point first learned in Spain. Of course the new actors on the democratic side in these countries were themselves capable of making and keeping bargains because of their previous political experience and socialization. Not surprisingly, to me at least, it was therefore not the revived traditional parties, but the new political organizations that emerged from civil society (MDF, SZDSZ, and FIDESZ), who played the major role in the negotiations on the democratic side. Regime moderates like Imre Pozsgay, who often had a great deal of voice in deciding whom to bargain with, implicitly knew what I am talking about. They needed partners capable not only of social support but also self-limitation. Only elites emerging from civil society, whose party names usually testified to their origins, were capable of both.

(Note that in Latin America parties inherited from the past were often in place and could play the requisite role.) But these elites had to rapidly transform themselves and their mode of action, because what the old ruling parties needed above all were rival political actors, capable of strategic considerations. Only parties or party-like elites could be trusted to provide enough security and guarantees for the ruling parties to be able to disengage and surrender most of their power. A mass movement, always having a fundamentalist wing, could not provide such guarantees. Such a mass movement was increasingly the much-feared idée fixe of leading Hungarian reform Communists, and events in Czechoslovakia eventually proved how right they could have been. Moreover, political parties could be possible partners in future governments, able to share in the burdensome responsibility of difficult economic decisions. Having relatively low legitimacy, they could not turn the struggle in terms of the older solidarity formula into that of legitimate society versus immoral power, "us" against "them." Indeed the lower the legitimacy of the new actors, as in Hungary in distinction to Poland, the more concessions had to be made to them (and fewer concessions could be asked for), so that democratic elections may legitimate the whole new political society in which the Communists hoped to be a leading part. Subsequent history, and in particular the electoral return to power of the ex-Communists in 1993 and 1994, show that this last expectation was not entirely based on illusions.

Having come from civil society did not stop many new party political actors from declaring that the politics of civil participation was only a matter of yesterday. In Hungary, efforts were made almost from the beginning to insulate political bargaining from societal pressure. At the National Round Table for example, at the insistence of the representatives of the ruling party, it was agreed to exclude the press and the public from all the sessions of the committees, followed by their exclusion, without prior agreement, from middle-level bargaining as well. Public participation in the negotiation was more or less nonexistent, and even press coverage turned out to be remarkably poor, in contradistinction to the Round Table in Poland, as well as the Hungarian standards of the preceding year.[64] While the ruling party's motivation seems clear in this matter, it is hard to avoid the feeling that at least some of the opposition parties did not fight hard enough for publicity, from a charitable point of view, perhaps because they considered themselves representative enough of Hungarian society or because they thought the press lacked the necessary technical competence to follow the negotiations in any case.

The weakening of associational life, though not the result of conscious strategy, complemented the exclusion of public discussion. The differentiation of new political organizations meant also that elites and militants were pulled away from civil organizations and into fledgling parties, thereby promoting an implosion of many of the movements that previously occupied the center stage. Moreover, there were also conscious efforts at demobilization, which were very much intensified when the new elites took charge of economic policies of stabilization that they saw potentially threatened by access-organized societal demands. Finally, with the upsurge of new ideologies, the new and specifically East European ideology of civil society had to compete with old ideologies revived from the past or imported from the West. The discourse thus followed but also justified the sociological regression: The elites that originally saw their action in terms of civil society stopped using the whole conception.

I believe that many of the intellectual objections to the use of the category of civil society generally reflect one or more of these ideologies. For the revolutionaries, who wanted to purge and punish, the idea of a self-limiting revolution was too limiting, the orientation to civil society was too legalistic and gradualist. For the new professional politicians, keeping channels of communication open to groups outside of parties and parliaments violated their narrow conception of democracy derived from not so much Western ideals as Western elite democratic practice. Cynically put, it also threatened their imagined new monopoly of power. For the liberal economists, who imagine themselves as bourgeois, after having called for civil society in their pamphlets as the only possible environment for a market economy, a society of unions, ecologists, consumer associations, and so on, came to appear as a luxury suitable only for developed market economies. For now a minimal civil society organized around the protection of property would do. Thus they are allied with the elite democrats wishing to keep politics isolated from societal inputs. Neither was apparently conscious of the fact that the paper-thin legitimacy acquired through a democratic election alone was not going to be sufficient for a population undergoing deep economic hardships. On the other side, the nationalists were interested in the imagined community of the whole, living off issues of the past, and not in the real communities that are confronting the challenges of the next century. They feared the modern postmaterial values around the new social movements most of all. Along with the advocates of class they tended to channel social protest, inadvertently or deliberately, in populist directions.

Incomparable harm could have been done had the converging trends seeking to obliterate the very problem of civil society succeeded. While a democratic transition can be formally completed with a marginalized civil society, the same is not true for democratic consolidation. I understand "transition to democracy" in the narrow sense, as the relatively rapid process that establishes and guarantees the "organic" rules (at the very least: electoral rule, the temporary structure of government, freedom of association and assembly, including party formation and activity, access to the media, and private security for people engaging in politics) for the holding of free, contested elections. In the broader sense the transition can also include the process of designing specific democratic institutions: For example, constitution making, but the final work of design may come well after the transition in the narrow sense is completed.

I understand the consolidation of democracy, along with others, as a process by which "democracy becomes the only game in town." But unlike interpreters who seek to explain the consolidation of democracy simply as an equilibrium resting on a desirable combination of interests and fears, for me democracy can be consolidated only when, in addition to a favorable interest constellation, a sufficiently large number of actors accept a given system as legitimate. In my view, civil society has an important role to play in the consolidation of democracy so defined. This is so for several reasons:

Adhering to Contract and Legality

After democratic institutions are in place, and especially within the radically altered geopolitical context, the strategic reasons for compromise with the elite of the old regime disappear and are forgotten. In this context, the *ideology* of civil society with its evolutionary and legal emphasis can help bar the way to attempts to radically and extralegally alter the framework within which former enemies can function as political opponents in a fair competition. While groups in civil society may indeed adopt neorevolutionary ideologies, those having the experience or memory of the long evolutionary march against Communism are more likely to retain the emphasis on self-limitation and rule of law.

Legitimacy

The governments elected in the first free election will be legitimate in the narrow legal sense of the term, which requires only that the established procedures be faithfully followed. The same is not necessarily true for the framework under which they were elected, when these have been produced by agreements among unelected elites. If the final constitutional design occurs relatively late in the process, its links to normal political processes of logrolling will be unfortunately too clear. Thus the "window of opportunity" for achieving the democratic legitimacy of the new system will be open only for a brief time. The quasi-traditional legitimacy that can eventually insulate constitutional orders of uncertain origin requires a long period of continuity and stability, which in the given context is the problem rather than the solution. Thus what I call the *sociological legitimacy* of the new government, in Max Weber's sense of the empirical belief in the validity and justification of an order, becomes all the more important. Democratic legitimacy, unlike Weber's three ideal types, cannot, however, be restricted merely to an administrative staff. Given the inevitable exclusion involved in electoral systems, and disappointments in the formation of coalition governments and programs, a wide variety of social elites (functional, local, and generational) will accept a given regime as legitimate only when they are capable of forming organized associations with political power or influence. Only sociological legitimacy in the long term can congeal into a political culture supportive of democracy and a given set of institutions.

The Ability to Wait

The first governments of the new democracies, especially, but not only, in East and Central Europe, have difficult economic decisions to make. As is well known, the (in my view) correct decisions (radical price reform, ending of subsidies, demonopolization, export-oriented restructuring, and privatization) imply a significant period in which the real income of the bulk of the population is drastically curtailed. The crumbling welfare institutions of the old regimes are not in the position to handle the resulting suffering, and their restructuring would itself lead to at least transitional pain. The inevitable social discontent is to be sure handled by the emerging party systems that typically produce alternation in power without alternation in the underlying policy (unless, as in Hungary in 1995 and Romania and Bulgaria somewhat later, policy alternation means radicalization). This "technique," rooted entirely in political society, has the effect of discrediting democratic institutions and process,[65] unless it converges with the judgment of elites—especially union leaderships but also local elites—outside of the government. Put another way, only those capable of waiting with their demands can accept a short but significant period of economic hardship, and only the organized are capable of waiting. Elites capable of trading short-term demands for long-term influence can do so only when rooted in relatively strong organizations of civil society. Nothing, however, can so easily block the consolidation of democracy, or deconsolidate it, as an excess of populist demand that overtaxes the redistributive capacities of the state.

FROM MOVEMENT TO INSTITUTION

Fortunately, the reports concerning the demise of civil society turned out to be premature. During the period when many of the older civil organizations became parties or imploded, political and economic processes initially on local and sectoral levels provided countless new opportunities and incentives for the formation of new organizations. Because these, despite their considerable number (one analyst reports the existence of more than forty thousand associations and foundations in Hungary in 1995), were not initially able to engage themselves in politics, political actors at first could safely disregard their existence. Nevertheless the new organizations soon established forms of national coordination among them, and relatively soon thereafter they forcefully indicated their intention to participate in national politics.[66] The discourse of civil society, too, now spread to groups and strata who never saw themselves in these terms before. How has this been possible, given the very real tendencies toward demobilization and exclusion? The answer lies both in the survival of the conception both in the region as well as (importantly) abroad and even more in the structural characteristics of the liberal democratic systems established in the region. Indeed, the discourse might have lost its social context, had not the constitutional arrangements facilitated in various ways and degrees the reemergence of civic associations and initiatives and their reinsertion into national politics.

The development of new civil organizations certainly did not follow as a lawful regularity from the establishment of a capitalist market economy. Nevertheless, the new political regime established in 1989–90 contributed a great deal—even if indirectly and unintentionally—to the formation of a large number of civil actors. It should be noted that the concept of civil society has been recently used in two distinct senses: to indicate a set of societal movements, initiatives, and forms of mobilization *and* to refer to a framework of settled institutions (rights, associations, publics). One could use different terms altogether to avoid confusion. In *Civil Society and Political Theory*[67] we chose, however, only a relative distinction to deal with the difference involved: civil society as movement *versus* civil society as institution. We did this because the differentiation is a fluid one: Mobilization always seeks at least some institutionalization as, for instance, in the August 31, 1980, Gdansk accords, and institutionalization is the precondition for new movements and initiatives. Alain Touraine nicely captured this relationship in his distinction between historical and social movements.[68] Even more fundamentally, the distinction is rooted in Cornelius Castoriadis's dualism of *société instituante* and *société instituée.*

For my present purposes it is important to stress this distinction, because it follows from it that demobilization is not automatically equal to atomization, to the obliteration of a politically significant civil society. Beyond reasons already mentioned, demobilization follows from the life cycles of movements, from the relative achievement of their goals, and we should not lament this fact unless we long for permanent revolution or permanent mobilization. But the choice is ultimately not between permanent mobilization and atomization (both are impossible) but levels and degrees of stability of institutionalization.

Liberal Institutionalization

Institutionalization of civil society in the sense of politically relevant and relatively stable associations and publics is achieved by the following institutions and practices:

1. guarantee of fundamental rights of association, assembly, speech, press, and coalition, which in turn presuppose;
2. establishment of a constitution that works as a fully legal document, one supported by the separation of powers, especially independent courts;

3. institutionalization of a politically accessible and also decentralized media of communication, relatively independent from both government and market;
4. political and economic decentralization, involving independent local and regional self-government and possibility and facilitation of local and small-scale forms of enterprise;
5. acceptance and recognition of the operation of national and international organizations (NGOs) and institutions dedicated to the monitoring and defense of rights (ombudsman, transnational courts); and
6. the financing of civil society associations.

These interrelated levels of institutions and practices promote the institutionalization of civil society defined in terms of associations and publics. While I am convinced that some relevant fulfillment of the first two criteria, rights and constitutionalism, leads to some level of institutionalization, only the fulfillment of most of the other criteria can lead to relatively higher levels of institutionalization. (At the end of the chapter I return to the question of a high level of institutionalization, which, according to some, involves additional constitutional prerequisites.) In Hungary, in fact, rights, constitutionalism, political and economic decentralization, and the ability of NGOs to operate have been securely established in the period between 1989–94 because of the activity of constitution makers, the legislature, and especially the Constitutional Court, which made clear from the outset that fundamental rights in Hungary will be strictly enforced as genuine legal norms. At the same time, the achievement, or partial achievement, of structures of consultation and of independent communication media did not happen as smoothly and required in the end collective action and civil remobilization. Channels of consultation were explicitly rejected by the constitution makers of 1990, and it was only under the impact of the October 1990 taxi- and truck-drivers' strike that forms of social partnership (the tripartite Council for Interest Coordination: ET) received new relevance. The electronic media had to withstand strong efforts at governmentalization, and it was only after the 1994 alternation in power that their greater autonomy was uneasily (and in my view still incompletely) enshrined in a new media law. Obviously, independent associations and publics when established could promote further institutionalization and thus the expansion of their own political role and influence. This indeed happened in the case of social consultation and the media law with organizations such as the Publicity Club and movements like the Democratic Charter playing the major role in the second case. Thus there are strong reasons, in Hungary at least, to disagree with Ralf Dahrendorf's thesis that the institutionalization of civil society will take incomparably longer than those of competitive political institutions and market economy.

On the basis of my study of the East and Central European cases, a relatively high level of institutionalization of civil society in the period of transition depends on several factors. One is again the politics of civil society before the transition, since a pattern of participation establishes political norms and organizational competence that can be called upon by an expanding circle of new organizations. Institutionalization depends in part on the demands made, and expected to be made, from below. But the relevant parts of the institutional design are affected also by the power relations at the site of negotiation and the ideologies shared by the participants. The more balanced the relations, the more actors will seek in context of future uncertainty a larger variety of channels of social participation and self-protection. But as János Kis rightly stresses, successful negotiations also presuppose relative consensus about the political framework of the future. This consensus can have various contents with respect to the level of institutionalization of civil society. The latter, in turn, has important consequences for the tasks of the consolidation of democracy.

The minimal criteria of rights and constitutionalism are of course also the minimal criteria required for a transition (in the wider sense, including the institutional design) to a constitutional democracy or polyarchy. Dahl might insist on relatively open and accessible media, but in light of international experience with both governmental and commercialized media that would be too demanding as a minimum condition. Of course the question is what *relatively* means. In Hungary the public sphere was relatively free even during the year when radio and TV were finally degraded to governmental organs, because the widely read written press was indeed independent. It may be therefore fair to say that at least some level of free communication is required if the minimal conditions of a polyarchy are to be met. At the same time the latter has two additional conditions that are less directly related to the institutionalization of civil society: (1) the organization of competitive elections; and (2) the design and plausible operation of a machinery of government in the narrow sense guaranteeing some accountability and responsiveness, as well as space for the functioning of a viable opposition.

I would therefore argue the following: Under East and Central European conditions, the more developed the institutionalization of civil society, and in particular those levels that do not belong to the minimum definition of democracy or polyarchy (i.e., levels 3 through 6), the stronger will be the consensus supporting the democratic design of free and competitive elections and accountable government, the higher will be the legitimacy and therefore the stability and quality of democracy.

I would like to demonstrate (though not "prove") this thesis in relation to some key dimensions of Hungarian experience:

Legitimacy, Channels of Consultation, Decentralization

Advocates of parliamentary sovereignty and radical economic stabilization agree in seeing societal demands as illegitimate and as sources of fiscal strain. According to their views, civil associations have no electoral legitimacy and can conceivably represent only unelected minorities. There is therefore no justification supposedly for giving a distinguished role to just those minority views that happen to have the good fortune to be organized. Such a role is supposed to be especially unfortunate, because organized interests are presumed to seek redistributive advantages for their members. This objection can be refuted on the theoretical level by stressing the difference between the political power of parties and elected representatives, as against the influence of movements and associations working through the societal public sphere. Moreover, it is also true that nationally coordinated organized interests are capable of restraining the redistributive demands of their members and will ordinarily try to do so when either their long-term interests or political trade-offs make this worthwhile. At the same time there is a good deal of empirical evidence indicating the negative side effects of decision making without consultation.

In Hungary the picture is relatively clear: Lack of consultation and political centralism can severely shake the legitimacy of governments, at least in the sociological if not the legal sense. During the first year of the first freely elected government, disregard of interest groups and attacks on the autonomy of local government led to a severe legitimacy deficit in the sociological sense. A culture of consultation and decentralization helps to establish political incentives for association building, but this is potentially a positive-sum game in relation to governmental power. After the dramatic social conflicts of the October 1990 taxi- and truck-drivers' strike, the institutions of social consultation (in particular the ET, the Council for the Coordination of Interests) received new life. This strike can be represented as the defense of particular corporate advantages against necessary steps of restoring budgetary integrity. It can be even said to have frightened the MDF government to such an extent that they would no longer dare to undertake reform measures that could run into determined popular opposition. But the strike was also, among other things, a protest against the introduction of austerity measures without consultation with those most concerned. And in this sense it achieved its purpose, for a time at least.

Significantly, the MDF government did not have to face another major challenge to its legitimacy for purely economic reasons. However, after the putschlike introduction (perhaps unavoidable) of the (Lajos) Bokros stabilization program in early 1995, the support for the Gyula Horn government plummeted. The existence of fora of interest coordination like the ET made a great contribution to the social peace of the period, even if the nongovernmental participants experienced this whole period as the failure of interest coordination.[69] While the introduction of some measures without prior consultation may be a precondition of their effectiveness, hopefully the wrong lesson, the avoidance of consultation and negotiation will not be drawn by policy makers. Recent agrarian protest (February–March 1997) and government response show that the bad instincts are still there, but that there is also some goodwill on both sides to resolve the contentious issues through negotiations.

Public Sphere and a Culture of Openness and Criticism

The governmentalization of media not only blocks access to alternative forms of opinion, it also deprives government of needed criticism. Moreover, under formerly state socialist conditions only independent media can present the point of view of government in a believable manner. The incredibly quick loss of popularity of the victors of the 1990 elections can be explained only by their attacks on local government and independent media, both of which found their own means and the political allies to resist. In the end, even the victory of the Antall-Boross government in the electronic media war contributed a great deal to its almost total political defeat in the 1994 elections. Open media are the precondition for the expansion of societal publics; but as associational participation, these too strengthen rather than weaken government. The lesson was learned by the new coalition, though not as fully as some might have hoped. Today Hungary has a media law that guarantees the plurality of the forms of institutionalization of the media and their independence from at least direct forms of governmental intervention. Unfortunately, instead of direct government intervention the current trend is toward the "partification" of media controls, on a pattern that resembles more discredited practices in Italy and Austria than the BBC or CBC mixed model that many of the reformers have hoped to establish. Thus, already during the first year of the operation of the new media law, one state-owned TV channel was licensed not to the highest bidder, but to one preferred by an ad hoc combination of the socialists and some of the right-wing parties. In any case, media channels or broadcasting segments farmed out to parties is not the best way to guarantee (as the Hungarian Constitutional Court once recognized) either the widest public access to different groups or especially the most open process of critical deliberation concerning issues of public relevance.

In the defense of the public sphere, the importance of monitoring agencies like the Publicity Club and civic movements like the Democratic Charter cannot be underestimated. Starting out in defense of free media, these institutions played a major role in blocking trends in Hungary toward authoritarianism, significant not because of popular support but because of the presence of such trends *within* the politics of the government between 1990 and 1994. Today it is a little too easy to say, in retrospect, that there never was an authoritarian danger in that period. It is, however, the task of institutions like the Publicity Club and of democratic citizen initiatives like the Charter, to demonstrate the illegitimacy of authoritarian reversion even if it has a good chance to fail within the given political and geopolitical environment. The consolidation of democracy relies precisely on swift public condemnation and protest against all authoritarian phenomena that can undermine committed support to democracy in the longer run.

With politicians relatively friendly to these movements in power between 1994 and 1998, these organizations faced the well-known dilemma of either atrophy or weakening a government that may have been (whatever its grave deficiencies) the best alternative at the moment. Characteristically for a movement, which undergoes life cycles, the Democratic Charter has been quiescent in the social-liberal period. The Publicity Club, equally characteristically for an established institution, has remained an alert defender of the free media also in this period, recently appealing to the Constitutional Court against an interpretation by the government of the new media law that threatened the public and open character of the electronic media.

Antipolitical Movements and Initiatives

Finally an area needs to be mentioned where orientation to civil society can endanger democratic consolidation. Some (though not all) of the civic movements share an antipolitical tradition and a hostility to parties that has now been often exacerbated because of the unenlightened policies of parliaments and governments. Nevertheless party systems in the very few countries where they are now in place have played an important role in the consolidation of democracy, specifically by making democratic politics compatible with the continuation of market-oriented reform. This role, actual or potential, can be endangered by fundamentalist or antipolitical versions of the politics of civil society. Such was the politics of LAET (association of those living below the minimum income), directed at the collective recall of the members of Parliament in 1993 through the use of the referendum. Such efforts, if successful, could have threatened the viability of parliamentary representation and pushed the country toward plebiscitary democracy.

Democratic Institutionalization?

Hungarian civil society, demobilized during the transitions, has been institutionalized during the period of the consolidation through the structures of liberal constitutionalism. Such an institutionalization guarantees, however, only a rather minimal civil society, and not necessarily one that will contribute to long-term democratic legitimacy through the formation of an active, participatory civic culture. We have seen that in Hungary, the main organ through which the actors of civil society can achieve national integration and national influence, the public sphere, that is, the sphere of the independent communication media, was under attack in the democratic period itself. Even today it may be only the party pluralization rather than the genuine independence of the media that is legally guaranteed through the so-called media law. Thus one cannot say, even in Hungary (one of the most fortunate of the new democracies), that the level of the institutionalization of democratic civil society has been particularly high.

Evidently institutionalization in itself is not enough. We again have to focus on the problem of achieving a type of institutionalization that would facilitate the emergence of a democratic, participatory civil society. That is the perhaps now old-fashioned stress to which the emphasis on civil society inevitably leads. Of course, a democratic civil society presupposes the long-term cultural developments that cannot be designed. But institutional design might be able to help with promoting an "opportunity structure" for forms of activity that can positively influence cultural development itself. If constitutionalism guarantees societal independence as such, an active democratic civil society may require the support of constitutional provisions that make the participation of groups, associations, and initiatives worthwhile.

In Hungary two such constitutional provisions have been stressed: the idea of a second parliamentary chamber rooted in civil associations and the expansion of the role of referenda. The first of these ideas revived notions from the armory of semiauthoritarian forms of corporatism. It was favored by some socialists seeking to give the unions an institutionalized foothold in parliamentary decision making and by some Christian Democrats wishing to do the same for the traditional churches. In a more democratic version, other advocates of corporatist ideas proposed the constitutionalization of social partnership, in other words, making interest aggregation compulsory in economic decision making.

The second idea, the stress on referenda, came from advocates of direct, popular, and plebiscitary democracy. Surprisingly, the two rather contradictory traditions (corporatism and direct democracy) were even combined, as in the case of Christian Democrats and members of the Small Holders who insisted on an item-by-item plebiscitary ratification of the emerging constitutional synthesis. Given a certain amount of justified skepticism that a parliamentary process dominated by parties would ever design institutions favorable to civil society, the eclecticism of civil society advocates was perhaps less than surprising. It was repeatedly proposed by the Small Holders and by a variety of civil associations that the latter too should participate in the process of constitution making, and the insistence on ratificatory referenda came as Parliament continued to disregard claims of civil participation in the drafting process.

The constitutional role of civil society became a salient issue in the period between 1994 and 1998, because the governing social liberal coalition embarked on a project of codifying Hungary's definitive constitution (the constitution of 1989–90 was understood by its own makers as a temporary one).[70] The parties of the ruling coalition opened up the process for the participation of the opposition parties. Given their parliamentary power and the additional support they could rally behind a project that would preserve in substance the regime structure established in the year of the change of systems (1989–90), those who supported innovations like a semipresidential system or the constitutionalization of corporatism found themselves initially in a rather weak position. Thus came the call from within Parliament to open the process beyond Parliament, for the organizations of "civil society," who as it happens supported the positions of parliamentary minorities on the disputed issues.

But which of the many thousands of associations, clubs, movements, umbrella organizations, and so on have the legitimacy to share in the *constituent* power? Once posed, this question could never be resolved satisfactorily, and it is not very surprising that the parliamentary advocates of such "civil" participation never really pressed their case, one that was not supported even by most of the opposition parties.

The appeal to referenda was born out of the same quandary, politically speaking, namely, parliamentary minorities seeking to overcome their minority status. The argument for such an appeal had, however, distinct historical, legal, and intellectual foundations. We should recall that the popular petition campaign and referendum on the election of the president in 1989 played an important role in correcting the results of elite bargaining processes and in giving Hungary the purest structure of parliamentary democracy in the whole region. I have described this set of events as the last hurrah of a civil society strategy under a still authoritarian regime form. Referenda therefore played an important role in Hungary's regime change. Moreover, the still valid 1989 law on referenda (unlike the Constitution of 1989–90 itself) requires that a new constitution must be ratified by a popular plebiscite, before it is validated.[71] Though there were disagreements on the question, this requirement was willingly conceded by the governing coalition. Once, however, several features of the proposed constitutional draft became controversial, it was objected that a really meaningful plebiscite could not involve a yes or no vote on the whole package without forcing people to accept or reject features that they actually objected to for the sake of features that they accepted or rejected even more strongly. Should not the mobilized population determine all features of its political constitution one by one?

Again, once posed, the alternative of constitution making through repeated referenda had to be rejected. Whereas any number of civil associations lacked the legitimacy to directly participate in constitutional creation, plebiscitary mobilization lacks the cognitive capability to draft rules. The end result of such constitution making could only be an incoherent and unworkable melange of opinions. Worse, those who proposed such a role of referenda ran the risk of fully discrediting this important democratic channel that could be an important corrective for the party political monopolization of participation under parliamentary democracy.

It may very well be the responsibility of the coalition that governed between 1994 and 1998 that forms of less-obtrusive public participation and consultation with respect to constitution making were not worked out. In Hungary there was, for example, much less of an attempt to educate and inform public opinion concerning constitutional issues than there was roughly at the same time in South Africa.[72] But civil society-based forms of the exertion of constituent power could not make up for this lack and had to prove self-defeating. In the end the advocates of such participation, not wishing to allow the social liberal coalition to take credit for giving the country its new constitution, only used their claims to bring down the project as a whole. Ironically, they succeeded in the effort only because a small group of socialist leaders too, around the prime minister and the minister of justice, who harbored corporatist ideas themselves, turned against their own parliamentary fraction and deprived it and the liberal coalition partner of the necessary majority, at the penultimate moment.

This tragicomic episode has an important lesson for us. The proposed political forms, direct civil participation in constitution making, and direct plebiscitary forms of constitutional consultation foreshadowed the corporatist and plebiscitary elements that their advocates hoped to enshrine in the constitution then in the making. These forms, each hoping to directly institutionalize the power (not the public, deliberative influence!) of civil society,[73] turned out to be incompatible with the logic of parliamentary democracy. Establishing a second chamber of corporate representation is incompatible with the one-person, one-vote principle. Moreover it threatens to freeze civil society, in itself a fluid and ever-changing field of associational life, because those initially admitted to corporate representation can maximize their power only if they exclude new entrants to the fora of bargaining. Democratic corporatism can be saved from such an outcome only through its informality and the ability of parliaments to bypass corporatist forms of intermediation if they wish to. The attempt to constitutionally enshrine corporatism made the posing of the more relevant constitutional problem, namely, the regulation and pluralization of lobbying activities, impossible by vastly overshooting the mark. By raising the specter of corporatism, liberal opinion was motivated to disregard the problem of pluralist access to the political process and the democratic requirements one may impose on those who are to have such access. Referenda of course, unlike corporatism, are potentially inclusive rather than exclusive. But they too represent threats to parliamentary democracy in contexts in which political parties, unaccustomed or unwilling to limit themselves, are ready to use referenda to contest each and every electoral and legislative outcome not to their liking. Referenda can be tamed not through informality like corporatism, but through having a subordinate role in the framework of parliamentary democracy. The Hungarian Constitutional

Court has played some role in redefining referenda in this spirit, and in particular in depriving them of the ability to openly or tacitly modify the existing constitutional structure.[74] It is unfortunate that the constitution makers of 1994–96 failed to produce a liberal democratic constitution that might have settled the relationship between parliamentary and direct democratic forms in a more definitive manner.

In order to be politically influential, civil society and its organizations must on the whole renounce the direct exercise of power, which is appropriate only in revolutionary situations. Revolutions, however, are rarely conducive to democracy. The civil society-based initiatives of Central Europe contributed to revolutionary results, but within the framework of legal continuity. For these results to remain open to further democratization, new openings for the influence of civil society will have to be found. But for this democracy to remain democratic, it will be equally important for civil actors of all types, from churches to unions, from voluntary associations to more tightly knit communities, to eschew all forms of populism and relearn, if need be, the great democratic art of political self-limitation.

Chapter 3

Revolution, Restoration, and Legitimation: Ideological Problems of the Transition from State Socialism

Did you want a revolution without revolution?
—Maximilien Robespierre[1]

In politics, words and their usage are more important than any other weapon.
—Reinhart Koselleck[2]

The idea of the "self-limiting revolution," internally linked to the project of the reconstruction of civil society, represents one of the major contributions of recent East European thought and action to political philosophy.[3] And yet from the outset, from the times of the first Solidarity, this idea was scornfully rejected by would-be radical revolutionaries, largely but not exclusively from the nationalist right. Of course, as long as the geopolitical reasons for strategic self-limitation, rooted in an intact Soviet imperium, continued to apply, it was not fully apparent that only a minority of intellectuals and movement militants promoted a self-limiting radicalism also on the basis of historical learning experiences and normative considerations. Given the strategic reasons, there was apparently no need to fully argue a case that would have contributed to ideological divisions within the opposition, divisions that were pragmatically unnecessary.

With the happy collapse of the geopolitical context of self-limitation the idea of radical revolution has clearly reappeared at least among some intellectuals and politicians. And yet, as the continued use of adjectives like peaceful, velvet, gentle, quiet, bloodless, negotiated, legal, and constitutional indicate, there has been, at least for a time, a reluctance, on a wide variety of grounds, to define or interpret the East European transitions as revolutions in the classical sense of the modern revolutionary tradition.

81

In what follows I will first reexamine the problem of what constitutes a revolution in its modern sense. Second, I will show how the presence of only some of the important criteria favors in principle at least the retention of the notion of self-limiting revolution and, focusing on Hungary, how this state of affairs has powerfully affected the legal-constitutional development of a post-Communist society. Third, I will consider the reasons why, mainly but not exclusively in the form of revolutionary restorationism, radical revolutionary ideology has nevertheless experienced a revival among political forces even in Hungary, perhaps the least revolutionary of East and East Central European societies. I will try to point to the political weakness of this revival as well as to the normative complex from which it nevertheless may continue to draw its energies. Finally I will try to show why the social scientific notion of "transition" and the liberal defense of the continuity of the *Rechtsstaat*, however justified in themselves, are unfortunately in themselves inadequate in the face of the challenge of revolution. I end by making a plea for an ideology that recognizes the originality and radicalism of the East European transformations, beyond mere imitation and restoration, and the need to distinguish this civil society-centered ideology from all concepts of radical revolution.

WHAT IS A REVOLUTION?

Even today,[4] I have little need to deny that in light of comparable transformations what occurred in 1989–91 in at least the three countries of East Central Europe was in varying degrees peaceful and bloodless, quiet and gentle, negotiated and legal. But were the transformations revolutions? Most authors who use these terms focus on the adjectives, not the substantive they qualify.[5] On the other hand, in light of rather cataclysmic change the newer consensus among Hungarian social scientists and at least some politicians that whatever occurred in Hungary certainly was not a revolution, seems also a bit one-sided, that is, not sufficiently complex and—for a while it seemed—premature.[6] Leaving aside political motivations, to which I will return, it seems that the uncertain guidance offered by most social science and some social scientific historiography (both well known in Hungary) are at least partially responsible for the confusion.

From a hermeneutic point of view, the social scientific literature on revolutions suffers at best from the subjectivism and arbitrariness of its definitions, at worst from confusion and inconsistency. From the exclusive point of view of external, scientific observers, analysts have not been able to decide, and especially convince one another, whether the concept of revolution should refer to all of history, or only to modern times, whether it should include violence or a reference to social movements. It has been difficult to decide whether the concept refers to the change of the form of government or only the possessors of political power. Amazingly enough some analysts solve this last problem by treating the two forms of change as if they were one. But there is hardly any consensus to treat revolutions as primarily political phenomena; to many interpreters they signify above all the transformation of the symbolic and legitimational core of a society. There are others still for whom change of symbols is entirely irrelevant. Most believe revolutions to be rapid transformations, but only some include success in the definition. There are even a few who attempt to give a temporal frame to the idea of success, for example, thirty days in the case of one rash analyst. Some definitions of revolution turn it into a general class concept with several subspecies, including coups, palace revolutions, military takeovers, and so on, and thus hundreds of exemplars in history; others confine the category to a very few cases, in particular the great revolutions of modernity. There are some, however, who even move back and forth between broad and narrow definitions as their implicitly political purposes apparently require.[7]

There have been notable efforts to bring order into the confusion. By using the independent variables of revolutionary situation (divided sovereignty) and revolutionary outcome (change of power blocs) and listing their various combinations, Charles Tilly has established continua between coups (revolutionary situation, but low degree of change), silent revolutions (no revolutionary situation but great change) and great revolutions.[8] This analysis remains helpful in showing the uneven range of application of the social scientific definition and pointing to the different elements great revolutions share with other phenomena at least some people will continue to call revolution. Yet given the inevitably political use of any concept of revolution this effort has its paradoxes. Can revolution really be a matter of degree, like being a little pregnant? More seriously, do coups, silent revolutions, and great revolutions really belong to a single genus other than social change itself? Silent revolutions need not be political events at all; coups may involve minimal change beyond replacing one group by a socially identical one. Does it make sense to call events and processes revolutions because of the requirements of a mere definition, if no one before, and especially no participants, understood them to be revolutions? Not that we ought to take the word of the participants alone.

It seems to me to serve no readily obvious purpose to construct a definition of revolution for any period other than modernity and to try to cover hundreds of events and processes other than the great revolutions.[9] Indeed most students of revolutions have been concerned only with these, and the relevant debate that concerns analysts of contemporary East Europe concerns the inclusion or exclusion of some major complexes of events that have played important roles in modern history, like the Glorious Revolution (predating the origin of the modern meaning of "revolution"), the American Revolution (supposedly not a "social" revolution), and the Hungarian Revolution of 1956 (not successful). To be sure definitions restricted to the great revolutions may also mislead. Theda Skocpol's definition of social revolution, namely, "rapid, basic transformations of a society's state and class structures . . . accompanied by and in part carried through by class based revolts from below," rightly distinguishes social revolutions from coups, rebellions, revolts, and transitions from one power block controlling the government to another. The same definition would, however, also disqualify the American Revolution.[10] Perhaps Skocpol would want to classify the latter as a political as against a social revolution, because it involved (presumably) no class conflict and change in class structure.[11] But what is the genus to which such political revolution and the French revolution, for example, belong, making both certainly revolutions and in terms of importance worthy of the adjective "great"? Skocpol's exclusion of issues of normative integration from her concept, including even the destruction and construction of constitutions in the sense of constitutive rules of a society, makes this question unanswerable.[12]

More useful in this context is S. N. Eisenstadt's insistence on the contrary position, namely, that the great revolutions involve above all a rapid, total rupture with the old symbolic core of society and the establishment of a new one.[13] He seeks to flesh out this notion by a long and complex list culled from a variety of sources: (1) violent change of political regime, its legitimation and symbols; (2) displacement of one ruling elite by another; (3) changes in all major institutional spheres, economy, and class, leading to modernization (including a market economy!); (4) postulate of novelty and radical break with past; and (5) millenarianism—desire to change human beings, including their personality—supplemented by the additional criteria of utopianism, revolutionary experience, and intense solidarity. In the process one inevitably gets the feeling that not only the American Revolution does not qualify, but that there has never been even a single great revolution![14]

Eisenstadt rightly seeks to restrict the meaning of revolution to contexts of modernity, but he does not lay any special emphasis on the modern use of the concept. Alain Touraine makes just this notion the center of his analysis. Like other social scientists he apparently proposes a simple definition: Revolutions are the destructions of old regimes based on privilege by movements in the name of democracy.[15] This definition, unlike most others in social science, combines social scientific analysis, in this case focusing on the contrast of tradition and modernity, with interpretations of the self-understanding of the actors; the reference to democracy takes seriously what the actors say regardless of the outcomes, in general hardly democratic. Unfortunately Touraine does not go very far in his interrogation of the revolutionary meaning of democracy and its connection to antidemocracy.[16] He nevertheless presupposes just this latter connection, which according to him gradually vitiates the democratic element as the history of revolutions proceeds.

Touraine postulates the end of revolution in our time. This thesis, however, is based on two separable, and potentially inconsistent, arguments. First, he argues that there are no longer old regimes anywhere. Today people suffer from modernizing authoritarian regimes or the side effects of modernization or both. Thus the so-called Islamic Revolution or Solidarity do not represent revolutions. Both struggled against different types of modernizing elites who themselves already destroyed old regimes. The social movements of the West oppose an excess of voluntaristic transformation, not lack of change. Second, he notes the rejection of revolution by collective actors in Latin America and East Europe because of the evident disassociation of democracy and revolution today, because of the undemocratic and primarily state-strengthening character of past great revolutions and, it seems, also the desire of revolutionaries even as late as the 1960s and 1970s to overthrow liberal democracies by undemocratic means.

But what if the actors actually use the term *revolution* as in the case of the Islamic Revolution and the Hungarian Revolution of 1956? The power of such usage need not be decisive, but we should note its strength all the same. Significantly and inconsistently, Touraine does not even contest it in the latter case.[17] The same issue of course arises for the events of 1989. Unfortunately, *antirevolution*, the term Touraine seems to prefer for the popular movements that sought to overthrow Communist regimes, reminds one too much of *counterrevolution* and, in any case, remains mere private usage.[18] Moreover, both of his separate arguments for the thesis of the end of revolution can be contested. As the literature on neopatrimonialism and neotraditionalism indicates, originally modernizing regimes indeed have had the propensity to harden into political and social frameworks experienced as conservative old regimes based on new forms of privilege.[19] And though the learning experiences Touraine postulates about the authoritarian logic of revolutions are real enough, it would be a great mistake to assume a linear and overly global model of collective learning in which what is learned by some movements and actors cannot be forgotten and must structure the self-understanding of all other relevant actors. Unfortunately in history everything learned must be constantly relearned, in the face of great temptations not to learn at all or even to unlearn.

Touraine is entirely right of course to pay attention to the self-interpretation of the participants and to structural change. The new intellectual history of the concept of revolution—developed by François Furet, Mona Ozouf, and their colleagues, by Reinhart Koselleck and the coauthors of *Geschichtliche Grundbegriffe*, and by Lynn Hunt and Keith Baker in this country—has demonstrated, in particular in the case of the French Revolution, the importance of the voice of the participants.[20] In particular these authors study the concepts, semantics, and rhetorics of revolution in the process of the emergence of a new and specifically modern political culture. They certainly do not neglect the structural changes involved in revolutions anymore than did their important forerunner Hannah Arendt. Indeed Furet specifically battles against a populist historiography uncritical of the representations of the actors. Nevertheless these analyses clearly complement objectivistic models of change that are in themselves unable to document the thresholds where social principles of organization enter into crisis.[21] The stress of this literature on the French Revolution hardly disqualifies it from the point of view of a more general or comparative theory. On the contrary, this stress establishes the semantic and rhetorical elements of a revolutionary tradition within which all subsequent self-interpretations of revolutionaries were to unfold.[22] To be sure the emergence of such a tradition complicates the problem of interpreting the self-representations of all later revolutions, since for them the experience of the new shared with the French was cast in terms inherited from a revolutionary tradition that itself was primarily constructed between 1789 and 1795.

In my view a heavily loaded term like *revolution* receives its meaning on four[23] interpretive levels: cognitive, phenomenological, hermeneutic, and legal-normative. Not only are these theoretically fundamental, but in each case we have a discourse on which we can rely. The first refers to how external observers would view a social process. It relies on the analytical discourse of social scientists and some historians. The second focuses on the experience of participants, their expectations and anxieties, expressed through semantic labeling as well as nonverbal symbolism, while the third stresses their interpretive activity linking their own actions to the tradition of modern revolutions. These two dimensions can be reconstructed from the participants' own discourse as well as from the works of hermeneutically inclined historians. Finally the legal-normative dimension focuses on the place the concept of revolution occupies in juridical discourse, as reproduced in particular by the legal analysis of both observers and participants. Of course these four dimensions are generally interrelated. Nevertheless, they can also be found in separation from one another. Significantly, while the American and French Revolutions could be and were "revolutions" in only three dimensions, all the modern revolutions after the French that we tend to consider "great" were revolutionary in all four of them. Let me therefore expand the meaning of each of the four dimensions.

Cognitive-Objective Level

Both structure and event can be studied from the point of view of external observers. What they study depends on their specific theories of course. In my view the most advanced theory of social structures today would locate revolutionary change on the level of social systems or subsystems. Revolutions from this point of view are replacements of social systems or subsystems by alternative ones, differently organized. Evidently, however, social systems cannot be replaced in toto. There is on this level always continuity and change. One difficulty for a systems theory of revolution would be to isolate organizational or coordinating principles or institutional cores in systems whose replacement would be a necessary and sufficient condition of revolution in that sphere. A second difficulty is that although it is not meaningless to speak of an agrarian, industrial, cultural, or educational revolution, our term *revolution* ordinarily refers to the political sphere. Thus it may be well advised to insist that revolution from the systemic point of view should refer first and foremost to the transformation of the political subsystem, thus to changes of one or more subsystems of which the political is always one.

A third difficulty for cognitive-objective, and especially system theoretical types of analysis of revolutions, one in my view less severe than the one of reliably establishing thresholds of transformation, is establishing their relevant time frame. Here focusing on events rather than structures may be helpful. From this point of view we can speak of revolutions when we can establish the importance of an event, or more likely a series of events, in accomplishing a change in question. In the leading social historical approaches today the relevant events are political, involve collective action though not necessarily collective violence, and lead (in my view) to an alteration of the form of government and not only the group that holds power. This last criterion would allow us to characterize the change in the political subsystem at least as a rapid one.

Nevertheless, even the shift to the level of events does not allow us to establish the necessary and sufficient thresholds for system transformation. The events of 1956 in Poland, for example, involved political action, collective actors, and change of government as well. But did the emergence of Wladyslaw Gomulka's regime change the form of government, the organizational principle of the political subsystem? We generally answer no, in spite of the fact that there were in this case political changes, indeed important ones. The dilemma is insoluble if we stay on the cognitive-objective level.

Phenomenological-Experiential Level

Social scientists are not in all respects privileged in relationship to the participants; they are well advised to take the point of view of actors seriously both when they describe their experience and when they define the meaning of their action. Revolutionary actors, as is well known, experience a vast acceleration of time in terms of boundless, in a sense "timeless," charismatic moments, freeing from social restraint, moral purification, and the dramatic expansion of the scope of solidarity and participation.[24] At such moments, as Walter Benjamin proposed, the historical dialectic stands still (*Dialektik im Stillstand*). Lynn Hunt rightly referred to this experience as the cult and celebration of a "mythic present."[25] Hence the importance of festivals and commemorations in all revolutions, which seek to capture and even institutionalize such unique experiences of time. In revolutions, the very language of actors undergoes important changes: Key terms of the old regime are tabooed, and there is a passion for the invention of new words, new terms, new verbal identifications. Towns and streets are renamed; symbols, emblems, and statutes are replaced on a wholesale basis.[26] The verbal construction of the community and a consensus based on a mythic present are, however, fragile; revolutionary semantics are full of anxiety. This is one of the roots of the recurring fear of enemies and conspiracies in all great revolutions.[27] For radical revolutionaries in action, the political universe is populated solely by wills, and each minor conspiracy is proof of the one great conspiracy.[28] There are to be sure other ways of dealing with the fragility of community and consensus. As Hannah Arendt showed, actors in revolutions shift their priorities from private to public happiness and freedom.[29] This shift favors the generation of power and the reduction of anxiety, thus the democratization of political life and the creation of new constitutions. Revolutionary experience thus has potentially both dark and light sides.

When actors describe their action as revolution, they are generally referring to the coexistence of experience, event, and structural change. Since they may be mistaken about structural change, it is certainly impossible to determine the presence of revolution merely by focusing on revolutionary involvement, experience, anxiety, or labeling. To be sure, the revolutionary involvement of actors is itself one force pushing structural changes beyond the relevant thresholds. But these thresholds cannot be determined by focusing on the consciousness of actors alone. Indeed actors are likely to experience disappointment even when from the observer's point of view such thresholds have been definitively passed, organizational principles altered. Revolutionary experience by its nature strives toward permanence and the continuation of revolution. This feature is linked to the anxiety concerning community and consensus and is incompatible not only with constitutionalism but also with the institutionalization of democracy.

Hermeneutic Level

Naming the event(s) of revolution does not exhaust the relevant semantics. Starting with the French Revolution, the discourse of those who experience revolution has been remarkably constant. While one reason for this is the similarity of revolutionary experience, a positive interpretive relation to and even identification with previous great revolutions plays an even more important role. Thus from the French to the Cuban Revolution the term *revolution* is often referred to in the singular, the actors call themselves "revolutionaries" and their opponents "counterrevolutionaries"; a wide variety of substantives too are qualified by the adjectives *revolutionary* and *counterrevolutionary.* Revolutionaries everywhere are not only dominated by fears of enemies and conspiracies, but they also claim to be fighting for the real, or historical or rational interests and needs of constituencies against their merely empirical interests. Until the Cuban Revolution at least it has been commonly under-stood by revolutionaries that their semantics, indeed their very actions, were derived from the Great French Revolution and its tradition, which they affirmed. Contrary to the hope of the author of the *18th of Brumaire,* even Marxist revolutions did not derive their poetry primarily from the future. Most, if not all, modern revolutionaries willingly assumed the label of Jacobinism and continued to see their defeats in terms of Thermidor, Bona-partism, and restoration. Even the songs "la Marseillaise" and "Ah, ça ira" were adopted by later revolutionaries, with different words to be sure.

The semantic potentials of the revolutionary tradition of course intensified and channeled the revolutionary experience. It also devalued for revolution-aries transformations that were incomplete from the point of view of the assumed model, or departed from its pattern. In terms of a philosophy of his-tory inherited from the French Revolution and systematized by Marx, revolu-tion in the singular involved total rupture with an existing state of affairs, but at the same time continued a process begun with the so-called bourgeois-democratic revolutions. The final goal was a completely unprecedented future—a fully emancipated society based on freedom and solidarity. Such a conception, based on a full-fledged philosophy of history, was at the heart of all revolutionary claims of legitimacy. From the point of view of this philoso-phy of history, very much influenced by the radical phase of the French Rev-olution, any attempt to complete the revolution in terms of settled institutions could be construed as betrayal and embezzlement. Within the revolutionary tradition, any revolution calls for a second or even permanent revolution, and even a revolution within the revolution.

Normative-Legal Level

Evidently the revolutionary tradition in terms of which most who called themselves revolutionaries interpreted their action has no room for events and processes that aim at closure and seek to avoid their own stylization as permanent. As Hannah Arendt recognized, the American Revolution, without a tradition of its own and because of its culmination in constitutionalism, is excluded from *the* tradition by both its critics and advocates. But other revo-lutions, like the Hungarian of 1848 or the German of 1918, would also barely qualify. The legal definition of revolution potentially provides a wider genus, with room for both the French and American types. According to Hans Kelsen, "a revolution . . . occurs whenever the legal order of a community is nullified and replaced by a new order in an illegitimate way, that is in a way not prescribed by the first order itself."[30] Kelsen considers it irrelevant from the legal point of view whether the actions involved are violent or nonviolent, are initiated by governments, rival elites, or the general population. He also includes coups d'état in his definition.

Even though Kelsen's definition remains a useful starting point, we must improve upon his own interpretation of it. It is only in terms of Kelsenian dogmatics that coups, involving a rupture in legality but not necessarily any further legal change, alter the identity of a legal system.[31] More serious are two other objections. First, one needs to distinguish between the abolition of a state (federation, secession, annexation) and the abolition of a constitution.[32] Thus Kelsen's definition is not complete even in its own terms; one needs to say instead something like "the legal order of an otherwise (especially territorially) continuous state." Second, according to Carl Schmitt's views, the definition does not even contain the necessary conditions of revolution, because whenever a constitution or even its key principle of amendment are replaced by the utilization of this very same amendment rule, the fact of revolution has only been disguised by legalistic fiction. Thus, if the argument concerning the inclusion of coups indicates that Kelsen's definition does not contain the sufficient conditions of revolution, Schmitt's argument implies that it contains a condition that is not even necessary, namely, a break in constitutional revision procedures.

One suspects that Schmitt tacitly replaced a legal by a political problematic and considered legal continuity to be a possible disguise for political revolution. Yet his argument has legal force as well. As H. L. A. Hart has shown, it is not the case, as Kelsen thought, that using a system's own rules for change necessarily leaves the original legal order intact, nor is there, as Schmitt and others maintained, a logical contradiction involved in using an amendment rule to amend itself.[33] From the legal point of view an order's identity can be totally transformed without a break in legality. In such a case, typically amendment rule 1 would be in effect, without a break, until amendment rule 2 is fully ratified according to the provisions of rule 1. Would such a scenario, involving both legal continuity and fundamental change of legal systems, amount to "revolution" in the legal sense?

Of course legal continuity can indeed disguise a political revolution. In my framework this would in effect mean only that a transformation can be judged to be a revolution on the one level, but not the other. Contrary to Schmitt's view, I would maintain that in such a context legal continuity would not be merely fictional and would have important consequences. Purges and retroactive justice, for example, become more difficult in the context of continuous legality.[34] On the other hand, complete legal discontinuity involving both a change of legal orders and the utilization of another method of constitutional change than the original system's rules of revision also has political effects that are not present when legal change is continuous. When an order is changed outside its own rules of change, there is inevitably a legal hiatus, ex lex, when the old order is no longer and the new one is not yet valid. A rupture, an empty space is opened up in constitutional legality. At such a time all government is merely provisional. Even more importantly, while a legally unbound and unregulated constituent power is not, as Schmitt thought, the ever-present correlative of a constitution, in moments of full legal discontinuity (but not when a system is completely changed according to its own amendment rule) just such a power emerges.[35]

We thus have three possible definitions of revolution in the legal sense: (1) the complete transformation of a legal order bypassing its own rules of revision; (2) the bypassing of a system's own rules of revision in political or legal change; and (3) the complete transformation of a legal order even if its own rule of revision is used. All lawyers should accept definition 1 as sufficient to indicate revolutionary transformation, but not necessarily the claim that either of its conditions is necessary for revolution in the legal sense to occur. In any case, when both conditions of this definition apply, the presence of a revolution in the legal sense will be incontestable. At the same time, lawyers, like extreme followers of Kelsen, would consider definition 2 necessary and sufficient; lawyers like Schmitt will do the same for definition 3. While I remain skeptical in relationship to the orthodox version of Kelsen's position because of its inability to distinguish coups from revolutions, Schmitt's position is less easy to dismiss. It seems to me that whenever systems are fully changed but according to their own rules of revision, the question of revolution in the legal sense will remain somewhat indeterminate and potentially contested. In such cases the legal interpretation of a set of events as a revolution will have to depend on judgments drawn from the other three dimensions of analysis, the cognitive-objective, the phenomenological-experiential, and/or the hermeneutic.

I do not define *revolution* or *great revolution* by the presence of all these dimensions of what constitutes a revolution. To be sure the great revolutions of modernity after the French shared all of the criteria, fully, while the American and French Revolutions had to do without a reference to the revolutionary tradition. The real issue facing the interpreters of new phenomena, the historians of present, is whether we might have adequate reason to call a set of events a revolution if only some of the dimensions are satisfied. It might appear that a full, exhaustive, and unambiguous satisfaction of a single dimension will allow us to make a definitive judgment concerning the presence of revolutionary change. While ordinarily this is not possible, even if it were, the result would not be conclusive in any case. The events leading to the formation of the U.S. Constitution in 1787 seem to satisfy the most demanding version of the legal meaning of revolution. The actions taken by the founders were in part extralegal, and they produced a new legal-political order. Yet with the exceptions of a very few supporters and opponents of the Constitution who insist on speaking of revolution and, more often counter-revolution in this case, the usage has not had much success even among lawyers themselves. In a different way, a social-scientific determination of the coordinating or organizing principles, institutional cores of systems, or even the identity of ruling groups within political subsystems on which the objective criteria of revolution depend is always a hypothesis disputable on the level of concept formation and of course falsifiable empirically. A definition on this level will always be contested from the outset, and its persuasive power will tacitly depend on how the other criteria of revolution are met. Most commonly we will encounter contexts in which the criteria of revolutionary change are met incompletely, as the examples of systemic change with some fundamental continuities à la Alexis de Tocqueville, or of comprehensive legal change using the system's own rules of revision, tend to show. Such cases will depend even more on the relatively convincing satisfaction of the criteria of revolution on the other levels. If a hard-nosed social scientist stays fully on Tocqueville's ground and accepts his argument, he or she will persist in calling the phenomenon the French Revolution (as he himself did), openly or tacitly, only because of the overwhelming presence of revolution in the experiential, semantic, and legal sense.

The real problems begin when in the case of many important event-complexes we find less than complete or fully unambiguous satisfaction of two or more criteria of revolution. These complexes will in my view leave the matter fundamentally contested, with the decision for or against using the concept of revolution (or counterrevolution) becoming first and foremost a political matter. Indeed even some political semantics implicitly concede the ambiguities involved with the adjectives recently used in front of revolution: self-limiting, gentle, velvet, and peaceful on the one side, and stolen, betrayed, embezzled, and interrupted on the other.

The East European transformations of 1989, both similar to and different than the great revolutions, raise especially difficult questions for students of revolutions. What is the meaning and what are some possible consequences when a series of events go beyond all possible meaning of reformism and indeed tend to qualify as revolutions in terms of what I call "objective" and in some countries "subjective" criteria, but involve both the absence and even more the conscious rejection of important components of the hermeneutic dimension, of the revolutionary tradition, and the conscious attempt to bypass or avoid revolution in the most complete legal sense of the term. I continue to be struck by the terms qualifying the use of revolution in 1989: on the one hand, legal, constitutional, and negotiated, which involve reservations with respect to the idea of absolute break and the laying of entirely new foundations; on the other hand, nonviolent, peaceful, gentle, velvet, and bloodless, which involve a rejection and attempted replacement of a semantics linked to the relentless destruction of enemies and the purification of self through violence, indeed of the whole language of friend and enemy conceived in class or national terms. Moreover, absences are as important as explicit rejections: Down to this day we do not encounter the noun *revolutionary* or its plural, or the adjective *revolutionary*, as in revolutionary justice, morals, law, and personality. A philosophy of history, liberal or Marxist, placing the events and the formation of a new society in a series of historical stages, is conspicuous by its absence, as is the even more important and characteristic poetry drawn from an imagined future. From the intellectual armory of great revolutions only the normative precipitates of the natural law tradition, universal rights, and democratic proceduralism are present; this is the one dimension of the original revolutionary imaginary that has disappeared from the revolutionary tradition itself and has everywhere become the part of a different tradition, that of settled constitutionalism.

I have always thought that the East European model of the self-limiting revolution anticipated this conceptual complexity and could continue to help to creatively organize the phenomenon even after the events. At the same time, for about two years now just this model has been under attack. What we have called self-limiting on the basis of both analysis and political principles, others now call embezzled or stolen. At issue first and foremost is a political and not social scientific conflict. More than nationalism even, the partial revival of radical revolutionary projects have come to characterize the programs of right-wing authoritarians throughout the region.[36] Interestingly, however, it is through a revolutionary rhetoric that right-wing authoritarianism has attracted the support of individuals and groups of a radical democratic persuasion. Liberals, who have also tended to tear apart the terms *self-limitation* and *revolution* and make their stand around the idea of self-limitation through the rule of law and constitutionalism, have remained curiously vulnerable to revolutionary radical attacks even where the population is on the whole unmoved by demagogy. The radicals tend to be strong in many new political parties and parliaments. The revival of the idea of radical revolution thus represents an important force in East Europe, a force, as I will show, inimical to the development of democracy. Its rise involves conflicts around all four criteria of revolution developed here. It can be studied only if one has full access to a given national discussion, in my case Hungary, to whose ideological conflicts I will now restrict myself.

SYSTEM CHANGE OR REVOLUTION IN HUNGARY?

The most common term Hungarians use for their political changes is *rendszerváltás,* literally exchange of systems. The term has endured in spite of the first democratically elected prime minister's and subsequently his party's stated preference for *rendszerváltozás,* change of system. One exchanges horses, not systems, József Antall liked to say. Possibly his party's, the MDF's one-time defense of a slower, less radical model of change was originally responsible for this preference. Equally likely, the introduction of the first term by the rival SZDSZ, championing rapid transformation, in its famous blue book[37] played a major role in the terminological conflict. Today the two terms are used almost interchangeably. Interestingly, the original terms easily survived the challenge of another verbally close rival, *rendszerváltoztatás*, which would have put the emphasis on the subject of transformation rather than merely the object that is exchanged or changed.[38]

Change of System and Subsystems

The idea of a change of systems without a global subject behind this process seems particularly adequate for Hungarian conditions.[39] While in all other countries of East and Central Europe one can register the decomposition of old structures and the neutralization of old systems in coordination, it is in Hungary that one can speak to the greatest extent of the emergence of a new subsystem as well as the overarching social system, even if the processes are hardly completed. Instead of a single party political system based on the nomenklatura model of selection, Hungary has a multiparty political system to a large extent based on free elections both on national and provincial levels. Even if the exact nature of the party system is not yet determined (polarized, mildly polarized vs. two rival coalitions, e.g.), based on a viable electoral law and fairly well-established parties it seems certainly as stable as new party systems introduced elsewhere in postwar Europe. Moreover, in spite of attempts to reestablish old forms of dependence and central control, Hungary already has a more autonomous system of local administration than some West European countries, whose models the ruling coalition could not impose because of the pressure of the opposition. Turning to the cultural system, instead of a model based on political constraint and strong mechanisms of censorship and self-censorship, the country has now a dynamic and active public sphere, in spite of new government pressures to instrumentalize the press and the media. The ability of the public sphere to fight these pressures has been remarkable. While the legal system is by no means fully altered, and the independence of the courts is still at issue, the Constitutional Court (the most successful in the region) has come to enjoy entirely new independence, representing thereby an important stepping-stone to constitutionalism. Compared with only a few years ago, a remarkable number of independent associations has emerged, and if their input into big politics has been limited, their sectoral and local role, expressed in part by the national media, should not be underestimated. Finally, and most crucially perhaps, in the economic sphere, despite the initial slowing down of the privatization of the state sector and early attempts to (temporarily?) restatize some industries that have earlier enjoyed a large measure of manager-led decentralization, Hungary has gone a long way from command structures and even the coordinating primacy of informal regulation toward the primacy of market forms of coordination.[40] Most crucial in this context has been "indirect privatization," in other words, the vast increase of new forms of private enterprise, using both domestic and foreign capital, thereby displacing the overall weight of ownership and employment in the direction of purely market-oriented forms.[41] To be sure one cannot fully determine on this level whether the thresholds between a primarily state-owned, redistributive, command economy, based on soft budgetary constraints to a market economy, has been definitively passed. Based on what has happened in the related political subsystem, one can say only that the chances of Hungary passing this threshold relatively soon, though not independent of policy choices, remain rather good.

The rate of change in the various subsystems is of course not the same. There is some consensus that while the political system of change is more or less completed, the economic lags far behind. And yet, in my view at least, the foundations for new central institutions and systems of coordination are laid down in all subsystems with the possible exception so far of the state administration that continues to control the larger part of the national economy. The statism of the ruling coalition has indeed reinforced this type of continuity, which significantly, has been registered for the great revolutions by some of their foremost students, beginning with Tocqueville.[42] To evaluate the meaning of this continuity, however, one must look at the system as a whole within which it persists.

While it remains controversial how to define the principle of organization for the societies of the Soviet type, I continue to stress in this context the general social primacy of a political prerogative or discretionary power.[43] In the Hungarian case this organizational principle, in my view, has been replaced by that of the liberal democratic rule of law, a principle hardly unchallenged or securely established. It is presently operating nevertheless. One need not in general approve of the direction of change in many of the subsystems of Hungarian society to note that the emergence of a *Rechtsstaat (jogállam)* where there was none before is an exchange of systems and that it is foolish to claim that nothing has changed.[44]

Just this is claimed by some: "[T]his system is still that system."[45] The evidence for this proposition is that many of the same people continue to occupy important positions in political, economic, and cultural life. The argument both exaggerates the centrality and number of those who have managed to convert their earlier power and position into new forms and, more importantly, confuses the issue of replacing structures, institutions, and mechanisms of coordination with that of replacing individuals. Those who state it are not deterred by the parallel between their own proposals and earlier Communist purges; in their view the historically cumulated effect of the old regime's purges and nomenklatura can be reversed only by new forms of social purification. The lustration laws of the Czech and Slovak Republic, as well as most likely Bulgaria, indicate that the problem is hardly a Hungarian one alone. And yet the focus on persons and elites may once again displace the real issue relevant to rapid system change: the transformation of institutions and the patterns of social interaction.[46]

To be sure one need not support quasi-revolutionary blacklists and purges to argue that little has changed in Hungary outside of the narrowly understood political system, the top of the social pyramid, as it were.[47] Another argument focuses on the survival of old elites, perhaps identifying this sociological category (rather than persons and jobholders taken individually) with structures and institutions against which the liberal opposition always concentrated its fire. But even this identification is wrong. Even elites can survive and play a very different historical role in the context of changes of institutions and mechanisms of coordination. In the case of state socialist societies, where the political system has been the hegemonic one in society, its complete transformation can leave nothing else intact, even if the changes of the various social subsystems lags behind that of the central political principle of organization.

To be sure, the persistence of the same officeholders, many of whom now owe their jobs to democratic national and even more local elections, can be extremely repulsive to those who have suffered. It is in this context that some radical fighters against the old regime now affirm their radical revolutionary intentions.[48] Undoubtedly, their radicalism feeds on the missing or disappointed subjective components of revolutionary transformation.

Absence of Revolutionary Experience

The term *rendszerváltás* is peculiarly adequate for Hungarian conditions not only because of what it says but also because of what it is silent about. It is a strangely colorless term capable of inspiring little passion or enthusiasm. It expresses the fact that many Hungarians, whenever they refer to the transformation as a revolution, feel obliged to add not only the words *constitutional* and *negotiated, peaceful,* and *bloodless* but also *quiet* and *sad.* At times these last adjectives are even applied to *rendszerváltás,* doubling the effect. And indeed when compared with most other countries, Poland with the history of Solidarity as a mass movement on the one hand, and the role of popular movements in East Germany, Czechoslovakia, Bulgaria, and even Russia at the time of the attempted putsch, the Hungarian population was strangely quiescent through the radical changes. There were to be sure key events in the transition, but these were either well-organized, peaceful demonstrations set in limited time frames,[49] or events in which elites encountered other elites. The petition campaign on the presidency in November 1989 was only a partial exception to the trend. Subsequently, increasingly low electoral participation also showed that Hungary's revolution was hardly joyful.

Evidently many leading politicians preferred a quiet, nonrevolutionary transformation in 1989–90. More than just strategic, geopolitical reasons were involved. The late Prime Minister Antall did occasionally use the term (peaceful or quiet) *revolution* for public consumption. In his circle he was, however, better known for his rather sardonic remark, apparently a rationalization of his statist conservatism, in the face of criticism, "You ought to have made a revolution."[50] Gáspár Miklós Tamás, a leading voice of the conservative-liberal wing of SZDSZ, did once upon a time affirm the revolutionary nature of non-reformist system change as part of a polemic against other members of his own party still insisting on a Polish-type radical reformism. But the idea of a social revolution filled him with horror, and he soon stopped speaking about revolution except in negative terms.[51] Finally, the core of the democratic opposition, originally advocates of a Polish type radical reformism, though the first to realize that the geopolitical reasons for self-limitation were disintegrating, nevertheless adhered to a strategy of self-limitation throughout the transition. While they were no longer ready to offer institutional concessions to the Communists, as was Antall's MDF almost until the bitter end, they tried to defeat such concessions only through a completely legal loophole, allowing referenda on even constitutional issues. Their normatively based opposition to radical revolution continued even as the strategic reasons for self-limitation evaporated, as they were first to recognize. They posited, moreover, the avoidance of reprivatization, political justice, and campaigns against jobholders as the necessary tokens of self-limitation that could not be sacrificed for reasons of fundamental principle to any mass revolutionary sentiments.[52]

The strategy of course affected the labeling. At the time of the key negotiations of 1989, almost no one (Tamás was the one exception I know of) spoke of the transition at hand as a revolution. After the "German" and "velvet" revolutions, some Hungarian authors and political actors began to occasionally use the term, as it were, retrospectively, but always with the adjectives already mentioned. Social scientists, however, remained consistently skeptical. They too preferred the term *rendszerváltás,* and if they needed a substitute they borrowed *transition* from Latin American discussions, *great transformation* from Karl Polanyi, or the half-serious term *refolution* (in the equally funny Hungarian, *reforradalom*) from Garton-Ash.[53] Many would agree with Akos Szilágyi, who extends the point to all of Eastern Europe, that the most revolutionary event has been the avoidance of revolution.[54] He suggests the terms *the avoided revolution* or even *antirevolutionary revolution* to describe the exchange of systems that he admits has occurred.

Even those who tended to use the term *revolution* in Hungary with various qualifying adjectives had at first no interest and even less ability to make up for the missing experience admitted by all. It is otherwise with a new terminological shift that I detected first in August 1990 and more intensively starting in October 1990 among members of the FKGP (the Independent Small Holders Party) deeply committed to the reprivatization of land. First it was merely proposed that the government should decide whether it is involved in a "peaceful transition" or a "peaceful revolution." In the latter case the government could demand the loyalty of the press and move against

Communist officeholders.[55] After the first decision of the Constitutional Court rejecting the reprivatization solely of land in October 1990, members of the same party began to openly speak of the impasse of the bloodless revolution and the beginning of the counterrevolution.[56] All these characterization were meant to mobilize a given constituency behind the program of reprivatization, which after the first relevant decision of the Court, now denounced as counterrevolutionary, could no longer be achieved supposedly through a bloodless revolution or exchange of systems. Were the speakers promoting a violent, second revolution? Interestingly enough, not openly as far as I could determine. At most members of the FKGP called for a new constitution or the abolition of the Constitutional Court or both. But the indirect reference declaiming the end of the bloodless revolution is revealing enough.

In 1991 and 1992 the populist movement wing of the MDF too got into trouble with some of the key (as it were, countermajoritarian) institutions of post-Communist Hungary, the press, the presidency, as well as the Constitutional Court, which would not give Parliament a free hand against these other institutions. The Court in particular continued to interfere with the reprivatization plans of the coalition, as well as with its attempts at retroactive political justice. It was in this context that some of the leading figures of MDF discovered that the negotiated arrangements played a major role in what amounted to a "stolen," or "betrayed," or "embezzled" revolution.[57] These adjectives, as well as the thinly disguised call for a second revolution,[58] of course belong to the classical vocabulary of the great revolutions. "It seems that there is a great price to pay for the bloodless character of the peaceful revolution, when the street is not possessed by the revolutionary people . . . is it a revolution at all?"[59] In the Hungarian context this tirade was directed against both those who insisted on keeping the rules of the game agreed upon at the Round Tables and later between the two major parties, MDF and SZDSZ, as well as the supposed beneficiaries of these rules, officeholders in the press and the media who have not come around to celebrate the coalition government. How can a revolution that has not happened be betrayed? The revolution did not happen because the elites betrayed the people and deprived it of its possible experience of victory, argued a leader of one such elite, the most important one. Power remained in the hands of old power holders, claimed the party controlling the new governmental power. Not surprisingly, their argument was supported by some who considered the Round Table agreements, the electoral law with its then 4 percent threshold, and the monopolization of the political field by merely six parties as betrayal from the outset.[60] On the one hand, they denounced the dictatorship of parties in Parliament, on the other, they declared their support for "this government, this parliament . . . if they too are in opposition to the Communism organized among and above us."[61]

Relationship to the Revolutionary Tradition

The advocates of a second revolution were thus not sure if they wished for a revolution of civil society from below or a state-led revolution from above. This dilemma is of course inherent in the whole Jacobin-Bolshevik tradition. Hungary's new Jacobins rejected this tradition all the same, even if some of their rhetorical devices—like István Csurka's constant talk of national and international conspiracy, Imre Kónya's implied distinction between the empirical and the authentic people, and the many different calls for a real or a second revolution—very much resembled intellectual devices of that tradition. But in Hungary, after forty years of a Bolshevik or neo-Bolshevik regime, any positive reference to its heritage remained off limits. This affected the semantics of key actors. No one described himself or herself as a revolutionary, nor were actions, institutions, events, or processes so described. The semantic revival inherent in the talk about conspiracy, enemies, and counter-revolution remained partial. All the same even the selective use was striking, given the fact that the most revolutionary rhetoric came from the most determined anti-Communists.

One explanation lay in the fact that Hungary has another revolutionary tradition, symbolized by the years 1848 and 1956, that indeed belongs to the central symbolic core of Hungarian politics. The power of their interrelated heritage is by no means exhausted. Every Hungarian regime since the Compromise of 1867 tried to use the symbols of 1848 for its own legitimating purposes; the commemoration of its initiating events on March 15, 1848, has been an important contested ritual from the nineteenth century to the Communist regime (which de-emphasized this holiday) to the dissidence of the 1980s (that tried to revive it).[62] Similarly, even small demonstrations on October 23 and June 16, two central dates commemorating 1956 and its bloody defeat, have been important for the opposition seeking to delegitimate the Kádárist regime. The official redefinition of 1956 as a national uprising, and the national reburial of Imre Nagy and his comrades on June 16, 1989, completed this process of delegitimation.

Nevertheless, reference to the heritage of 1848 and even more 1956 has not been easy in Hungary.[63] To an extent they both belonged to the classical tradition of revolutions, and attempts to redefine them within the context of the new East European politics of self-limitation have not been particularly convincing. Lajos Kossuth and his collaborators were not "constitutional revolutionaries" in the contemporary sense since there was no modern constitution whose rules they could use for change, and they in any case extralegally dethroned the House of Hapsburg even if reluctantly and rather late in the process.[64] Nor was the idea of revolutionary dictatorship far from their minds once they were in open war with foreign invaders. Similarly, while it may have been technically correct (and politically understandable in 1986) to make the workers councils after the second Soviet intervention in November 1956 into forerunners of the self-limiting revolution of Solidarity, the parallel remained artificial and selective given the whole context of 1956.[65] Neither 1848–49 nor especially 1956 could be made sense of within a model of nonviolence. Moreover, in 1989 no important political force was willing to revive crucial aspects of the political programs of 1956, especially the elements of direct and industrial democracy and dual power. The influence of the radical democratic ideas of Istvan Bibó, the leading political philosopher of 1956, was rather small in 1989, in spite of his great importance for both the populist writers and the democratic opposition of the 1980s.

Most importantly, both 1848 and 1956 had the character of national struggles of liberation. The domestic enemies of the revolutions had in both cases overwhelmingly powerful foreign supporters. In 1989, on the other hand, the international context only facilitated the transformation whose internal enemies had no significant foreign support. Indeed the late Kádárist regime helped to dramatically destabilize the sources of whatever support they could have had (in the GDR for example). This points to the fact that the transformation of 1989 did not even have major, readily identifiable internal enemies. The reformist Kádárist and especially post-Kádárist regime has, to the end, managed to avoid a scenario in which "we" the people would be arrayed against "them," the power structure.[66] Finally, all attempts to put the West and the United States in the place a foreign power dedicated to slowing down the pace of transformation and the survival of Communist officeholders is bound to seem ridiculous to a largely pro-Western and pro-American population and is indeed ridiculous at least as far as changes in Hungary are concerned.[67]

Using Hannah Arendt's categories, but rejecting her specific conclusions, 1956 in any case represented more revolution in the sense of liberation than in that of laying the foundations for a new political order. While new and old institutions did begin to emerge or reemerge, the relationship among these and the pattern of future development were entirely unclear at the time outside military force disrupted the whole experiment. For this reason, the tradition of the extremely short-lived 1956 revolution provides absolutely no guidance or framework of orientation for those who seek to act in the present. Indeed one can derive entirely opposite models from it, street violence or self-limitation, party pluralism or council democracy, alliance with reform Communists or utter hostility toward them, and so forth.

The context for the revival of the traditions of 1848 and 1956, to the great chagrin of the some surviving veterans of the latter, is entirely missing in 1989 and after.[68] The symbolism and the commemoration of these revolutions could be and were used to delegitimate the Kádárist regime without providing anything like positive symbolic identifications, not to speak of strategic guidance to the actors of 1989. If it is true, as Tamás Hofer argues, that the peaceful demonstrations were meant to and did frighten the regime by recalling the specter of 1956, there is little evidence that the option of an open rebellion in the streets was any less frightening to the immense majority of the population. In this context 1956 represented a negative scenario for both sides, regime and opposition. The shared positive scenario was a negotiated and legal transfer of power, following both the actual Polish model as well as all major oppositional programs.

It is not incorrect to note that Hungary's population was in a conservative rather than revolutionary mood in 1989.[69] The victory of MDF, originally promising a slow transition with a soft landing, was built upon this premise. The fact that the freely elected parliament chose as the main national holiday one commemorating the existence of the Hungarian state (St. Stephen's Day, August 20) over March 15 and October 23, and the emblem with the crown of Hungarian kings over the Kossuth emblem, presupposed a mood not particularly committed to revolutionary symbolism, and sought to canalize it in the statist-traditional and antisecular and antirepublican direction favored by some elements of the ruling coalition, notably the Christian Democrats and the group around the prime minister. The disappointment of some veterans of 1956 had to be great, but in context of the prevailing national mood of 1989–90 they could do little to revive their cause especially since the then most radical force for system change, the liberal SZDSZ and FIDESZ, were willing to integrate only those 56ers who accepted the program of a self limiting, peaceful and above all fully legal exchange of systems. More radical would-be heirs of 1956 were to come up above all against the last of these limitations; their aspirations based on memories of open and violent conflict with the Communists were incompatible with the legal and constitutional limits agreed upon by the combined opposition, enshrined in the Round Table agreements, and on the whole enforced by Hungary's active Constitutional court.

Legality and Revolution

The Hungarian Constitutional Court is a major protagonist of post Communist Hungary. In an early (summer 1990) discussion with a group of Western academics, its president, László Sólyom lamented the restorationist spirit of the parliament, and he jokingly added that it is the Court that would have to be revolutionary.[70] The decisions against the death penalty and against a centralized system of computerized collection of data on each individual affirm this "revolutionary," or rather innovative aspiration. But the Court by no means admits that what occurred in Hungary is a revolution in the legal sense. According to a report issued by the president of the Court on the first year of the institution, political changes in Hungary were paradoxical: revolution under the control of the Constitutional Court, whose task is to guard human rights during the transformation.[71] But a constitutional court can only play such guardian's role if it has a constitution to refer to at the very moment of revolutionary transformation. Indeed the Hungarian Court assumes the real-

ity of a continuous constitution development. As a result it was only logical
that it further defined its view of the paradox of the Hungarian change of systems. In a justly famous decision totally rejecting the retroactive abolition of
the statute of limitations for cases of murder, maiming, and treason, the Court
has affirmed that "[T]he exchange of systems *[rendszerváltás]* took place on
the basis of legality. . . . The Constitution and the organic laws that inaugurated revolutionary changes from the political point of view took place in a
formally unimpeachable manner through adhering to the lawmaking rules of
the previous legal order."[72] To be sure the Court declares the revised constitution of October 23, 1989, as "in practice" a new one, inaugurating a qualitatively new legal and political system, one defined as that of an independent,
democratic rule of law state *(jogállam)*. This in the Court's view is the meaning of *rendszerváltás* from the point of view of constitutional law.[73] For this
reason too, the Court considers *jogállami forradalom* (literally *rechtsstaatliche
Revolution*, rule of law revolution) to be an acceptable rendition of the meaning of the exchange of systems.[74] This idea, however, is called paradoxical. And
no wonder: It entails both that the system change first establishes a
Rechtsstaat, which comes into being only gradually, and yet that it takes place
from the beginning wholly on the grounds of a *Rechtsstaat*. "A rule of law state
cannot be created by violating the rule of law."[75] Though the *Rechtsstaat* can
be only established gradually, in the sense of bringing the whole legal system
under the sway of the new constitution, it is a duty of all organs of government to manage all present and future change entirely within the framework
of the rule of law. Thus the Court is committing itself to the complex proposition that although there is a moment in the change of systems when a
Rechtsstaat does not yet exist, or exists only as a goal, only by acting at all
moments of the transformation as if the rule of law already existed, can we
bring the rule of law about. This proposition evidently breaks not only with
the strictest legal definition of revolution but seeks thereby to vitiate the historical logic of political revolutions as well. The Court does this not because
of its attachment to mere legalisms, but because of its conviction that only by
defending the rule of law in an uncompromising manner can it be a guardian
of human rights in the midst of dramatic political changes.

The formula "political revolution on the basis of legality" not only expresses
the meaning of the differing levels of the Hungarian *rendszerváltás* but is
equally a restatement, on the level of constitutional law, of the East Central
European project of a self-limiting revolution. This translation of the project
into the language of law makes it clearer than ever before. In spite of the fact
that the change of systems inaugurates a new legal and constitutional order,
from a legal and constitutional point of view the Court seems to argue, echo-
ing Kelsen's definition, that it is not a revolution. The principle of identity of
the legal order was transformed but only according to its own rules of legal
and constitutional change. This admission, however, does not mean for the

Court as for Kelsen that the old legal order survives as the foundation of the new one. Closer to Hart's more persuasive argument, the Court asserts the compatibility of using the amendment rules of the old system and creating an entirely new one. Thus the self-limiting revolution limits itself, its desire for substantive justice in particular, by submitting to the rule of law. It is this self-limitation in fact that inaugurates a new legal order, the rule of law, that could not emerge any other way. In relationship to a modern authoritarian system curiously, where the primacy of the prerogative implies legal nihilism, the self-limiting revolution is on the legal level both less revolutionary and more radical than a radical revolution could be. It is less revolutionary because it presupposes legal continuity. But it is more radical because it breaks with legal nihilism immediately, while a radical revolution could only produce, in the short term at least, a "legal" condition outside of all law. This paradoxical proposition, in spite of its fundamental cogency, is evidently a difficult one to accept especially by those drawn to radical revolution.

While the Constitutional Court clearly dominates—and in a legal sense even decides—the discussion about the meaning of the exchange of systems in constitutional law, almost all of its assumptions have been challenged. It is to begin with denied that a *Rechtsstaat* can be produced only by its own methods. Where it does not exist, according to Csurka and his followers, it can be established only by methods different than those of the rule of law. A break with the legality of the old regime is needed, and the methods of the rule of law prohibit such a break. Legal continuity of any kind implies that the old regime too was one of the rules of law. One can moreover establish the rule of law too early, delaying transformation, and therefore the emergence of a system in which the rule of law is something other than a cover for old power and officeholders.[76] To appeal to the principle of the rule of law where there is not yet a *Rechtsstaat* means to block the efforts of Parliament at a real systemic change, the completion of the peaceful transition by a complete change of systems. While the retroactive legislation proposed by the ruling coalition sought to disconnect the country from the previous system, the Court's rule of law wizardry reaffirms an essential continuity.[77] The sponsor of this legislation rejected by the Court believes for example that in a revolutionary process, in an exceptional situation, it would be better to pay more attention to the people's sense of justice and the substantive principle of justice than to apply mechanisms appropriate only to long-standing rule-of-law states or to appeal to the principles of the rule of law that can be used only manipulatively.[78]

It is not only right-wing radicals who resent the apparent shielding of the guilty by the principle of the rule of law used by Constitutional Court. It should be mentioned that a significant number of the deputies even of the liberal SZDSZ actually wished to vote for the Zétényi-Takács bill, and periodically editorialists for the liberal *Beszélö*,[79] such as W. András Nagy and Ferenc Köszeg, attack "the white gloved" practice of the Court, that would have made even the Nuremberg Trials impossible.[80] These voices forget that both liberal parties have explicitly renounced retroactive political justice from the outset. More importantly, they disregard the fact that the Hungarian population has at all stages of the transition (demonstrations, referenda, elections) opted for precisely the combination of change of systems and the rule of law and never a choice between them.[81] To opt for revolution and substantive justice in the present situation can only be the choice of a self-appointed radical elite (or elites). Moreover the Constitutional Court's argument, that the rule of law is precisely the break with the past, points to an emphasis on replacing structures rather than campaigning against individuals, an emphasis that the liberal parties themselves were the first to introduce. Finally, the application of the rule of law in the present need not assume that the past regime was itself a *Rechtsstaat,* thus assume any legal continuity with it. It is for the sake of the legal security of the present, and not to legally reinterpret the past, that the Court insists on a legally grounded transition. Continuity exists only to the extent that past regulations can become unconstitutional only by the decision of the Court.[82] Nor did the Court claim that a *Rechtsstaat* was already in existence, only that it was a process that the government is bound to promote above all by its full adherence at all times to the relevant principles.[83]

Such reasoning has little effect on those who consider the negotiated transition a betrayal of revolution and a legal, or *rechtsstaatliche,* revolution a contradiction in terms.[84] In its most extreme form such an argument denounces the constitution as still Communist or Stalinist, and the Court as composed of holdovers and appointees of the old regime.[85] These two propositions are evidently false. In a less extreme version, the argument stresses the transitional, patchwork, and temporary nature of the constitution that does not allow for the self-confident decisions of the Court and the corresponding need for a new constitution.[86] This argument, though clearly rejected by the Court in all of its parts,[87] is more serious and has been in part raised by liberal lawyers as well.[88] The constitution still contains a few unfortunate continuities with its predecessor, like the amendment rule by which the latter was transformed with its implied doctrine of parliamentary sovereignty. More serious are unclarities concerning the separation of powers, the absence of adequate guidance on the question of property, and "economic constitutionalism" and uncertainties in the catalogue of rights. But these continuities and unclarities do not in fact mean that the Court does not have a modern document to work with. Be that as it may, the burden of interpretation and the charge of judicial activism cannot be avoided by any court that is sufficiently strong to do its job.[89]

In my view, the problem with the constitution is more the patchwork and exclusionary nature of the constitution-making process that included different fora of elites, but deprived the population, and even the public sphere, of genuine discussion and participation. It is for this reason that the legitimacy of the document, and with it that of court decisions, becomes periodically vulnera-

ble.[90] On this Csurka is right; the declaration of the new constitution on October 23, 1989, and we might add the two party agreements of April 1990, were
acts supported by little legitimacy, in spite of the authority of the unelected
Round Table behind the first and an adequate number of freely elected mandates (not, however, votes!) behind the second. It would have been better, from
the point of view of the legitimacy of the constitution-making process, if the
Round Table would have been able to restrict itself to negotiating a few organic
laws needed to guarantee the transition, as the opposition originally wished,
and if the SZDSZ and MDF agreements led to a democratically supported new
constitution. On the other hand, if a constitution would not have been produced in 1989, Hungary too might have missed the constitution-making
moment as did Czechoslovakia, with well-known consequences.

It was, however, in any case unfortunate that the makers of the interim constitution used the old, entirely parliamentarian amendment rule for this purpose, instead of first amending this rule itself to make it more democratic.[91]
Even an interim constitution could have been democratically ratified. I know
of at least two alternative suggestions, each transgressing the model of a legal
exchange of systems. The first was an early call for a Constituent Assembly in
1988–89 made by elements of MDF close to Imre Pozsgay's wing of reform
Communists. This would have been formally the cleanest solution, and for
this reason many who are hardly associated with the MDF or reform Communists recall it favorably to this day. Yet very likely, since at the time oppositional political organizations were weak and unknown, such a model would
have left the process, as in Bulgaria, in the hands of Communist officials. It is
unfair to disregard this consideration of the SZDSZ who opposed the formula
and preferred Polish-style negotiations for a few organic laws.[92] According to
a second such suggestion, after the free elections the new parliament could
have disregarded all earlier agreements and rules and turned itself into a sovereign constituent assembly.[93] The ever renewed calls for a new constitution
by Csurka and *Magyar Fórum* operate within this model. The conception corresponds to the desire of many members of the ruling coalition to govern
through a majoritarian model of parliamentary sovereignty alone, without
the limitations of constitutional courts, presidents, and public opinion. It does
not even have the virtue of the first suggestion of breaking with the model of
a purely parliamentarian structure of constitution making, inherited from
Communist constitutions. But of course each of these models is exposed to
the dilemmas of revolutionary constitution making and the dangers of failure
leading to permanent revolution in the juridical sense.

At the same time, continuing with the existing constitution as indicated by
the wishes of some members of the Court, the government, and political realities, or continuing the patchwork process of wholesale amendments begun by
the Round Table and the MDF-SZDSZ agreements, may yield a technically
adequate document.[94] Yet neither of these approaches can yield a high level of

legitimacy for constitutionalism and especially, for a long time, the foundations of genuine identification with the constitution, what Jürgen Habermas
called constitutional patriotism. In this respect the adjectives *legal* and *constitutional* in front of the word *revolution*, implying continuity and self-limitation, do seem to involve some important costs as well as undeniable benefits.
These costs could be intensified, if a radical revolutionary project managed to
exploit the weaknesses of constitutionalism and political legitimacy.

THE RETURN OF RADICAL REVOLUTION?

There is remarkable consensus in Hungary according to which the change of
systems did not take a revolutionary path. My analysis confirms this consensus by demonstrating that only in some dimensions did the transformation
correspond to the model of modern revolutions. At the same time I have
shown that there is no agreement on whether the avoidance of revolution has
been desirable. The views of those minorities that lament the "embezzlement"
or "betrayal" of revolution before it could occur would not in themselves add
up to much unless they were parts of a general political program to which they
could contribute. There was such a program in Hungary, one of revolutionary-restorationist étatism.[95] Though now defeated, its representatives continue to have a parliamentary presence. They have already had a significant
effect on developments and may yet develop into a modern European
extreme-right formation, like those of their allies Jean-Marie LePen and Jorg
Haider. Had they not linked their message to an obsolete form of nationalist
xenophobia, the danger they presented to Hungarian democracy could have
been more formidable. In the actual case, only their strong presence in the
right-wing government until 1994, even after the exclusion of the symbolic
figure of István Csurka, represented a threat to liberal democratic institutions.
Having the effect of driving all their enemies together, they wound up strongly
contributing to the reaction (including the formidable social movement of the
Democratic Charter) that led to the victory of the ex-ruling party, the MSZP
(Hungarian Socialist Party) and to the formation of the Socialist Liberal coalition. It is still an open question whether they may again contribute to such a
result, through pushing the current center-right government to the right.
Much depends on how seriously they adhere to the ideology to which they
have owed their ability to mobilize in the past and to what extent they can rid
themselves of the conceptual elements that have interfered with the extent of
this mobilization.

Between 1990 and 1994, at the height of radical right politics in Hungary,
there were four projects that *taken together* pointed to a radical revolutionary
direction, or reinforced a revolutionary populist sensibility: (1) restoration;
(2) purges leading to elite change; (3) political justice; and (4) authoritarian

state strengthening. Singly taken, these four are not exclusively the projects of the populist right, but their combination is, and this combination was strongly present in the governmental coalition of 1990–94. That coalition came to power on the basis of a clever combination of conservative themes with the idea of systemic change. But in power, given popular dissatisfaction with the way things were and with the government's performance, as well as the relatively modest appeal of its favorite themes of religion, nation, and family, even authoritarian-traditional components of the coalition became increasingly attracted by revolutionary themes.[96] Many of its members thus compulsively talked as if not they, but someone else, were in power.[97] This ploy too has been historically common in radical revolutions. But the four projects that I have in mind were not mere ploys; they were taken dead seriously by at least some of their proponents.

Restoration

The importance in the given context of the concept of restoration was first called to my attention by L. Sólyom shortly after he became president of the recently formed Hungarian Constitutional Court.[98] Sólyom's contrast between a restorationist parliament and a revolutionary court was, however, doubly misleading. We have seen that the Court has been primarily the guardian of legality rather than the agent of innovation. At the same time under the peculiar conditions of the Hungarian change of systems revolution and restoration belong conceptually together and are not alternatives as Sólyom thought.[99] The rage to restore, also noticed by François Furet,[100] first of all depended on diverse interests. The restorers greatly differed about what they wished to restore. The focal points have ranged from the restoration of the 1947 post-land reform ownership of land (FKGP), the semicompulsory religious education and church real estate of the same period but in large part inherited from before the war (KDNP), the symbolism of the violation of Hungary by the treaty of Trianon, and even that of a just war against Soviet Communism (MDF). In a sense, the first two of these parties in themselves restore elements of pre-Communist political reality. More quietly the largely intact state apparatus too would have liked to restore something, specifically its own role and open dominance in both prewar and late Kádárist epochs, willingly dressed up in the imagery of traditional pre–World War II etatism and paternalism.[101] Finally, veterans and partisans of 1956 wished to restore at least the symbols, and to some extent the programs, of that revolution. Only the liberals had little wish to restore anything, given the backward and deformed nature of pre-Communist liberal, democratic, and capitalist institutions.[102]

As a pamphlet of the liberal SZDSZ rightly assumed, 1937, 1947, and 1987 do not represent symbols and arrangements supported by any general consensus, to say the least. Even 1956, as we have seen, did not inspire much enthusiasm. Equally important, the adherents of these dates, or rather of the four different targets of restoration, disagreed among themselves and often rejected one another's specific dreams. Thus the idea of restoration could not make any more clear than its previous incarnations what exactly should be restored and where to stop.[103] As I see it, only revolutionary legitimacy had a chance to reconcile, perhaps only temporarily, the differences among the restorationists, by focusing on the element of a fervently desired break, disguising the dimension of restoration, and leaving the question of determining the content of the "popular-national tradition" to be restored to a future political elite recruited from the different restorationist factions, after the desired break with the commonly despised present could be effected.[104]

But if the restorationists needed revolution, revolutionaries without a positive model of the future could not do without restoration. Since the main revolutionary heritage of the West could not be referred to because of its link to the history and ideology of the Communist regimes and the specific Hungarian revolutionary traditions were, as wholes, clearly inapplicable in the present, only a highly selective use of these traditions and their semantic potentials was possible. But leaving out the philosophy of history of both revolutionary traditions (liberal and socialist!) that implied a progression of historical stages and a picture of the just society projected into the future, the very building blocks of revolutionary legitimacy, left these traditions impoverished. Moreover, without this philosophy of history the temporal relationship sustaining the difference between revolution and restoration, from the point of view of either, was gone. *Forward* and *backward* became meaningless terms. The road was open to try to replace, in a traditionalist but certainly not traditional manner, the future by the past as the orientation point of a revolutionary-restorationist philosophy of history. The question was "only" whether an imagined past can become a focus for mobilization any more than an imagined future. If not, the revival of other semantic aspects of the revolutionary tradition, in particular the whole vocabulary of enemies, conspiracy, and betrayed revolution, would remain rather shallow.

So would the cry of counterrevolution on the part of the restorationists. Were they themselves counterrevolutionary? Some critics think so. In an interesting train of thought, Pál Szalai recalls that the old regime's depiction of 1956 as a counterrevolution used to be countered by the 56ers by pointing out that the idea of giving back any property to former owners was explicitly, and repeatedly, rejected by the revolution that, after all, had a strong working-class, industrial democratic component. But what then is the meaning of the call for *reprivatization*, if not counterrevolution, asks Szalai.[105]

The only opportunity to actually restore came up in relation to state property. All sides assumed that dismantling of the state socialist system must entail the dramatic reduction of property in the hands of a state that owned not only the means of production but much of the land and real estate as well. There is a large variety of possible models of privatization competing with each other primarily in terms of supposed speed, efficiency, as well as possible negative side effects. The so-called reprivatization appeals above all to the sense of justice: Those who have been unjustly expropriated should now be the beneficiaries of privatization, whether or not their renewed ownership could possibly serve any other social purpose. Only as long as this issue was on the table did restorationism have some kind of identifiable social content.

The arguments on behalf of reprivatization avoided the question, not only of efficiency but of whether the "original" owners they support acquired their property justly, whether or not reprivatization could be just with respect to new owners (e.g., members of collective farms) who themselves had committed no wrong and whose livelihood and way of life were bound up with the property in question, and whether it was just to "compensate" people who lost only property and not others whose suffering was physical and emotional. Indeed the model of justice inherent in it, arbitrarily based on some kind of temporal baseline considered natural,[106] was never confronted with other conceptions of justice. For these reasons, reprivatization was never popular in Hungary. But it was a central feature of the programs of two restorationist factions that could in theory at least mobilize relatively large numbers behind their respective projects. The FKGP, the Small Holders, sought reprivatization of land expropriated after 1947 from people who to an important extent benefited from expropriations between 1945 and 1947, and in some cases even earlier, from the expropriation of Jewish property. Somewhat at odds with this, the KDNP, the Christian Democrats, sought the restoration of confiscated church property. To remove the contradiction among allies, the latter soon refocused their demands concerning real estate, which once allowed the church or churches to carry out educational and charitable functions. Each project could count on some support from below, from former small owners and their heirs, on the one side, and especially older believers, on the other. The MDF government reluctantly supported these projects of its coalition partners that were unpopular among the economic experts (who wished to generate income through privatization and who wished to support economically viable owners primarily) and among their local politicians.

The Constitutional Court, however, probably not contrary to the secret wishes of Prime Minister Antall, found a way to defuse these proposals. After rejecting a full reprivatization scheme, it allowed a moderate compensation scheme for landed property and a partial but extensive restoration of church real estate to take place. These steps, though denounced as counterrevolutionary by the most extreme counterrevolutionaries, had the effect of beginning the split of the two parties that supported reprivatization. The enhanced revolutionary or counterrevolutionary rhetoric occasioned by the decisions disguised only the growing weakness of the project of restoration.

Nevertheless, restorationism is not simply identical to counterrevolution. The rejection of anything resembling "Bolshevism" as well as religious ethics pushed many adherents of the restorationist position, and originally parts of at least one party of the coalition (the KDNP), in the direction of Joseph de Maistre's "contrary of the revolution," rather than "contrary revolution," meaning the rejection of revolutionary semantics in the name of nonviolence and legality.[107] When severely blocked, however, as in the case of the repeated rejection and eventually drastic modification of the reprivatization program of the FKGP by the Constitutional Court, the language of some (if not all) of the very same people could easily change. It is this shift that I have documented by bringing up declarations and warnings of right-wing politicians that the bloodless revolution has reached a dead end and that the (Communist) counterrevolution is now triumphant. Even the staid Christian Democrats, not satisfied with their victory on the question of church property, have adopted a militant language and strategy in the face of their perceived failure to greatly penetrate the media and popular culture. But who were the counterrevolutionaries in the literal sense of the term? Some of the militants of the much smaller of the two heirs of the old state party, the MSZMP, could be so described especially after their leader's approval of the Moscow putsch. But keeping the different objects to be restored in mind, the term also fit many restorationist revolutionaries. It was a special piquancy of the situation that both types screamed counterrevolution against real and imagined enemies and offenses. This linguistic revival that vividly recalls the Communist usage of the term *counterrevolution* regarding first and foremost 1956 would hurt its adherents more than help them, were there no convergences with other projects.

Unfortunately there were. The problem with the restorationist-revolution was never that it could have in fact restored a whole form of life, Miklós Horthy's or Ferenc Rakosi's, István Bethlen's or János Kádár's Hungary.[108] Hungarian society was simply too different than its predecessors for that. From the time the property question was settled through compromise, the ideology of restoration could at best provide a legitimating cover for other authoritarian strategies.[109]

Purges of Elites

In Hungary as well as Poland, it is the right wing that wished to accelerate the replacement of former officeholders by new individuals, supposedly untainted by the past.[110] Both in Poland and in Hungary the Round Table agreements have been considered responsible for a type of transition that allowed members of the old elite to save or convert its power. The Polish right excluded from the negotiations declaimed, ahistorically, against a red-pink alliance. The MDF's radicals, very much part of the negotiations in which the SZDSZ was more intransigent than they, later saw fit to pretend that there was always a red-liberal alliance protecting the old elites.[111] Indeed, the MDF has made the promise of "spring cleaning" one of its most effective campaign slogans, which helped the party get rid of a certain collaborationist image acquired in 1989, at the conclusion of the National Round Table and during the referendum campaign that followed. It should be added, however, that the program of "spring cleaning," violating the party's earlier promises, was always directed against persons rather than institutions; it was in other words understood not in the sense of eliminating whole administrative structures as required by a change of the existing paternalist-statist system, but as the removal of jobholders from a range of institutions.[112] In practice furthermore after the election, the resulting policy has spared all officials who have joined the parties of the ruling coalition, or managed to establish links with the government on a new basis. And while the extent of actual firings may not have been numerically great, they were visible enough and involved a number significant enough to put officials, managers, and expert employees on notice that lukewarm support for governmental programs and joining or even slightly favoring opposition parties cannot be to their advantage to say the least.[113]

In Hungary individuals, even talented ones, thus had to learn how to adapt to different political rulers. Already good at that sort of thing, most office and jobholders survived. It was moreover a mere fiction (unlike in Germany, with its reserve army of un- or under- or unfavorably employed) that there existed a whole alternative, well-trained corps of replacements, untainted by the past, ready to assume the relevant positions. But when it concerned the survival in office of people with high levels of public visibility especially in the press, in the media, in culture and performing arts, and in politics, the results justly infuriated the victims of the past and their self-appointed spokesmen. In some areas this has led to campaigns for the removal of individuals who were by no means always ones with significant history of political collaboration with the old regime.[114]

Who was in fact exposed to such campaigns? The crucial variable turned out to be conflict with the government of 1990–94, and certainly not at the level of collaboration in the past. Most exposed were those in position to interfere with the political projects of the ruling coalition, especially members of the press and the electronic media, and officeholders in those areas where a network of second-stringers who supported the governmental parties and were willing to become governmental clients was actually available and ready. Thus, even where there was a great deal to lose for all concerned, in particular in the area of economic and industrial management, the government has often been ruthless. A common pattern has been denunciation first by extreme right supporters of the government, followed by government action using transparently weak justification, as in the case of the young president of the National Bank, György Surányi, who after the 1994 change of government returned to this post. That dramatic economic success, to be sure rare in Hungary, is no guarantee of preserving a position is showed by his case, as well as the earlier firing of the director of the famous record company Hungaroton. Expertise is the last refuge of Bolshevism, maintained some of the new revolutionaries, inadvertently recalling many a Bolshevik campaign.[115] The point of all this was not only to remove Communists, or even liberals from positions but to put reliable clients of MDF in their place. Imre Kónya's lament, that the victors of the system change, that is, the activists of MDF, have not yet sufficiently benefited from their victory, had to be redressed.

The counterselective structure of appointment and promotion under Communist regimes is well known. It may be less well known that in its last decade the Kádárist regime demanded in most areas only minimal and verbal political adherence and in fact went at least part of the way toward establishing the beginnings of a system of meritocratic appointments. The problem lay more with the institutions than with the personnel. Accordingly, rejecting the model of revolutions, and especially that of the Communist taking of power in Hungary, all major political parties of the transition at one time at least declared their own full adherence to meritocratic selection and their rejection of all political lists and blackballing. But the government, and especially the MDF and the FKGP, were under pressure from their own base, which included many job seekers, some capable, others less so. Only a new process of political counterselection could fully satisfy these strata. But how was such a thing to be justified in a period when one should have concentrated all talent behind economic restructuring and recovery? Here the revolutionary slogans of elite change (acceleration, spring-cleaning, etc.) coming from below played an important role. They were moreover met halfway by the response of the new governing elite from above. Stung by criticisms that pointed out the inconsistency of preserving much of the state apparatus that makes a genuine system change far more difficult and the firing of managers whose expertise may not be in doubt, some leaders responded by pointing to enemies in the sphere where all this was repeatedly pointed out, the sphere of culture. In the manner of good revolutionaries from 1793 to 1917 and beyond, an independent cultural realm, one not instrumentalized by the government, was the last thing they could accept.[116] Highly sensitive to criticisms concerning the survival of old elites in their rank, they shifted the focus not to institutions, but to surviving elites that were presumed to support the other side. To the critics who lamented the slowness of system change in some or all spheres, they were again ready to sacrifice persons (of their choosing) rather than institutions (which they came to rather like).

Political Justice

Political justice was closely related to questions of purges of personnel, but it was even more symbiotically linked with a revolutionary discourse. The close relation is evident of course for the "lustration" bills passed in Czechoslovakia and Bulgaria, where retroactive justice would bar the road to public employment.[117] Even in Hungary, where in the case of the retroactive Zétényi-Takács bill aimed at the murderers, torturers, and "traitors" of the period between December 1944 (thus including "treason" against the Arrow Cross government!) and May 1990, the connection was more difficult to see technically; some proponents of the legislation saw it as a way of breaking the surviving power of the Communist "new class."[118] The project of political justice very much helped to intensify the revolutionary stakes. Unlike purges, political justice in the context of a change of systems implies revolution in its own domain, a (revolutionary) break in legality. This is the case, because while the firing of present state employees after an election can be arguably construed as a question of mere policy,[119] the punishing of individuals for their past acts under the old regime requires an answer to the delicate question: By what law should they be judged? Most of the relevant acts (if we do not count December 1944 to April 1945) were not crimes or wrongs by the factual legal system of the time, and the laws of the present were not yet written. The ban against retroactive legislation is fundamental for the rule of law, breaking that ban implies that at present there is no *Rechtsstaat*. Using the "rubber paragraphs" of politically inspired and often changed Communist statutes or governmental decrees, as in the case of the treason paragraph of the Hungarian criminal code that the Zétényi bill relied on, would have meant using the devices of a system permanently based on something inherited from revolutionary justice, the dominance of political prerogative over law. Such reliance too can only weaken the respect for law in the present, because the legislation in question should have been abolished as part of the move to a rule of law constitutional state rather than used. Evidently the new democracies do not have sufficiently well-established and respected legal systems to risk the absurdities of the arrest of security chiefs in formerly East German territory for crimes they supposedly committed against a country, the Federal Republic, which they harmed only in capacity of serving what was then an existing and internationally recognized state (one I personally happened to hate, but so what?).

Moreover, the periodically revived proposal to establish special committees and tribunals to investigate and adjudicate claims and accusations in terms of either laws that were yet to be written, or natural law, or pre-1947 law, or the bypassing of all laws by tribunals guided only by their own sense of justice, all belonged specifically to the species of revolutionary political justice, dangerously incompatible with the rule of law and constitutionalism, and therefore the protection of fundamental rights. Such proposals, often made right after the free elections, soon became moot in Hungary. But according to the Constitutional Court, in a more subtle way, the attempted retroactive extension of already expired statutes of limitation and the intended political instrumental-

ization of duly constituted courts would have also violated the legal and constitutional character of the exchange of systems and displaced the whole
process toward a revolutionary break in legality. The rebellious reception of
the Court's decision and the references to substantive justice, natural law, and
the people's natural sense of justice, as well as the claim that the Court's word
ought not to be final, all explicitly championed the elevation of a politically
based revolutionary legality above the rule of law, its guardian, and the constitution itself.[120]

There are pragmatic as well as normative difficulties in the face of political
justice. In an ex–Soviet-type society, in principle at least a very large number
of people could be affected by the application of such justice, in both criminal and civil cases. That could create legal chaos. But it is equally possible that
courts would in the end condemn very few people, thus greatly diminishing
popular support for the rule of law and independent courts. This surely would
have been the case for the Zétényi-Takács bill in Hungary, resisted from the
outset by the legal profession in general and judges in particular. For these reasons the government and the ministry of justice sought to escape responsibility for such a program, hiding behind the coalition parties, especially the
MDF. Nevertheless, the repeated intrusion of the issue in the public space in
and of itself promoted a revolutionary discourse that came in handy for actors
who felt constrained by the "legal" character of the "revolution." The FKGP, for
example, became interested in political justice only to help counter the Court's
decision on the question of land reprivatization, hoping to show the crimi-
nality of post-1947 (but not pre-1947!) expropriations, which would supposedly make current expropriation of collectives and at least some of their originally landless members into acts of justice.

Of course, in Hungary and elsewhere the victims and their sympathizers
and, unfortunately, people hoping to exploit them demanded retribution for
very real acts of injustice. And indeed justice in the substantive sense is for
many easier to understand than the rule of law. It is hard to understand that
the choice between them is ultimately not between law and morality, but
between two different moralities, one based on human rights and the other on
revolutionary, substantive moral wisdom. Given the magnitude of some
crimes, it is hard to accept that they could come under any statute of limitation. Even for some liberals, it was hard to see why the Nuremberg precedents
should not apply to the executioners of the post-'56 retribution. The demand
for substantive justice thus not only presupposes a revolutionary rupture, it
also recruits adherents for a revolutionary discourse among people who are
not attracted by its other components, semantic or programmatic. By speaking and appealing to the simple sense of justice of ordinary people this
demand has a better chance to put normative muscle into a revolutionary
project than idle dreams of restoration alone.

Authoritarian State Strengthening

Tocqueville's insight about the state-strengthening logic of revolutions has been amply confirmed by social historians for the great revolutions in the tradition of the French.[121] Could systemic change directed against authoritarian states avoid this logic? If such was the aim of the East European strategy of the self-limiting revolution, the actual changes in East Europe in 1989–90 have all raised the specter of new forms of statism, responding to a variety of economic and political problems. While most critics of authoritarianism feared in particular the institution of presidentialism, as the Hungarian case shows, parliamentarianism too is not automatically incompatible with statism, indeed with forms of authoritarianism.[122] It is well-known of course that Parliament, in its classical form, was meant to be a mediation between civil society and state power, aggregating the wills of the former and controlling and limiting the latter.[123] In spite of great changes in form, modern parliaments, at least in West Europe and North America, continue to exercise these two interrelated functions. But, under current East European conditions, claims of a purely parliamentary sovereignty as well as the practice of majoritarian democracy interfere with both of them. They produce the aspiration toward what would be semipermanent constituent assembly, with implicitly revolutionary practice, in need of revolutionary legitimation. In Hungary, at least, such was the backdoor through which revolutionary statism could have reentered in the transition.

In the celebration about the first free parliamentary elections many East Europeans active in new political parties, as I have shown, forgot about all earlier demands for the devolution of power and the practice of democracy on the level of civil society. Increasingly, leading political figures redefined democratic legitimacy purely in terms of the results of national parliamentary elections. Who elected unions to interfere in economic policy?—asked G. M. Tamás, then an economic liberal. Who elected the press to become an independent fourth branch of government?—asked I. Csurka. The questioners did not realize, or in the second case did not care, that with the loss of power of institutions of civil society, Parliament's own source of power, its mediating role with respect to the state administration, would be itself decisively weakened.

In Hungary, for example, action followed the words, action to the detriment of civil society. First, the governing parties have attempted to impose a centralistic organization of local self-government, in this respect continuing the heritage of both old regimes, the Horthyist and Kádárist, along with some of the symbolism of the former. If these attempts succeeded only in part, this was because of the two-thirds rule, which the coalition tried to bypass in vain, and which put the liberal parties in the position to negotiate a compromise. Hungary's local thanks for these efforts of the coalition were registered by its resounding electoral defeat in local elections. Second, the parliamentary parties not only eliminated as pseudo-democratic a constitutional provision requiring a period of public discussion before legislative enactment of a statute, but under pressure of the coalition refused to replace it with required consultations with genuinely concerned social organizations. Third, there has been an attempt by the MDF to "parliamentize" the press and the electronic media, first by distributing influence exclusively among the parliamentary parties, as Csurka repeatedly proposed, and, with the failure of this attempt, to "governmentalize" at least part of it through control of the economic privatization process. It is astonishing how a press extremely respectful and initially only mildly critical of the government and the coalition has been depicted over and over as dominated by their "enemies," with effects that have harmed the freedom of the press, in spite of the eventual failure of government to control the printed press at least. Soon, the relative independence of television and radio, achieved in an agreement with the opposition, became the main target of attacks. After two years of courageous resistance of the president of the republic, the government succeeded in appointing new vice presidents in the role of political commissars and later firing the capable presidents of radio and television, thereby taking over and politicizing the electronic media.

While the ruling parties had only mixed success in achieving their specific goals, they have managed to greatly reduce the potential influence of civil society on Parliament. This they did at a time when, as a result of the agreement of MDF and SZDSZ, governmental power was greatly strengthened through the constitutional provisions of a constructive no confidence vote and the elimination of the responsibility of individual ministers. Hungary has in effect become a Kanzlerdemokratie in the German mode, where controlling or pressuring government through Parliament has become exceedingly difficult. Without open channels of outside pressure, it was easy for government to turn the parties of the coalition into voting machines. Unfortunately, too many deputies, even of the opposition, consider such instrumentalization of parliamentary work, incompatible with the very principle of free representation, normal. Even parliamentary committees became fully and routinely instrumentalized. Thus the constitutional committee repeatedly disregarded the obvious unconstitutionality of statutes; the cultural committee never did defend the independence of culture. Disregarding opposition members in wholly adversarial settings, as during the interrogation of the president of TV, these committees now only did the bidding of the government. Moreover, with the press and the media greatly weakened and cast in the role of the government's enemies, the opposition could not play the role of controlling the government through appeals to the public sphere.

Thus, the exercise of parliamentary sovereignty has only led to an increasingly impotent Parliament. Public opinion surveys and the results of local and by-elections have in the meantime documented the massive delegitimation of the originally victorious coalition parties in particular and, unfortunately, through low electoral turnout especially, the party system and Parliament in general.

One response of the coalition parties in Parliament to loss of power and legitimacy had been an increasing commitment to anti-Communist revolutionary rhetoric linked to backward looking legislation: reprivatization and political justice. Formally, the same frustration has led to developing the most dangerous potential of the model of parliamentary sovereignty and to try to turn Parliament into an unlimited quasi-constituent assembly. Only in this way could the power of rival, countermajoritarian institutions be further reduced and revolutionary legitimacy, compensating for the loss of democratic legitimacy, be plausibly claimed.

The formative, potent fiction of the Hungarian *rendszerváltás* has been that there is no constituent power or assembly; the old (illegitimate) Parliament, instructed in large part (but not on all points) by the (self-elected) National Round Table, only amended (i.e., rewrote the bulk of) the constitutional rules under which its successor was elected. Amazingly enough the rule under which Parliament can amend the constitution by a simple two-thirds majority was not itself amended. It is precisely this background that leads to the illusion of constituent powers. If its delegitimation motivates the present Parliament to try to turn itself into something like the constitutive assembly that never was in fact assembled, the two-thirds rule, which it has already used in 1990 to massively amend the constitution, gives it the precedent that it can do so, to the detriment of genuine constitutionalism. If this strategy were to succeed however Hungary would move from the model of constitutional and legal change of systems to one in which permanent revolution in the constitutional sense may become the alternative to producing a settled constitution.

But there are evident roadblocks in the way of the strategy. The only examples of successful constitution making by the present Parliament have relied upon consensus with the parties of the opposition, needed for two-thirds majorities. These agreements are increasingly difficult to obtain, as the conflicts with the opposition become increasingly polarized. But not impossible, as the case of several votes (each requiring only 51 percent) show: FIDESZ abstained in the case of the coalition's bill on the reprivatization of church property, and SZDSZ abstained on the Zétényi-Takács bill.[124] These examples show that a restorationist or radical revolutionary rhetoric represents ways in which the opposition can be split, with constituent power regained.

The second roadblock is that of the constitution itself, or more exactly, the Constitutional Court. While the coalition parties have routinely disregarded constitutionality in their legislation (which in a way amounts to trying to pass constitutional amendments by only 50 percent plus 1 of the vote!) their track record with the Court has been embarrassingly poor. Evidently, they would have to eliminate or intimidate the Court in order to succeed in their quasi-revolutionary mission. But the Court has remained more or less firm in the face of intimidation, and the reluctant revolutionaries have not dared to sponsor constitutional legislation to limit the powers of constitutional review. However, in their press (as I have documented in the case of *Magyar Fórum*) they continue a steady campaign against the Court and the constitution.

The third hindrance in the way of parliamentary revolutionaries has been the president of the republic, Arpád Göncz, against whom the radicals of the right have concentrated so many of their attacks. Despite some court decisions that have evidently narrowed his powers, he has skillfully used his ability to ask for constitutional review and his right to deny countersigning appointments and dismissals to thwart the authoritarian designs of the coalition. Here too the coalition does not have the two-thirds vote needed to impeach the president or to redefine his powers or even to give the Court the power to decide single contentious cases involving the separation of powers.[125]

In my view a concentrated strategy against these roadblocks would have been possible only if the coalition parties themselves had dared to explicitly formulate their mission as a revolutionary and constituent one, against the existing constitution.[126] Evidently, however, the support within these parties for quasi-revolutionary reprivatization and political justice did not stretch this far. The real revolutionary populists may have for a time won the rhetorical battle within the MDF and its parliamentary fraction. But they have not won unlimited support for a revolutionary program. The prime minister was careful to manipulate the radicals within limits of his own choosing, and though he almost lost this dangerous game, in the end he managed to exclude Csurka (who was forced to reveal that he had once been listed as an agent with the code name of Rasputin) if not Csurkism from his party. The radical populists of the Small Holders have also been excluded from the coalition and their own parliamentary fraction, which along with the KDNP remained a tool in the hands of the conservative prime minister, who only occasionally plays with a revolutionary rhetoric. But the excluded Small Holders around party President József Torgyán did not support the radicals of MDF, thus both remained relatively weak in Parliament except on certain symbolic issues when the government allowed revolutionary playacting. Thus if Csurka and his friends (or for that matter Torgyán's following) wanted to promote a second revolution, they had no other option than to turn to the streets. In this they were, however, helped, up to a point, by the real beneficiaries of the claim of parliamentary sovereignty, the top officials of the state administration.

It is of course the state administration, still deeply penetrating the economy, that had tenaciously protected its operatives in the past and was most vulnerable to charges of preserving or converting the power of old officials. From a structural point of view this organization, benefiting from the intended and unintended statist policies of the government, has become the most important holdover from the old regime. Ultimately, the government's instrumentalization of Parliament has refurbished the power of top bureaucratic officialdom. Thus they had reason to try to deflect popular anger from themselves, in other directions. Such efforts could be well described as the cynical Tocquevillianism of the apparatus, which involved a recognition and manipulation of the administration-strengthening power of radical revolutionary projects and mobilization.

Prime Minister Antall and his second minister of the interior, Peter Boross, were virtuosos of cynical Tocquevillianism. They and their experts always must have known that the Constitutional Court would reject many of the schemes of reprivatization and political justice. It was in their power to submit better legislation or no legislation at all in these areas. Similarly, they have always understood that the parliamentary opposition and President Árpád Göncz could dramatically slow down, if not entirely block, their schemes of full takeover of radio and television. It was in their power to make compromises highly beneficial to the government, as television under Elemér Hankiss already showed. It is difficult to escape the impression that it was not the specific goal but the corresponding crisis that was sought by the government, to deflect both from its own difficulties in policy making and management of the economy and from the growing, clientelistic administrative apparatus that would be the natural target of the critics of insufficient systemic change. Under pressure, as after the disastrous defeat of the coalition in local elections and during the taxi drivers' and truckers' strike of October 1990, cynical Tocquevillianism went so far as to actually promote street disorders and confrontations. At that time Balázs Horvath, the first MDF minister of the interior, was observed waving to and encouraging from the Parliament building a counterdemonstration of MDF supporters. His clownish performance did not help him keep his job as Hungary's top cop.[127] Yet, with the popular support of the government at an all-time low, after a potentially even more violent demonstration on March 15, 1992, against the presidents of radio and television, which included both disgruntled 56ers promising to arm themselves and skinheads, and where journalists and liberal figures were in fact attacked, Minister Boross again expressed a great deal of understanding for the demonstrators. He glossed over any threat to individuals who, according to him, should have avoided their own provocative presence at the event.[128] The policemen on the scene, who did nothing to keep order and to protect those attacked, understood their chief's attitude. An even worse repetition of the same scenario occurred in October 1992, when the president of the republic himself was a target of mass disruption during a ceremony in front of Parliament honoring the 1956 revolution.

All these efforts could of course be chalked up to merely traditional authoritarianism, shared by all Hungarian regimes of the past. And indeed, as far as the prime minister was concerned such an explanation suffices, with the proviso that traditional Hungarian authoritarians in the past have routinely made

use of right-wing radicals for whom privately they only had severe con-
tempt.[129] While Istvan Bethlen, the greatest interwar prime minister, was to
personally experience (and to condemn!) the disastrous results of such a policy, Antall had obviously not learned the lesson of his father's generation very
well. In his time it was indeed a part of the governmental coalition—and not
forces outside of them as in Bethlen's day—who produced a typically revolutionary justification for the new authoritarian trends. According to them (I.
Csurka) there can be no fully democratic way to democracy, because the last
forty years have so deformed the population, so damaged its popular-national
(nép-nemzeti) identity, that the empirical voice of the people whether through
direct participation, or through the press, or through social organizations,
cannot be taken as its true voice, at least for the present.[130] According to others (Minister of Education Bertalan Andrásfalvy), full freedom of choice in
matters of religious education could not in itself lead to freedom for a population socialized under a secular and antireligious regime. Thus "the people"
must be represented and even defended against the empirical people, which
must be forced to be free, not only in terms of immediate compulsion but also
long-term socialization.[131] It is just this concern with long-term resocializa-
tion so incompatible with cultural freedom that represents a break with conservative ideologies and establishes the revolutionary bona fides of many of
the right-wing ideologues.

The various projects of restoration, purges of elites, political justice, and
state strengthening represented a curious yet coherent mixture. Taken
together they sought to remedy the supposedly insufficiently revolutionary
nature of the Hungarian exchange of systems. The project of restoration was
to provide symbolic substitutes for the spent components of the revolutionary tradition. The project of elite purge hoped to make up for the supposed
slowness of systemic change in the different subsystems of society. The project of political justice sought to chip away at, while parliamentary absolutist
attempts sought to entirely eliminate, the legal and constitutional foundations
of the regime change. None of these, however, were able to produce a revolutionary experience of either liberation or public freedom for anything more
than select, and even sectarian, constituencies. Even the determined use of
selected elements of classical revolutionary semantics, the talk of betrayal and
counterrevolution, the drummed up fear of enemies and conspiracies, and the
timid call for a second—perhaps this time bloody, noisy, extralegal—revolution have done little to manipulate the relevant public sentiments. Inevitably
the impression is left that, when the work of the streets reached its limits, the
second revolution would have to be after all executed from above.[132]

"Revolutions from above," however, bring up only the worst memories in
ex–Soviet-type societies. This is the Achilles' heel of the whole radical revolutionary project. Each of its elements has, moreover, its built-in contradiction:
Restoration was too ambiguous with respect to what was to be restored and

how far it all was to go; mere purges of elites on the basis of political selection could not have changed the institutions and social mechanisms and endangered economic functioning besides; political justice would have produced a climate of uncertainty and fear that was itself deeply feared by almost everyone; and state strengthening via attempts at parliamentary absolutism weakened Parliament and ultimately the government itself.[133] In this context various fragments of traditional revolutionary semantics was used not only to legitimate the projects and establish symbolic links between their different adherents and to try to drum up popular support but also to help manage the resulting conflicts. The revival of revolutionary semantics organized around a "friend-enemy" complex was especially slated to play this role. The power of this language in a form that stressed class may have been spent, but in its right-wing populist form it retains a wide horizon of possible application.

THE LIBERAL REJECTION OF RADICAL REVOLUTION AND THE PROBLEM OF LEGITIMACY

Given the revival of radical revolutionary discourse on the right, the support of a few liberals, and many more others who merely found themselves in a liberal party of some quasi-revolutionary projects like elite purges, political justice, parliamentary sovereignty, and the taming of the Court, are highly dubious, whatever the complex motivations involved. While only radicals of the right bought in to the whole package here described, support for their individual projects could only contribute to their cause. Fortunately, the prevalent attitude among liberals, despite the embarrassing abstentions of FIDESZ on church property and SZDSZ on political justice, was rejection of the whole radical revolutionary complex, of its semantics as well as its strategic components. Was this rejection based on sufficient hermeneutic sensitivity and a truly competitive philosophical posture? I am not convinced.[134]

In its details the liberal response is convincing enough. First, on the level of social science it is demonstrated that Hungary did not have a revolution, nor was (or is) the country in a revolutionary situation. András Bozóki, for example, argues that the Hungarian *rendszerváltás,* more than a reform but less than a revolution, belongs to the species of negotiated transitions encountered in recent literature on Southern Europe and Latin America. Of course it could be objected that the tasks of system change as a whole, and in particular the replacement of resource-constrained shortage economies define rather unique tasks for Soviet-type societies, unlike any encountered elsewhere. But the primary change did occur in the political system, and in Hungary its transformation indeed resembled "pacted" transitions elsewhere. To be sure this mode of analysis cannot answer the question why, unlike in the Southern European and Latin American transitions, so many people nevertheless speak of revolution, or even whether a revolution under the specific East European circumstances would have been desirable. Bozóki after all cannot expect everyone to share his apparent admiration for how the elites have "managed the transition above the head of society."[135]

Some leaders, advisors, and sympathizers of FIDESZ do go a step further. Not having been themselves attracted by revolutionary rhetorics, they reject such language as a species of modernist ideology, as an example of the grand ideological narratives that postmodernism is leaving behind.[136] Unfortunately when other leaders of FIDESZ replace ideologies and politics as a mission by pragmatism and political professionalism only, they free themselves of principles along with revolutionary demagogy. In the best case others of their colleagues do opt for a normative position: the defense of the classical *Rechtsstaat*. As György Bence apparently maintained at a Prague conference on political justice, we must make up our minds whether we want *Rechtsstaat* or revolution.[137] After the Court's rejection of the Zétényi-Takács bill, Peter Hack of SZDSZ repeated this argument, not noticing that the decision linked the form of the *Rechtsstaat with* revolution in the political sense.[138] Apparently, the Court was aware of the fact that however important maintaining the form of the *Rechtsstaat* from the point of view of the legal validity of the transition, on the level of political legitimation, such a reference was nevertheless insufficient. While people may indeed give their lives for the rule of law where it does not exist, where it does exist, its motivating power is unfortunately rather weak.

Gáspár Miklós Tamás battles the restorationist-revolutionaries in the name of a wider principle: the tradition of modernity. He thus rejects all restorationist and revolutionary politics that would endanger the results of Hungary's admittedly one-sided modernization, the product both of socialism and forms of liberal opposition to it. Since the population has shown itself time and time again to be conservative regarding these achievements (secularization, status equality, individualism, expert cultures, plurality of forms of life, and so on), restorationist adventures can take only a neo-Bolshevik, elitist, demagogic form.[139]

Responding to such popular "conservatism," leaders of SZDSZ, such as János Kis, now argue that the party should redefine its message in the sense that "the period of great political shocks associated with the change of regime has ended and what now follows is the quiet exploitation of possibilities created by this change of regime." In particular Kis proposes that the liberals should clearly renounce once again any future campaigns and purges against jobholders, explicitly including the clients of MDF who recently attained their position through quasi-purges.[140]

As accurately as Tamás's thesis seems to gauge popular sentiment and political behavior, the idea of a conservative attitude with respect to those products of the old regime that we can defend by West European liberal principles is easily cancelled out by a rhetoric that focuses on all the negative aspects of the Communist past, which require a radical break. Here too, moreover, as in the case of an argument anchored in the unconditional defense of the *Rechtsstaat,* one senses the dominance of the idea of the imitation of the already existing forms of modernity, an idea that carries little normative weight, and, for its success, depends entirely on successful imitation of only one quality of Western life, the most difficult to imitate, the standard of living. And while to his credit, Tamás is one of the very few liberal leaders in Hungary who mentions the need in some respects to surpass even the West, whose democracy is evidently not complete, he is able to propose ideas of democratic innovation only on the level of detail and not overall conception.[141]

As plausible, moreover, as Kis's centrist, evolutionary strategy may be, it too leaves out of consideration what he himself has noted, namely, that the population is unhappy with the present government and Parliament not only because of the element of insecurity in everyday life intensified by political hysteria from above, but also because the change of systems has not visibly taken place in everyday life.[142] Reassuring officeholders on the middle levels cannot address this second concern, and indeed may intensify it.

Periodically, liberal leaders, such as Kis, Miklós Haraszti, Bálint Magyar, and others, revive the appeal to an independent civil society, in part as a way to combat the popular perception that nothing has changed, and even more that nothing can change in everyday life.[143] But more characteristically they revive this conception once again when they are ready to do battle against new forms of authoritarianism, and little demonstrates as yet their view of the actual place of this concept in a positive program of the democratization of society. The concept still seems to be primarily a polemical one, and not yet a way of thematizing a possible path for democratic innovation. But will it be all too easy to think once again that the Democratic Charter, the Publicity Club, the Independent Forum of Jurists, and the like are needed only as long the wrong people are in power, until our turn comes? After the first experience of relevant groups of the population with the ideology of civil society, with its early dominance followed by relative amnesia in political circles, a mere mention of this category does not redress the legitimation problems of political society, problems that the liberal opposition inevitably shares.

The liberal answers are to be sure quite adequate in relationship to the specific revolutionary projects they address. The defense of the *Rechtsstaat* versus political justice; the defense of modernity against restoration; the idea of ending the period of quasi-revolutionary change against the call for purges; the rediscovery of civil society against statism; and, finally, the appeal to the dispassionate language of social science against revolutionary semantics, are all convincing in their own right. But they do not get to the root of the problem, on which the revival of radical revolution manages to feed, despite its relatively low popular appeal at present. I have in mind the legitimation problem of the Hungarian change of systems that liberal writers certainly perceive, but, in my view never successfully address, and especially respond to.

Analytically speaking, the legitimation complex contains both the problem of legitimacy in the normative sense, referring to the validity of a political order, and that of legitimation in the sociological sense, referring to the support or at least motivated acceptance of an order by a given population, or at least politically significant parts of it. Moreover, each of these aspects can refer to a political system or regime and to a specific government. What makes the Hungarian legitimation complex difficult to interpret[144] is that while in the normative sense, the government, and in the sociological sense, the new regime, can be considered legitimate, in the normative sense, the system, and in the sociological sense, the government, have serious legitimation problems. The government between 1990 and 1994, created through free elections and parliamentary coalition formation, did satisfy the criteria of legal procedural and democratic legitimacy. Nevertheless it has, through most of its existence, suffered from the erosion of popular support. And while the new system created as the result of the *rendszerváltás* enjoys general, if not particularly passionate, acceptance, attached to its origins is a degree of illegitimacy that goes beyond the perplexities of beginning an order at a time when the rules of the old do not, and the rules of the new do not yet apply.[145] Thus there are two distinct areas of legitimation problems:

1. Aside from having to undertake economic measures that are inevitably unpopular and the failure to achieve quick, corresponding results,[146] the government of 1990–94 had exacerbated its legitimacy deficit in at least two important ways. First, the population reacted very negatively to the emergence of petty party political rivalry in political society at a time when it is evident that cooperation and consensus in the search for common problems would be mandatory. The idea of a great coalition of the three parties emerging from civil society (MDF, SZDSZ, and FIDESZ) was highly popular at the time of the elections, and the reasons for avoiding this option are not clear to the population. Even less clear are the attacks on the press, the president of the republic, and the Constitutional Court by the coalition. It is tough furthermore to be asked to neglect your interests to the benefit of the country, when the ruling coalition so blatantly followed its own and not the country's, as in the case of reprivatization. Second, when a new system of property and the resulting inequalities are produced by conscious political design,[147] but without popular participation or even parliamentary consensus, it was easy to come to the conclusion that the government represented the interests of very narrow constituencies. For all organized groups and institutions, from local governments and unions and professional associations to single issue initiatives and elements of new social movements, their exclu-

sion from decisions touching on their vital needs and interests has been a particularly disliked feature of the new state of affairs.[148]

2. The normative legitimation deficit of the new system was (and is still) a function of the already mentioned difficulties with the constitution and its founding. Being rooted in the old constitution carries only the minimum of a procedural, legal legitimacy to an extent vitiated by the fact that the original constitution was a Communist one that no one took seriously until the beginning of the transition itself.[149] Furthermore, the constituent work of self-selected elites, of the old Parliament, and the two parties of the April 1990 pact that received less than 50 percent of the vote in the most complete electoral round, the first round of the parliamentary election, were clearly unable to generate any new legitimacy. One might say that a bashful revolutionary legitimation that dressed itself in the colors of modern competitive party politics could not be sufficient to ground a new constitution. Nor was it especially convincing, in light especially of low levels of later electoral participation, to argue that the free elections somehow retroactively validated the rules under which they took place. In my view only the petition campaign and the referendum of fall 1989 can be said to have contributed an element of genuine democratic legitimacy to the new system, obviously insufficient in itself.

The revival of revolutionary discourse began with the sociological problems of the legitimation of the first freely elected government, from either the point of view of those highly disappointed with its policies, or that of circles of the ruling coalition frightened and angered by their loss of popularity. Paradoxically even a combination of these views was possible, one that asserts that the governmental coalition is somehow itself in opposition to some kind of hidden rulers. Only a common enemy had to be found for these different politics to be united. This incoherent discourse gains its minimal coherence and normative claims not from ravings about a New York–Tel Aviv axis, but from its critical reference of the legitimation problems of the "founding," which, accordingly, only a new, genuinely radical and unlimited revolutionary round could now remedy.

It seems to me that a liberal and democratic answer to the revolutionary exploitation of legitimation deficits needs to address itself to both levels of the problem. These pertain ultimately to the crisis of civil society, on the one hand, and the difficulties of constitutionalism, on the other.

I have already mentioned the rediscovery of civil society by liberal politicians and claimed that in my view this renewed stress is desirable if still unconvincing and insufficient. More has to be said about the details of how a complementary relationship of civil and political society is imagined in their programs. Liberalism must demonstrate that its motivational energies in a democratic age are not restricted to opposition to authoritarianism. This goes also, and even especially, for the use of the concept of civil society, after the intellectual amnesia surrounding this concept in 1989 and 1990.

But the issue of constitution making represents an even greater difficulty for liberals in Hungary and other East European countries. For liberal constitutionalism the sole principle of normative validity is the legal (self-) limitation of all political power and the resulting protection of the private spheres from political penetration. Accordingly, all one needs to stress is having or obtaining a constitutional document that fully achieves these goals, a document that could be produced by simply imitating what has worked in constitutions elsewhere. I would suggest that L. Sólyom's insistence that Hungary already has a fully adequate constitution, while in many respects correct, underemphasizes the very difficulties of his own court, which seeks to be an active defender of human rights under conditions of a less than fully legitimate constitutional document. Even Mátyás Eörsi's proposal, which implies the country simply needs a third round of elite agreements to produce such a document, focuses only on the object to be attained, a coherent liberal document, and is not concerned with the democratic character of attaining it. Both arguments are examples of a liberal theory of constitutionalism.[150] But now that the right radical critique of the constitution has emerged, neither argument is adequate. Csurka is unfortunately right: The way the constitution was originally constructed bypassed democratic participation and even democratic procedures, and more elite agreement cannot remedy its procedural problems. Even, or especially, liberals can no longer afford not to pay attention to the procedures of making and revising constitutions.[151] Unfortunately, a narrowly liberal argument, not having linked up with a democratic understanding of constitutionalism, opens the door to demands of genuine revolutionary legitimacy that turns "the perplexities of foundation" into an advantage by seeking to speak in the name of the demos in a future moment when all law falls silent.

It is for this reason that I am skeptical about some of the ideological choices of the liberal parties between 1990 and 1994. I do understand of course that these groups, earlier the most determined force for total systemic change, eschewed nevertheless a revolutionary vocabulary and most of the time even the very term *revolution*. The revival of the uses of this language and its subtextual presuppositions, which I detailed amply, confirm this judgment. I am not certain, however, that it was sufficient to save from the genuinely creative East European idea of self-limiting revolution, around which the earlier democratic opposition organized itself, a notion of self-limitation that chokes off one's own political imagination and normative self-justification in favor of models drawn solely from the West from its often questionable empirical practices even more than from its norms. Indeed it is to be only regretted that in the desire to imitate one renounces (with a very few exceptions) the possibility of normative innovation, which ought to be easier in the case of constitution creation than in that of settled constitutions. From the new challenges and types of conflict in the West alone, it could have been learned that existing constitutions are neither democratic nor liberal enough, and that the idea of a self-limiting revolution, with its new combination of democratic and liberal elements centered around the notion of civil society, could enrich our common normative heritage.

Chapter 4

Dilemmas of the Power to Make Constitutions in East Europe

Many years after the dramatic events of 1989 let us recall the outcome of Hannah Arendt's analysis of revolutions.[1] According to her, in modern times, the history of revolution was dominated by the antinomic paradigms of a permanent revolution that fails to make a new beginning of freedom and a conservative revolution that forgets its very origins, or converts them into mere tradition. This diagnosis has certainly not lost its power. It is no longer too early to speak of outcomes in East Europe, and especially of the self-interpretations of the actors themselves who, whether or not they used the term *revolution,* have reproduced the very antinomy Arendt analyzed. This time it was elements of a new nationalist right who clamored for a total break with the past and the indefinite prolongation of radical revolution, while the liberals and the remnants of a democratic left, who have done far more to change the earlier regime, now affirmed continuity and the rule of law. Once again a third possibility, a combination of revolution and constitutionalism, of public freedom and fundamental rights, seems to have been excluded. The leading slogans were "restoration" for the revolutionaries and "imitation" for the liberals, with very few people recognizing the necessity or even the possibility of innovation, of new historical creation.

Arendt of course insisted on the establishment of a *novus ordo seclorum* as the most important task of modern revolutions. We should recall that she believed not only that successful constitution making alone could fulfill this task but also that a republican constitution could provide a way of transcending the antinomy of permanent revolution and revolutionary amnesia. For this to occur two fundamental problems had to be solved, that of the democratic origins of the new regime (a constitution had to be the result of a people constituting a government rather than the work of a government) and that of preserving public freedom beyond the dramatic beginnings.

Are these two problems soluble? Does the solution of one require that of the other? Yet can a satisfactory solution of one be incompatible with that of the other? Assuming for example the revolutionary democratic origins of the constitution, can any attempt to *institutionalize* the public freedom to make constitutions be anything but an illegitimate occupation of the place of the people, as the source of institutions, prior to all constitutions. Can, however, the institutionalization of constitutional politics within constitutions be anything but a mere technical device (i.e., amendment rule) unless an internal relation to a legitimate founding can be established?

Arendt's original solution to the problem of institutionalizing public freedom, a Jeffersonian argument for revolutionary citizen councils, is not only obsolete but was self-contradictory in the first place. This solution amounts to maintaining within a settled constitution the process and the practice that is supposed to be its only legitimate source. A directly participatory council republic implies a constitution that is not constituted at all, because its sovereign source is always present, in the midst of political action. This idea was not far from the permanent revolution that in fact filled Arendt herself with fear. What attracted her about councils was nevertheless not limited to the hope that a participatory level of local government could be somehow included within the administrative hierarchy of the modern state, as even now in contemporary New England. But she was hardly optimistic about her preferred option, the admittedly aristocratic solution of the organization of a republic of councils. In fact, by placing the emergence of such politics at historical ruptures when "the dialectic stood still" *(Dialektik im Stillstand),* by in effect removing the periodic eruption of democracy from historical time, she tacitly admitted defeat.

A second Jeffersonian solution, to which she sometimes referred, that of a new constitutional convention or an institutionalized revolution in every generation, did not suffer from the same internal contradiction. The settled constitution and the liberated power of the sovereign would not have to impossibly coexist in this scheme: Each would be dominant during its relevant moment, longer or briefer. But Arendt was right to be wary of this option, because, as she showed in detail, one of the most difficult tasks in politics was that of establishing a legitimate authority after breaks in legality that periodic self-annihilation of constitutions would surely risk.[2]

Two theoretical options are at the moment available to think beyond the antinomies of permanent and conservative, social and political revolutions. These correspond to Arendt's ambivalent emphasis on public freedom, on the one hand, and legal continuity, on the other. The first retraces the road of her one successful revolution, the American, and argues (against her verdict) that the eighteenth-century experience of public freedom was successfully institutionalized in a *dualism* of constitutional and normal politics.[3] In this conception, constitutional politics refers to movements of citizens, publicly participating through extraordinary political forms, oriented primarily to constitution making or revising. The second conception, directly focusing on the revolutions of 1989, argues that in East Central Europe at least a new program of self-limitation has emerged, one capable of combining radical social change and the making of free constitutions in a program of legal continuity.[4]

While the two conceptions are linked together by the idea of self-limitation, there are crucial differences between them. The philosophical core of Bruce Ackerman's argument is based on the eighteenth-century American theory of popular sovereignty, according to which valid constitutions and constitutional revisions are acts of the sovereign people outside of all duly constituted legislatures.[5] In contrast, battling against the European theory of a unified constituent power capable of exercising all dimensions of sovereignty, Ulrich Preuss applauds precisely the absence of a reference in East Central Europe to the sovereign people as the subject of constitution making and stresses its replacement by a pluralistic emphasis on the organized collectivities of civil society. While Ackerman seeks to defend a genuine form of revolutionary legitimacy, Preuss seems to prefer the idea of constitutional continuity propagated by the new constitution makers as the shield of not just stability and legality, but also constitutional innovation.

I believe that the two perspectives, born in different constitutional traditions, may be more complementary than it would first appear. The democratic consistency of the American idea of constitution making power, which unlike the European theory of the *pouvoir constituant* rightly excludes legislative and executive powers from the constitutional convention, does not benefit from being linked to a claim of having a privileged access to the mythical entity, the sovereign people. It is also true that it would be impossible to justify (as Carl Schmitt repeatedly argued) the substantial alteration of a constitution whose origins are linked to a noninstitutionalized form of popular sovereignty, by a merely political process under that constitution, including the utilization of the amendment rule. Thus the conception not only calls for repeated revolutions because of its very logic but makes the task of *institutionalizing* public freedom hopeless from the start. On the other hand, it is not clear what could make a piecemeal, fragmented legally continuous process, which Preuss has in mind, legitimate in the democratic sense. While scaling down the stress on the *sovereign constituent power* opens up the option of democratic constitution-making acts in the future, within a model of legal continuity, it is not clear from where those acts would receive their full authority except the constitution itself. But a constitution must first possess this heightened authority in order that it be borrowed. It is not clear by what authority the process of piecemeal constitution making could be closed, leading to that differentiation between constitution and legislation on which Ackerman rightly insists. Thus, even if we cannot and should not any longer insist on the sovereignty of the source of the new order, we are nevertheless forced to stress the special legitimation requirements of the process of its creation. This much should be saved from Ackerman's insight concerning the origin of constitutions that is at the base of his formulation of his conception of dualistic politics.

The two conceptions of Preuss and Ackerman share the idea of democratic constitutional politics whose referent is civil society and its public sphere rather than either established legislative bodies or the atomized population, a politics having an elective affinity for the dimension of fundamental law making. This politics, worthy of institutionalization in settled constitutions, represents in my view the centerpiece of a theory of *democratic constitutionalism*. Nevertheless, the two theories cannot be simply superadded or synthesized because of their rather different conceptual presuppositions. Thus I prefer to follow the logic of each, as somewhat corrected or tempered by the other. Although in the next chapter I will work with the model of legal continuity and consider how it could be democratically legitimated, in the current one I consider the dualistic democratic program and try to asses how much of it can survive under the specific East European processes of political transition.

Relying on the American discussion, I will first explore some of the theoretical reasons for insisting on the somewhat unusual notion of democratic constitutionalism. Second, focusing on the dilemmas of constitution making in East Europe, I will examine the political conditions of the possibility of such, in my view, innovative version of constitutionalism. Third, to judge in a preliminary way the actual correspondence of outcomes to this project, I will present and critically analyze the amendment rules of several new constitutions and their origin in specific patterns of constitution making.

DEMOCRATIC CONSTITUTIONALISM

We define constitutionalism as a political form in which a body of fundamental laws not only establishes the powers of government but institutionalizes important limits for its operation.[6] Ordinarily, these limits are understood in the liberal sense, as disabilities of the legislature and, by implication, the executive. They are supposed to affirm the existence or carve out and stabilize a realm differentiated from the state, that is, civil society understood in the rather defensive liberal sense. Fundamental rights, civil rights as well as political rights understood on the model of civil rights, that is, freedoms and liberties, represent the major building blocks of liberal constitutionalism. Constitutionalism in the liberal sense, along with the judicial review that enforces it, is often understood to be in conflict with democracy. This common understanding is in part mistaken, and not only because limitation and self-limitation in politics can often be forms of empowerment. While conflicts between liberalism and democracy, between rights and political participation, are indeed possible, they are hardly what is automatically involved when rights of minorities or individuals are defended against legislatures or executives. Most supposed instances of conflict between liberal constitutionalism and democracy are such only from a narrow legal point of view that identifies modern political systems as democratic, following civic textbooks, which provide only the official narratives concerning the workings of government. From a sociological point of view, many of the same conflicts turn out to be between liberal rights and oligarchic-statist claims of governments having various degrees of democratic legitimacy.[7]

If, however, we understand constitutionalism as first and foremost limitations on the modern state and not on democratic forms of power, and if, moreover, we entertain the possibility of a three-sided conflict between liberal, democratic, and statist principles, a second dimension of constitutionalism comes to the fore, one involving a defense of democratic participation in the face of the state, whose logic involves not only the drive for efficiency[8] but also the perpetuation of existing prerogatives and powers of officials. Next to and in addition to liberal constitutionalism there is a need to assert the imperatives of democratic constitutionalism.[9]

In the recent literature on American constitutionalism and judicial review, two important and, in my view, complementary attempts have been made to establish the idea of democratic constitutionalism. In J. H. Ely's *Democracy and Distrust*,[10] judicial review by unelected, life-term officials without democratic accountability is justified by the needs of keeping the democratic procedures open, a task that cannot in general be left to elected officials with an interest in closing the process to their own benefit. As important as this emphasis may be, Ely's argument can be faulted for leaving untouched the internal mechanism of the "democratic" process and protecting the citizen only on the input side as voter (who is to have equal access) and the output side as beneficiary (who is to receive equal treatment). It is in this context that we should locate Ackerman's "Neo-federalism." Ackerman attempts to go beyond Ely (whom he treats somewhat unfairly) by discovering in *The Federalist Papers* a program for a dualistic politics in which constitutional politics represents a more democratic, if extraordinary option next to normal, in his view, interest group pluralistic politics. While Ackerman can be rightly criticized for conceding too much of normal politics to a version of pluralism without democratic principle,[11] it is his insistence on a radical democratic constitutional politics that acquires special relevance today. Indeed, while Ely's understanding of the democratic correction of normal politics, because it is still focused on the defense of rights even if democratic political rights, can still be contained under an expanded notion of liberal constitutionalism, Ackerman's reassertion of a form of power within its sphere more democratic than normal electoral and parliamentary politics establishes the equal status of democratic constitutionalism.

At least in principle. The operation of the framework of American constitutionalism does not in any obvious manner leave much room for an element of radical democracy. In particular it seems to me difficult to identify judicial review as such as intrinsically involved in provoking a radical democratic response.[12] In fact, the ambiguity between principle and pragmatism is already in Ackerman's major source. The principle at least of the superior, constituent power of the people is indeed present in *The Federalist Papers*.[13] Ackerman, following Gordon Wood, is right to describe it as the culmination of a generation of revolutionary experience.[14] The incorporation of this principle in the constitution is, however, balanced by the desire to also build in the foundations of a traditional legitimacy.[15] Thus it could be said that the early defenders of the U.S. Constitution used the principle of the democratic superiority of the constituent power over the legislatures to bring the whole period of constitutional politics to an end and to establish the legislatures all the more firmly.[16] In any case, if the making of the U.S. Constitution was legitimated by a new American, revolutionary-democratic principle, this principle was built into the settled constitution at best in a contradictory manner. This is shown by the uneasy status of constitutional conventions in Article V of the Federal Constitution, an article that restores the role of ordinary legislatures in constitutional politics as its major option.[17] And while in great, quasi-revolutionary moments of U.S. history, the amendment process—especially in the post–Civil War period, though without the direct provocation of judicial review—could play a radical democratic role, during most of this history the traditional element in constitutional legitimacy, stressed by Arendt, certainly has come to the fore.[18] Dualistic democratic politics today seems to be more of the basis of an immanent criticism than a description of the actual framework of our constitutional reality. Ackerman's critics seem to be right to point this out, even if they cannot thereby vitiate the normative interest of the dualistic program.[19]

Is the program, however, viable on the level of normative-theoretical considerations? Let us concede to the critics of all radical democracy that any attempt to establish large-scale popular participation on the level of normal politics is doomed to fail in modern societies; it is scarcely thinkable, given all relevant empirical experience, that a democratic constituency in a large-scale, complex society with radical time constraints not delegate day-to-day control over legislation, execution, and adjudication to specialized political bodies, that is, organs of the state.[20] Assuming, though not here demonstrating a discourse theoretical conception of the plurality of democracies,[21] the dualistic fallback position provided by Ackerman becomes all the more attractive. There are in fact important reasons why constitutional politics can and therefore should involve a wider and more democratic form of participation than normal politics. Let me enumerate and briefly discuss some of these reasons.

Plurality of Democracies

On the most abstract and entirely normative level I would stress the need to combine different forms and types of democracy. Assuming a discursive theory of democratic legitimacy, I wish at the same time to maintain the impossibility of fully and definitively embodying the normative-rational presuppositions of discourse, in empirical institutions of public life. For reasons that are in part contingent (e.g., the stress on private happiness in a modern cultures) and in part theoretical (e.g., time constraints) all types democratic institutions of public life have forms of exclusion, constraints of discussion, and probable asymmetries among participants built into them. However, the forms that nondemocracy takes within various types of democracy are significantly different. Thus in principle (other things being equal) it is highly desirable to combine in a given constitutional framework different types of democratic institutions and processes, for example, direct and representative, centralistic and federal, civil and political.

Separation of Normal and Constitutional Channels

The idea of the plurality of democracy has special relevance to the problem of democratic constitutionalism, because it is highly desirable that constitution making and revision operate on a different democratic "channel" than normal legislative politics. In this context, the argument of *The Federalist*, systematizing the already prevalent American rejection of parliamentary constitution making and revision, remains the best starting point. It is still lamentably true that this idea is poorly understood by many Europeans. According to Madison, whenever legislatures retain the power of constitutional revision, they are in position to establish themselves as oligarchical replacements of the power they claim to only represent.[22] Evidently, when questions of changing the operations or institutional relationships of the legislature are the themes for constitutional revision, the legislature should not be in the position to judge the issue on its own behalf. Even more importantly, if constitutionalism is to be a limit on the operations of primarily the legislative branch of government, it is unwise to put the same legislatures in the position to alter the relevant limits according to its own lights alone.[23] Whether a constitutional convention doubles as a legislative and policy-making body, or working legislatures retain constitution-making powers, the interest divisions of ordinary politics permeate a process in which principles should have the dominant role. In times of rapid change and dislocation either variant (e.g., the Convention Nationale and the Long Parliament) can lead to dictatorship. In this context, restrictions on the legislature, like the need to produce qualified majorities, change nothing in principle and link the avoidance of ill effects only to contingent electoral outcomes. Putting constituent powers in the hands of legislatures alone can lead to either a frivolous use of constitutional revision, producing patchwork constitutions without legitimacy, or to the great constitutional inflexibility of even supposedly entirely flexible constitutions (to avoid potential constitutional chaos), or even to bizarre combinations of these two options: total inflexibility in some areas and frivolous use of amendments in others.

The Democratic Surplus of Constitutional Politics

The democratic legitimacy of the normal operations of the state would be weakened if the state and its agencies maintain the same type of control over the making of the rules as they possess under these rules over ordinary legislation. On the other hand, democratic legitimacy would be clearly strengthened if the extraordinary processes of constitutional rule making could in principle involve a widening of democratic participation. However, neither populist (Madison, Sieyès) nor existential-political (Schmitt) arguments for the normative superiority of constituent politics are acceptable today. Constitutional politics has a privileged access neither to "We the people" nor to the deepest layers of our political identity. Nor is it a good idea to elevate constitutional politics by linking normal politics under liberal democracies exclusively to liberal as opposed to democratic standards.[24] What is true is that constitutional politics is legally superior in the sense of trumping all other political forms of decision making. Beyond this, because of its extraordinary nature constitutional politics has a chance, if only potentially, to promote the public participation of individuals otherwise dedicated to private happiness and whose political involvement is inevitably a shifting one. While organization outside the sitting legislature may create nothing more than simply another legislature, constitutional politics limited to a relatively few broad issues of principle could be and often is organized to give the direct democratic element a greater (though fortunately rarely an exclusive) role. Yet the democratic surplus of constitutional politics lies on a still more fundamental level. Assuming that democracy is most fundamentally deliberation and dialogue, much depends on the structure of the public sphere in which discussion is institutionalized. Here Jürgen Habermas's path-breaking 1962 work on the public[25] can easily mislead those who follow him: The structure of parliamentary publicity never was and never could be based on the unconstrained communication possible in the cultural or literary public sphere that is located in civil society rather than the state. Above all in parliaments the complexity of the types of issues and the constraint of decision making lead to formal and substantive limitations of the time available for debate.[26] Given the relative specificity and lesser complexity of the parameters involved especially in constitutional revision, and even constitution making, as well as the lesser demand for quick decision making than in the case of policy questions, con-

stitutional politics can in principle take place in the far less-constrained public sphere(s) of civil society. Even special legislatures and expert commissions
involved in constitution making need not isolate themselves from an ongoing
public discussion in which those most concerned can participate in an organized manner. The legitimacy of a constitution, as the whole American experience from 1776 to the final ratification of the Bill of Rights indicates, has
much to gain from a long and open period of public discussion of the basic
principles.[27]

Constitution as Space of Freedom and as Tradition

Even if opposed to the idea of the veneration of constitutions in civil cults, we
should not give up the desideratum of constitutional stability, important for
both the limiting and identity-forming functions of constitutions. The very
possibility of a "constitutional patriotism," *Verfassungspatriotismus* (Habermas), depends not only on democratic legitimacy of constitutions but on their
stability as well. Starting with the reply of *Federalist* #49 to Jefferson, the democratic claims of constitutional politics have been typically rejected on behalf
of stability. Indeed the discussion even today is under the shadow of Jefferson
and Madison's long debate.[28] Three issues are, however, conflated in the reference to Jefferson, who came to believe not only in democratic, but also frequent and potentially total, hence revolutionary, revisions of the existing constitution: the level of difficulty, the democratic character, and operating on
dual or plural political tracks. The level of difficulty, however, does not
directly vary with the democratic character of the process of constitutional
revision, nor with its legal operation on a separate and higher legal track.
Indeed a purely parliamentary procedure, in my sense not sufficiently democratic, is certainly the easiest and quickest way to change a constitution. One
could, however, imagine a dualistic process more easy procedurally (e.g., simple majorities in two assemblies) than a monistic parliamentary procedure
(one, e.g., involving a highly qualified majority). The dangers of bypassing sitting parliaments are real, but when these dangers are particularly grave (they
were not in 1787), this assembly can be included in a pluralistic process.
Moreover, only Jefferson's own preferred road, frequent constitutional conventions, potentially implies repetition of the convention of 1787, that is,
turning a commission to amend into the power to make a completely new
constitution. It is possible to eliminate this option, or better still to make any
recourse to it procedurally far more difficult than other procedures of amendment.[29] Thus, it is possible to keep the process of even frequent revision
entirely within the constitution, a point disregarded by Madison in *Federalist*
#49, but insisted on by Hamilton in #85, in a different context.[30]

For now these arguments will suffice to make the idea of dualistic politics
worth discussing. I would like to repeat that I am skeptical with respect to

the claim that politics in the United States at present actually takes this form. To be sure, occasionally in American history constitutional revision (but not linked to judicial review) and more often judicial review (linked to changes in the political culture, and even movements, but not to constitutional revision) have provided links between extraordinary levels of public involvement and commitment and constitutional politics in a broader sense than simply revising the written constitution. Moreover, since the constitution itself has not successfully institutionalized two tracks in our political life, extraordinary politics has repeatedly established links to normal political processes as well. Does this speak for a continuum between extraordinary and ordinary, constitutional and normal politics? Perhaps. But this may be because our channels for extraordinary politics are relatively closed on the constitutional level, because of the formidable difficulties involved in the use of Article V, and the related tendency of the Supreme Court to monopolize constitutional politics.[31] There is nevertheless still a strong case to be made for the assumption that constitutional politics and public politics in the full sense have great potential affinity. The trouble is that where the link is not now well established it is difficult to foresee the use of existing procedures of constitutional revision to produce a fundamental shift toward the institutionalization of dualistic politics. Legislatures are generally reluctant to give up even minor powers, and the power to amend constitutions is a major power indeed. Except in revolutions, the amendment process may be the most difficult to amend.[32]

CONSTITUTION MAKING IN EASTERN EUROPE

Here lies the link between the theory presented so far and the "revolutions" of East Central Europe. Not only does 1989 represent a year of extraordinary democratic, in some sense revolutionary politics, but it is also a year that begins a new epoch of constitution making. The need to make new constitutions should once again raise the question of how the new or renewed meaning of public life could be incorporated in fundamental law.

It certainly lies within the power of the new constitution makers (more so than in the case of politicians under well-established constitutions) to institutionalize a future dualistic politics in which constitutional politics would carry a democratic surplus. The likelihood of their doing so is another matter. Aside from the constellations of interests involved, much depends in this context on the self-understanding of current constitution makers, which means not only their ideological assumptions in general but also interpretations that arise during the course of the process of constitution making. In turn constitution making procedures depend not only on ideology and interest, but, significantly, also on the specific type of transition to democracy.

To begin with, however, the initial ideological assumptions are burdened by ambiguities. The leading ideas of the day, "restoration" and "imitation," certainly do not point to innovative forms of democratic constitutionalism. At the same time, however, all current constitution makers face a special need, namely, to increase the reserves of democratic legitimacy. Mere imitation of institutional frameworks elsewhere is hard to raise to the level of a norm, especially when these have already shown their negative sides as well as their inflexibility in the face of novel historical challenges. The imitation of liberal institutions seems especially difficult in strongly democratizing contexts, where the idea of democratic revolution has become for the first time fully conscious, and where popular strata are ill prepared to forget their needs and interests. At the same time, restoration is an inherently divisive and unstable goal in complex societies with, to say the least, complex histories. In fact only in some uniquely fortunate modern historical constellations could a deficit of democratic legitimacy be compensated for by a species of traditional legitimation, based not only on the traditionalization of the present but on a relatively problematic relationship to the past. Thus I would maintain that democratic constitutionalism as presented here represents one possible way to redress the emergent legitimation problems of the new democracies.[33] Its key assumption is the limitation of the power of the state through the dualistic distinction of constituant versus constitué (or better still constitutional politics versus normal politics) institutionalized in the constitution itself around the democratic power to revise and amend. Whether this advantage in future legitimation potential is grasped at all (some of us worked hard to convince constitutional politicians of this) and whether it will outweigh short-term interest considerations is again a big question.

But whatever the actors might otherwise desire to include in their constitutions, their actual choices are in part structured by the framework of constitution-making procedures in which they act. These affect in particular the type of constitutionally formalized solution to the problem of constitutional change that can be justified, to themselves, to other actors, and to the public. This dimension is important especially because a common framework of constitution making and its need for justification can help the convergence of choices rooted in different ideologies.

Let me try to demonstrate the strong potential linkage between method of constitution making and the possibilities of instituting dualistic democracy. I begin with a simple contrast of constitutions created by sovereign assemblies and those produced by ordinary parliaments.[34] The former is the only option when there is a full revolutionary break, but it can be opted for in principle even when there is legal continuity. There is at least a strong elective affinity between negotiated transitions and the latter option, parliamentary constitution making, even if the negotiators may, under specific circumstances, decide to call a constitutional assembly, as in Bulgaria.[35]

Revolutionary constituent assemblies and assemblies that imitate them typically enact their work in the name of the sovereign (the people, the nation, the class, or the faithful). In contexts of breaks in legality they have little option. Even revolutionary legitimacy, claiming knowledge of an imagined future, must act in the name of the assumed beneficiaries of that future. It is, however, inconsistent with such sovereign claims to establish a constitution whose essential aspects (structure of regime, table of rights, amendment rule) could be changed through the ordinary political process, including the routine use of the revision rule. An amendment rule that allowed this would devalue the always precarious claims of legitimacy by a group of people either self-chosen or elected according to rules chosen by itself or another unelected group.[36] In order that the work of the *constituant* not be abrogated by the *constitué*, Carl Schmitt went so far as to recommend that sovereign assemblies should create constitutions unchangeable in their essentials. The actual historical record, as in the case of the Constituent Assembly of 1789–1791, indicates only constitutions that are very difficult to change by constitutional means.[37] With a little exaggeration, the Communist revolutions and the unwritten constitutional structures (Hans Kelsen's constitutions in the material sense) they established fit into this pattern. Without any procedures of orderly change, these have been exposed only (but not infrequently) to coups and palace revolutions.[38] Of course, as shown by the example of the insurrection of 1792, which replaced the constitutional monarchy by a republic, constitutions cannot logically proscribe revolutionary change (only failed revolutions), and their extreme rigidity may indeed invite these. Pace Ackerman, however, a constitution also cannot reliably institutionalize revolutions and indeed does not need to since when a revolution becomes possible it needs no authorization, and when successful, justifies itself in other than legal terms.[39] Thus to Ackerman's probable chagrin I am forced to draw the conclusion that constitutions established in the name of the popular sovereign by constituent assemblies are not likely to institutionalize genuine constitutional space for a dualistic politics[40] because of their tendency to *overly insulate* the constitution and to leave, as a result, little room for constitutional politics.[41]

On the other hand, and here I take the example of the Westminster Parliament as my guide, it is extremely difficult for an ordinary legislative body using ordinary parliamentary procedures to insulate its decisions at all against changes by a future legislative body exactly like it. I accept the famous arguments of H. L. A. Hart, according to which neither the possibility nor the impossibility of constitutional insulation through an amendment rule can be derived from the premise of parliamentary sovereignty. Moreover, in the legal sense, Parliament's current rule of change (the vote of 50 percent plus 1 members) could be used to produce a more difficult one that could be technically insulated from easy reversal through self-reference.[42] But Parliament is only, legally speaking, the sovereign; politically the United Kingdom is of course a popular sovereignty.[43] A constitutional change enacted by Parliament does not have the imprimatur of the sovereign people, and easy repeal turns out to be part of its condition of political possibility. (The more permanent a usurpation of the power of the popular sovereign, the more unacceptable, I would think. A centennial act would be much worse to democrats and republicans than a septennial act.) Even if we accept A. V. Dicey's argument that Parliament is always simultaneously a constituent assembly the same result follows: It is unacceptable for a constituent assembly to tie the hands of a future constituent assembly. If the point is, however, that since the future assembly's hands will be tied it will not be a constituent assembly, the question will inevitably be: What makes the two parliaments so fundamentally different from one another besides the will of the first? Why won't the will of the second not to be bound count for as much as that of the first to bind? Thus, speaking politically, the arguments for greater constitutional insulation of the acts of Parliament than the restrictions to which the original Parliament is exposed will generally be difficult to justify. If, however, future parliaments are not so restricted, constitution making will hardly be distinguished among their ordinary activities. Where sovereign assemblies tend to block the road to dualism by almost prohibiting constitutional politics,[44] ordinary parliaments that produce constitutions tend do the same by leveling the difference between constitutional and normal politics.

What could make a difference between present and future parliaments could of course be the enhanced legitimacy of the decision of the first, whose source may be (to stay within Ackerman's terms, but only for the moment) the mobilized and publicly documented will of the political sovereign, the British population. This brings me to my second conclusion: Ordinary political processes cannot institutionalize dualistic politics, based on the relative insulation of the constitution *unless* solving the difficult problem of legitimation for their constituent role.

We are ready to turn back to East and Central Europe, with their peculiar "revolutions against the Revolution." The simultaneous desire for radical change and the radical rejection of the revolutionary tradition biased all the cases, where new popular forces were initially strong or quickly became stronger to negotiated transition paths of legal continuity. In terms of what has been said so far, we should expect not only parliamentary constitution making in these settings but the need to solve the legitimation problems involved in the sufficient insulation of the constituent work of the relevant assemblies. The legitimation problems that would be ordinarily present in such a model of constitution making are in fact exacerbated by the particular historical and ideological context of the "revolutions against the Revolution."

I see three great problem areas: the relationship of the power to make constitutions to the old constitutions, the problem of the identity of the constitution-making instance, and the problem of the presence of elements of the future normal politics in current constitutional politics. These three contexts indicate grave legitimation problems that make it difficult but not perhaps impossible to establish a dualistic structure in the new constitution, in the future *pouvoir constitué*. In conclusion, I want to explore the status of constitutional insulation and constitutional politics within constitutions in terms of the actually emerging amendment rules of some select East and Central European regimes. I will analyze these in relation to the specific constitution-making process and the different paths of transition. Let me take these issues in turn.

The Old *Constitué* in the *Constituant*

Constitution makers in Europe have good reason to fear the revival of the old idea of *le pouvoir constituant*. In Carl Schmitt's version for example, this idea involves democracy by way of affective identification with leaders or elites, as well as a dark and potentially violent reservation in the face of all duly constituted authority. Even Hannah Arendt's transmutation of the principle into that of public freedom does not dispose of all doubts, since it depended on a historically unique example of the inherited constituted bodies of American political society that anticipated the new principle and could be therefore simply integrated in the new constitutional order. Although confronting old regimes far less attractive than the one faced by Sieyès, the East European constitution makers, conscious of history, had all the more reason to fear the strong temptation to adopt his notion that the constituent power is in the state of nature, that all previous legality is fully null and void in the presence of the *pouvoir constituant*. As Arendt showed, this idea was logically connected to a claim of plenitude of powers by subsequent constituent assemblies and the logic of permanent revolution and, we might add, legal nihilism.

The East Europeans of 1989 faced, however, a new situation. At a time when the military forces in the hands of the old regime were still intact, Sieyès's slogan, with its concomitant implication that all power must belong to a new constituent assembly, would have been a call for civil war. Moreover the "gentle" and "legal" revolutionaries had equally good normative as well as strategic reasons to avoid this road, since they explicitly rejected the Jacobin-Bolshevik tradition of the revolution in which it always culminated.

It was, however, difficult to reject revolutionary legitimacy while accomplishing something like a revolution. The circle was squared by tentatively postulating the legitimacy of the old constitution and by using its method of amendment to produce a new one. Thus the East European constitutional actors, first at the various roundtables, sought to avoid precisely a condition of the state of nature, outside of all law by postulating constitutional continuity with the old regimes, that left legislative and executive power, whatever their actual value, transitionally in old hands.[45] Thus, in Poland, Hungary,

Bulgaria, and in the former GDR, the democratic oppositions sought to carry out "legal" and "constitutional" revolutions.[46]

But the use of the old constitution was based on a double fiction. The old written constitutions were only fictionally the constitutions of Soviet-type societies. In reality they were forms of window dressing on an unwritten constitution in which the Communist Party is the only sovereign, and its various organs, the actual possessors of power. At the moment the rules of the old formal constitution were used for the first time for real, a break in the actual structure of constitutionality has arguably occurred. In some countries, though not in all, this break can be actually dated. In the GDR, for example, the government formed under the "old" constitution could be considered a provisional government. Nevertheless, these breaks were not visible since the transformation of the status of the old paper constitutions was never enacted or even raised to public consciousness. Moreover, in Hungary and Poland, where the old regimes began to take some reluctant measures toward constitutionalism before any negotiations (that is, turning their paper constitutions into real ones, hence in some respects actually attempting to make them less liberal!), even the moment of a break, however plausible, logically is difficult to locate in time. Indeed, even later when the adherence of the old parliaments to the work of roundtables was achieved through the rather old-style pressure of the Communist parties, the use of the rules of the old written constitution could still be portrayed as fictional.

It is worth keeping in mind one of Carl Schmitt's key theses, that whatever the formal limits of the amending process, its procedures cannot be used—for both logical and fundamental political reasons—to amend a constitution out of existence and to create a new one.[47] When this can be done, it is because the old constitution is already politically dead. The legal procedure of massively amending the constitution in this case seems to amount to only so much play-acting, which can have social psychological motivations but certainly no legal justification.[48] In this context it would be the first use of the amendment procedure to introduce or eliminate any key provision, in fundamental contradiction with the spirit of Communist constitutionalism that would signify a constitutional break, that would be merely disguised by procedural continuity.

Fictions, however, can have important consequences, in the present case both positive and negative. In the Polish and Hungarian contexts, for example, the apparent constitutional continuity provided for a transition within unchallenged rules that allowed both sides, still (for different reasons) far more equal than in Czechoslovakia, to agree upon the terms that would vastly diminish (Poland) or largely eliminate (Hungary) the powers of one of them. This was only possible if the losing side did not have to fear revolutionary justice and the populist utilization of revolutionary semantics. The constitutional transition provided a genuinely legal model of justice and a semantics of self-limitation for all sides. Not only the losers gained in this. As they knew from the history of revolutions, the winners too, indeed the whole society, had good reason to fear the triumph of a revolutionary logic.

Thus, the determined use of fictions turned them into legal realities.[49] But the consequences were not only positive, from the point of view of the consolidation of a future democracy. Fictional procedures continued to hide what was in fact taking place. In order to accomplish their goals, the roundtables had to assume the double constitutional reality of Soviet type societies and could not entrust the fate of the agreements to the goodwill of packed or unpacked, but fundamentally Communist parliaments. It was assumed throughout that the Communist Party would get the necessary (two-thirds) parliamentary votes, more or less in the old way. When, however, the fiction turned into the actual procedure, instances that should not have had voice in the outcome managed to do so. When the old Parliament in Hungary modified the Round Table's electoral formula (to the wrongly supposed advantage of the ex-ruling party), this act revealed the weakness of the Round Table compromise, or the continued ability of the Communists to manipulate a double constitutional reality. Of course both sides could now play the formal political game suddenly for real. Thus the Hungarian opposition (within the opposition) could use a recent law on referenda (February 1989), passed by the last Kádárist Parliament, to in effect amend[50] the constitution beyond the roundtable agreements, just as this old Parliament used its prerogatives to alter some of the same agreements as well.[51]

Finally, and most significantly in the present context, the fiction of continuity came to imply that nowhere, not even in Hungary, were all important features of the inherited constitutions actually changed. All the constitutions that were presidential remained so, while in Hungary, where a parliamentary system proper existed, it turned out to be impossible to introduce a presidential one. Only Poland, where the presidency was strengthened and a new chamber of Parliament was introduced as a trade-off, was an exception to the trend. Equally important, and highly unfortunate in my view, in most countries the old (if originally a merely formal) status of Parliament in Communist countries as a quasi-constitutive assembly was maintained by preserving the old method of constitutional amendment.[52] This fact confirms another of Schmitt's insights, according to which it would be highly implausible to use the method of amendment to essentially alter the amendment procedure itself.[53] Thus if the use of the existing amending procedure to replace a constitution may only disguise a very real break, the survival of this procedure points to the incompleteness of this break in a fundamental area, helping to produce a form of parliamentary sovereignty rather than democratic constitutionalism.

The consequences of using the old *constitué* in the new constituent process were also ambiguous for political legitimacy. On the one side a species of legal legitimation was achieved, according to which the emerging changes were not merely the work of groups (with poor legitimation claims), but of a variety of contending forces that subordinated their will at all times to the requirements of legality. On the other side the claim of continuity with the old constitution had to involve a blurring of the line between a formal constitution that was now used for the first time and the actual operative constitution of the Communist regimes. Continuity with the latter could of course only reduce the legitimacy of the new enterprise. Unfortunately, the occasional reliance in the formative period on the double constitutional reality of the old regime only reinforced this highly questionable type of continuity.[54]

The Identity of the *Constituant*

Evidently, then in several countries the use of the old constitutional rules to frame the transition blocked the emergence of the classical *pouvoir constituant* of European revolutions, along with its political embodiment, the sovereign constituent assembly. This outcome, however, did not settle the question of the identity of the instance that was to draw up the new constitution. While the Communist Parties and their ministers of justice everywhere assumed that the old parliaments would do just fine in this role, the thorough illegitimacy of these organs soon made such proposals irrelevant. But the new parliaments that could perhaps assume the responsibility, could only come into being on the basis of at least some new constitutional framework, even if a temporary one. Who was to establish such a framework was all the more important, because temporary arrangements, if seriously used, often tend to find their way into the more permanent ones.

According to Ulrich Preuss, the *pouvoir constituant* in the Central European countries at least was replaced by civil society as the key system of reference of the constitution-making process. Here was then a second answer of the East Europeans to Sieyès: Constitution making need not be in the state of nature during the transitions not only because it assumes the constitutional rules of the previous system, but also to the extent that it refers as its ground of validity not to the unified but unstructured people, but to the organized groups, bodies, and institutions of civil society. In this depiction civil society somehow becomes the stand in for the *pouvoir constituant,* and the alternative framework to a unitary sovereignty. There are two ways to interpret this claim, in relation to East European experience. On the one side, a stronger version of the argument refers to the instance of the roundtables that refused the status of constituent assemblies, and where a plurality of participants acted not according to the logic of power, but to the open-ended discursive processes characteristic of civil society. Preuss's own experience with the Central Round Table of the GDR represents the empirical background for this version.

In a more plausible weaker version, civil society would not be seen as a substitute for both the *pouvoir constituant* and the constituent assembly. Rather, concern for civil society, which may exist only in a rather undeveloped form, leads only to the renunciation of the model of a unified, unlimited sovereign constitution-making power. While theoretically this merely negative determination would also leave the door open for the participation of the groups of civil society in a major constitution-making instance as in the GDR, it may also lead, and in Hungary did lead, to a pluralization (fragmentation?) of the constituent process, with each instance acting within the limits of existing law. This meant that a bewildering array of instances could, and did, play a role in the constituent process: the National Round Table, the old Parliament, the referendum of November 1989, the negotiators of MDF and SZDSZ (the two leading parties after the free election), the new Parliament, and last, but certainly not least, the Constitutional Court.

To be sure both of the options had their drawbacks. The presence of many equal partners probably reduced in East Germany the political weight of the few organizations with actually and potentially greater following, thus no one was in the end in the position to fight for the acceptance of the constitution formulated.[55] The constitution makers, in their refusal to act strategically, were defenseless against of those groups that were willing to do so. Breaking their self-limitation and accepting governmental responsibility made the groups of civil society represented at the Round Table only weaker still.

In Hungary the renunciation of a classical constituent power and constituent assembly[56] empowered an incipient pluralistic, but political rather than civil society. Here two political organizations were dominant within the opposition from the beginning of the National Round Table, and there was little problem of enacting most of what they agreed upon, especially given the simple parliamentary process of amendment taken over from the Communist constitution. On the other hand, the two most important stages of constitution making, the agreements of the National Round Table (September 1989) and the MDF-SZDSZ pact (April 1990), smacked of exclusionary elite compromise that was corrected only in the first case by a national referendum (November 1989), which became, under the provisions of existing law, another constitution-making (rather than only ratifying) instance. The plurality of constitution-making instances, as well as of the political forces that played the most important role, may have represented some, but only some, of the plurality of a slowly institutionalized civil society. From a legal point of view, however, this type of process led at the same time to important inconsistencies of formulation, weakening the coherence, and identity-forming power of the constitution. This had the unfortunate consequence of putting the appropriately strong Constitutional Court and later processes of constitutional review in a difficult position. Given the context of a patchwork constitutional document, which nevertheless does amount to a minimum basis of a liberal constitutionalism, the Court had to inevitably become overactive and, in the view of a number of people,[57] perhaps overly creative and overly political. A high level of court activism on behalf of rights, however justified, becomes precarious when, as I will show, the constitution whatever its qualities otherwise has insufficient democratic legitimacy.

To sum up this section: As important as (1) the break with a unified constituent power, (2) the establishment of the role of constitution-making instances other than sitting parliaments, and (3) the involvement in the process of unconstrained, extended public discussion may all be, both the establishment of a public body relying on open, discursive processes of interaction but without any strategic capabilities as the central constitution-making instance as well as the bypassing of a central instance altogether represent difficult and perhaps counterproductive institutionalizations of these desiderata.[58] As the German and Hungarian examples show, reliance on the roundtables to produce the final constitution of a new democracy leads to a difficult-to-solve dilemma. These bodies, with all their key virtues, not having been elected, do not have democratic legitimacy. An attempt to legitimate them through their internal procedures, as in Germany, seems to produce a process of public communication without genuine strategic capacities. The roundtable as a public legitimates through purely discursive criteria only at the cost of surrendering its decision-making and enforcing capacities. On the other hand an all too ready acceptance of the strategic tasks of the roundtable as in Hungary, perhaps required to push through the compromise decisions of the negotiating actors, reveals an atmosphere of elite bargaining that is difficult to normatively justify. The use of the double constitutional reality of a Communist regime did lead to the enactment of the decisions of such a forum, but at the cost of further tainting the origins of the new constitution.

The New *Constitué* in the *Constituant* and the Problem of Legitimacy

Thus it is not surprising that irrespective of the level of the success of the roundtables in drafting and enacting a new constitution, constitution making continues after the passing of these institutions. As a result in most countries there was a subsequent return to parliamentary constitution making. Only in one roundtable country, Bulgaria, was a method of a more classical constitutional assembly chosen. But while there are differences between the constituent assemblies and regular parliaments that have been freely (in Poland, partially freely) elected (regarding division of labor, house rules, length of tenure) in one respect they are not different: They combine constitutional and policy interests, constituent and legislative powers. Deeply involved in the processes and conflicts of ordinary politics, and in the position to tailor constitutional requirements to party political needs visible after the first election, it is indeed an open question whether and how such bodies can generate democratic legitimacy for the constitutions they produce.[59] What is wrong with all of them is that they incorporate too many of the interests of an already constituted future politics in the politics of constitution making. In such a context, even the principled arguments of the actors tend to appear as mere rationalizations for self-interest.

The problem has come up already at some of the roundtables, especially those that began to show the beginnings of party formation. Whatever else these forums would do, they would have to produce an electoral rule for the first democratic elections. But electoral rules favor one actor or another, and as was clear in the Hungarian case, incipient political parties favor rules that they assume (rightly or wrongly) favor them. Their own behavior brought to their consciousness their lack of legitimacy to undertake acts that will have asymmetrical distributional consequences. They knew that the losers and the excluded will immediately ask them by what right they chose these particular rules and how the new exclusions can be justified when the rules guaranteed the continued presence of the Communists in political life.

And indeed the Hungarian and East German actors of the Round Tables were obsessed with their lack of legitimacy.[60] Granted, the Polish participants were unconcerned by this problem.[61] Unlike the much smaller groups in Hungary and the GDR, Solidarity after all had a charismatic central figure and nationally known leaders, as well as vast reserves of more or less active social support to draw on as a result of its ten-year struggle as the one big movement of Polish society. According to terms defined at the end of chapter 3, they hoped to substitute their very real empirical or sociological legitimacy (that only the Polish democratic opposition possessed) for legitimacy in the normative legal sense, which was missing here as well. Solidarity representatives were no more chosen in democratic elections than their counterparts elsewhere. It was a negotiating partner that possessed only sovereign power, but no legitimacy (in either sense) that chose the representatives of Solidarity and Lech Walesa as its democratic interlocutor. As all dualistic proposals from Adam Michnik's "New Evolutionism" (1976) to János Kis's "Social Contract" (1987) assumed, a historic compromise with Communist power had to be legitimated in part by a merely negative legitimacy: In the given geopolitical setting this is the best that we can do. In the dramatically changed historical circumstances of a year later, this negative legitimacy disappeared, opening up a serious legitimation deficit for the previous agreement. In the end, the circumstances of a bargain between old and new elites, in which, as it turned out, initially some important things were conceded to the Communists, clearly helped to erode the very real social support of the first post-Communist government in Poland.

The lack of legitimacy of all sides, of government and opposition, of Round Table and Parliament, was clearly faced at the Hungarian Round Table. But the first response, that none was needed, could only suffice as long as the Round Table and the parliamentary acts based on it could be restricted to a democratic minimum needed for regulating the transition. When even this minimum came to imply the full-scale rewriting of the constitution this position collapsed. Strategic elite bargaining could not be justified especially when the geopolitical reasons for deal making with the Communists were no longer pertinent and when the elites assumed functions to which the first freely elected parliament would have better claim.

So the actors had to consider the means by which their legitimacy could be increased. What other legitimating options were there?

1. All the Round Tables, even the Czechoslovak one, which was clearly a one-sided affair, renounced revolutionary legitimacy, which would have involved a claim of complete identity with the people in whose name and future interest a total rupture with the past would have been announced. This option, equivalent to a claim of fully sovereign constituent power, was unacceptable in "revolutions against the Revolution."

2. The Hungarian Round Table claimed a potential, retroactive democratic legitimacy. If, as the argument went, the population voted under the new electoral rules, within the new procedural framework, this would, after the fact, legitimate the agreements. Such a tacit form of democratic legitimation, on which all democratic normal politics relies to some extent, is very doubtful in the case of constitution making. With the partial and indirect exception of the important referendum of November 1989, the electorate was not asked to vote on the new constitution, but to vote under it or to stay politically passive. Under such conditions, low levels of participation in the first year of free elections as in Hungary had to have devastating consequences for the legitimacy of the system.

3. The Round Table of the GDR, like its Hungarian forerunner, claimed neither revolutionary nor any other form of strictly political legitimacy; it passed no decrees nor otherwise formally exercised political power. The new elites relied instead on their power of persuasion in the reconstructed public sphere, a "power" rooted in the superiority of a powerless morality over an immoral power.[62] Unlike its Hungarian counterpart, the GDR Round Table sought, however, to produce a new constitution from the outset, by a method that would partially break with the Communist as well West German models of constitution making by requiring not only a two-thirds majority of the *Volkskammer* but a popular-plebiscitary ratification of the document as well.[63] Thus the actors sought to derive the legitimacy of the constitution from a combination of two democratic methods: a process of communication free of domination among elites and plebiscitary, direct democratic ratification involving the rest of the population.

4. To the extent that constitution making must involve actors capable of strategic action as well as decisions that can be enforced, hence actors of political and not merely civil society, the primary instance can involve

only a public sphere with significant formal, material, and temporal limits. It is for this reason that a Rawlsian veil of ignorance rather than a
model of undistorted communication seems to be the best source of the
claim that political society can make for the legitimacy of its constituent
activity. While no actors clearly thematized this requirement, the roundtables sought to portray their activities as if they operated under a modified veil of ignorance (in an empirical sense, and not in Rawls's sense of
hypothetical interrogation of a set of results that could have been produced without particular interests having played a role). In this context,
it helped of course that the parties to the various East European roundtables were not linked to clearly identifiable social constituencies, that
they were not parties of interest representation but rather of diverse but
inchoate political philosophies. Even their specific interests as parties
were less suspect to the extent that there was good reason to believe that
the actors could be seriously mistaken concerning them. When in the
case of the Hungarian debate about electoral rules each party clearly
sought to institutionalize what it imagined was its particular interest, the
fact that they were actually, and obviously ignorant concerning the content of these[64] made the resulting compromise still fit, if barely, under a
conceivable veil of ignorance, especially since the best democratic arguments could be marshaled behind a mixed system of proportional representation and individual mandates, combining both a relatively accurate representation of the voters' wishes with the responsibility of
individual representatives to their constituencies.[65] What immediately
became illegitimate, however, was a form of agreement based on the
linking of anticipatory knowledge with the power capable of bringing
about results in line with particular interests. When the veil of ignorance
was clearly lifted, when an agreement was made that clearly indicated
specific winners and losers, as in the case of the presumed deal between
the conservative parties and the Communists concerning the presidency,
it was possible to delegitimate and defeat the outcome.

Most pertinent to the presence of future political interests in the constitution-making process is the argument concerning the veil of ignorance. We
should note, however, that this argument works only in the early stages of the
process in the case of constitution making in negotiated transitions that
involve ordinary parliaments. To the extent that the job of constitution making failed, or was put off, or had to be restarted because of the questionable
circumstances of the original drafting and enactment, the tacit or open appeal
to a veil of ignorance had to become increasingly hollow. The presence of
political parties that now could predict the effect of specific rules on their performance, the operation of powerful institutions like the presidency and the
constitutional court that knew how to influence the process in line with their

interest, and the clearer attachment of constituencies to parties meant that from now on new publicly viable justifications had to emerge if the window of opportunity for new constitution making, if it were to reopen at all, were to be used successfully. And yet it was also with the passing of time and the discovery of the weaknesses of the early constitutional arrangements in countries like Poland and Hungary that the need to produce more coherent and more legitimate constitutions became impossible to evade.

Thus constitution makers are forced to look to sources of legitimacy beyond claims of the veil of ignorance covering the procedures. Elsewhere, I will emphasize publicity, the plurality of democratic channels, and meeting demanding consensus requirements in addition to staunch adherence to legality and the veil of ignorance (in a limited empirical sense) as such principles of legitimation.[66] Even when these demanding requirements cannot or will not be met, however, the imperfect documents and their low level of legitimacy will require redress by other channels of constitutional politics. If the window of opportunity for constitution making cannot be opened up, or if a new effort fails, it becomes willy-nilly the task of amendment procedures and constitutional courts to carry out the ongoing reform of the constitution. The balance between the two options determines the relationship of democratic and liberal constitutionalism in the new regime. Where the former, constitutional review dominates, and the court in question does a good job under the given circumstances, the legitimation problems can be addressed by the slow development of a species of traditional legitimacy that will be administered by a specialized group of lawyers, the guardians of the constitution. A country could do worse than to evolve a republican system in a somewhat traditionalized version. But what a court cannot do is to contribute to the expansion of democratic constitutionalism, not only because that would decrease its own power, but also because a court cannot easily produce a new rule of change for a constitution. Within a constitution, only the use of an amendment rule can produce a new amendment rule. And while such a use too would require the solution of the problem of democratic legitimacy, it may be nevertheless easier to satisfy demands of consensus and publicity for individual amendments than for a constitution as a whole. Such use of amendments can in principle increase the weight of democratic constitutionalism in a given regime. But whether or not this is possible depends on the amendment rule in place.

The *Constituant* in the *Constitué*

I return to my original question concerning the current chances of democratic constitutionalism, of dualistic politics, of incorporating some of the political spirit of the remarkable transitions in settled constitutions. Considering today's politics in the new democracies, it would be a mistake to confine the idea of extraordinary public politics to the constitutional track, or even to

confine constitutional politics to the amendment process. The battle for freedom of the press and media in Hungary, between 1990 and 1994, pitted, for
example, the organizations of civil society against the government, with issues
at stake belonging to both normal and constitutional politics. The defense of
the presidency and of the Constitutional Court against parts of the ruling
coalition involved constitutional politics, even if this defense took place without producing new constitutional provisions defining the roles of these public law institutions.[67]

As we have seen (in chapter 2), moreover, the politics of civil society itself
depends on institutionalization, especially, but not only, in constitutions. Different countries of course satisfy to various extents and in different ways the
demands and the potentialities of such institutionalization on which the
future of dualistic politics will in part depend. But this future will also depend
on how constitutional politics in the more limited sense is institutionalized.

While extraordinary politics of public involvement could occur on various
channels, the politics of constitution creation and revision has a greater affinity with this politics than any other channel. If all politics has elements of the
normal and the extraordinary, the center of gravity of constitutional politics
alone lies decisively on the side of extraordinary public involvement. And, of
all possible forms of constitutional politics, the processes of constitution making and amending are privileged in this context, because, of these, the former
can institutionalize (rather than merely occasion) extraordinary politics as a
long-term possibility, while the latter in some of its forms is just this politics
institutionalized. Amendment rules are especially important, because they not
only represent the key option for democratic constitutional politics but also
determine to a significant extent to which constitutional politics will be practiced outside of a formalized higher political tract. It is then extremely worthwhile to examine the fate of amendment rules and processes in a select group
of East European constitutions or constitutional drafts chosen to illustrate the
basic types available to constitution makers.[68] I will pay special attention to
the link of constitution-making procedure (and transition path) to amendment rules to illustrate the difficulties to be overcome if inadequate amendment rules were themselves to be amended.

From Antinomic to Monistic Rule: Hungary

No country in East Europe has followed the Westminster model of parliamentary sovereignty without a written constitution protected by the insulation of an amendment rule. If for the moment we leave aside the key difference of a strong, very un-British Constitutional Court, Hungary seems to
come closest to this model.[69] Its constitution, by now the only one to preserve
the original amendment rule of the Communist paper constitution, categor-
ically states in the section dealing with the parliament that "the National

Assembly a) creates the Constitution of the Hungarian Republic" (*The Constitution of the Hungarian Republic*, par. 19, [3a]). To be sure the same section also ordains that "[t]o change the Constitution . . . the votes of two thirds of the parliamentary representatives is required." But this restriction, under contemporary conditions, is only a political one and does not alter the sovereign, constituent role assigned to the unicameral Parliament or National Assembly (par. 24, [3]). In addition to what is considered constitutional in the strict sense, the Constitution contains also a series of special laws, dealing mostly with the regulation of materially constitutional topics like local government, elections, and the Constitutional Court, laws that the National Assembly can change even more easily, with the two-thirds vote of merely those present, assuming a quorum of one-half plus one of the members. Since such legislation, unlike amendments, is liable to constitutional review, the Parliament's sovereign authority seems to be diminished in these cases. But since nothing on the formal level would stop Parliament from repassing a rejected "two-thirds law" as a constitutional amendment, the restriction is more apparent than real.

The rule is a characteristic product of negotiated transition in which several stages of constitution making benefited from an easy rule centered in a single institution, and where no constitution makers possessed sufficient legitimacy to try to insulate their product from future changes. Once the first freely elected parliamentarians, already relying on a workable if imperfect constitutional document, chose to bypass the making of a new constitution in favor of another mere amendment, the longer term survival of this rule was ensured. It is tough to expect from an assembly (early in its tenure) to adopt rules that would restrict its own freedom of action, and it did not have sufficient legitimacy (late in its tenure) to do the same favor for their successors.

Yet the monopoly of a purely parliamentary revision rule was not, in the beginning, a foregone conclusion. Referenda represented for a while a procedure of amendment in competition with parliamentary sovereignty, leading to an *antinomic* structure of sovereignty. According to the law on referenda, Act XVII of June 1, 1989, redefined as a "two-thirds law" by the Constitution in 1989 and 1990 (19[5]), a new constitution is to be ratified by a popular referendum. The Constitution itself is silent about this requirement and was indeed enacted in October 1989 without a referendum. But perhaps mindful of the law as well as the intention of many of the Round Table participants to agree upon only the organic laws needed for genuinely free elections, this very Constitution was presented as a massive amendment, and by implication as a merely interim constitution. To quote the text, this constitution was to remain in effect only until "the *acceptance* of our country's *new* Constitution" (Preamble, my emphasis). As the example shows, this restriction is more apparent than real, because nothing could stop future parliaments, formally speaking, from adopting new constitutions in the form of massive amendments that need no ratification. Undoubtedly the subterfuge would and *already did* contribute to legitimation problems of new constitutions.[70]

At the same time it remained an open matter for a while whether referenda alone could modify the Constitution. The law on referenda does not limit plebiscites in this respect. Nor does the Constitution do so in any definitive manner,[71] and indeed it states in the very beginning that the Hungarian people "exercises popular sovereignty by way of its elective representatives as well as directly" (2[2]). In fact, the idea of constitutional change through referenda already played a role in political practice. The Referendum of November 1989, in effect, abolished the extraordinary procedures for the first free election of the president, in favor of parliamentary selection.[72] In July 1990 another referendum took place, which would have restored the direct election of the president had the participation threshold been met. The Constitutional Court allowed these referenda to be carried out and affirmed the result of the first, and there is no sign that it would have rejected a positive result in the case of the second. In 1993, however, during an attempt to recall Parliament by an organization of the poor, the LAET, and in effect order new elections through a referendum, the Court decided that referenda cannot amend the Constitution because of what was now asserted (without sufficient textual support) as the primacy of parliamentarianism in the exercise of popular sovereignty in the Hungarian system.[73] With this step from a model that was in effect an antinomic one, the Court restored the monistic character of the constitution amendment rule, inherited from the Communist paper constitution.

Evidently, however, members of the Court hate the present amendment rule, charitably because of the opportunities it presents for constant constitutional tinkering (and delegitimation) through normal politics, and, less charitably, because it provides a relatively easy method of overruling court decisions, especially in the case of two-thirds laws when the votes are prima facie available for an amendment. In fact only one Court decision has been overruled by amendment. But there has been much and repeated tinkering, starting with the massive amendments of 1990. This practice has interfered with bringing the regime change, constitutionally speaking, to a proper closing. Even more seriously, the electoral rule has always given (and will probably always give) the first two parties among six a two-thirds majority. When these parties make a deal as in 1990, or enter into a coalition as in 1994, the charge of "constitutional dictatorship" comes naturally to the other parties. The response to such charges can be total constitutional inflexibility. When the social liberal coalition entered into a set of compromise arrangements with the opposition in 1995 to make a new constitution, the price was a unilateral renunciation of the power to amend the current constitution, which, however, turned out to survive after all. When this moratorium was itself renounced, a few amendments were pushed through in spite of the loud protests of four parliamentary parties, hardly an ideal way to do constitutional politics.

Here lies the reason why the apparently very flexible amendment rule has hardly been used to trump adverse Constitutional Court decisions even when the parliamentary votes were available. The apparent power of Parliament to amend the Constitution is not backed up by sufficient legitimacy to dare to challenge the Court, and the illusion of parliamentary sovereignty blinds the ruling parties concerning the necessity and the required means of building public support to undertake important amendments. Under these circumstances, the Court retains a significant dimension of sovereign power that not only leads to rulings in the defense of rights but also to decisions that in effect shape and reshape the structure of power. As we will see in chapter 5, such decisions are by no means always democracy reinforcing as one would require of a body without its own democratic legitimacy.

Thus the tasks in Hungary seem clear: At the very least the old amendment rule should be used one more time, to amend itself. The aim, however, should not be only what the Court desires, namely, to make the rule simply much more difficult. Inevitably, a change could bring the period of initial constitution making to a close, only by making the rule somewhat more difficult. More important would be to reduce its monistic and to increase its democratic features. Three available proposals offer to do this, which, however, should not be combined in a single rule affecting all amendments, if Hungary is to avoid having a rule of forbidding difficulty. The first would simply require referenda to ratify changes in the Constitution. The second would require two parliaments to ratify a given change (with or without compulsory dissolution of the first). The third would elect an ad hoc or semipermanent parliamentary chamber according to an electoral rule not based on parties (individual races or single transferable voting in single districts) that would have to concur in amendments. Each of these formulas could reduce the qualification of the parliamentary majority to counteract somewhat the increased level of difficulty. Each could be restricted to the essential components of the Constitution and thus allow, for the sake of efficiency, Parliament to amend everything else in the current way. What is most important is that in different ways each formula would increase the democratic legitimacy of essential constitutional revisions. The first would do so through the element of direct democracy. The second would make the proposed change a possible stake in a democratic election. And the third would bring in another dimension of interest, primarily local, into a democratic process in which parties have attained overwhelming influence.[74]

From Monism to Bicameralism: Poland

Poland has a bicameral parliament with a Senate as a result of the Round Table compromise, and thus one of the possible solutions in Hungary comes here more naturally. And yet, as the other classical country of the negotiated transition,

Poland started out in April 1989, when the Round Table agreements were ratified, with constitution making through the repeated use of the inherited amendment rule, located in the original lower house of Parliament, the Sejm. Nevertheless, the special nature of this first democratic transition from Communism
made for a development different than the Hungarian one from the outset. Since
the Round Table compromise included nondemocratic elements, it could not be
constitutionalized. Thus Poland could not put off constitution making in favor
of a regime of repeated amendments, as did Hungary, after the new elections.
Secondly, the body that had the constitutional right to amend or to enact a new
constitution (according to the amended Constitution of 1952, whose amendment rule was retained) was the so-called contractual Sejm, with only one-third
of the freely elected members and thus a low level of democratic legitimacy. Thus
the Senate could immediately register its moral, if not legal, claim to play the pre-
dominant role in Constitution making.[75] While the short-term result was the
failure of parallel and conflicting efforts to make a new constitution,[76] one legal
and the other legitimate, the end result had to be the formal inclusion of both
chambers in constitutional politics. Finally, the Polish Round Table established a
new office, a strong presidency as a sort of insurance policy for members of the
old regime, and the last Communist Parliament further strengthened this office
in April 1989.[77] The presidency was strengthened still more in September 1990
by adding direct election to the office, a failed move ostensibly designed to stop
Walesa's conquest of the office. In his hands, the directly elected presidency, well
in place before any constitutional draft could be adopted, represented yet another
important counterweight to parliamentary sovereignty.[78]

The inclusion of the Senate occurred, however, in a dualistic manner that
presupposed the differentiation between amendment rules and procedure to
produce an entirely new constitution.[79] The original text of Article 106 of the
amended Constitution of 1952[80] states that "The Constitution may be
amended only by a law passed by the Sejm . . . by a majority of at least two-
thirds of the votes." Focusing on the term *only by a law,* the rule was interpreted (redefined) as requiring that all other conditions of law making had to
be satisfied.[81] These included two important requirements: The bill had to be
submitted to the Senate, which could reject or amend it, and the president had
a right to use his suspensive veto powers. Thus the amendment rule was not a
monistic, unicameral one, strictly speaking, from the beginning of the first
Solidarity government. Given, however, the possibility, that by a two-thirds
vote the Sejm could reaffirm the original amendment if vetoed, or reject the
Senate's changes, the predominance of the lower house was certainly preserved.[82] This is borne out in the subsequent conflicts over amendments, with
the Sejm repeatedly pushing through constitutional bills in spite of Senate
opposition.[83] Thus a constitution-making channel, in effect quite like that of
Hungary, relying on a series of structural amendments, continued to operate
in Poland for an extended period, until May 1994 at least.[84]

But constitutional politics was to acquire a second channel. Using the same amendment rule, despite the opposition of the Senate, the Sejm forced through a new constitution-making procedure in April 1992.[85] This rule mandated a mixed Extraordinary Constitutional Committee of the Sejm and Senate, in which the former dominated, to propose the draft of the new constitution to the National Assembly, the joint sitting of the two chambers, which would have to pass the constitution by successive two-thirds votes and send the approved draft to the president for his approval or amendments. The latter's amendments would have to approved by again two-thirds, and the bill as a whole had to be again passed in a third reading with the same majority. After all this the president was required to submit the document to a binding referendum without a threshold of participation.[86] While this rule itself was later amended in May 1994,[87] it remained the basis of the procedure that led to success in 1997.[88] Note, however, that its coming into being did not displace the Sejm-centered amendment rule, or consign it to the making of only minor amendments. The important interim Little Constitution of October 1992 that dealt with the whole machinery of government and reaffirmed the original amendment rule itself emerged as a result of this amendment procedure in which the Sejm and its drafting commission dominated. And this happened after the (mixed) Constitutional committee of the (joint) National Assembly was already formed and had begun its deliberations!

The ambiguity of course could have undermined the project of making a new constitution. Why would the Sejm concede a constitution it did not fully want, if it could use the amendment rule to introduce one piecemeal that it wanted? Could even the search for greater legitimacy outweigh the desire for lower house dominance of the project? At the very least, the ability of the Sejm to control the amendment process was a potential source of pressure and subversion. It appears that this strategic dilemma became moot only after 1993 when the same coalition dominated both chambers vitiating the old rivalry between them. If the power to amend was in fact also shifted to the National Assembly, it would have also happened at this time expressing a new, cooperative relation between the two similarly composed chambers. That move would have removed a structural impediment from the making of the new constitution.

Quite characteristically, given the existence of a strong presidency from April 1989, the president had a role in both the amendment process and the production of a new constitution. Formally this role was only that of less than a genuine suspensive veto in both cases. In the case of constitution making, he could offer only amendments that would have to be approved by the same two-thirds margin as the constitution itself. Thus the power of the National Assembly was in no way diminished. In the case of amendments, the president did apparently have, even after the power shifted to the National Assembly, the power of suspensive veto. But since the Sejm (or later the National Assembly) could override the veto by the same majority that the amendment had to acquire, this power too was at best only to delay. In fact several amendments were passed over presidential objections. Nevertheless, the office with its strong formal powers, patronage, and access to the media could pursue its goals informally. Revisions of the constitution-making rule in March 1994 were achieved by President Walesa in this way. This aspect was important, since the president could be expected to try to institutionalize (or preserve) aspects of presidential or semipresidential government that the Sejm, or even the National Assembly, was bound to resist. Here was a second built-in difficulty of the dualistic structure of Polish constitutional politics.

As long as the making of the new constitution was on the agenda, demands for the expansion of its democratic character focused on its procedures. The focus tended to be on the Constitutional Committee receiving popular drafts, beyond the many proposals that groupings of fifty-six deputies and senators could and did submit.[89] Such proposal for extraparliamentary participation became all the stronger, when representatives of about a third of the electorate found themselves outside of Parliament (to be sure because of their own poor strategic choices, in context of the given electoral law). What the constitution-making body thus gained in freedom of action, it lost on the level of legitimacy (in the sociological sense, since in the normative legal sense it was beyond dispute). Thus proposals to expand participation had to be taken very seriously. While Walesa's proposal to give the right of popular constitutional initiative to 100,000 signatories along with rights of being heard on the Constitutional Committee was rejected, similar rights were in the end given to 500,000 signers and their representatives. Ill-conceived plans for corporatist representation and preconstitutional referenda on basic principles were, however, allowed to wither through tokenism (some representatives of social groups and excluded parties received symbolic representation, and the National Assembly reserved the right to call preconstitutional referenda).[90] With more than a million signatures behind it, the Solidarity Union did manage to have its constitutional draft received, and parts of this draft did find their way into the final document.

With a new president after 1994, the hurdle of presidential interference too was overcome. The new constitution of 1997, enacted by the National Assembly[91] (after some popular participation and discussion as well as attempts at compromise) and ratified in a referendum, could now have a very different amendment structure than before. The new option turned out to be, unsurprisingly, a bicameral one with a distinctly stronger role for the Senate. But a place is found for direct democratic referenda as well. Even with these new elements of pluralism, the new rule is not a difficult one, and is even less so regarding more peripheral constitutional matters. According to Article 235, an amendment is submitted by one-fifth of the Sejm, or the Senate, or by the president; it needs to be accepted by two-thirds of the Sejm and a majority of the Senate; and changes in the structure of government, fundamental rights, or the amendment rule itself may require approval in a referendum if the majority (not the losing minority!) of the Sejm or the president so moves and more than half of the Senate agrees. It seems to me that it would be difficult to pass essential changes in these dimensions of the constitution without a referendum, if public opinion required it. The example confirms what we have assumed, that a primarily parliamentary process of constitution making that is able to satisfy additional conditions of democratic legitimacy is likely to institute a model of amendments that is consistent with both constitutional insulation and the expansion of democratic participation in constitutional politics.

Rigid Constitutions and Democratic Constitutionalism in Bulgaria and Romania

I now come to two cases where new constitutions were produced by constituent assemblies relatively early in the process of transformation. Bulgaria and Romania have been commonly seen as representing almost the diametrical opposite of constitutional development in Poland and Hungary with their evolutionary, piecemeal, flexible patterns of development. From a point of view that is far more concerned with constitutional learning than with normativity ("learning not to learn") and the institutionalization of a two-track model of constitutionalism, Stephen Holmes and Cass Sunstein expressed unambigous preference for the Polish and Hungarian model, and the current state of constitutionalism in these countries seems to support their judgment. But given the many differences between the four countries and their legal traditions, we should not avail ourselves of such easy evidence and attribute the outcome to a model of constitution making alone. There may be many positive features of Bulgarian and Romanian constitutional developments, moreover, from which even Poles and Hungarians could learn.[92]

According to Holmes and Sunstein, Bulgaria and Romania produced complete and well-insulated constitutions in the early stages of the process, primarily because of their domination by Communist politicians. In various guises, elites of the old regime wished accordingly to produce constitutions while they were still in charge, in order to insulate their "ill-gotten gains" from future challenge. In order to succeed, they had to make the constitutions as inflexible as possible, thereby gravely damaging the learning capacities of the new regimes.

The two authors are on the whole right concerning who dominated the process, but they are not completely right. In Bulgaria without some opposition agreement, the constitutional project of the BSP (Bulgarian Socialist Party) could not have succeeded and the moderate opposition gained many important concessions both at the Round Table and at the Grand National Assembly [Ralitsa]. In Romania, the National Salvation Front (NSF) did dominate the process, but its institutional links to the past were broken by the insurrection. Thus it is not completely accurate to refer to this elite as "the Communists." The description that it was the Communists who wanted a new constitution to be adopted early is right for Bulgaria. Here the elections after the Round Table were incredibly rushed as well, in order that the opposition remained unorganized and relatively weak in the constituent assembly. In Romania, however, because of the legal break, there was no inherited constitutional reality to amend and use, and long delays would have lengthened only the dictatorship of the provisional government, hardly desirable under the circumstances. Any expansion of this government, given the weakness of other forces, could have happened only on terms dominated by the NSF. The constitution-making effort thus came when it more or less was supposed to, after a revolution in the legal sense, and could not restrict itself to a few amendments, given the lack of a valid constitution at the time capable of functioning.[93]

There is, moreover, little that expresses specifically Communist preferences in the constitutions. There are nationalist components, like the Bulgarian ban on ethnic parties or the Romanian exclusion of politics aiming at federalism or territorial autonomy or even modifying the national language (in the direction of bilingualism, e.g.), but these features too could have been included on the wishes of many other political tendencies. Equally important: There is also little in the texts that specifically protects ill-gotten gains, unless Holmes and Sunstein have in mind constitutionalism itself, which of course guarantees the rights (including property rights) and political participation of all individuals, regardless of their political past. But even here I must note that the legal continuity and the constitutionalism of the Polish and Hungarian transitions offered similar or even better protection: It was Bulgaria that had a lustration process rather than Poland or Hungary.

What remains of the critical argument is the undoubtedly valid point concerning the link between early constitution making by constituent assemblies and the greater inflexibility of constitutions. Even here I should repeat my thesis, that the flexibility of piecemeal constitution making was coupled with severe legitimation problems that at times could have developed into full-fledged constitutional crises. Moreover, the dedifferentiation of constitutional and normal politics in step-by-step constitution making that Holmes and Sunstein argue for, can easily mean that instead of learning from unsuccessful arrangements, parties will change arrangements, even successful ones (like the independent status of the public prosecutor in Hungary currently under attack) for short-term political gain. Constitutional incoherence can just as easily be the result of a fragmented path like Hungary's and (until 1997) Poland's as genuine constitutional learning.

Are the Bulgarian and Romanian constitutions truly inflexible? Not if we compare them with constitutions like that of 1791, or even 1787, or, to take a much later case, the current German Grundgesetz, with its many entirely unchangeable provisions. But these extreme comparisons do not help, because the constitutions in question could still be too rigid for what should be periods of democratic design in countries without any democratic experience. The Bulgarian Constitution's chapter 9 divides the amendment process along two tracts. According to the first, the unicameral National Assembly can amend the constitution after three readings in which the positive vote is three-quarters of all representatives. If the measure fails but receives more than two-thirds support, it can be resubmitted after two months and then passed with only two-thirds support. I disagree with Holmes and Sunstein that this is a particularly demanding procedure. It is certainly less demanding than the Polish amendment rule in effect until 1994 (or 1997), which also mandated three readings of the bill, with the second chamber and the president having a role.[94] But I cannot see why this formula is in itself much more difficult than even the Hungarian one, unless we think that a two-month delay is particularly meaningful for constitutional amendments.[95]

However, in Bulgaria there is a second procedure that involves the election of a special Grand National Assembly (in effect the Constitutional Assembly),[96] to which alone the following issues are entrusted: (1) the adoption of a new constitution; (2) questions related to "changing (or changes in?) the state structure and form of government"[97]; (3) the legal validity of the constitution; (4) the status of treaties as part of the constitution; (5) the nonalienability of fundamental rights and the protection of some right even if states of war or emergency are declared; and, logically enough, (6) changes in the chapter dealing with amendments. A Grand National Assembly is to be called upon the initiative of at least two-thirds of the deputies and entertains only proposals supported by at least half of the deputies or the president. While one such proposal could be the writing of a new constitution, the last restriction implies that the Grand National Assembly could not become a "runaway convention." Only in some respects would it resemble a constitutional assembly: It is in session for at least two, but no more than five, months. Unlike a constitutional assembly, it would not fully dispose over its procedures and would have to make decisions by a two-thirds majority of all its members.

It is hard to object to such a differentiation of tracts of constitutional amendment without knowing its meaning.[98] The rule is unfortunately not formulated particularly well and omits specifying what is exactly meant by "changes" in the state structure and form of government and which chapters or paragraphs of the Constitution that are thus off limits to the ordinary processes of change. If the passage means only things like "unitary state" and "republican" or even "parliamentary form of government," there would remain a great number of changes in the governing structure and even structure of the state that the ordinary process of amendment could achieve. But the passage could also mean all articles dealing with the governmental form and state structure, and in this case there would be little that might be excluded from it. To take as an example, in spring 1997 it became clear that the direct election of a president from the opposition can produce a severe crisis if the government remains in the hands of a party with, as the French say, a much earlier democratic mandate. In my view at least, in the future, such a difficulty could be solved if the president would formally have the right to a one-time dissolution of Parliament, which could be restricted as in effect, though not in law, in France, to the period following his election. Highly knowledgeable Bulgarian friends could not tell me for certain whether normal Parliament could actually try to pass (and succeed in passing in the face of possible court challenge) such an amendment that could be interpreted either as shifting to a semipresidential system or as improving the functioning of an already semipresidential system.[99]

Of course, in the case of constitutions with elements that are unchangeable or even with multileveled amendment structures, constitutional courts must guard over the integrity of amendments. Such systems can, indeed, have "unconstitutional amendments"[100] and perforce constitutional review of lower-level amendments. As far as I can tell there have been very few attempts at constitutional amendment in Bulgaria, and thus we cannot yet know what the two-tiered system will really mean. It could mean in the future a tremendous strengthening of the Constitutional Court. The fact, however, that there have been few amendments can be taken to be a proof of the rigidity of the constitutional regime. On the other side, we should notice that the two-tiered regime allows for the expansion of democratic participation when important constitutional issues are at stake. Moreover, it does not do this through a devaluing of parliamentary democracy by plebiscitary practices, to which Holmes and Sunstein rightly object. What the system provides for is an electoral campaign primarily around constitutional issues that would not only educate the population to these but give them a role in decision through their representatives, avoiding the incoherence that amendments through plebiscites may produce.

If in the future, as it is quite possible, interpretation of the Bulgarian Constitution establishes its relatively flexible character, this might be seen as at odds with my thesis that sovereign constituent assemblies tend to produce constitutions that close the door to constitutional politics. I would "save the phenomena," however, by pointing to the legitimation deficit at the origins of this particular Constitution. The Bulgarian Communists had the power to push through a rapid timetable for constitution making, but their very doing so weakened their legitimacy. We can thus explain the many concessions to the opposition, some of whom nevertheless remained quite dissatisfied. Some deputies of the Grand National Assembly went on a hunger strike, and the president did not add his signature to the constitution. The framers were afraid to call a referendum to legitimate their work. No wonder perhaps, that they could not bring themselves to the point of detailing what was really enshrined in the document. The more they openly restricted future parlia-

ments, the less legitimate their effort would have become. Thus it will be relatively easy for a future court, if it wishes, to interpret what is enshrined in a
relatively narrow fashion. They will certainly not be restrained by the spirit of
the founders acting in the name of the popular sovereign.[101]

I do, however, see the Romanian constitution-making process as one dominated by a sovereign constituent assembly, appealing to revolutionary legitimacy.[102] Whatever we think of the National Salvation Front, it did overthrow
Nicolae Ceausescu, or was the only organized force to appear when his regime
was overthrown. The claim of representing the revolutionary will of the people could not be challenged; there was no rival group to raise an alternative
claim. The scenario of constitution making followed the classical revolutionary democratic model: insurrection, legal rupture, provisional government,
emergency decrees, calling an election of a constituent assembly, constitution,
and popular ratification. Unlike in Bulgaria, no one seriously challenged this
scenario, or the identity of those who generated it. In both the elections for the
assembly and the ratifying referendum the front won overwhelmingly. While
its methods at the constituent assembly were dictatorial and heavy-handed, it
was evident that everything accomplished could have been accomplished in a
more elegant and civilized fashion as well.

Clearly, I do not wish to apologize for the group around Ion Iliescu. They
imposed a constitution on a society that was not yet ready to resist, or to participate. In principle they might have proceeded differently. They could have
made a provisional constitution and waited for partners and rivals to emerge
with whom the new constitution could have been negotiated. But no such
project was formulated within Romanian society. This too contributed to the
legitimacy of the only available scenario: revolutionary democratic constitution making.

If my original hypothesis about this very model of constitution making
was right, one would justly expect a constitution well insulated against
future claims of change. The framers had both the incentive (they generally
do) and the claims of legitimacy to protect their work, if need be, against
future generations who might need a revolution of their own to overcome
these claims. By and large the Romanian Constitution of 1991 supports the
hypothesis. Its revision rule is the most difficult in the region, and even this
rule is limited by a number of unchangeable provisions. According to Articles 146, 147, and 148, changes in the Constitution can be initiated by the
president, one-fourth of the members of either chamber, or a large number
of voters (500,000) that have to sufficiently represent at least half the counties. At least two-thirds of each chamber must approve, or failing this, three-
fourths of the two chambers meeting together. Finally, a referendum must
ratify any change of the Constitution. The unitary character of government,
territorial integrity, the national language, as well as the republican form of
government, political pluralism, and independence of the system of justice

cannot be the subject of revision; nor can amendments eliminate basic rights or their legal guarantees.

Several of the provisions supposedly unchangeable are quite clear, especially those against any kind of diminution of the authority of the central state. But since none of the relevant constitutional passages are enumerated, who can tell what is unchangeable with respect to "political pluralism"? And here the answer available in the Bulgarian case cannot help much, because according to the Constitution (Article 145), any judgment of unconstitutionality by the Constitutional Court can be reversed by two-thirds vote of each chamber, the same vote more or less that is required to pass an amendment in the first place.[103] With this said, however, the difficulties in the amendment rule with respect to what is changeable are quite formidable, at least when compared with any other rule in the region. And indeed Romania has not amended, as far as I can tell, the constitution even once since its promulgation in 1991.[104] This does not mean total constitutional inflexibility. In 1995 a large number of government-sponsored statutes were declared unconstitutional. This meant either that the Court was using the opportunity to mold the constitution, or more likely, given its structural weakness, it was resisting the attempts on the part of the legislature to amend the constitution in the guise of ordinary statutes.[105] In either case we would have the hijacking of the constitutional channel by ordinary politics, something that revolutionary constitution makers provoke through the inflexible constitutions they tend to prefer.

The picture that emerges here does not allow a simple decision between parliamentary constitution making and sovereign constitutional assemblies. In each case, we have seen a successful and a less than successful variant. The parliamentary model is plagued by legitimation problems and the related disappearance of any veil of ignorance differentiating normal and constitutional politics. Nevertheless, as the Polish case shows, the legitimation deficit can be addressed if the opportunity for constitution making is genuinely opened up by the development of electoral, parliamentary, and coalition politics.[106] It may take good fortune for the latter to happen, as the failure of Hungarian constitution making between 1994 and 1998 will show.[107]

The revolutionary democratic model suffers not from legitimation problems as much as a tendency to close off *both* future learning and constitutional politics. Paradoxically, legitimation problems in the beginning, as in the case of Bulgaria, can contribute to the relatively greater flexibility of this model, to be sure recoverable in that case only through interpretation. Since democratic legitimacy is superior to its absence, the parliamentary road as in Poland seems to be the preferable option among the four. Nevertheless, from another point of view, that of constitutionalism, which is vital for the consolidation of democracy, Hungary and Bulgaria have not been behind Poland, and all three have been significantly ahead of Romania. This is expressed by the ability of Parliament to override Constitutional Court decisions, used on several occasions in Romania, but not in Poland where the new constitution abolishes this option altogether. What ties the three Round Table countries together in my view, as against Romania, the one country of revolution in the legal sense, is the model of legal continuity within which their transitions took place. Even the Bulgarian constitutional assembly operated, unclassically, within a negotiated framework that at all times adhered to the rules of existing legality. It is to this model of legal continuity that I will now turn.

Chapter 5

Constitution and Continuity in the East European Transitions

CONTINUITY AND ITS CRISIS

Creating New Constitutions

After the change of regimes, in a modern society, the normative integration of a new order depends in great measure on the creation of a constitutional framework. For such a framework to command legitimacy from the outset, it must be relatively broadly accepted, or must at the very least involve consensus among leading political groupings rather than being imposed by force by one of them. Yet the cost of consensus must not be too high on the level of the "design" of the constitutional document. For a constitution to be effective, it must coherently anchor the legislative, executive, and judicial processes of the political system in legally rigorous procedures and decision rules. To be legitimate, by liberal and democratic criteria, fundamental law ought to incorporate a full set of civil and political rights, as well as mechanisms guaranteeing the democratic and public character of the political process. A constitution will be coupled with constitutionalism only if mechanisms are provided ensuring the compliance of the branches of power with fundamental law. Thus, constitutional review, and usually constitutional courts, are necessary, even if not sufficient, requirements for the development of the practice of constitutionalism.[1]

Constitutionalism in a broad sense is a precondition of the consolidation of democracy, almost tautologically so. For actors to accept democracy "as the only game in town," they must have a realistic belief that others will also accept it and act accordingly. For political interests to accept others to exercise governmental power, even when they may have the means to resist, is possible only if there is a plausible expectation that those who rule will do so within a framework that protects the rules of the game and that they can have a fair chance to

167

come to power in the future using the same rules. Constitutionalism, the application of the rule of law to the structure of government, means precisely the submission t laws that are not at the immediate disposal of the rulers. It means that a relatively constant set of rules will be adhered to when coming to power, when exercising power, and when leaving positions of power. When all sides of an otherwise conflictual political field respect a constitutional order and use only its own rules in trying to change it, democracy is consolidated.

Constitutionalism, however, is hard to achieve when an old political order is abandoned and a new one is being designed. The violence, the raw exercise of political power that is so often held to be unavoidable when making new beginnings, can create institutions that are exposed to similar violence when the power constellation changes. It is during the violent beginnings that democratic forces need constitutionalism the most, thus at the very time when it is the most difficult to establish.

In the post-1989 societies of East and Central Europe, facing rapid economic transformation and potentially deep social, ideological, and even cultural divisions, the importance of producing a widely accepted, secure, and operational constitutional framework can hardly be overestimated. Given the history of statist penetration of the economy and the surviving preponderance of state property, present and future market actors desperately need the protection of a fundamental legal framework beyond the day-to-day discretion of governments and parliaments.[2] All the countries in the region inherit strong paternalistic and clientelistic propensities, which in the short term can be battled only by a rigorous system of "economic constitutionalism" enforced by the courts.[3] Moreover, sophisticated institutional designs that are capable of moderating strong social cleavages rooted in differences of ethnicity and worldview as well as (increasing) social inequality can function only if they are agreed upon on the level of the most fundamental rules of the game, that is, constitutional settlement. Finally, given a political situation that is in some respects revolutionary, only constitutional protections can securely limit the sovereign powers of legislatures that are inevitably tempted to assert extraordinary prerogatives and to turn themselves into quasi-permanent constituent assemblies.[4] Thus the task of making or producing a valid and accepted constitutional arrangement remains logically, politically, and normatively a preeminent one for those wishing to avoid the destructive logic of yet another permanent revolution, which could only reinstitute another authoritarian system, perhaps in different colors. Constitutional synthesis is a necessary though certainly not sufficient condition for the completion of a successful transition from a Communist to a democratic regime. To achieve the operation of such a framework according to the norms of constitutionalism is equally important.[5]

Can constitutionalism, however, be created or designed? This question hides actually two interrelated perplexities. Can constitutions be created at all?

And if the answer is affirmative, by what rules, procedures, or processes are they to be made or designed if they are to secure constitutionalism? Evidently just any arbitrary procedure of constitution making cannot and indeed will not be accepted. Yet the end of one constitutional reality before the new one has been established seems to inevitably produce a kind of legal vacuum that would tend to leave us no other option than such arbitrary (to some, violent)[6] act of beginning. It is this dilemma that produces the claim that perhaps constitutions cannot be made in spite of empirical historical evidence to the contrary. Fortunately, such "evidence" never much constrained G. W. F. Hegel:

> "Who is to frame the constitution?" This question seems clear, but closer inspection shows at once that it is meaningless, for it presupposes no constitution there, but only an agglomeration of atomic individuals. . . . But if the question presupposes an already existent constitution, then it is not about framing but only altering a constitution, and the very presupposition of a constitution directly implies that its alteration may come about only by constitutional means. In any case, however, it is absolutely essential that the constitution should not be regarded as something made.[7]

> [T]he constitution of any given nation depends in general of the character of its self-consciousness. . . . The proposal to give a constitution—even one more or less rational in content—to a nation *a priori* would be a happy thought overlooking precisely the factor in a constitution that makes it more or less an *ens rationis*. Hence every nation has the constitution appropriate and suitable for it. . . . A constitution is not just manufactured; it is the work of centuries. . . . A nation's constitution must embody its feeling for its rights and its position, otherwise there may a constitution there in a merely external way, but it is meaningless and valueless.[8]

Evidently, it has not skipped Hegel's attention that many constitutions were actually made during the epoch of the French Revolution; indeed he specifically refers to the failure of Napoleon to create a constitution for Spain. More generally he had to have in mind his own critique of revolutionary rationalism culminating in violence and terror. Accordingly, written constitutions can be made or designed by constitution makers, but such efforts will lead not to genuine constitutions that are actually adhered to, that is to say, constitutionalism, but to instability and violence ("the fury of destruction") followed by efforts at restoration.

Hegel's argument was of course anticipated by Edmund Burke, writing amazingly enough before the Reign of Terror, and in that version has influenced countless authors of the last two centuries. Even Alexis de Tocqueville and Hannah Arendt, who unlike Hegel were deeply impressed by the success of the Americans to produce new constitutions, repeated versions of the same basic argument as it pertained to the French case. Arendt's critique of the Abbé Sieyès, who, according to her, placed the *pouvoir constituant* in a state of nature of atomized individuals, is identical to Hegel's objections to constitution making ex nihilo. Moreover, for Arendt, the long and evolutionary English road to constitutionalism even without a written, insulated constitution was preferable to all continental attempts to design a constitution by either experts or even the mobilized population.⁹ In this too she followed Burke and Hegel, the latter otherwise no friend of the Common Law. According to Arendt, even the American effort at constitution making succeeded in one of its tasks, the foundation of constitutional government (i.e., constitutionalism), because, as Tocqueville was first to see, it was the work of preconstituted political bodies that were the source of the constitutional initiative of 1787, bodies that fully survived, with intact state constitutions, the crafting of the federal regime. Even on the level of content, many of the state constitutions anticipated some of the key "innovations" of the Philadelphia Convention. Thus, in this argument, the apparent counterevidence of American constitution making seems to support rather than undermine the Hegelian thesis. Finally, Tocqueville's warnings against the imitation of the successful U.S. Constitution, either in the case of Mexico or (less insistently) France, has exactly the same logic as Hegel's suspicion of rational, a priori constitution construction as applied to the case of Spain, for example.¹⁰

And yet the Americans themselves did make [a] new constitution[s]; they did successfully found a new secular order. It is precisely the act of founding a new political order, and not the establishment of new constitutional doctrines, that Tocqueville and Arendt consider the specific innovation of the American Revolution.¹¹ They do not for a moment accept the Southern theory according to which the Federal Constitution was merely a treaty,¹² an interpretation that, despite its resounding defeat in the Civil War, continued to be taken seriously by European advocates of undivided, sovereign constituent power.¹³ Both stress the importance of drafting, making, creating in this process of foundation, which in the U.S. context at least they systematically distinguish from violence. Moreover, we should note the part of the Hegelian conception that neither Tocqueville nor Arendt specifically take up, but in light of U.S. history evidently reject: the idea that constitution making in order to be successful must be based on the rules of revision of the inherited constitution. The Philadelphia Convention, no less than the French Constituent Assembly, rejected such a requirement after due consideration.¹⁴ Thus, the continuity of U.S. constitution making was on the levels of political bodies (stressed by Arendt) and political culture (stressed by Tocqueville), both of which linked the past and the future of the states through the constituent process. It is on these levels, and not on the level of constitutional-legal continuity, that the American Revolution incorporated a conservative moment.¹⁵ The Americans neither relied on the voluntaristic imagery of the *pouvoir constituant* creating the new constitution ex nihilo and a model of citizenship derived (implausibly) solely from the constitution itself, nor anticipated to their great fortune a form of identity rooted in a prepolitical reality like the ethnic nation. Their constitution(s) were the work, as Arendt has shown so well, of people politically organized.¹⁶

Arendt's analysis does not fully escape the thrust of the full Hegelian argument, which stressed full legal as well as political continuity. She admits that the solution of the problem of the origin of the power to make a constitution was not automatically that of the origin of the authority of law, which, according to her, was as troublesome in America as it was in France.[17] Could the solution of only one of these problems avoid the collapse of the constituent into the state of nature and the logic of permanent revolution? In the United States the answer was apparently a positive one. But the preconditions for this answer, legitimate and viable republican forms of government on the provincial level at the moment of federal constitution making, could not be generally duplicated elsewhere in the face of crumbling old regimes.[18]

Continuity in Constitution Making in the Transitions

A Hegelian stress on constitutional continuity as against constitutional creation seems especially out of place in East and Central Europe. Let me repeat that Hegel's focus was on the actual working constitutions of political regimes, and he did not in effect consider nonworking and unworkable legal documents to be constitutions at all. Using this standard, we come up against the rather intractable state of affairs that there was no possibility of any organic development of liberal-democratic constitutions from the actually operative, unwritten constitution of Soviet-type societies, involving the thoroughgoing juridical primacy and dominance of discretionary power, the very opposite of "constitutionalism." None of the established bodies of the existing regimes had the legitimacy, moreover, to become the sources of a new power to make constitutions. None of them could be allowed to survive within the new structure of power unless totally transformed. Finally, none of the political traditions developed in the forty to seventy years of the relevant regimes involving pervasive authoritarianism and clientelism could be used as parts of a liberal-democratic constitutional synthesis.[19]

At the same time, despite superficial appearances, the constitutional ideas of East and Central European cultural or "value" conservatives also could not satisfy the demands of Hegel's conception. Any attempt to return to the supposed models, precedents, and legal rules to the pre-Communist epoch, which have had no institutional existence for one to two generations, would involve all the paradoxes of restorations and would not in principle be able to avoid the dilemmas of rupture and constitution making ex nihilo. Indeed, any vision of restoration is inevitably just as abstract and rationalistic with respect to the actual institutions, traditions, and political cultures that have emerged in long "intervening periods" of Communist regimes as constitutional images based on rationalistic construction or blind imitation.

Given the inadequacy of Communist institutions for constitutional development, East and Central Europeans seemed to have been stuck with one of three equally precarious models of discontinuity: restoration, imitation, or rationalistic constitutional design, which, in spite of their very different normative assumptions, may all be equally unlikely to succeed. Yet in my view there always was room for innovation instead, specifically in the method of constitution making itself, that was indeed exploited in many of the countries.

We have seen that the continuity thesis can be differentiated into different strands involving the continuity of political bodies, political culture, and law, all of which were insisted upon by Hegel. In Arendt's version (the one I will use here) this differentiation reduces to the one between source of power and source of legal authority. The analytical separation implies the possibility of reversing the choice of the American constitution makers and building the element of continuity primarily on the dimension of law, hoping thereby to avoid a legal state of nature. Indeed, in 1989–90 most Central and East European constitution makers initially made the opposite choice of the Philadelphia Convention and the *Assemblée Constituante* and chose to preserve and use the rules of revision of their inherited constitutions. In the process, however, unlike the drafters of Philadelphia, they hoped to obliterate or change beyond recognition all their inherited institutions. If organized political bodies, the associations and movements of a fledgling civil society, did participate in constitutional change, these (unlike the associations of U.S. political society) were without any legal and constitutional status under the old regimes. And conversely, the inherited Communist parliaments that were to ratify the results in terms of the requirements of continuity were to disappear in the new constitutions and were to be replaced by entirely new, freely elected bodies. The act of ratification of the old parliaments furthermore was not supposed to be based on their own power, but was to involve only the exercise of legal, procedural requirements. Power, on the other hand, was exercised by bodies without any legal status, the Round Tables of Poland, Hungary, Czechoslovakia, Bulgaria, and initially the GDR, composed of the ruling party and variously defined oppositions. These bodies, however, were to be entirely provisional, without being provisional governments.[20]

In the period between 1989 and 1990 at least, few Central Europeans would have accepted Hans Kelsen's thesis that using a constitution's own rule of revision necessarily involves the persistence of the original constitutional identity.[21] They were far closer to H. L. A. Hart's argument showing that logically at least all elements of a constitution, including its very amendment rule, could be changed by using the original amendment rule, thereby achieving an entirely new legal order.[22] This argument is especially impressive in demonstrating the possibility of total legal change without any legal hiatus whatsoever. Undoubtedly, this is what some Polish and Hungarian constitution makers had in mind when they pursued the road of amendments toward the production of entirely new constitutions.[23] But even their Czechoslovak and Bulgarian colleagues stayed within the same argumentative structure.

They envisaged constitutional assemblies that would (followers of Carl Schmitt would say "illogically") continue to use the revision rules of the old constitutions, at least until this rule yielded a new method of ratification as well as new constitutions.

Evidently, more than mere legal issues were involved in choosing the road of amendment as against a direct rupture in fundamental legality. The Central and East European transformations, as veritable "revolutions" against "the" Revolution, involved learning from and innovative response to the history of modern revolutions, and in particular the heritage of permanent revolution left to them by the Bolsheviks. It is for this reason, and not because of any links on the level of the history of ideas, that the reflections of Hegel, Tocqueville, and Arendt on the relationship of modern revolutions and constitution making help us understand the project and the dilemmas of the new constitution makers. Evidently they sought to accomplish the task of founding new political orders without violence and the wholesale violation of rights. They (Romania was the most clear exception) have responded to the normative "perplexities of founding a new regime" by resolutely avoiding the legal state of nature that Arendt linked to the logic of revolution and dictatorship. Without knowing, they replied on the level of action to the Burkean warning that total rupture with and uncompromising hatred of the recent past leads to loss of identity and vulnerability to demagogic dictatorship.

In all this, East Central European democratic oppositions were helped by *the one original theory of transition* that emerged from the region, the Polish and later Hungarian conception of "new evolutionism," or "self-limiting revolution," which assumed from the outset that the changes in the periphery of the Soviet imperium would have to be rooted in the rebuilding of civil society rather than in a direct struggle for state power. Thus, the road to transformation would have to be at all stages negotiated, involving as a result continuities with the existing system. Even if this idea was proposed originally for geostrategic reasons, some actors within the democratic oppositions, reflecting on the history of revolutions, developed a normative, "internal" relationship to it.[24] From the August 1980 agreements in Gdansk to the Round Table agreements of early 1989, the main line of the Polish opposition followed such a legal and negotiated strategy.

Paradoxically, by the time the success of the strategy indicated to other countries that the geopolitical reasons for self-limitation no longer existed, the institutional innovation crystallized around formal Round Table negotiations had already taken hold in at least four other countries. Whether the actors followed normative conviction, only reexpressed the rejection of violence by whole populations, or thought the method merely convenient for the peaceful disengagement from formal power of a Communist Party that still controlled the means of violence, the consensus around the method of self-limiting system change was maintained.[25] When it became clear that no substantive political concessions had to be made to the outgoing regime as in Poland,[26] formal (rather than substantive) constitutional continuity came to be the sole dimension on which the strategy of self-limitation was to subsequently rest.[27] The threat to constitutionalism through the violence of new beginnings was thereby effectively overcome; if the founders themselves submitted to the rule of law at all times, every one else would have little justification, subsequently, to undertake extralegal actions. As the Hungarian Constitutional Court was to assert, the rule of law can be created only through the rule of law from the very outset.

Evidently in the relevant countries, the constitutionalization of the self-limiting revolution certainly did work to the extent that large-scale violence and the massive destruction of rights so characteristic of all revolutions involving social and economic stakes like the transformations in East Central Europe were indeed avoided. Romania, where there was a full rupture of the legal-constitutional order,[28] serves as the instructive counterexample even if most (but not all!) of the fighting came first and the formal abrogation of the old constitution second. It seems, unfortunately, that the Russian model, which has now definitely entered the path of legal rupture, will continue to give us further indirect evidence of the merits of legal continuity, even if this method could no longer be followed in that country.

And yet the legal basis of systemic change on the ground of constitutional continuity was peculiar to say the least. The constitutions of Soviet-type societies were quite evidently fictional.[29] They were parts of the characteristic double constitutional reality of each country, which involved the inorganic juxtaposition of two dimensions. First, there was the already mentioned unwritten authoritarian constitutional practice of the dominant party-state that was effectively used without, however, any trace of constitutionalism. And second, every single Communist country also had a written but unused constitution, formally democratic, that was produced for little more than (in part external) public relations. The written constitutions were strange documents from a formal point of view. They tended to contain only the weakest references ("the leading role of the Party") to the operative constitutional reality, but even these were contradictory in terms of the main thrust of the documents. The latter tended to affirm, in terms of a Marxian rejection of the separation of powers but in countries with rubber-stamp parliaments, a kind of extreme parliamentary sovereignty that had no place for any kind of constitutional review.[30] The foundations of constitutionalism were thus absent from the written documents as well as from the very different unwritten practice. And yet elements pointing in that direction were also included in the texts, completely different than the actual practice, like the independence of the public prosecutor from the government, a homage to a very liberal dimension of late Russian imperial legal practice. Finally, in federal states like Czechoslovakia and Yugoslavia, the written constitutions contained federal or confederal provisions that would have been (and were to be) wholly unworkable, but were of little consequence as long as the unwritten and highly centralistic constitutional practice was intact.

The fictional written constitutions of the Soviet type were thus compliments paid by authoritarian vice to democratic virtue. They were, however, not entirely without political consequences even under the old regimes. Constitutional concessions could be used as symbolic payments to purchase the goodwill of some groups inclined to such coin, as in the case of Slovak nationalist sentiment in the turbulent days of 1968–69. Constitutional changes seeking to bring the written constitutions closer to the unwritten one could be the context for protesting against the latter, as in the case of Poland in 1975 and Hungary in 1988. Human rights provisions, along with international treaty obligations, could become the basis of well-publicized appeals by fledgling oppositions, notably KOR in Poland, Charta 77 in Czechoslovakia, the democratic opposition in Hungary, and the religious opposition in the GDR. The fact that in four countries at least oppositions already appealed to the Communist constitutions made their use in the transition process all the more plausible. What was once merely fictional by this time acquired a measure of normative reality rooted in action. On a more formal level, the most important thing about the old written constitutions was that they each had relatively clear amendment provisions, and thus fictional constitutions could in principle be used to produce real ones.

In spite of all this, the strategy of legal continuity with a past whose actual constitutional order was that of a dictatorship remained difficult to justify. The key achievement of this strategy, that of constitutionalism, which meant a greater adherence to the rule of law by organs of government than ever before in these countries, thus lay on precarious foundations. From the point of view of liberal constitutionalism, it was hoped that in time regular adherence would help to produce new motivations. But time is what many of the countries did not have.

The Crisis of Constitutional Continuity

Today the method of constitution making on the basis of legal continuity seems to be in shambles. Some theorists consider it largely responsible for the difficulties of East and Central European constitution makers.[31] Others, originally seeing the method as innovative, have since come to de-emphasize it.[32] It seems that there was perhaps no alternative to "fixing one's boat in an open sea" or repeating Baron Münchhausen's feat of pulling himself out of a swamp by his own hair ("bootstrapping").[33] A first look at the results seems to fully support these views. In Czechoslovakia the intractable "federal" amendment provisions of the inherited constitution played a role in the dissolution of the federation.[34] Subsequently, new constitutions were produced by the freely elected legislatures of the Slovak and Czech Republics, breaking with inherited legality by accomplishing the breakup of the federal state without a referendum.[35] The newly elected GDR Volkskammer did not even debate the new constitutional draft given to it by the Round Table. In the process of avoiding the enactment of a new constitution this parliament carried out not only its own, but also the country's self-annihilation.[36] In Bulgaria a new constitution was created, but by a constituent assembly. To be sure, here the rules of revision of the inherited constitution were maintained until legally replaced. But the new Bulgarian constitution has had legitimation problems from the beginning, best symbolized by the hunger strike of a large group of opposition deputies against enacting it, who claimed unconvincingly but powerfully that the constitution and especially its difficult amendment procedures were fruits of Communist imposition.[37] Partially analogously, a new constitution was created in Hungary through two major and some minor stages of using the method of amendments. But here too, the legitimacy of the constitution was repeatedly challenged and in fact some elements of undesirable continuity with the old constitution, notably the revision rule itself, were maintained. When between 1994 and 1998 there was a determined attempt to draft a new constitution, the whole effort came to nothing because of the triumph of short-run political interests. Finally in Russia, the whole method of constitution making through amendments produced an inconsistent monster with hundreds of revisions that came crashing down in October 1993, perhaps symbolizing the end of an epoch in which revolutions were confined within inherited legality.

To be sure the results represent hardly a clear-cut defeat for the strategy of legal continuity. In Poland the legal continuity was never violated, and yet some important pieces of a constitutional synthesis did emerge in the first five years. To be sure the process threatened to repeatedly come to an end without producing a coherent relation without the powers of the president and those of Parliament. Yet, in 1997 an effort to create an entirely new constitution approved by a referendum did come to successful conclusion. In Russia, where the same strategy was abandoned, an independent constituent assembly operating outside of the sitting Parliament in the U.S. style in June–July 1993 could also not produce an acceptable result. The president who called this council could no more accept the inevitable concessions to the subunits of the federation than he could live with the parliamentary republic the sitting legislature would have produced.[38] The collapse of the method of continuity, and the clash of the (semi) legitimacy of the president with the (semi) legality of Parliament were coupled with massive violence. Thus on December 12, 1993, only Boris Yeltsin was in the position to repeat Napoleon's alleged dictum, "je suis le pouvoir constituant." Yet it remains definitely unclear whether the ratification of his draft on that day (coupled with the weak showing of reform parties) could produce anything more than a constitution of the (inevitably temporary) winners.

Thus we need not waste time on stressing the superiority of the Central European patterns, which have all avoided large-scale violence to a scenario of complete rupture, such as the one in Russia. In fact upon closer examination it turns out that most of the countries that embarked on a strategy of continuity did not abandon it, and thus in these countries we cannot speak of complete failure. The Bulgarian transition shows that it was possible to combine complete legal continuity and full innovation. Yet even in the Polish and Hungarian cases the method of amendments produced constitutional frameworks at least temporarily workable. In the case of the GDR the shift from the inherited legality to the law of the GFR, by way of a treaty ratified by both parliaments, never involved legal discontinuity. Here, the method of continuity could have facilitated a process by which the constitution of the Federal Republic as a whole was fully replaced, according to its own internal rule (Article 146 of the *Grundgesetz*). While the option chosen was different, it too was based on an internal possibility of the *Grundgesetz* (Article 23). Thus one cannot speak of the failure of the method of continuity in Germany, but at best one can regret that, of the options it made available, perhaps the wrong one, or the wrong combination, was chosen.[39] Finally, the Czech and Slovak Republics in the end smoothly shifted from the continuity of the source of law, the inherited constitution, to the continuity of legitimate bodies, the two republican parliaments that had already exercised power for more than two years. In other words, the amended old constitution that could not be used to save the federation did prove adequate for the task of electing, in fully contested elections, two legitimate republican assemblies that assumed, in each case, unrestricted constituent powers.[40]

It may not be too early to draw a preliminary balance sheet:

1. It seems that wherever the identity of the state was in doubt, the method of legal continuity led to failure to produce a new constitution for the inherited state unit. This was the case in Czechoslovakia where the largely unworkable revision rule of the previously federated state did not allow the making of a new constitution. Here indeed the requirement that the constituent assembly operate under inherited rules (bicameral structure, the difficult amendment rule giving veto power to 31 out of 150 deputies in the upper house) turned out to be illogical.[41] But under different legal and political circumstances the method of continuity failed to produce a new constitution in other previously federated states like Russia and Yugoslavia, as well as under a state whose citizens wished unity with another one, the GDR.

2. We have only two instances of full-fledged revolutionary breaks in constitutional legality, Romania and Russia. Significantly, in these instances the complete abandonment of old constitutions was linked to large-scale violence, even elements of a civil war.[42] In both cases new constitutions

emerged, but in each case these are constitutions imposed by a dominant group, a fact that is all too evident in their internally authoritarian, presidential features. With the rapid change of political constellations, one has reason to believe that the legitimacy of these constitutions too will be difficult to maintain, in spite of popular ratification. The fact that before ratification in Russia the government permitted no public debate on the constitution even by the contending electoral parties potentially undermines legitimacy from the beginning.

3. In the three instances where the method of continuity was maintained to the end, in Poland, Hungary, and Bulgaria, the extent to which the emerging constitutional syntheses are new, and legitimate depended on specific national political constellations. It seems that when in Bulgaria such a process produced a supposedly final, or rather difficult to amend, synthesis too early (when new political forces have not yet fully crystallized), there were inevitably the greatest problems of legitimacy. But it was also possible to miss the constitution-making moment as initially in Poland, where Lech Walesa's campaign to break up the Solidarity block in 1990 fragmented the power that could have then passed one of the available drafts. To be sure the window of constitution-making opportunity can reopen.[43] In the intermediate Hungarian case, the problems of which I will examine later, the present constitution, created in stages, is certainly not perfect in terms of either coherence or liberal and democratic criteria.[44] In particular the inadequacy and latent ambivalence of the revision rule inherited from the past is clear.[45] Nevertheless, in terms of contents, this constitution is already workable and could be easily improved. At the same time, the legitimacy of the constitutional order in the normative if not the sociological sense,[46] which has been contested by right-wing advocates of a second revolution, cannot be easily increased by more constitutional tinkering.

It seems that the very process that helped to avert violence and massive illegality in some countries has exposed the amended or new constitutions to revolutionary challenges that contest their legitimacy. Such challenges to the negotiated transitions and the interim or new constitutions have been significant in Poland, Bulgaria, and Hungary even if the forces behind them, elements of the radical right, repeatedly experienced electoral defeat in each of these countries. At any future moment of instability, the right that now links the decline of its electoral fortunes precisely to the constitutionalist avoidance of a real revolution can remount its challenge. The specter of permanent revolution has not yet been banished. At the same time, from other points of view than the radical right, one can claim as well that the self-limiting revolution was not revolutionary enough and that the legal-constitutional acceptance of parts of the past involved too many concessions to "tradition" and "continuity."

Many interpreters who continue to admit the dangers of radical revolution now also call our attention to the liabilities of system change through continuity, meaning both a transition negotiated at all stages and the absence of a legal break in constitutionality. Focusing on only the major points, these are:

1. The fiction of legal continuity allows ample opportunity for old elites to conserve their earlier positions, under the cover of the rule of law. This points to the bad alternative of either limiting the rule of law or doing nothing about the "conversion" of nomenklatura power (Kis).[47] The conversion of power and the legal protection of the political activity for former elites prepares the electoral return of post-Communist groupings in the face of popular dissatisfaction with reform (Smolar).[48]
2. The appearance of continuity helps a revaluation of the earlier Communist regime, resulting in a loss of memory and a weakening of historical consciousness. The absence of a revolution interferes with a full thematization of the crimes of the past and the assessment of full responsibility for them (Smolar).[49]
3. The fiction of constitutional continuity tends to produce the illusion that legal continuity in all areas of regulation is in itself positive and all legal vacuums must be abhorred. As a result, inevitably, a whole series of authoritarian regulations, laws, and even governmental orders survive that continue to have repressive implications and can be used by new forms of authoritarian statism.[50]
4. In a continuous transition, the population is demobilized, does not participate in its own liberation, does not come to think of the democratic republic as its own creation, and, consequently, can easily become alienated from democratic politics in the face of later difficulties (Kis).[51]
5. The new constitution does not emerge as the result of democratic participation. Thus the new system lacks a fundamental source of legitimacy that would be the basis of the emergence of a tradition based on moral conviction that could stabilize the constitutional order in the future (Kis).[52]

I myself have stressed four of these aspects (1, 2, 4, and 5), originally thematized by the radical right in Hungary at least, under the headings of the desire for purges, political justice, the recovery of revolutionary experience, and the contestation of the legitimacy of the new regime.[53] It is significant that liberal writers such as János Kis and Aleksander Smolar do recognize the force of some combination of these criticisms coming from the right. The third point significantly has not been stressed by right-wing critics, undoubtedly because their opposition to constitutional continuity most certainly does not extend to continuities in authoritarian regulations in general. Instead, it is liberal writers and politicians, fearing the renewal of authoritarianism in different colors, that are likely to make this particular point.

At issue is not the sociological importance of each of the arguments. They all correspond to specific and genuine experiences and injuries of whole strata of society, and, ideologically, the arguments coming from the right have already played a role in mobilization. I am here only interested in their applicability to the problem of constitutional continuity and the extent to which they would now justify the rejection of the strategy of "self-limitation." My specific responses to the five arguments follow:

1. The democratic opposition in Hungary at least has rightly stressed that they wish a radical exchange of institutions and not of large groups of persons per se. Aside from the corresponding sentiments of the population, preferring through the whole period expert leadership and management to yet another campaign of purges, two considerations support the original liberal point of view. First, no counterelite of experts is available to occupy the relevant positions, only less-successful members of the same system of partially meritocratic, partially politocratic selection. Second, large-scale purges lead to appointments by state organs and almost inevitably to a renewal in new colors of just the political clientelism one seeks to abolish. It is better to concentrate on the demolition of these structures by fostering meritocratic and market-oriented forms of selection even if these unfortunately or fortunately will not be able to weed out ex-Communist officials as a stratum, without regard to merit and demerit. Moreover, since the transitions were negotiated and the ability of successor parties to compete electorally was guaranteed, there is little justification for now complaining that they are doing this successfully. Did they really have greater resources in Poland than the liberal parties of the government? Or did the former help prepare their own defeat by their disunity and their move to the right, which astonishingly allowed the post-Communists to win in the center of the electoral spectrum?

2. The task of coming to terms with the past is that of cultural reflection, not of law; that of intellectuals, historians, publicists, and reflecting ordinary citizens, not of lawyers, judges, and policemen. When such a task is taken over by a legal system, reflection is cut short by the exercise of power and the legal system itself is inevitably perverted.[54]

3. In spite of the fact that even the Hungarian Constitutional Court at times has tended to extend the idea of constitutional continuity to the idea that all legal rupture is per se undesirable and even dangerous, the interpretation is mistaken. It is undoubtedly inevitable that the Court should insist on old statutes and decrees remaining in effect until they are formally replaced by Parliament or declared unconstitutional by the Court itself. But there is rarely a convincing reason for the maintenance of legal provisions recognized as unconstitutional. The absence of relevant new

legislation in itself is not enough of a reason, because the absence of specific legal regulation in a given context does not automatically have negative consequences. A legal vacuum in one area (e.g., media regulation)
could be amply compensated by the fact that there is regulation in other
related areas (e.g., constitutional law, labor law, contract law). Constitutional continuity can just as much provide a stable framework in which
the oppressive aspects of the old legality are abolished without damage
to civil rights, as a model for the compulsive maintenance of even unconstitutional regulation until replaced by Parliament.

4. The negotiated character of the transitions did demobilize movements,
   though in Hungary the form that negotiations took was as much the
   result of the low level of mobilization of society. Nevertheless, as the
   Czechoslovak example shows, mass activity could proceed together with
   negotiations and the procedural continuity of the legal system. To be
   sure this example also shows that when it came to constitution making a
   year later, the method of continuity in the given bi-national context
   turned out to be incompatible with constitution making reduced to "an
   activity of government."[55] The representatives of a mobilized Czech and
   Slovak population, on the whole opposed to separation, could have perhaps succeeded where the experts representing the two governments
   failed. But can one create such a mobilization and such a revolutionary
   experience from above?

5. The Hungarian case indeed seems to show that the method of continuity
   has had difficulty in producing a fully legitimate new constitution that
   would have presupposed the kind of democratic experience and participation to which János Kis refers. But was the method of continuity itself
   or constitution making restricted to the level of political society primarily
   responsible for this outcome? In my view, in this context, too, Arendt was
   closer to the truth when, in the spirit of Tom Paine, she maintained that
   constitutions as acts of governments and their experts are no substitutes
   for constitutions constituting governments.[56] But in what sense could
   constitutions become the acts of a people in a model of legal continuity?

I agree with Kis's subtle argument that the change of regimes was characterized by legal, procedural continuity in the context of a genuine break or
vacuum in legitimacy. At the time of the Round Table agreements the old
institutions no longer had political legitimacy, and the unelected parties of the
opposition had to admit that they too had no democratic credentials of any
type. I would only add that without a philosophy of history, the participants
also could not claim a revolutionary legitimacy derived from the poetry of the
future. Thus it was all important to produce democratic legitimacy for the
new constitutional arrangements, a requirement that the method of continuity as practiced in Hungary so far did not satisfy.

At issue is not some kind of Kelsenian continuity of the original Communist legal system. Even if they cannot regard their constitution as their own work, Hungarians rightly do not regard this document as simply the same old constitution. But it is a fact that the new constitution being rooted in the old constitution's rule of revision carries only a minimum of a procedural, legal legitimacy that is pace Max Weber, much too shallow without a wider, democratic (though also procedural) legitimacy. Furthermore, the constituent work of self-selected elites, of the old Parliament, and the two parties of the April 1990 pact that received less than 50 percent of the vote in the most complete electoral round, the first round of the parliamentary election, or even the highly activist quasi-constitution-making activity of the Constitutional Court are clearly unable to generate any new legitimacy in a strongly democratizing setting.[57] While the acceptability of the constitution is very much enhanced by the fact that it indeed was at two stages at least the result of bargaining and not imposition by any one of the parties or groupings, the importance of this fact is diminished when the population feels alienated from the political elite as a whole. It is not especially convincing, in light especially of low levels of later electoral participation, to argue that the free elections somehow retroactively validate the rules under which they took place. While in forthright claims of revolutionary legitimacy a future can retroactively legitimate the past,[58] a bashful revolutionary legitimation that dresses itself in the colors of modern competitive party politics, but hides various levels of elite bargaining, cannot be sufficient to ground a new constitution.

I am not claiming the absence of belief in the validity of the new regime, of legitimacy in the sociological sense. The fact of replacing the Communist and ultimately foreign-imposed regime and having established a national one that resembles the Western democracies already carries generalized support. So does the old "negative" legitimacy in a new form: Many Hungarians, for example, are rightly convinced that given unavoidable constraints their country is still in a relatively acceptable condition especially when compared with others on the road from state socialism. While these sources of acceptance can produce an empirical belief in the validity of a regime, they do not add up to its legitimacy in the normative sense, which exists in modern societies only when strong democratic arguments that can be marshaled to demonstrate this validity. Democratic legitimacy in the normative sense can become especially important in the face of potential conflicts and crises to which the constitutional system remains exposed. In such contexts, even the refurbishing of an inevitably threatened empirical legitimacy depends on the normative resources that can be mobilized by the defenders of the new regime.

Two questions therefore should be asked. The first is whether the practice of constitutionalism can compensate for an initial deficit in the democratic legitimacy of a constitution. And if not, secondly, whether democratic legitimacy of a constitutional construction created through continuity with a rejected old regime can be significantly reconstructed midstream without damage to constitutionalism, without the threat of a "second revolution."[59]

THE HUNGARIAN CASE

Constitutionalism and Constitutional Court

The Hungarian case, as it has developed since the drafting of the constitution, is the ideal terrain for an examination of the thesis that constitutional continuity with a rejected Communist old regime can produce a system of the rule of law supported by democratic legitimacy. Only here was the method of amendments consistently followed at all stages that both presupposed a constitutional framework for constitution making and produced a more or less new constitution. More importantly, here was the most determined and rigorous attempt to turn the constitution into a working, legal document as a limiting framework for political power, implying the establishment of constitutionalism along with a new constitution. It is the combination of the method of continuity with a very early assertion of constitutionalism in the strong sense that makes the Hungarian case so decisive for those seeking to test both the innovative aspects and the pitfalls of a self-limiting revolution in the legal sense.[60]

The agency that is first and foremost dedicated to the establishment of constitutionalism in Hungary is the Constitutional Court.[61] Indeed, most analyses of constitutional developments in this country, and in Central Europe in general, tend to focus on the activity of this new Constitutional Court. Given the patchwork nature of the new Hungarian Constitution and the variety of semilegitimate instances that have produced it, the most attractive and to Westerners (especially Americans and Germans) the most recognizable feature of the constituent process has been the series of remarkable decisions of this court. These decisions evidently produced some elements of the current constitution through a creative interpretive process.[62] More importantly, however, the Court's practice has introduced liberal constitutionalism in the strong sense of actually restraining the actions of the executive and legislature in the name of fundamental legality.[63]

The Hungarian Constitutional Court has defined its own activity as that of the guardian of human rights in the midst of quasi-revolutionary transformation, a task accomplished by maintaining legal continuity and security during the political replacement of one system by another. This stance involved a strong insistence on the principle that "one cannot create a rule of law state with methods other than the rule of law."[64] For the Court this meant that although the specifically *revolutionary* aspect of the Hungarian system change was establishing a *Rechtsstaat* where there was none before, it was nevertheless the duty of all governmental organs to act from the beginning *as if* a

Rechtsstaat had already existed.[65] This insistence that defined the self-limiting feature of the system change was made possible by the legally continuous nature of the transition that was based on treating the inherited constitution *as if* it were actually the basic law of the land. It is important to stress that the Court considers the establishment of the *Rechtsstaat* to be a radical break with the past. Implicit in the Court's judgment is the idea, that in view of the legal nihilism of the old regime inherited from its revolutionary past and maintained in the paternalist-conservative epoch as well, a new revolutionary vacuum in constitutionality would in fact represent continuity with the "legal order" of the past. This continuity would be, I would add, with the unwritten, operative rather than the written, inoperative constitution. To repeat: Any kind of revolutionary legality would in this argument represent no break at all with the inherited pattern of legality. In such a context, paradoxically, it is the insistence on (ultimately fictional) continuity (or continuity with a fiction, the old constitution) that produces a radical break, while an apparently radical break maintains the existing state of affairs. The best part of the activity of the Court is based on this difficult, paradoxical, but in my view *true* proposition.

It is hardly disputable that the Court has indeed been a strong defender of human rights in the transition.[66] It has eliminated capital punishment and personal identity numbers, declared the unconstitutionality of a law providing for retroactive (political) justice, and severely limited the *re*privatization of state property, all in the face of a largely hostile legislative majority that never abandoned its belief in a purely parliamentarian notion of sovereignty interpreted in a majoritarian sense. Those who present the record of the Court as simply a success story find ample evidence to justify their positions in these elements of the record.[67] To be sure, from the point of view of the defenders of political retribution and full reprivatization this very history is that of the abuse of legitimate power, in some versions by a creation (and even creature) of the last Communist government, in other versions by a product of a difficult and contradictory transitional period.[68] It has, however, not been difficult for the Court and its defenders to refute these arguments, which were in any case based on a very questionable historical reconstruction of the transition and the surrounding negotiations. Themselves among the architects of the various pacts, the leaders of the right-wing government, like József Antall, were in no position to support such criticisms of the Court.[69]

Yet from another point of view as well, one that focuses on keeping the democratic process open as one of the key roles of judicial review,[70] the Court has not been particularly successful. It failed to protect the independence of electronic media from governmental control, apparently not understanding the deep, potential threat to electoral politics in a new and inexperienced democracy. Moreover the Court refused to fully defend the ability of the president of the republic to insist on consensus in areas where the democratic nature of the transition could very well depend on it (appointment and dismissal of the heads of radio and television, command of the armed forces). Here too the majority of the judges seem to have been unaware of the dangers that ruling majorities could present to the democratic process and the democracy reinforcing feature of the consensus that even a relatively weak president is capable of imposing in constitutionally appropriate contexts.[71] Indeed in the discussions around the presidency and the media, the Court has been inclined to assert a majoritarian interpretation of the constitution belied by many provisions of the text, including the ones that have established such a strong Constitutional Court.[72] Thus, while an effective defender of liberal constitutionalism, the Court has not been equally committed to democratic constitutionalism (which is not to be confused with an inclination to defer to parliamentary majorities).[73]

Only when facing a government much less to its taste, the socialist liberal coalition of 1994–98, did the Court rediscover the need to protect the democratic process even against the parliamentary majority. In 1997 it was entirely right to decide that it was wrong of the government and Parliament to try to subvert a petition and popular referendum initiative (however stupid and manipulative the actual cause may have been) by suddenly ordering its own referendum on somewhat different questions, after the required number of signatures had been submitted.[74] But even this decision was somewhat tainted by a previous one, in which the Court supported the right of Parliament to quash a referendum sponsored by a small, hard-line Communist successor party. It will be interesting to see if the Court will be willing to keep the democratic process open, if need be, against the center right government formed in 1998.

To be sure the record of the Court, apparently ambiguous from almost any political point of view, could be seen as an effective back and forth movement from decisions where the defense of fundamental rights must be asserted even against the governing national democratic majority, to decisions where the prerogatives of this majority should be conceded if the Court is to preserve its own effectiveness. Furthermore, it may be a testimony of its status above politics that no political side is fully satisfied with all of its decisions. However, such an independent profile certainly ought not be achieved merely by allowing different political sides to alternatively influence the decisions of the Court.[75] Indeed, in the Court's own view of itself its decisions are not influenced by any outside forces. Instead, aside from the letter and the spirit of the Constitution ("the invisible constitution"), the Court's decisions are supposedly determined only by the structure of precedents created by its own activity as the country's first case law court.[76] And yet it is precisely in this important dimension of its activity, in adhering to the general framework of its own precedents, that the Court's inconsistencies have come into sharpest relief.[77] Within a relatively short period in each instance, its two sets of decisions, on reprivatization and on the fate of a 1974 governmental order on control of radio and television, have been each plagued by important inconsistencies. In the former case, the Court initially forbade full reprivatization of land among other things because this would be unfair to nonowners and would violate the legal equality of collective forms of property. Subsequent decisions then proceeded to forget these two reservations, or to bypass them by masking partial reprivatization as "novation of old promises."[78] In the latter case the Court initially declared the 1974 order giving the government control over the media unconstitutional and gave Parliament six months to produce a new law on the media. When such a new law was not produced within the allotted time, the Court then proceeded to leave in effect the still unconstitutional regulation indefinitely, thereby removing all pressure on the government to change a legal state of affairs that very much suits it on the eve of general elections.[79] Let me admit that in both cases the Court faced a strong campaign by the governmental parties that involved coordinated and uncoordinated forms of parliamentary and extraparliamentary pressure. Yet nothing indicates that the judges were particularly frightened by these campaigns![80]

Further grave inconsistencies followed in the period of the socialist liberal coalition. The decisions concerning referenda represent only one example of this. More fatefully for the future, after allowing the previous government to interpret social rights as mere goals of the state that cannot be judicially enforced especially in a difficult economic setting, the Court now suddenly became a doctrinaire defender of "acquired rights" in an economic context fraught with potential fiscal disaster.[81] While in the end, the Court decisions did not really affect the success of the stabilization program of 1995, and may have even provided a safety valve for channeling discontent, this was hardly what was intended. The political costs to the liberal SZDSZ, which was the main force behind the radical steps, turned out to be considerable.

The Hungarian Constitutional Court has been often accused of an overly high degree of judicial activism, in the sense of both the supposed arbitrariness of some of its interpretations and its willingness to overrule the acts of the democratically elected Parliament.[82] However, both the incomplete nature of at least parts of the constitution and the repeated unwillingness of the parliamentary majorities and ministers of justice to make even a serious attempt to tailor normal legislation to constitutional requirements and the tendency of Parliament to illegitimately slip into the role of a constituent assembly leave the Court little alternative.[83] Evidently, to be the guardian of human rights in a political "revolution" is a difficult task indeed, one that requires activism. So does the assertion of "constitutionalism" in what is still, inevitably, the process of the creation of the constitution itself. Equally important are the features of the new Hungarian Constitution that produce a very strong form of executive power, depriving Parliament of its role as a counterweight, leaving the Court as the most important limitation of governmental power. Instead of being a reason for the weakness of government as for example Stephen Holmes seems to think, the activism of the Court is in fact a reflex of a potentially much too unlimited executive power.[84]

Nevertheless, judicial review does raise problems from the point of view of democratic legitimacy even under a normally functioning liberal democracy. These problems, moreover, are inevitably exacerbated by the unavoidable activism of the Hungarian court in the context defined by *the weak democratic legitimacy of the constitutional document*.[85] The problem is not with activism as such, but with the normative weakness of the document to which it refers.

In my view the Court has managed its own potential constitutional crisis, rooted in its unavoidable activism made precarious by weak constitutional legitimacy, by selectively conceding the claims of the present holders of power. This has been done in the manner of the jurists of the nineteenth-century *Rechtsstaat* through a trade-off that involved a firm defense of liberal rights and the tendency to accept political discretion on the level of the governmental process. Thus, the extension of the idea of constitutional continuity to the idea that the Court should guard against all legal vacuums even at the cost of (temporarily) maintaining authoritarian regulations as in the media case may not be as much the result of deep legal conviction as a form of self-protection (or protection of the constitutional order) in the face of the potential authoritarian (and extraconstitutional) response by the government. Even under the social liberal coalition the Court was careful not to go too far in opposing the government, especially when the outcome would have been obviously harmful to the country. After condemning the effort of the government to subvert a legitimate referendum, it closed its eyes to the procedural maneuvering that in the end blocked any referendum on the really disputed questions.[86]

This "solution," however, protects the Court (and perhaps the constitution) at the cost of further weakening the democratic legitimacy of the whole constitutional system. Such a system can be legitimate today only if it preserves the democratic nature of the political process (which includes its openness and cannot be restricted to its majoritarian character) as well as the fundamental rights of the citizens. Thus, starting with a constitutional document with little *initial* democratic legitimacy, which necessarily weakens the legitimacy of judicial review itself, the Court, unwilling or unable to fully recognize this difficulty, winds up by weakening the democratic process that the constitution is supposed to protect. In the process, however, it weakens the second most important justification[87] of countermajoritarian judicial review in a democratic society, namely, that the democratic process can be protected in no other way against its own undemocratic potential.[88]

Refurbishing the Legitimacy of the Constitutional Order: In Search of a Theory

There are conceptions, and not only of East European authoritarians and right-wing radicals, according to which the whole early experience of constitutional synthesis, rigorous constitutionalism, and judicial review on behalf of

human rights as typified by Hungarian practice has been based on a fundamental mistake. According to Stephen Holmes's views at one time, the only
major task of the present was to let governments and parliamentary majorities govern. This apparently entails punishing at least some ex-Communist
officials after tugs of war with their squeamish or pragmatic defenders and
returning property to former owners irrespective of moral and economic considerations as long as the government's political interests require it.[89] It is perhaps because of his fears for the success of the transition to market economy
that Holmes considered the formation of strong government the top priority,
rather than either constitutional synthesis or the strengthening of civil society.
Without knowing it perhaps, he has only repeated the thesis of right-wing
authoritarians and populist radicals, who, at least in Hungary, wished for (different versions) of a majoritarian-authoritarian resolution of all major issues
of the day by a Parliament doubling as a permanent constituent assembly,[90] as
the only road to a future constitutional government where it presently does
not exist. How else is one to contextualize Holmes's all too great toleration of
parliaments dominated by anti-Communist witch-hunters against anti-anti-
Communist courts and presidents representing either human rights (apparently a useless luxury in his view) or mere efficiency (a necessary evil, it
seems)? How else indeed are we to make sense of his comparison of constitutional courts, in particular the one in Hungary, as "unelected"*(sic)* and secret
bodies, with the politburos of the Communist regimes?[91] What are we to make
of his evidently fallacious blanket assumption that decommunization is in
general popular in the former Communist countries and could therefore lend
an "aura of legitimacy to the government as a whole"?

The case is somewhat more complicated with Holmes's thesis that constitutionalism deprives governments of the power to redivide property according to their political preferences. Only so can the so-called nomenklatura or
"spontaneous" privatization be blocked.[92] This point is right as far as it goes.
But when Holmes, in a later essay, seems to interpret his argument in the sense
of an advocacy of full reprivatization,[93] a policy that very few governments in
the area actually wished to impose, we are left to wonder whether this type of
government strengthening can actually lead to an effective system of property,
as he also wishes. Moreover, the result of such policy, also inevitably unjust
and inconsistent,[94] could only be (as the German government came to realize)
long-term legal uncertainty dramatically interfering with the larger privatization process.[95]

Holmes has unfortunately forgotten to address the important argument of
his colleague Jon Elster, according to whom in Eastern Europe marketization
and constitutionalism belong inevitably together, and reform dictatorships of
any stripe are doomed to fail.[96] On this point, the argument of István Csurka
and his supporters in Hungary was at least more consistent, since they, unlike
Holmes, do not wish for radical marketization of the economy. But Holmes

amazingly enough has also forgotten his own earlier and rather eloquent demonstration showing that constitutionalism and perforce judicial review do not represent a zero-sum game with respect to the power of government.[97] Constitutional limits can be enabling to the extent that a government, forced to respect a rational division of powers and forced to desist from interventions into the spheres of society protected by rights, becomes both more legitimate and more capable of action within its own well-defined sphere. This is an important lesson that Holmes once learned from Niklas Luhmann.[98] In Hungary, with or without the Court, the government has been repeatedly weakened by its own inability to concentrate on the sphere of its proper constitutional authority. The Court's actions, especially if more consistent and rigorous, could have helped rechannel the government's activity and concentration to areas of policy making of greater interest to the population than symbolic issues like retroactive justice, reprivatization, and battles over the media.[99]

Thus the task in Hungary at least was not to go "back to the drawing board" in search of a more statist or authoritarian constitution, but forward to strengthen the legitimacy of a constitution and a constitutional practice that already has some significant achievements to their credit. There have been four important proposals seeking to address the constitutional difficulties of new democracies that respond to or are highly relevant to the specific problems of the Hungarian case. They are liberal (nondemocratic, nonrevolutionary); democratic-revolutionary (nonliberal); liberal-democratic-revolutionary; and liberal-democratic (non- or postrevolutionary).[100]

Liberal

The president of the Hungarian Constitutional Court, László Sólyom, at one time at least openly renounced the need for a *democratic* legitimation of his body, whose members, elected through a two-thirds parliamentary vote, serve for nine years. He is proud of the fact that in a political revolution legal continuity has been maintained, and he sees no need whatsoever to create an entirely new constitution. As already mentioned, for Sólyom, as for the Hungarian Court as a whole, a rule-of-law state can be created only through the means of the rule of law. Thus in the legal sense he rejects a *revolutionary* model of transformation. According to him the present constitution, open to self-revision of course, is a sufficient basis for the fullest possible development of constitutionalism. Sólyom evidently fears, with some reason given the attacks on the Court's decisions, that a future constituent power could eliminate important provisions of rights from a new document or decisively weaken the powers of judicial review.[101] Thus a completely new constitution could only be worse than the present one.[102] Instead of democratic legitimation Sólyom proposes two sources of the legitimacy of the court's practice: the internal coherence of decisions, and gradual adherence to European constitutional norms. As desirable, however, as these criteria may be, they do not in themselves solve the potential legitimation problems of the Court and of the present constitution. Coherence in itself cannot produce normative obligation.[103] Moreover, as I have shown, under the pressure of democratic legitimation, in the face of a Parliament with greater (though by no means adequate) democratic legitimacy, the internal coherence of the Court's structure of precedents has suffered. Finally, general European or international standards exist only in the case of rights, but not in the case of governmental powers or democratic procedures. Adherence to European norms can thus legitimate only a part, however important, of the Court's practice. Thus, the Court's self-understanding may be partially responsible for a state of affairs in which this institution has been a more effective guardian of human rights than of democratic procedures.[104]

Of course one cannot expect a court operating under a given constitutional text and seeking to legitimate its mode of jurisprudence to admit that the difficulties of this jurisprudence are rooted in the very text to be eventually made sacred or in the way it was originally produced. Nevertheless, it would take extreme blindness not to realize that Sólyom's nondemocratic claims of legitimacy could become extremely precarious, if the attacks on the Court's decisions began to mobilize the support of those whose economic situation has been worsened during the system change. Where the Court's own self-understanding tacitly counts on the traditionalization of both the constitution and its own practice—that is, on time and good luck in other words—right-wing radicalism seeks to thoroughly discredit such a tradition even before it could form.

Democratic-Revolutionary

It is important to notice that the political philosophy of the more sophisticated Hungarian right-wing radicals, such as István Csurka, is a *revolutionary* (national) *democratic* one.[105] *Liberalism* from this point of view is the ideology of a stratum that inherited its wealth from the Communist era. To Csurka, a rule-of-law state, where it does not exist, can indeed only be created through means other than the rule of law.[106] To apply the technology of the *Rechtsstaat* before a revolutionary transformation of power and property has been effected, means to help preserve the prerevolutionary, that is, Communist, status quo.[107] According to Csurka even the most perfect court applying the most perfect constitution would inevitably stand in the way of a radical change of systems that necessarily must be unjust toward those who achieved their power and property through past injustice. But the constitution is to him only a heavily amended version of the Communist constitution—both its origins and its internal structure remain shrouded in ambiguity. Moreover, the Court itself was, he argues, a product of a transitional epoch and of transitional agreements that allowed the old ruling party to control the terms and the choice of some of the members. A strong Constitutional Court was therefore understood by each side, the old regime and the opposition, as a potential form of protection from a state power whose possession was at the time still highly uncertain. After a democratic election, however, according to Csurka, the same institution only protects the old ruling elite from the new, legitimate government and parliamentary majority. This majority may be "forced from the road of legality and constitutionality" by the actions of the Court designed to protect them.[108]

Csurka's position should not be understood as merely a cynical rejection of "legality and constitutionality." He has periodically made the argument that the country could receive a legitimate constitution only through a constituent assembly. When the actual development did not go his way, he quite consistently transferred his constituent claims to the democratically elected Parliament, or to its majority, which just happened to be in the hands of his own party. If the constitution was created by a variety of nondemocratically elected or selected bodies, and in a small part (in his view under Western economic pressure) through the pact of the leaders of the two major parties of the new Parliament, then any attempt to bind the sovereign Parliament by an undemocratic constitution should be rejected by both democratic and revolutionary standards.[109] The Constitutional Court can earn its authority (never a democratic one) only through self-limitation, by staying out of the way of the democratic revolutionaries. To be sure, Csurka does not tell us when the time will come finally for settled constitutionalism and the judicial review based on it. A permanent revolution does not particularly frighten him.

Liberal-Democratic-Revolutionary

The Arendtian rejection of permanent revolution in favor of a constitution-making one is clearly at the heart of Bruce Ackerman's democratic, liberal, *and* revolutionary argument. He sees no virtue in the specific political programs of the East European right: reprivatization and political justice.[110] More importantly, he seeks to defend the *liberal* and *democratic* features of the democratic revolution by arguing in favor of separating constituent and normal legislatures, thereby depriving each of the power of the sovereign constituent assembly of European history. Not only does he propose a constitution liberal in its contents, but by insisting on a timely closure of the constituent and therefore revolutionary process, he in effect argues for the early establishment of liberal forms of the protection of rights. Nevertheless, some of his arguments are similar to those of the right. He too rejects constitution making through the amendment process, the work of the Round Tables and the patchwork plurality of constitution-making instances. Even if unlike the right, Ackerman is in substantive agreement with the decisions of the Hungarian Constitutional Court, he is extremely critical of the practice of abstract normative control that brings the judges into direct conflict with Parliament. He fears that irrespective of the merit of the Court's positions, Parliament will try to destroy "such a politically exposed institution," operating on the basis of a "soft constitution." He recommends more prudence to the Court (a suggestion accepted even before it was made) and normative control only when concrete cases come up. He does not consider the harm that already would have been done had the Court adopted from the beginning the diffident posture he now considers appropriate. How else could the country have been saved from the irreversible evils of full reprivatization and political justice?

The gist of Ackerman's argument, which he wishes to apply to all East European countries, has to do with producing a hard, that is, democratically legitimate, constitution. In terms of his broader theory[111] this is possible only when revolutionary, popular mobilization unites behind the work of a constituent assembly that bypasses the normal legislature. Undoubtedly at some moments in some countries (perhaps in Czechoslovakia in 1989–90 where there was such a movement, and where the existing constitution was unworkable) this method has much to recommend it. But what if a country has more than one potentially powerful mass movement, as in the case of Russia? In such a context, the proposal can easily turn into an advocacy of civil war. And what if it there is no mass movement behind radical change? This was and remains the situation in Hungary. Should it be drummed up from above? In this context the actual constitution-making process in Hungary was part of political bargaining between old and new elites, and within the new one arising from civil society. Does Ackerman propose (like Csurka) that such bargains be simply abrogated by the one elite that merely has a few more deputies than its opposition? In general, as perceptively as Ackerman has criticized some aspects of the constitutional practice of the Hungarian court, his solutions both with respect to judicial review and constitution making have an air of unreality in the case of this particular country. Without the Court's activism, Hungary would not have been able to satisfy even a minimum of liberalism. And there is little chance of anyone (the Court, the Parliament, any of the important parties, or an independent movement) successfully calling for a constitution-making process, entirely bypassing both the Parliament and the existing constitution.

Evidently Ackerman once hoped to have leaders like Walesa or Yeltsin, ahead of mass movements, somehow take charge of the constituent process as modern equivalents of Washington.[112] But Washington was not the dominant figure in the making of the U.S. Constitution, and Walesa and Yeltsin are no Washingtons. More importantly, the social consensus that allowed a variety of different U.S assemblies to at least accept if not fully support a particular type of constitution made by a special convention is missing in most East European countries, and especially Russia. The fate of the constituent assembly Yeltsin called, followed by his subsequent direct assumption of constituent powers á la Bonaparte, should put to rest a model of constitution making directly imported from U.S. history.[113]

Liberal-Democratic

Finally, the democratic-liberal but non- or post-revolutionary option first articulated by Ulrich Preuss makes a virtue of the self-limitation of the East European constitution makers. Making explicit what was only implicit in Sólyom's liberal position, Preuss at one time applauded the stress of the constitution makers on legal continuity as well as their reliance on a diverse set of instances, all rooted in civil society. Only thus was the emergence of a unified *pouvoir constituant* and the destructive logic of historical revolutions avoided. Preuss was fully aware of the element of collective learning from the history of revolutions needed in stopping revolutions against the revolution from turning into counterrevolutions. Given the scope of the transformation and its potential social cost, the task cannot be solved (as Ackerman would have it) by imitating the American Revolution. If the logic of the French and Russian Revolutions is to be avoided, new means had to be devised. Initially Preuss believed that most countries of Central Europe at least were successful in such effort precisely through their self-conscious renunciation of a constituent power outside of all law.

But the objections that can be raised against the liberal theses can be raised in this case as well. Undoubtedly, by referring to civil society, Preuss sought to give his conception democratic content. Unfortunately, it seems that where civil society rather than political parties remained the main force behind the Round Table and constitution making (the GDR to which Preuss explicitly refers),[114] there was not enough political force behind the acceptance of the new constitution.[115] In Hungary (not treated by Preuss), where on the other hand a more or less new constitution was generated through the work of the Round Table, the constitution-making role of civil society (that one had the right to expect in 1988, the greatest year of self-organization from below) was in fact displaced by that of political parties.[116] Moreover, Preuss's position, if applied to Hungary, would be open to the objection that a patchwork and never-concluded constituent process cannot produce or fully legitimate a constitution needed for vigorous judicial review. Yet the latter is the sine qua non of constitutionalism in a formerly authoritarian setting where everyone has become long accustomed to living under a potentially unchecked governmental prerogative.

Of course, the liberal-democratic postrevolutionary position need not imply that the constituent process is a more or less complete aside from creative use of constitutional review and an occasional constitutional amendment. Here the stress on democratic legitimacy inherent in the civil society argument points to important differences with Sólyom's thesis. If the constitutional document is not yet consistent or complete, if civil society has not yet fully participated in the constituent process, a new phase of this process (the necessity of which is recognized by many liberal lawyers and philosophers in

Hungary) would present an important opportunity for integrating a new procedure of discussion, framing, and ratification.

What are the prospects of success of the four options in constitutional politics, and is there a chance of synthesis between some of them? The purely liberal, nondemocratic option could potentially succeed if other dimensions of political and economic processes were to sufficiently contribute to requisite stability. Under such conditions, there would be little opening for the calculated illegality of the sovereign that Csurka hints at, or for the destruction of the Court that Ackerman fears. After a while possibly the initial absence of democratic legitimacy could be compensated by the traditionalization, and even sacralization of the constitution. Unfortunately, this option would be relatively impotent, given its unwillingness to firmly defend the openness of the democratic process, against the project of a semiauthoritarian or at least a highly oligarchic version of democracy.[117] And it would become extremely vulnerable in moments of serious political crisis to challenges to the constitutional order as a whole. The non- or antiliberal revolutionary-democratic option on the contrary counts on just such a crisis for its success. Given a dramatic division of society, this option, with its already well-developed friend-enemy schemata and its ideology of "revolution from above," would turn increasingly authoritarian, pointing to dictatorship or civil war. One can be rather certain that as a full-blown model the liberal-democratic revolutionary option has little prospect in any country, above all in Hungary, despite the attractiveness of some of its normative features. Given the pragmatism of Hungarian society and politics, it is difficult to believe that if the purely liberal model based on continuity had a good chance to survive, the political forces needed to produce the kind of liberal constitution Ackerman would like would wish to fully open up the question of constitution making. At best, Ackerman's option as a whole would be a relevant alternative for liberal democratic politics in the face of either total constitutional impasse or the danger of a radical turn to the right. But as the events in Russia have shown, even in such contexts the chances of success may be slim, even if one can hardly fault the group around Yeltsin for having tried to follow, for a moment, something like the U.S. federal model of constitution making.

In Hungary most certainly, in the present and foreseeable context, democratic politics can be best served by focusing on the liberal-democratic option that does not require a complete constitutional rupture and continues to operate within the method of continuity. This is all the more justified, because such option can incorporate the best features of the two other liberal proposals. It already shares the purely liberal model's stress on continuity, rule of law at all instances, and does not run the risk, as does Ackerman's proposal, of losing important features like a strong constitutional court from the present document.[118] Like Ackerman's proposal, however, this solution might involve both a democratic relegitimation of the constitution and important new additions to it.

Nevertheless synthesis between the two liberal democratic proposals remains apparently difficult, especially on a deeper level. The two proposals do fortunately agree in what they expect from constitutions: Aside from the defense of rights and the guarantee of democratic procedures they both hope for the development of a constitutional patriotism as an alternative framework of social identity to the nation or the ethnos. Nevertheless, although both imply a stress on democratic participation, the loci of this are presented in apparently incompatible ways: extraordinary revolutionary activity in the one case and normal communication processes of civil society on the other. Moreover, the two approaches remain very different in their relationship to the problem of rupture and continuity, because of their very different fears: the dangers of violence (feared by the nonrevolutionary option) and the loss of legitimacy (feared by Ackerman).

Ackerman's model, derived from an interpretation of the American revolutionary experience, seeks to establish a moment of revolutionary rupture and synthesis as the unambiguous origin of the new constitution. Ackerman has in mind a program of popular mobilization led by a charismatic individual pushing through a new constitution in the face of parties, factions, groups representing social division, and a merely normal politics. Only when a constitution is ratified does the revolution come to an end, but then it does come to an end allowing normal politics to recommence. This interpretation of the U.S. experience fails to give us guidance (as already implied) in societies without established and uncontested local and provincial governments, torn by deep cleavages and in the midst of transformations where the whole socioeconomic structure is at stake. More dangerously still, in very different contexts than its original, the recommendation may very well wind up solving the problem of constitutional legitimacy at the cost of destructive violence, and in the end, more constitutional instability.

The liberal-democratic postrevolutionary model builds on East Europe's own experience and not historical analogies. It too has serious problems, however. Unlike Ackerman's constitutional convention that only exposes its synthesis to public discussion and ratification, Preuss's original referent, the democratic public sphere of civil society, is not capable of producing constitutions directly. The failure (even if overdetermined) of the GDR Round Table he advised and analyzed teaches the right lesson. A democratic public ought to influence the politics of constitution making but should not seek to become its central organ. Moreover, neither a pluralistic civil society-based process nor the method of revision through amendments has an obvious ending. In new situations, new groups will arise that did not participate in the constitution-making process. Even simply proposing another round of constitution making[119] does not address the question of whether there will be new such rounds in the near future, and eventually at what cost. One needs to reflect like Ackerman both on what is needed to bring the process to an always provisional close and how future access can be opened up in such a way that civil society preserves a potential influence over constitutional change. In my view there is a need to distinguish the ratification procedures needed to "complete" constitution making and the procedures of future revision. Here, the U.S. model still seems to be a good guide. But in any case, much will depend on the future (and hopefully changed) revision structure of the constitution that ought not be prohibitively difficult in a democracy[120] and yet cannot be left up to single-session parliamentary majorities, however qualified.[121]

Whatever the difficulties, in context of the possibilities of constitutional development in Hungary on the eve of a new constitution-making effort in 1994, a synthesis was at least theoretically possible between the two liberal democratic positions, Ackerman's and the one I derived from Preuss's writings of three years ago. Three types of desiderata needed to be satisfied:

1. For the sake of legal security, to avoid instability and potential revolutionary illegality and violence, the original East European method of constitution making, through continuity, needed to be itself continued. This is the necessary Burkean-Hegelian moment of constitution making, implying an acceptance of one's immediate past, and thereby the avoidance of a severe crisis of social identity. It has the additional virtue of being able to protect to an important extent the considerable constitutional achievements of the process of transition itself. Admittedly this road up until now in Hungary has tended to produce some elements of undesirable continuity with the past, like a process of purely parliamentary, single-session constitutional revision. But this consequence is not unavoidable. Following Hart's argument, even an amendment rule can be used to fully change itself without self-contradiction. When this is done, the principle of legality triumphs.

2. While the newly elected Parliament could not be expected to voluntarily defer to another constitution-making body, as some of the losers in the election of 1994 suggested, it remains a valid insight that the creation, ratification, and revision processes of a constitution should not be left up to a single parliament alone. Especially when normal party politics emerges, constitutions should be both protected against temporary, short-range interests and kept open to the creative input of a wider range of social forces. This is the Madisonian insight that Ackerman rightly insists on. There is a variety of ways of accomplishing this objective and some of these can even be combined.[122] But the first step would have to be the use of the inherited amendment rule that fudges the distinction between producing a new constitution and revision, to produce a new rule for constitution drafting, enactment, and ratification. It is this new rule that would have the burden of satisfying the demands of democratic legitimacy that intensified during the process of piecemeal constitu-

tional change through using the original amendment rule. With the creation of a new rule of constitution making, a way would be found that the current rule of amendment not be used to subvert the entire process.

3. Finally, in a strongly democratizing setting it is illusory that an effective and popularly accepted constitution can be created through the formal political process alone. The "final" round of constitution making, both before and after parliamentary approval and before popular ratification, should provide an opportunity also for the less-formalized participation of the public by individuals and concerned organizations. This is the Tocquevillian moment of constitution making, necessary if the document should in the future become the founding document for constitutional patriotism. Hannah Arendt rightly stressed that the U.S. founders could achieve future stability and even a reflective form of sacralization for their constitution based on the power of memory, because of their remarkable capacity to look upon their own activity "with the eyes of centuries to come." It was such a vision that led them to seek a beginning that could incorporate its own principle, and they found this in the principle of public discussion and the inclusion of different levels of deliberation.[123] Even if Arendt introduced public discussion and deliberation to deal with the problem of discontinuity, such participation is by no means incompatible with the method of radical change within legal continuity. Even today the principle of publicity is hardly obsolete. Not only a future constitutional patriotism but also the much needed short-term legitimacy of the constitution would be greatly facilitated by democratic participation in its genesis.

Chapter 6

Refurbishing the Legitimacy of the New Regime: Constitution-Making Endgame in Hungary and Poland

The parallels between the Polish and the Hungarian roads from Communism are astonishing. These are the two countries where, under the impact of economic difficulties and democratic oppositions, regimes of the Soviet type were significantly liberalized in the 1980s.[1] The idea of the reconstruction of civil society, formulated also in Czechoslovakia, became a politics (as against an antipolitics) only in Poland and Hungary. They were the two countries of classic Round Tables, with rough parity between the negotiating sides. During the first elections, under quite different rules, the two parties of the old regime performed more or less similarly in terms of share of the vote: equally poorly. In neither country, for example, was the reconstructed Communist Party capable of winning more than one freely contested seat in individual districts.

In 1993 and 1994, however, the ex-Communists (polling 25 percent and 33 percent, respectively) came back into power in both countries (but not in the Czech and Slovak Republics!), and they carried out neoliberal economic policies. Yet in 1997 and 1998 (polling more or less as before) the very same parties were no longer strong enough to form a government and gave way to center right coalitions. Finally, and most relevantly in the present context, both countries have followed a pattern of piecemeal constitution making for several years, through the use of relatively flexible amendment rules. Yet in 1993 and 1994, in Poland and Hungary both, the window of opportunity for the passing of a new constitution was suddenly wide open, surprisingly enough with the ex-Communist parties, now with democratic legitimacy, apparently in position once again to dominate the process.

Undoubtedly one could and should also stress the differences between the two transitions. Poland had a much more powerful democratic movement that inherited the mantle of uniquely political mass struggles going back to 1976, 1975, and even 1971. What equalized the power of the two oppositions in the respective countries during the negotiations was that the Polish transi-

199

tion came first, operating in a world of formidable uncertainty, while the Hungarian transition could greatly benefit from the knowledge that a non-Communist government was possible in the strategically most important country in the region, Poland itself. This led to another difference: In Hungary, unlike Poland, no undemocratic structural concessions and no strong presidency had to be conceded to the Communists. The first Polish Parliament, elected only in part freely, had to make the effort to draft a new constitution, precisely because of the semidemocratic structure bequeathed by the Round Table. But for the same reason, it was in a weaker symbolic position to gain the passage of a constitution than its Hungarian counterpart would have been. At roughly the same time, however, the latter, already having a democratic constitution, could, in my view at least, mistakenly satisfy itself with another big amendment round.

In party politics too there were important differences. The new Hungarian parties formed early, and Parliament was structured around a more or less stable system of six parties after each of three elections. Government too has been very stable throughout the period. In Poland, because of the unique status of the one great movement—Solidarity—party formation was an initially slow one, followed by fragmentation rather than effective pluralization. Only after 1993 did a more coherent system of parties emerge, in part because of mistaken strategic choices by the right wing of the whole political spectrum, which failed to unite in party coalitions capable of passing the required electoral thresholds. Governments as a result have been much less stable in Poland, with many more prime ministers than in Hungary, and there was one more general election as well. Whereas in Hungary a clear-cut parliamentary regime emerged in late 1989, in Poland the structure of government initially involved a combination of semipresidential and parliamentary elements with unclear boundaries. While Hungarian development was not free of constitutional conflicts, in Poland these conflicts were deeper and far more frequent.

Thus the constitution-making effort in Poland in 1993 and after was propelled by serious structural as well as legitimation problems. As I see it, in Hungary in 1994 at issue was primarily, though not exclusively, constitutional legitimacy. As a result, while no serious constitutional politician or analyst in Poland could maintain that the country did not need a new constitution, such a view was often expressed and was quite respectable in Hungary. This brings me to the final difference: Hungary, unlike Poland, had a strong Constitutional Court whose members and advocates were becoming very much accustomed to an evolutionary pattern of constitution making presided over by this body. The fundamentally nondemocratic, indeed aristocratic idea, namely, "let the Court do it, it is their business," as a friend of mine once said to me, emerged during the course of experience with an unusually strong court at a time when the country was taking its very first steps historically toward constitutionalism in the modern sense.

From this short comparison between Poland and Hungary alone, the reader may assume that the different fates of constitution making in the two countries could have been predicted. This perception is strengthened by the fact that the outcome is already known. The Poles did manage to draft, enact, and ratify a new constitution; the Hungarians did not. But all that follows from the differences mentioned so far is that Poland would have a better chance than Hungary to achieve the result. It was not predetermined that the first country would necessarily succeed in making a new constitution, or that the second would inevitably fail.

WHY NEW CONSTITUTIONS?

When eventually the whole effort came crashing down, many of the leaders of Hungarian government tried to avoid their responsibility and to downplay the whole event by insisting that there was no "compulsion" to produce a constitution *(alkotmányozási kényszer)* anyway. This was long the position of the Constitutional Court, and some commentators were quick to note their triumph, and the victory of their so-called invisible constitution, meaning their ability to dominate the evolution of the actual rules of the game through interpretation.[2]

In fact the claim that there was no compulsion to make a constitution was a red herring that disguised a variety of political motivations. Let me therefore state from the outset that in a rigorous sense there can be no *legal necessity* to produce a *new* written constitution *as long as there is a currently valid document with a workable amendment rule.* Only constitutions like the *Grundgesetz* of the Federal Republic of Germany with important unalterable features constitute possible exceptions to this rule. In theory Hungary, for example, could be transformed into the hereditary possession of the House of Hapsburg (at least on paper) by a two-thirds vote of Parliament under Article 24(3) of the current constitution.[3] Thus even those who desired radical changes could claim without contradiction that there is no constitution-making compulsion. At the same time, and this is crucial, there may be *good reasons* to produce a new written constitution even where one wants (as against the above example) to preserve an existing political structure. Not only dissatisfaction with a given constitutional regime but also the desire to strengthen it through the increase of its legitimacy can be the motivation for the production of a new written constitution, which under such circumstances would have to be accomplished under the existing legal framework.

But was the problem of legitimation, or relegitimation, a common one for Poland and Hungary, sufficient to motivate the making of an entirely new constitution? Whether or not it would have been in practice, it is important to note the additional legal and political considerations that played a role in the two countries that could reinforce the argument from democratic legitimacy. What each country had in 1993–94 was an interim or transitional constitutional document, formally speaking. In its preamble the 1989–90 heavily revised Hungarian Constitution postulates its own provisional status and promises in effect the drafting of an entirely new constitution.[4] The Little Constitution of Poland of 1992 defined its own validity "pending the passing of a new Constitution," and was also understood as an interim basic law.[5]

Interim promises to enact new constitutions are not always kept, and at times perhaps should not be. The history of the *Grundgesetz* that survived the unification of Germany, despite the implicit promise of its original Article 146, is a case in point.[6] Nevertheless, such a promise, along with the symbolic fact that the 1989–90 Hungarian Constitution was, formally speaking, a set of amendments of the country's 1949 Stalinist constitution, could not be entirely disregarded.

The situation in Poland was similar, only worse. The revisions of 1989, 1990, and after, including the Little Constitution of 1992, were also amendments of a Communist constitution, one that dated back to 1952. Moreover, neither of the first two parliaments participating in constitution making through amendment was freely or entirely freely elected in Poland. In Hungary this was only true of the first parliament, which enacted the comprehensive draft of 1989. Though both processes were fragmented, the Polish one was much more so, with the inevitable uncertainties, inconsistencies, and textual tensions involved. Unlike the Hungarian document, moreover, the Polish amendments did not cover all relevant topics and did not add up to a complete interim constitution. Given the imposed character of some of the 1989 compromise and the strong presidency that emerged from it, step-by-step amendments in a different spirit had significant difficulty in transforming the document in a consistent and coherent way, especially after the full possibilities of a presidency reluctantly conceded to General Wojciech Jaruzelski came to be exploited by his successor, Lech Walesa. Evidently, the features imposed at the time of the origins of the Polish document prohibited the formation of an aura of legitimacy even more than in the case of its Hungarian counterpart. Significantly, in Hungary an active constitutional review by the powerful court managed to lend the document a legal as well as ritual aura of authority. In Poland the Constitutional Tribunal, a product of the late Communist epoch, was much weaker, and its decisions were not final.[7]

Granted, an active constitutional review in Hungary, in the context of a soft (less than fully democratic) constitutional background, was itself a structural strain of the Hungarian constitutional inheritance of 1994. This was especially obvious whenever, as in 1994, the parliamentary majority was capable of modifying the Constitution as well as pass on its own the so-called two-thirds laws, including the law on the Constitutional Court, under only slightly less demanding procedural requirements (relative versus absolute qualified major-

ity). Such efforts could easily involve putting Parliament on a potential collision course with the Constitutional Court.[8] Given the clever maneuvering of
the Court and its president, Lászlo Sólyom, in contrast with the aggressive and
openly self-aggrandizing behavior of President Walesa, the structural conflict
potential of the Hungarian constitution did not reach anywhere near the level
of the open conflicts within the Polish semipresidential regime.[9] While the
question *quis custodiet ipsos custodes?* is relevant to either case, as to all constitutional democracies, the Hungarian Court turned out to be, unsurprisingly,
a less dangerous "guardian of the constitution" than the Polish president, who
operated in a framework with an extremely weak Constitutional Tribunal. But
this is not to say that its great powers where unproblematic in a democracy,
especially one with weak initial legitimacy for its patchwork constitution.

We can safely say that although the heavily amended constitutions of the
two countries were challenged by serious legitimation as well as structural
problems, each of these were more severe in the Polish than the Hungarian
case. From this it does not follow that there was no need to produce a new
constitution in Hungary, only that the need in Poland was greater. What
united the paths of the countries nevertheless had to do above all with politics, not problems with legality or legitimacy. In 1993 and 1994, respectively,
coalitions came to power with the expressed intention of drafting and enacting new constitutions that would supersede the interim documents, and with
the political power to back up these intentions. Note that the goal in neither
case was said to be the production of materially new constitutions or new
political regimes. Rather, the two governing coalitions claimed that they
aimed to put the new regimes established in 1989 and 1990 on more stable
and legitimate constitutional foundations. The new constitutions would be
new in Hans Kelsen's formal sense only, and even in this sense they would be
established fully within frameworks of legal continuity.[10]

To be sure, the allegedly conservative or evolutionary character of the Polish constitutional project was not as clear as that of its Hungarian counterpart. This has to do with the fact that the presidentialist components even of
the Little Constitution were (thanks to the efforts of the anti-Communist
Walesa) survivals from a moment when the Communist Party could still
impose some of its specific constitutional ideas, in this case a strong presidency that was as a result inorganically combined with parliamentary government. The constitutional project of 1993–94 aimed at reducing, if not entirely
eliminating these presidentialist features. But even in this context, a strong
argument could be made that the project would only codify the evolutionary
line of development that—starting to a limited extent with the Little Constitution—involved a step-by-step weakening of presidential powers. Significantly, after the Constitution was ratified in 1997, some of its most vocal
opponents were to criticize it for an evolutionary approach that "only consolidated, codified, and sorted out the existing governmental playing field . . .

legitimized an already evolved legal and institutional order, giving it the rank of a constitutional order."[11]

WHO IS TO EXERCISE CONSTITUENT POWERS?

In terms of reopening the window of opportunity for constitution making, it was most important that the new coalitions had full constitution-making majorities in Parliament, that is, the required two-thirds of the votes in the relevant chambers.[12] This state of affairs, that the opposition parties in and out of Parliament in Hungary at least described as a potential "constitutional dictatorship," filled them with apprehension concerning the very real option that the new coalitions would use their numerical advantage to impose a constitutional settlement entirely of their own choice.[13] In my view, given their rather narrow two-thirds majority in Poland, and even more important the relatively weak social base of voters behind the super majorities in both countries (36 percent in Poland, 54 percent in Hungary), such imposition faced formidable difficulties—especially since the governmental parties recognized in each case the legal requirement of popular ratification after parliamentary enactment.

Note that the government's numerical edge and its immediate social support were even weaker in Poland than in Hungary. On the other hand there were fewer and weaker parliamentary opponents of the constitution-making effort in Poland, since much of the right suffered a complete electoral disaster because of its failed political strategy and the subsequent fragmentation of its vote. But the legitimation problems of the old state-party returning to power were the same in both countries, and this fact required extreme caution when it came to constitution making. Thus in both countries formulas with elaborate input for nongovernmental forces were offered to the opposition, and in Poland, where most of political right found itself outside of Parliament, this meant first of all a role for extraparliamentary formations and procedures as well.

There were a lot of reasons that the oppositions in both countries were reluctant to accept offers of participation. Producing a new constitution would concede a big public relations victory to the government. Some of the opposition parties, notably Freedom Union (FU) in Poland and FIDESZ in Hungary, were willing to accept this cost as long as their own involvement would be substantial, and as long as the coalitions would basically support liberal democratic parliamentary regimes, if need be against the wishes of traditional forces within the "post-Communist" parties. But others on the right, religious or populist parties, dissatisfied with the nonrevolutionary nature of the whole process of regime change, wished for qualitatively new types of constitution, variously involving elements of corporatism (in Hungary: in the form of a second parliamentary chamber based on churches and unions), the constitutional establishment of religion or religious morals (demanded especially in Poland), and stronger presidentialism (the demand of Walesa's circle and of József Torgyán, the leader of the Small Holders). Since there was little chance that such innovations would be adopted under the given coalitions, the advocates of these views tended to prefer delaying constitution making until they themselves had the requisite majorities. What they wanted least was the relegitimation and solidification of the existing arrangements. Paradoxically, therefore, it was those who wished for a materially new constitution that in 1993 and 1994 opposed or wished to slow down the process of constitution making, while those who wished to preserve and fortify the liberal democratic regimes emerging from the 1989 change of regimes hoped to do this through enacting a new, coherent, and fully legitimate basic law.

It is in this context that we must understand the parallel proposals in both countries for independent constituent assemblies, full participation of extra-parliamentary parties and self-chosen organizations of "civil society" in the drafting, as well as demands for consultative referenda on major issues before drafts were voted on.[14] As defensible as some of these ideas may be in themselves and in other historical situations, in the given contexts their function was to slow down and sow confusion. Given the free, democratic elections of parliaments, the likelihood of these giving away one of their fundamental constitutionally secured prerogatives to other elected bodies was zero. Such a delegation to constituent assemblies, structurally revolutionary instances capable of making their own rules, would have risked (as in Russia in 1993!) the method of legal continuity so important for these transitions. Less dramatically, in the European tradition, the election of a constituent assembly had to be preceded by parliamentary dissolution, clearly not in the interest of governing coalitions. As against such extreme options, at least the Polish National Assembly formula (uniting the two ordinary parliamentary chambers in a single assembly, in effect since April 1992) had the promise of preserving legal continuity in a more than just ordinary procedural setting. The Hungarian parliamentary formula did not have this advantage and required decisive steps to achieve a legitimate constituent status for the sitting Parliament. But it was entirely unrealistic to imagine, and no one actually imagined this, that parties having been recently elected under largely liberal democratic programs to parliaments with the established legal right to enact constitutions would risk elections to constituent assemblies where entirely different constitutional ideas may dominate.

The situation was somewhat different with demands for directly involving extraparliamentary parties and great nonparty organizations in the drafting process. These organizations, unlike members of a hypothetical constituent assembly, had no electoral legitimacy at all behind their various populist, corporatist, and traditionalist constitutional demands. The most that should have been claimed was that the ideas of such groups had the right to be taken seriously as ideas, along with other suggestions by even smaller groups and even individuals. The place for such consideration and potential influence was the public sphere rather than organizations and committees utilizing legitimate power.

In Hungary, because of the roughly representative nature of the Parliament, the argument against including small groups with uncertain membership more or less sufficed. The Polish context was, however, significantly different in that roughly 35 percent of the electorate, including about 20 percent that voted for Catholic parties, found itself unrepresented in Parliament. Here a way could have been found of including these parties in the parliamentary structure of compromise. But if they were included, there was little ground to exclude the far more powerful civil organizations, Solidarity and the Church, that disposed over far greater memberships, social influence, and potential political power.

Finally consultative referenda as part of the drafting process would not only have been unwieldy and time consuming, they were not at all suited for the tasks of constitution making because of their strong potential of voting in entirely incompatible elements into drafts. Here too it was better to rely on public discussion and the ultimate fail-safe device of ratificatory referenda. If the constitution makers in Hungary and Poland were to be faulted, it is not for avoiding constituent assemblies, or blocking the formal involvement of civil society, or for contesting the option of consultative referenda, but for not promoting a full-scale public discussion of the salient issues of constitution making.[15]

The various demands for greater participation brought attention to the underlying issue: If the constitution-making process is to produce a constitution with strong democratic legitimacy, it would have to be itself based on a fully legitimate procedure. Parliamentary constitution making, recalling ideas of parliamentary sovereignty, inevitably runs into the problem of justifying a sovereign legislature tying the hands of another legislature of exactly the same status. This problem cannot be avoided if a crucial aspect of producing new written constitutions in the formal sense is to be satisfied, namely, insulating the constitutional product and with it constitutionalism from change by simple majorities. The prima facie legitimation problems of parliamentary constitution making, having to do with a mere constitué (Parliament or "government") usurping the place of the constituant (the people) have been well noted in the two main traditions of designing constitutions, the U.S. and the French. Even the Polish National Assembly formula has been used in its home country, namely, France, primarily for amendments, and not for new constitutional synthesis. The salience of this formula is in any case reduced when the same forces have overwhelming advantage in both legislative chambers. Thus the coalitions in both Poland and Hungary faced the problem of increasing the legitimacy of a method that in itself tended to suggest both majoritarian fiat and an institution unilaterally producing rules for its relations with other branches, as well as the electorate. They responded by accepting not only the need for ratificatory referenda (i.e., including the electorate), but in Hungary at least also important consensus requirements (thus avoiding the charge of majoritarian fiat).

These very real steps to enhance their legitimacy, as mere organs of government, were not yet sufficient for parliaments to entirely deny the implicit or explicit participation of other political branches in the process: the government and the Constitutional Court in Hungary, and the presidency in Poland. The fundamental weakness of parliamentary constitution making, and this is another way to look at its problems of legitimation, is the inability of differentiating between ordinary and constitutional politics. The greater legitimacy needed for the supreme law of the land cannot be achieved when it is perceived as a product of ordinary political processes of majority decision or pragmatic compromise. And conversely the processes that help to raise the legitimacy of the constitution-making process—in my view, consensus, publicity, and plurality of democratic channels (see the last chapter)—only when taken together can help to fully differentiate constitutional politics even in ordinary parliaments from ordinary legislation. The less such legitimation needs are attended to, the less differentiated are the two politics: ordinary and constitutional. And the less differentiated, the less insulated constitutional politics becomes, the less the justification for excluding other democratic branches from their role in making, amending, and creatively reinterpreting constitutions. When such an exclusion does not fully succeed, the success of the efforts comes to depend not only on the good-faith roles of the relevant oppositional parties on which consensual constitution making must depend, as well as on the approval in ratificatory referenda so that the effort can claim the name of the sovereign people, but also on the ability of nonparliamentary political branches to practice the politics of self-limitation. The success of parliamentary constitution making thus easily comes to depend on instances other than parliamentary majorities; a difficult-to-avoid consequence of the built-in legitimation problems of this constitution-making model whose primary subject is a regularly elected parliament.

METHODS OF CONSTITUTION MAKING

The actual procedures of constitution drafting, enacting, and approval adopted in the two countries addressed the problem of legitimacy in different ways. In Poland the method of constitution making was approved far earlier than in Hungary, obviously because the unfinished nature of the interim constitutional document and repeated battles between the branches required it. The first effort between 1990 and 1991 failed among other things because of the absence of a rule coordinating the drafting processes in the Sejm, which at that time still had the *legal* prerogative to produce a constitution and the freely elected Senate that claimed, equally plausibly, to have the only really *legitimate* authority to do so.[16]

After the elections of 1991, there was no longer such a fateful divergence between legality and legitimacy since both chambers were now freely elected.

Yet there was little justification beyond the inherited legal rule in existence to leave one of these chambers out of the fundamental task of constitution making. When the effort was restarted, the National Assembly formula that was adopted had the role not only of including the Senate and Sejm in a single assembly but of creating a procedure formally differentiated from ordinary legislation.[17] The formula, moreover, was designed to deal precisely with the potential differences between the two chambers and to enforce their cooperation both in the drafting committee and the plenary sessions that would have to adopt their drafts. Unfortunately, this second stage of Polish constitution making, characterized no longer by battles between Sejm and Senate, was hampered by extreme party fragmentation as well as battles between the president and Parliament. Thus it was to succeed no better than the first stage of 1989–91.

It is important to note again that the new procedure was set up before the old procedure in place was actually abandoned; as we have seen (in chapter 4) the Little Constitution of August 1992 was still created using the method of Sejm-dominated amendments. Thus the new constitutional committee was bypassed at the moment it was formed: an inauspicious start for its existence. As this example shows, the existence of two channels for constitution drafting was a serious liability, because whenever the consensual requirements of the new, more extensive procedure proved too daunting, there was a readily available easier channel to solve structural problems. As long as, moreover, one chamber could hope to continue to dominate constitutional politics through the amendment formula, its representatives in particular were less interested in compromise than they otherwise might have been. Thus the francophone National Assembly formula, adopted in April 1992, could reduce the dominance of the Sejm only if a new consensual relationship emerged not only between the two chambers but among the parties represented in each of them. This eventually happened, but not until the elections of 1993.

The 1992 rule that indeed survived the election of a new Parliament and change of government in 1993, mandated a mixed Extraordinary Constitutional Committee of the Sejm and Senate, in which the former dominated, to propose the draft of the new constitution to the National Assembly, the joint sitting of the two chambers. This expanded assembly would have to pass the constitution by successive two-thirds votes and send the approved draft to the president for his approval or amendments. The latter's amendments would have to approved by again two-thirds, and the bill as a whole had to be again passed in a third reading with the same majority. After all this the president was required to submit the document to a binding referendum without a threshold of participation.[18]

The rule was not approved without a struggle even in 1992. President Walesa in particular supported a proposal that would have established a Constitutional Committee in which delegates of the president, the government, the Constitutional Tribunal and the Supreme Court would have received more representatives together (thirteen) than would the lower chamber itself (twelve). The presidential proposal was rejected in favor of a committee composed of forty-six deputies of the Sejm and ten senators, with the representatives of president, government, and Constitutional Tribunal receiving a non-voting participant status.[19] Even this compromise went beyond the purely parliamentary form established in Hungary. On the other hand, in Poland in 1992, given the relatively equal status of nine to ten parties in both chambers, no artificial measures were needed to shore up the opposition and enforce consensus requirements. Voting was apparently by individuals and not by parties, and by simple majority. The meaning of this individualistic formula entirely changed after 1994 when the parliamentary map was totally transformed with the governmental parties having slightly fewer than two-thirds of the seats in the Sejm but slightly more than two-thirds of the votes in the National Assembly. In the new context, proportional representation of the parliamentary forces in the Constitutional Committee produced a situation in which the governmental parties controlled thirty-six out of fifty-six of the seats.[20] In this situation even a moderate expert of the opposition like Osiatynski raised the specter of a democratic return to autocratic rule, reminiscent of the cry of "constitutional dictatorship" in Hungary.[21]

The real problem was that many oppositional parties were not represented in Parliament at all, and two that were, the Freedom Union (FU) and the Union of Labor (UP), had little disagreement with the secular and parliamentarist ideas of the majority. Thus no concessions to parliamentary consensus requirements could have improved upon the basic situation that parties and organizations not in agreement with these constitutional premises found themselves mainly outside of Parliament (to be sure because of their own poor strategic choices, in context of the given electoral law). Thus as long as the making of the new constitution was on the agenda, demands for the expansion of its democratic character had to focus on somehow involving groups, initiatives, and procedures outside of Parliament, with all the democratic theoretical and legal technical problems associated with such involvement. The solution tended to be the Constitutional Committee receiving popular drafts, beyond the many proposals that groupings of fifty-six deputies and senators could and did submit.[22]

These demands were already heard at the time of the National Assembly's first Constitutional Committee of 1992–93, which was unable to aggregate the opinions of its member parties and became entirely dependent on external submissions before the dissolution of Parliament in 1993 by Walesa. Such proposal for extraparliamentary participation became all the stronger, when representatives of about a third of the electorate found themselves outside of Parliament after 1993. The same elections that helped to overcome the long-standing battle over constitutional politics between the Sejm and Senate externalized some of the same conflicts as a battle between the legislature and extraparliamentary forces. What the constitution-making body thus gained in freedom of action, it was in danger of losing on the level of legitimacy (in the sociological sense, since in the legal sense its authority was beyond dispute).

Thus unlike in Hungary where all major political forces were represented in Parliament, in Poland proposals to expand participation had to be taken much more seriously. This was all the more true because the proposals came not only from important parties but also from the Solidarity union. The appeal of such "citizen initiatives" became so great that President Walesa, who earlier expressed his intention to be the president of "the excluded 35 percent," abandoned the draft produced by his own experts (too liberal in his view) and put his authority behind popular constitutional initiatives.[23] Initially, Walesa's proposal to give the right of popular constitutional initiative to 100,000 signatories, along with rights of being heard on the Constitutional Committee, was rejected. But after Walesa and Aleksander Kwasniewski, the latter at that time chairman of the Constitutional Commission, managed to compromise on this issue in April 1994, similar rights were given to 500,000 signers and their representatives in a consensual amendment of the constitution-making procedure.[24] Nevertheless, while those with accepted draft proposals were to receive symbolic representation on the Committee, more general plans for corporate representation and preconstitutional referenda on basic principles were allowed to wither through tokenism. Some representatives of social groups and excluded parties received a symbolic hearing without of course voting power, and the National Assembly reserved the right to call but never did call preconstitutional referenda.[25] Thus the only formal expansion of the process that could matter was the consideration of the proposal of the Solidarity union, with more than a million signatures as well as Walesa's support behind it. Solidarity, by this time well on the political right, was still a major social and political force, and its proposals could be disregarded only by putting the popular ratification process at risk.

In Hungary there was no unified process of constitution making at work during the first democratic Parliament of 1990–94. As some of the architects of the extensive MDF-SZDSZ agreement now recognize, the moment of pacting by the major parties in 1990 would have been the optimal time when a liberal democratic constitution could have been enacted. What occurred instead was only another process of wholesale constitutional revision, anticipating (in a more consistent version) the kind of changes achieved by Poland's Little Constitution. It was at this time that the constructive no confidence vote and the abolition of the individual parliamentary responsibility of ministers were included in the constitutional text. Along with the elimination of a large number of laws from the list of laws needing qualified majority for passage, the MDF-SZDSZ constitutional agreements gave the country an uncommonly strong executive structure ("chancellor democracy"). If that departure from the Constitution of 1989 could be agreed upon, it is certainly likely that a whole constitutional synthesis also could have been negotiated. But perhaps there was too much desire to exclude the other parliamentary parties from this bargaining process and too little trust between the two major ones to undertake a genuinely consensual project of constitution making. Subsequent polarization could be used to prove the skeptics right, but polarization could have been perhaps avoided through a genuinely consensual effort. In any case, the very same polarization made constitution making during the rest of the parliamentary period nearly impossible, giving the Constitutional Court and its interpretations the opportunity to step into the breech.

The coalition parties that came into power in 1994 were determined not to make their forerunners' mistakes. Their pact with the opposition was to be a comprehensive constitutional agreement in which all parliamentary parties who wished to participate could. The experts of the coalition parties recognized from the beginning that the process of renewed constitution making had to be justified by more exacting standards than what ordinary parliaments need to generally refer to in cases of legislation.

The agreement reached eventually by all six parliamentary parties implicitly emphasized two such standards: multiparty consensus and legal continuity.[26] To begin with, the current Constitution was amended as to require the vote of 80 percent of all parliamentary deputies to agree to the detailed rules of constitution making, which would in turn be incorporated in the House Rules (bylaws) of Parliament. In turn, these rules of constitution making set up even higher consensus requirements. The original plans of the coalition would have set up a constitution drafting committee where the coalition parties needed only the votes of one opposition party (or of a few oppositional MPs) to submit a draft to the parliamentary plenum.[27] The eventual agreement set up a committee with equal (four) representation of all parties. Moreover, now the votes of five parliamentary parties (each voting by majority) and at least two-thirds of all committee members were needed to agree on any item and to pass on a constitutional draft to the assembly as a whole. The biggest party, the MSZP, which had 54 percent of the parliamentary seats, continued to be protected against any outcome it alone opposed, since the parliamentary rule of approval remained two-thirds of all deputies. But no one, not even the parliamentary majority, was allowed to amend drafts and proposals without the agreement of the new committee, which is at least five parties. Thus unlike in Poland, the parties of the coalition renounced proceeding in the Constitution Drafting Committee by principles of majority rule, or even according to their proportional weight in Parliament.

Again unlike in Poland, the agreement sought to restrict initiation and participation to parliamentary parties: Only the government or parliamentary party groups could submit proposals to the drafting committee, and only the committee could submit a draft to Parliament. Moreover, the sessions of the drafting committee were to be closed to the public, unless the committee specifically decided to hold an open hearing. Perhaps this should have been done the other way around. The stipulations immediately exposed the parties to criticisms by all those wishing to participate who were now excluded. Criticisms last heard after the MDF-SZDSZ pact of 1990 were now revived, despite the efforts of the coalition. But now the pacting parties involved all the parliamentary parties, after the last holdout, the Small Holders (FKGP), decided to add their name to the agreement and join the drafting committee. Unlike in Poland, organizations outside Parliament, so much weaker than the Polish Church or Solidarity, lost the only means whereby their demands could have been heard, the support of sympathetic party organizations.

The danger in Hungary to the process came not from extraparliamentary forces, but from the potential difficulties of passing a new constitution through such heavy consensus requirements. However, a wide party consensus was not the only means by which the agreement sought to ground constitutional legitimacy. In a clever but principled move that made decision making compatible with the heavy consensus requirements, it was agreed that where consensus on a new constitutional item fails, the relevant component of the 1989–90 constitution would remain in effect. Thus the method of political change through legal continuity, which was characteristic of the whole Hungarian system change, was not only continued but was raised to a norm. The document to be created in 1995–96 would thus not be a materially new basic law with respect to the regime structure produced by the system change, but its completion in a democratically expanded process,[28] thereby finally severing the umbilical cord (in my view: the old revision rule that kept the process open and unfinished) between itself and the inherited, never previously used Communist constitution.[29]

Finally, the parties of the coalition unilaterally declared that during the constitution-making process they would desist from using the amendment rule of the current constitution. That Parliament had to stop its frequent recourse to constitutional amendments became clear after the uproar surrounding two such efforts soon after the 1994 elections. We have seen that in the Polish case, the ability of the Sejm to amend could easily interfere with the work of the National Assembly. In Hungary, the formula of constitution making agreed upon was even less compatible with such an activity. Since it was stipulated that in absence of five-party agreement the old Constitution's relevant component would be maintained, the coalition parties could not keep their prerogative of modifying the old constitution according to the qualified majority they still controlled. Such amendments would now imply the subversion of consensus, and the very possibility of making them could become a hidden instrument of pressure. If in other words the currently valid Constitution could still be easily amended by the coalition, they could use this procedure as a roundabout way to adopt components of the new constitution without five-party support.

Thus the parties agreed, though without formal enactment, that during the period of the making of the new Constitution the inherited one too would be modified only according to the new rules agreed upon. What they did not take into account was that the moratorium on constitutional amendments would strengthen another branch of power, the Constitutional Court, whose decisions could find their way into the new Constitution through the formula that made the current document, along with its valid interpretations, the point of fallback in case of failure of consensus.

PARLIAMENTARY CONSTITUTION
MAKING AND ITS RIVALS

Constitution making by Parliament, a mere constitué, a branch of duly constituted government, was very much exposed to the potential interference of other branches of power: the presidency, the government, and the Constitutional Court. In Poland, where the Constitutional Tribunal was weak and the ministers were less independent of Parliament than in Hungary,[30] it was the presidency that represented the major threat of intervention. This was a credible threat for three fundamental reasons. First, at least as long as Walesa was in office (1990 to 1995), he and his subordinates strongly advocated a presidential regime, or a semipresidential one with a very strong presidency, which was at variance with the view of each and every parliamentary majority in the Sejm, as well as the very logic of parliamentary constitution making. Second, both the April 1989 amendments and the Little Constitution gave the president significant powers (suspensive veto, right of dissolution never clearly defined, role in appointments, and so on) that could be used to formally and informally influence the process of constitution making. And third, Walesa's personality was such that one could expect from him to use his powers all the way up to, and even beyond, the limits of legality.

Given the existence of a strong presidency, the president secured a formal role in the amendment process and was to acquire a similar one in the production of a new constitution. It does not follow from the nature of presidential or semipresidential regimes that there be such a role. In Poland it was a result of the diffuse and expandable nature of the president's powers and a model of constitution making that was understood, especially in the beginning, as simply a species of law making. As I have argued, the leveling of the distance between legislative and constitutive powers was ultimately responsible for this state of affairs. Accordingly, if the president could veto laws, then he could also veto constitutional laws. Yet in reality Walesa's powers turned out to be less significant than at first sight both in the case of amending the constitution and of producing a new one. In the case of constitution making, he could offer only amendments that would have to be approved by the same two-thirds margin as the constitution itself. Thus the power of the National Assembly was in no way diminished. In the case of amendments, the president did apparently have, even after the power shifted to the National Assembly, the power of suspensive veto. But since the Sejm (or later the National Assembly) could override the veto by the same majority that the amendment had to acquire, this power served at best only to delay. In fact several amendments were passed over presidential objections. Nevertheless, the office with its strong formal powers, patronage, and access to the media could pursue its goals informally. Revisions of the constitution-making rule in March 1994, which expanded the right of constitutional initiative, were achieved by President Walesa in this way.

Walesa was not, however, satisfied with a formal and ultimately precarious role in the process of actual enactment. He wished to clearly inject himself into the constitution-drafting process as well. And though he repeatedly failed to attain in this respect the specific objectives he sought, he always managed to create enough dissension and confusion that repeatedly threatened to derail the whole process. He was clearly a sponsor of the presidential draft of the Senate in 1991 that helped to defeat the Sejm draft, the only one that could have been legally adopted. The end result was that neither draft had a chance. He used his veto as well as informal powers to force the makers of the Little Constitution back to a path where they could neither reduce the presidential elements in the draft as much as they wanted nor unambiguously strengthen the government against presidentially sponsored projects of parliamentary dissolution. Finally he tried to formally get representation for his office in the drafting process of the new Constitution, but managed to get only a nonvoting, though still significant, presence.

Beyond seeking formal influence over drafting, President Walesa used informal sources of pressure as well. Undoubtedly he influenced the Constitutional Committee in 1992 to abandon drafting its own document and to become dependent on outside drafts, one of which would be submitted by the president's office.[31] After 1993, he fought hard and partially successfully for the acceptance of popular drafts and eventually threw his support behind the one submitted by the Solidarity union. At all times his objective was the achievement of a strong presidency, though he was forced to put up with a process that each step managed to weaken presidential powers. In the face of such a trend, from 1993 he also made the cultural and social program of the right his own, and it is on this level that he and his allies were to put their stamp on the draft in formation.

Such partial success was never enough for Walesa, however. Whenever he did not seem to get his way he openly threatened everything from legal manipulation of the unclear rules of parliamentary dissolution to a "Yeltsin solution," that is, using force against the parliamentary majority. These threats were serious enough for Parliament in January 1995, remembering the dissolution of

1993, to amend the Little Constitution over Walesa's veto in such a way that dissolutions were made more difficult and parliamentary rather than presidential caretaker governments were provided for after successful dissolution.[32]

Though in the last phase of Walesa's presidency, Kwasniewski, as the socialist chair of the Constitutional Committee, managed to bargain with him effectively, Walesa made it clear that he would in any case use his office to campaign against the plebiscitary ratification of any document that did not fully conform to his objectives. This threat was all the more credible since he would be able to rely on the forces of the Solidarity union and the Catholic Church in opposing any genuinely liberal constitution. But the threat would be carried out only when it could no longer be truly effective, when Walesa was no longer president.

It seems to be clear in retrospect that the defeat of Walesa in the presidential elections of 1995 was essential if the parliamentary constitution-making project was to succeed. The election of Kwasniewski to the presidency was to be sure initially somewhat ambiguous from the very same point of view. Though on record as favoring a parliamentary system, he began to slightly change his perspective as his own chances of election to the presidency looked increasingly good. This may have helped his dealings with Walesa, and vice versa, he could use the need to deal with the president as an excuse for moderating his earlier views. Yet after his election, President Kwasniewski did try once again (remarkably enough) to pressure the committee to strengthen the presidency in the constitutional draft under consideration. Significantly, however, the committee, still dominated by his own party, found it relatively easy to refuse this proposal.[33] Kwasniewski, in light of his earlier supposedly principled stance, was not in a good position to publicly fight for his new institutional interests, nor could he ally himself with the forces of the right against his own coalition.

Thus on balance, Kwasniewski's presidency became a spur rather than a hindrance to parliamentary constitution making. Having been strongly identified with the whole project since 1993, he wished above all for a great public relations triumph and the legitimacy he and his party would gain, nationally and internationally, in being the major author of a liberal democratic constitution. Thus when his absence from the head of the Constitutional Committee led to a slowing down of the project in Parliament, he reportedly was willing to use the threat (never really serious, and certainly not legal) of calling an independent constituent assembly to complete the job.[34] Finally, he used all of his official authority and personal powers of persuasion to help achieve ratification. He did this on behalf of a document that was to significantly reduce the powers of his own office. Nothing could have been further from the behavior of his post-Communist counterparts in Hungary, who were to use their governmental powers first to compromise, and finally to defeat parliamentary constitution making.

In Hungary too, even if far less visibly, other branches of power could not be entirely excluded when one branch assumed the major responsibility for constitution making. In Hungary parliamentary constitution making had to come to terms with the efforts of the executive branch, acting through the Ministry of Justice and the Constitutional Court. Neither instance of course formally claimed constituent powers. Yet the Ministry of Justice in particular had a lot of difficulty with the notion that even an imperfect constitution produced by a democratically elected body open to public scrutiny would be preferable to however perfect a document drawn up by their own in-house experts that would be somehow forced through by the parliamentary majority. Presumably, the interest of the more enlightened advisors of the ministry was only to produce a draft that would be the all-important reference point for all further discussions.[35] This idea was indeed fed to the press and even some international fora, but it too was stillborn. The last thing the parties of the system change of 1989, including and even especially the coalition partner Alliance of Free Democrats (SZDSZ), wished for was that the current MSZP minister of justice repeat the unsuccessful efforts of his predecessor from 1988 to dominate the constitution-making effort from the ministry.

In fact the particular terms of consensual constitution making to which the MSZP rather reluctantly agreed made the efforts of Minister of Justice Pál Vastagh and his team irrelevant. The agreement put the existing Constitution rather than any new draft in the center of the current project. The most that could be done with the ministry's rather eclectic text, which had some good points and some extremely questionable ones, was to let the representatives of the MSZP submit their ideas point by point, hoping to achieve an extremely unlikely five-party consensus in each instance.

The Constitutional Court, which more or less admittedly considered constitutional development to be mainly its own job, was a more formidable adversary, even though never claiming any role in drafting a constitution. Even the Constitutional Court did not wish for a return to the unstable dualistic option of 1990–1994, according to which first the Parliament and later the Court massively engaged themselves in piecemeal constitutional change. Instead of that arrangement, however, the Court unexpectedly was given one much more to its liking. As we have seen, in order not to subvert the formula of constitution making, in which the inherited Constitution remained the base, the coalition parties informally pledged a moratorium on further amendment of the current Constitution on the basis of their qualified majority. Thus the coalition parties informally agreed that during the period of the making of the new Constitution the inherited one too would be modified only according to the new rules agreed upon.[36]

They did not realize that a moratorium on constitution amending made sense only if the Constitutional Court refrained from revision through interpretation. Unfortunately few outside the Court initially realized the potential implications. The moratorium on amendments, however justified in itself, suddenly gave the Court what it always wanted, even if temporarily: a constitution almost impossible to change. Thus constitutional review became for a period not only final in the sense that there was no legal appeal or parliamentary override that could trump it; it was for the moment not even subordinated to the Constitution's amending power.

The refurbished power of the Constitutional Court was not merely a potential one. In fact this power was soon used to destroy significant parts of the Bokros economic program of 1995, the only program of a government that, however, remained secure in its parliamentary position.[37]

There was nevertheless a gap between what the Court could do in principle and what it could dare to do politically. It is abstractly true that when no longer subordinate to the Constitution's amending power, the Constitutional Court itself gains quasi-constituent powers.[38] The statement of President Sólyom, that the Court did not need to be worried about parliamentary reversals because it, unlike the U.S. Supreme Court and Parliament itself, possessed revolutionary legitimacy (!) reflected precisely such a claim.[39] Accordingly, the power to mold the new Constitution and evade consensus requirements by modifying the old Constitution voluntary surrendered by the coalition parties, was now implicitly obtained by the Court, the surviving half of the dualistic Constitution revising arrangements of 1990–94. The fact that the inherited Constitution was to continue unless five parties agreed to change it also established the Court's interpretations of that Constitution as permanent unless the agreement of five parties or new decisions by the Court itself explicitly superseded these.[40] This claimed power was not without effects on the potential constitutional outcome. Its decisions against the Bokros program gained the Court significant influence over the development of social rights in the drafting of the constitution.

Thus while the constitution makers debated and discussed, the Court, in the eyes of its critics, could apparently continue its practice of developing the Constitution through interpretation. But in actual politics this practice had its limits. The Court could not look forward to a long-term evolutionary perspective that would make it the true author of the "material constitution." The parties to the agreement have agreed that the end of the tenure of the Parliament elected in 1994 represents the outer limits of the current constitution-making effort. This deadline posed a challenge to the Court and those who may have wished to use it as the instrument of their constituent activity. If there were no consensus on new constitutional essentials, the old Constitution would remain valid. If the whole effort collapsed, the same would be true and the moratorium on amendments would be renounced. Let us recall that the old Constitution did contain one item that the Constitutional Court feared and detested but could not itself eliminate through interpretation: the old parliamentary amendment rule that was still formally valid and would again recover its effectiveness unless it were consensually changed in the parliamentary constitution-making effort.[41]

Moreover, many of the judges were nearing the end of their terms in the mid- and late 1990s. The method of their election was one with extreme consensus requirements,[42] and it needed to be changed if the Court was to be able to recruit judges who were not faceless bureaucrats. Given the difficulties with the nomination process, the quorum requirements of the Court could be endangered. But reform of the nomination and appointment too would have much been easier to accomplish within comprehensive constitutional legislation, because the parties that gave up their prerogative to nominate could not have been otherwise compensated.

The Constitutional Court too faced a dilemma. It could take a short-term approach, interfere (one way or another) with the constitution-making effort, exercise its powers at their highest possible peak, and be prepared for a time when the current coalition renounced its self-imposed moratorium on amendments or the existing electoral rule would put yet another majority potentially in a position where it could reverse court decisions through constitutional amendments. In the face of such dangers, it is fair to say that the Court did not contribute to the bringing down of the constitution-making effort, as the government was to do and as the Polish presidency under Walesa almost succeed in doing. After the uproar concerning its intervention in the domain of social rights, activist interpretation was in fact scaled down. Even the controversial decision of the Court in 1997 denying the right of Parliament to subvert a fully legal popular referendum was a piece of conservative interpretation, from the constitutional point of view.[43] The Hungarian constitution-making effort's failure cannot be blamed on the Constitutional Court.

FAILURE IN HUNGARY AND SUCCESS IN POLAND

In spite of grave signs of danger coming from the government, some of the parties, and initially the Constitutional Court, the Hungarian parliamentary drafting committee did move ahead with its work. Unfortunately the drafting process was split apart. A set of guidelines was to be produced first, and only after their approval would a constitutional text be formalized. Thus the document submitted to Parliament in May 1996, and, after more than ninety amendments from the floor were incorporated, once again in June, represented only a set of detailed guidelines for the final draft.[44] The guidelines were conspicuously successful in preserving the structure of the constitution of the regime change and in clarifying and resolving at least some of the troublesome issues.

In its preamble, the document defines Parliament as the agent of constitution making together with the community of citizens of the Hungarian Republic. Even this confusing formulation (the politically irrelevant 1997 draft constitution[45] was to speak of the community of citizens alone) was an improvement over the interim Constitution that indicated Parliament alone as its subject. The proposal made a clear decision for a parliamentary regime, as against a presidential one, but not for parliamentary sovereignty. Popular sovereignty was said to operate primarily through elected representatives, but it was (confusingly) added that in specific cases referenda could be held.[46] Accordingly, the extensive right of petition and the powers of referenda in the interim constitution and in the current law on referenda (1989 [XVII]) were to be specified and slightly reduced. The proposal and all its successors decided against a second parliamentary chamber, whether corporatist or territorial in its organization, even in temporary functions like presidential elections or constitutional change. Evidently, the chamber engaged in constitution making was not predisposed to share its powers with any other legislative body.

At the same time, the strong powers of government with respect to Parliament were kept through the constructive no-confidence vote and the absence of individual parliamentary responsibility of ministers. The relatively weak powers of the president were not to be increased, and the coalition failed[47] in pushing through a manner of election that would enforce consensus and make the president a little more independent on the parliamentary majority. Thus after the failure of consensus in two voting rounds the president would still be elected by a simple majority (Guidelines A. 3a). The governmental parties also failed to eliminate significant powers of the Constitutional Court (MJ Proposal, 80ff) that would retain both prior and posterior constitutional review as well as review triggered by ordinary citizen action. Only two powers would have been lost by the Court. The first was the ability to take up cases on its own initiative, not a very significant loss given the extensive list of those retaining standing (Guidelines A VI.1b). The second was the right to review decisions of the Supreme Court, the highest court of appeal.[48] The coalition also failed to put through (see MJ Proposal, 87) a method for the election of Constitutional Court justices other than the unworkable one of nomination through party parity and election through two-thirds parliamentary vote. The reason for this failure probably had to do with the grave difficulties of achieving through a procedure requiring agreement of five parties the replacement of a structure in which there were extensive veto opportunities for even small oppositional parties.

Finally, among the important achievements of the guidelines was the redefinition of social rights as goals or obligations of the state that would not be enforceable by court decisions against the government (Guidelines A. 2f and 2g). When many members of Parliament considered the document insufficiently sensitive to the requirements of social justice, several relevant amendments were submitted. Among these were several state goals, such as right to the basic health care, that were now again defined as subjective entitlements of citizens, yet the important distinction was preserved. The right to work was, for example, cleverly reconceptualized by Mihály Bihari in such a way that full employment remained "only" an obligatory goal of the government (Guidelines B. II. 1f). Even more importantly, habeas corpus found its way among the approved amendments on the wishes of FIDESZ, which had fought for this since 1990. So did the right against any type of discrimination, whatever its basis (Guidelines A II.1.f. pars. 5 and 6). The table of rights that emerged from these efforts was in most respects a thoroughly modern and, on the whole, a legally enforceable one.[49]

In my view at least, a serious failing of the guidelines was the inability to clearly redefine the electoral rules in the direction of greater proportionality. These rules were constitutionalized only on a very high level of abstraction that required a mixed system but not a specific variety of one. Thus the rule remained open to relatively easy modification in the future with a qualified majority. Given, moreover, the likelihood of the continuation of the highly disproportional electoral rule, the relative silence of the document on constitutional politics is even more striking. Admittedly, the proposal confirms (perhaps illogically) that the new Constitution itself would have to be passed according to current rules by a two-thirds parliamentary vote followed by a ratificatory referendum, a risky project in Hungary given repeated problems with turnout. But even this requirement is missing in the case of amendments under the constitution that was proposed. The greatest failing of the guidelines was the apparent inability to say more about the all-important future constitution revision rule beyond stating that it would have to be made more demanding than the current one.

Thus it can be said that the drafting committee failed to propose a way of insulating the Constitution from future parliamentary efforts that could again level the distinction between constitutional and ordinary legislation. In fact the committee did consider three options for ratifying constitutional amendment drafts that pass by a two-thirds vote: (1) subsequent parliamentary dissolution and confirmation by the next Parliament; (2) confirmation by referenda; and (3) nullification by referenda, if a sufficient number of parliamentary votes or other possible instances like the president of the republic call for it.[50] The first approach of course would make the passing of amendments unlikely except at the end of a parliamentary cycle, while, given problems with electoral turnout, the third approach might have turned out to be identical to the current arrangement in which Parliament has the monopoly. Apparently in 1996 none of these options had the support of five parties. Unfortunately, the possibility was not seriously considered that the three approaches could have been combined in relation to amendments of different parts of the constitutional document. Though the drafters did not wish to make any part of the Constitution unchangeable, they might have seen the importance of shielding some provisions to a higher extent than others. Unfortunately they did not, though the possibility was called to their attention.[51]

The inability of the parties to agree on a new amendment rule that reliably interfered with ad hoc amendments and gave other instances and procedures other than parliamentary ones a role in constitution revising had serious implications. The closure of the period of regime change was one of the most important objectives of the current constitution-making effort, and without a new, more difficult amendment rule this goal could not be achieved. If the effort were challenged, it should have been because of this omission. Had that happened, however, the problem could have been corrected easily enough. For example, the amendment rule of the rather academic 1997 draft, which represented the final product of the work of the committee and its experts, provided for the possibility of nullification through referenda [pars. 185 and 186]. This provision, which also denied the president and the Constitutional Court any role in the review of amendments,[52] could have been adopted already in 1996. The result would have been marginally better than the current arrangements, with forces other than Parliament having gained at least a potential role in constitutional politics.

But in any case the project in fact did not fail in 1996 because of the genuine flaws and omissions of the guidelines. When it came to voting, the drafting committee first introduced the set of amendments that were presumably consensual among the parties and that were required to ensure passage for the guidelines as a whole. What then happened was nothing short of spectacular. Not only did many members of the Small Holders evidently boycott the session, but so did many Christian Democrats who sympathized with some of their issues (direct election of the president, a corporate second chamber, use of referenda to pass parts and not only the whole of the draft) as well as many members of the MDF (now free of its centrists). Because of these absences the two-thirds of the votes of all the MPs could be achieved only if almost all of the remaining fractions fully supported the amendments and the amended draft. Such support was indeed forthcoming from the SZDSZ fraction and from the relatively few opposition deputies (mainly from FIDESZ and the MDNP: a right of center breakaway from the MDF) who were present, and indeed from the large majority of socialist members as well who followed the instructions of their parliamentary leadership. But the amendments (and therefore draft guidelines that were never even voted on) failed by a mere five votes because of the unexpected but certainly coordinated negative votes and abstentions of the ministers and party leaders of the stronger governmental party, the MSZP.

As one participant, the ex-minister of the interior, Imre Konya (MDNP), remarked in *Magyar Narancs* (July 4), it sometimes can happen in a parliamentary regime that a party votes against its government. But a government voting against its parliamentary party, and on a cardinal issue, has never happened anywhere as far as anyone could remember. The excuse of Gyula Horn and his colleagues was that the guidelines did not define Hungary as a "social" rule-of-law state and that they did not mandate compulsory social bargaining in economic issues. This was laughable, since the socialist delegation has played a prominent role in drafting the guidelines, and the decision of the government members to vote against these discredited their long and serious work because of one matter that was merely symbolic (the adjective "social") and another ("social partnership") that is regulated almost everywhere in the world, including the most developed welfare states, through statutes or informal practices. Moreover, since a five-party agreement on such departures from the 1989–90 Constitution was extremely unlikely, insisting on it now with such vehemence could mean only that Horn and Vastagh never accepted in good faith the constitution-making procedures that their party signed and that the Parliament ratified by more than the necessary 80 percent of the votes (which at that time did include the socialist ministers and party leaders). Obviously, they could have stopped the process early when they saw that they could not influence the committee regarding their wishes. By letting it proceed in a normal, if time-consuming manner, and bringing down only the final result, Horn and his colleagues unmistakably indicated their hostility to the whole process of parliamentary and consensual constitution making.

They were not alone. All those who unsuccessfully fought for a materially new (presidentialist, corporatist, and so on) constitution, and who objected to the method of constitution making that was adopted, were on their side. As many representatives of the Small Holders and socialists close to the ex-official unions came to admit, the adherence to the regime structure of the Round Table, which the drafting procedures were based on, seemed in itself injurious to these forces, if for divergent reasons. They objected to an original process and outcome in which the three new parties of the regime change—the MDF (under Antall), SZDSZ, and FIDESZ—played the dominant role, conveniently forgetting that the Round Table agreements were as much the work of the reform wing of the socialists and that the Small Holders were one of the sponsors with SZDSZ of the referendum campaign against the direct election of the presidency. Whatever the historical merits of their arguments, these spokesmen now believed that the current constellation of forces no longer required the dominant role of SZDSZ, FIDESZ, and the remnants of the Antallist MDF now grouped in the MDNP in the constitution-making process. But the agreements of 1995 even now implied that at least two of these parties (the Antallists in MDNP were not included in the process because of the veto of the MDF), FIDESZ and SZDSZ together, were in position to protect the public law structure established in 1989–90. Thus these agreements had to be brought down.

Of course the socialist leaders agreed to the parliamentary consensual procedures in June 1995, and so did eventually the Small Holders. But in one year there was an important shift in party alignments. The formation of the MDNP pushed the remaining MDF to the right by taking away the more moderate followers of József Antall. The continued strength of the FKGP in the polls at that time kept alive the option of a right-wing replacement of the current government in which the new MDF and the Christian Democrats at least could participate. Many forces in the MSZP, certainly a minority, considered their government's own economic package to be inspired by the liberal SZDSZ ultimately, and they had considerable sympathy for the right-wing parties that denounced this program from the left. To some of them a coalition with the Christian Democrats would have been more desirable than one with the liberals. And these forces have been strengthened by the inevitably negative public response to the pain caused by the government's stabilization program. Thus just as the forces of the right were split between wishing to draw to the center with FIDESZ and the new MDNP or to the right with the Small Holders, so were the forces of the left that saw the choice between the center and with their then-coalition partner SZDSZ and the left where paradoxically the right-wing parties with neostate socialist economic views were to be found.

Thus the socialist leaders could feel free to repudiate the agreements of 1995 because they had new potential support, even if largely outside their own members of Parliament. After their vote brought down the constitutional guidelines, they were immediately greeted by Torgyan and Agnes Maczo Nagy (minutes of parliamentary debate of June 27). Voting statistics were even more revealing. Counting all deputies of each party, and thus absences as negative votes, 85 percent of FIDESZ, 84 percent of SZDSZ, and 63 percent of MSZP supported the amendments to the guidelines. In the case of the Christian Democrats and the MDF, that figure was only 39 percent and 41 percent, respectively. Thus it was an implicitly new alignment of parties that brought down the proposal, with the right-wing parties allied with the socialist apparatus arraigned against the still stronger (but not sufficiently strong) parties of the regime change: the SZDSZ, the FIDESZ, the remnants of the Antall MDF in the MDNP, and nota bene the modern sectors of the MSZP following their parliamentary leadership. We should not assume, moreover, that the run-of-the-mill socialist deputies (131 in all!) merely stumbled into opposing their top leaders over an issue that they did not understand. They were quite aware internally that Horn and Vastagh wanted the plan to be voted down. When the party leadership formally recommended to the fraction that this be done, they were decisively defeated in an open vote. In the end Horn and Vastagh were strong enough to prevail only because they were part of an alliance in their obstruction, a pink and gray (rather than red and black) left-right alliance.

In Poland it was an implicit socialist liberal alliance that succeeded in drafting and enacting a constitution. This success was above all based on a parliamentary weakness, even absence of the right, a different state of affairs than in Hungary. But mindful of the great forces that could oppose ratification, the church and Solidarity, the constitution makers did make concessions to forces not in Parliament. In the end, they could not come to an agreement with the forces opposed to a liberal democratic constitution, but their mostly symbolic concessions helped to reduce the effectiveness of this opposition when it came to ratification. The resulting document passed with a 451 to 40 vote majority in the National Assembly and ratified by a vote of 57 percent versus 46 percent in a national referendum with relatively low participation of 43 percent.

The new document had several important strengths that addressed the structural difficulties faced by the new regime:

1. First and foremost, the new Constitution established a parliamentary system, with only residual semipresidential elements. The Little Constitution to be sure already moderated the strong presidency produced by the Round Table, but the outcome left a great deal of room for presidential intervention when the parliamentary majority was weak. Thus as Leszek Lech Garlicki argues, the arrangement permitted two possible scenarios of executive and legislative relations—a parliamentary one and a presidential one—in my view reminiscent more of Weimar than the arrangements of the Fifth Republic to which Walesa preferred to appeal.[53] The Constitution of 1997 now eliminated the presidential scenario. To be sure the president is still elected as before, for five years, with the possibility of one reelection, directly by the population, according to the same rules. He can be removed only by impeachment (two-thirds vote of the National Assembly and conviction by the State Tribunal). He retained his veto power except in the case of the budget, but the vote to override a veto was reduced from two-thirds to three-fifths. A reduction of the Senate's veto powers was also ordained, producing a more asymmetrical brand of bicameralism, a requirement of genuinely parliamentary government. With the disappearance of the nonconstructive vote of confidence, the president's power to dissolve Parliament was severely limited, and he would not be able to name his own caretaker presidential cabinet à la Weimar. The president has lost his special relation to the appointment of the ministers of Defense, Foreign Affairs, and Security, and his role in appointments and other state functions was now tied to ministerial countersignatures. In line with the strengthening of the Constitutional Tribunal, the president did receive one important new function: to submit legislation to the Constitutional Review on grounds of potential violation of the Constitution. Moreover, he received the right to appoint the presidents of the top tribunals from among candidates proposed by the general assemblies of the courts.[54]

2. The Constitution not only strengthened the Parliament versus the president but also the government versus the Parliament. The only possibility of a no-confidence vote removing the government was now a constructive one, in other words, a replacement must be agreed upon by the majority that wishes to dismiss a current prime minister. Furthermore,

individual ministerial responsibility was abolished; thus the Parliament lost its ability to bring down government on a retail basis, bypassing the constructive vote of no-confidence.[55]

3. Even more importantly, given the strengthening of government, the Constitution made a distinct attempt to also strengthen constitutional review. Two years after the adoption of the text, Parliament shall lose the right to override adverse decisions by the Constitutional Tribunal.[56] Moreover, the circle of those with standing is vastly expanded by establishing the right of constitutional complaint (Article 79) of all those citizens whose rights are adversely affected by a purportedly unconstitutional statutes or decrees applied by the courts. Unfortunately the right of constitutional complaint does not apply to court decisions not based on unconstitutional statutes or decrees.[57] At least on a declaratory level it is, however, established that judges are first and foremost subject to the constitution, that thereby becomes the supreme law. Skeptics like Pawel Spiewak are right to stress that the model of constitutional review established is not a very strong one.[58] But it is certainly stronger than its predecessor, and, as the only somewhat less skeptical Ewa Letowska stresses, the actual role of the institution in the future will depend on its own actions, as well as relevant public attitudes.[59]

4. After various inconclusive and incomplete attempts to establish a Charter of Rights and Freedoms, the Constitution of 1997 established a more or less modern catalogue of rights. The idea so foreign to Americans, that rights can be limited by statute, is unfortunately kept. More disturbing even is the idea, undoubtedly a concession to the religious right, that rights can be limited by law in the name of a select group of "higher values," such as natural environment, health, and public morals.[60] On the plus side the table of rights established is fully comprehensive, while making an important distinction between rights that are fully judicable and those that are closer to goals of the state whose satisfaction depends on factors the courts cannot control. While the list of fully judicable social rights is rather large, the Constitution makes clear that only a minimum threshold of supports can be recognized by the courts as a full entitlement.[61] In addition, the important institution of the ombudsman was retained.

5. Finally the constitution raised proportional representation to a constitutional status and established what some consider a middle strong amendment rule.[62] After initiation by relatively few members (one-fifth) of the Senate or the Sejm, or the president, two-thirds of the Sejm can amend the Constitution as long as a majority of all members of the Senate agree ("absolute majority"). Referenda can be initiated only in case of amendments touching on fundamental rights and freedoms. In my view, given existing electoral patterns and the fact that the Senate does

not represent a specific constellation of interests, with the exception of the domain of rights the rule amounts to an easy parliamentary amendment regime, little different than what has existed since 1989. The constitutionalization of proportional representation (along with the strategic learning experiences of the parties) is important precisely in this context. If the easy adoption of highly disproportional electoral systems will be impossible even in the long run, we can assume that governments will not easily attain the two-thirds majority required to continue tinkering with the Constitution and endanger the boundary between constitutional and ordinary politics so important for constitutionalism.[63]

These provisions establish more or less the liberal parliamentary regime sought by the socialists and the liberals in Parliament between 1993 and 1994. To the extent the drafts of the right, especially the extraparliamentary forces, played a role, this was on the level of symbolic components of the Constitution with uncertain legal status. Elements of the preamble, some of the social and "cultural" rights (hardly judicable) represent the main concessions to the Catholic Episcopate especially. Instead of a formula of state neutrality on matters of religion, a formula of amicable cooperation between church and state was adopted. To the Church, however, these concessions were in any case hardly enough. Many bishops lamented that the God mentioned in the preamble is really the "god of the philosophers," not of Christianity. They were disturbed that natural law was not established as higher than positive law, as if any modern constitution could subordinate itself and its officials to the interpreters of natural law, presumably the Church itself.[64] But most of all the Church was disturbed that the Constitution did not establish a kind of right-to-life provision they sought. For these reasons, in the end the Catholic Episcopate violated its promise not to campaign against the Constitution.[65] In spite of their efforts, and the efforts of the Solidarity union as well as former President Walesa, the document was nevertheless ratified.

THE PROBLEM OF LEGITIMACY IN THE TWO COUNTRIES

The 1997 and 1998 elections brought new forces to power in both Poland and Hungary: Each involved a right-of-center alliance, bringing together a right-wing force (Solidarity in Poland, the Small Holders in Hungary) with a liberal or partially liberal party (Freedom Union in Poland, FIDESZ in Hungary). Though the power relations among the coalition partners is different, what is similar is that in each case one partner supported a liberal democratic constitution in the preceding parliamentary period, while the other partner was its determined opponent. Moreover, neither coalition today has a constitution-amending two-thirds majority. Thus in both countries the Constitution in place, the 1989–90 document in Hungary and the 1997 Constitution in Poland, are likely to survive and be solidified.

In Hungary this means, on the positive side, on the side of normal politics, the continuation of an effective parliamentary regime of five to six parties, allowing stable governments and relatively smooth alternations in power. On the negative side, the side of constitutional politics, there will be undoubtedly a continuation in the future of a tense relationship between parliamentary sovereignty and judicial constitution making. The current government is to the Court's liking, but because of the survival of the parity rule in nomination and the need for a qualified majority to finalize appointments, new conflicts between the Court and the opposition are possible. Today the four parties of the right can nominate judges, but the MSZP and the SZDSZ have more than the one-third votes required to block nonconsensual appointments of justices. Strangely enough this basic situation did not change as a result of the 1998 elections. Thus as members retire, the very functioning of the Court can be endangered. This is serious, because whatever legitimacy the Hungarian constitutional settlement has been able to slowly acquire was through the ritualized and traditionalized ministry of the constitution through court interpretations.

As of today, the current Constitution cannot be said to enjoy a high level of acceptance and support. And this means that the failure of consensus pursued for reasons of enhanced legitimacy left Hungary with the still open-ended constitution of the regime change, with its easy, parliamentary amendment rule, its electoral rule allowing the emergence of overwhelming majorities, with its built-in conflict between court and Parliament, and between constitutionalism and democracy, with a long-term potential for the "constitutional dictatorship" of whoever holds two-thirds of the seats.

In Poland far less attention has been paid to satisfying demanding consensus requirements for constitution making. Since the right-wing parties were outside of Parliament, token concessions to extraparliamentary forces allowed socialists and liberals, the main actors behind the effort (here as well as in Hungary), to produce their constitution. This Constitution solved some of the major problems of the previous constitutional arrangements, hostage to a mixed decision for parliamentarism and presidentialism. Today Poland, like Hungary, is a parliamentary republic with many of the same institutions. It will be interesting to see in the long term whether strong parliamentary and governmental power is better balanced by a combination of a weaker presidency and stronger Constitutional Court as in Hungary, or a stronger presidency and weaker Constitutional Tribunal as in Poland. We have no principled reason to prefer the Hungarian formula, where after the failure of constitution making, the search for legitimacy might in the end produce a republic of judges.

But the Polish settlement does have its Achilles' heel. Many Hungarians undoubtedly admire the way socialists and liberals in Poland pushed through their constitutional scheme, under presidential leadership, and wish that they had done so when possessing an overwhelming parliamentary majority. Yet in Hungary at least, such an imposed constitution would have had far greater legitimation problems than the interim constitution of the regime change that was adopted in a quasi-revolutionary time and in whose making a large number of social forces did after all participate. Little would have been gained from forcing through the change and much could have been lost. Of course the Polish interim constitution, with its built-in time bombs, had to be changed, and it could be argued that this necessary change could not be made hostage to political parties and civil organizations that would use the search for consensus to either impose their own ideas or shipwreck the whole project. Nevertheless, to major forces in Polish society, including the Church, Solidarity, and its offspring, the current major governmental party, the Constitution of 1997, is an imposed and illegitimate product. It is still difficult to see today under what conditions Poles with different political and cultural persuasions will be able to regard this impressive document as fully their own.

Chapter 7

Forms of Constitution Making and Theories of Democracy

There are still those who think that constitution making is simply the hour of the lawyers. Indeed all constitutional texts in modern times have been drafted by lawyers. But behind them are the most important political actors and forces of a given society. To some interpreters therefore, constitution making represents the hour of the political, of political politics, of *le pouvoir constituant*. In such a conception, whoever holds the "constituent power" or acts in its name hires the lawyers. Does the method of constitution making matter? Either way it may be deemed epiphenomenal, a formalistic facade for the activity of experts or for the elemental self-expression of an unlimited sovereign power.[1]

A constitution is the normatively established structure of a political regime, including above all the powers to make, execute, interpret, and adjudicate law, and the forms of limitation on these powers. In this "material" sense (Hans Kelsen) all political systems have a constitution, whether established by customary or positive law.[2] Kelsen rightly distinguishes from the material constitution, constitutions in the formal sense established as frameworks of *positive, written,* and *legal* norms, *insulated* from ordinary laws by a formal revision rule that makes constitutional change more difficult than ordinary legislation.[3]

Constitutions in the formal sense exist only in modern societies, and even then not necessarily. Where they do exist their aim seems to many to be the stability and relative permanence of the material constitution. In fact, as the example of Great Britain shows, a material constitution rooted in custom, precedent, and unprotected statute can at times be far more stable and inflexible than many written constitutions. H. L. A. Hart's analysis demonstrates this point with respect to custom, or the regime of primary rules that do not contain laws of change.[4] Laws of change, amendment rules in the case of constitutional law, are in principle rules of both insulation and reflexive adaptation. Their purpose thus cannot simply be the achievement of stability. In fact historically, written constitutions of a legal character with relatively difficult

229

amendment rules emerged in the context of the liberal struggle against absolutism or at least arbitrary government. Their aim was to constitute a new form of power that would be legally limited by its constitution. The eighteenth- and nineteenth-century ideal of liberal constitutionalism aimed not at constitutional stability as such, but the stability of a regime where the rule of law restricted in important ways all-important holders of political power.[5] Constitutionalism is possible without a constitution in the formal sense, but it is certainly strongly reinforced by written, legal constitutions and relatively difficult amendment rules.

From the point of view of constitutionalism the origins of the constitution are highly relevant. As Friedrich Hayek has maintained, one can defend the insulation of constitutional law from the will of legitimate legislatures in the name of a higher law incorporated in and defended by constitutional contents like fundamental rights and the separation of powers. Popular attachment to constitutionalism may be still largely based on such premises, above all in the United States. But in an epoch of the secularization of political ideas and the positivization of law, arguments based on natural law or even fundamental human rights appear increasingly unconvincing especially to the strata expected to interpret and uphold the law on the basis of an internal attitude of conviction, the legal profession including the judiciary. For this reason, a theory of constitutional legitimacy linked to the notion of the democratic origin of the constitution can be especially important in justifying constitutionalist forms of protection against elected representatives, in particular amendment rules and judicial review.

From the point of view of democratic theories that recognize the importance of written constitutions, it is of course even more important that constitution making be itself democratic. Most democratic theories do not and cannot recognize any source of legitimacy other than direct or electoral participation by all full members of the political community. If it is important that the rules of the game provide for democratic participation, it is equally or even more important that these rules themselves emerge in a democratic process. Moreover, since constitutional rules have distributional consequences, a decision concerning these cannot be left to elites or privileged minorities. Since consensus will be difficult on many legislative issues that will in fact be decided by narrow majorities, it is especially important that the rules under which legislation takes place incorporate a relatively high level of consensus. Finally, given the compromises with nondemocracy that "normal" politics under liberal democracies inevitably involve, it seems especially important that the constituent process itself be democratic in a relatively strong sense.

It is nevertheless true that any democracy is conceivable only according to some rules. Thus one easily runs into the problem of cicularity when one demands that constitutions be made democratically. The circle cannot be broken by a reference to a formless and preprocedural quasi-natural popular sovereign or constituent power. Some interpreters have therefore called attention to an element of irreducible factuality at the basis of the validity of our constitutional rules,[6] while many others have insisted on an unavoidable moment of violence at moments of constitutional foundation.[7]

Evidently, however, nondemocratic procedures of constitution making cannot be justified today; the figure of the "law giver," the nonparticipant architect of constitutions, can no longer be plausibly revived. But it seems at the same time that we cannot eliminate, for logical reasons, an element of nondemocracy prior to all democratic procedures of producing a democratic constitution.

Let us consider one instructive example, the making of the Fourth French Republic. In the summer of 1945, six months after the Liberation, the provisional government called the first election for a national assembly and at the same time addressed two questions to the population in a referendum: (1) Should the new assembly be a Constituent Assembly, in session only during the drafting of a constitution, for a maximum of six months? And if yes, (2) Should the new government be a provisional one, for the duration of constitution making? The affirmative answers that actually followed meant the abrogation of the already interrupted Third Republic and its 1875 Constitution. The assembly elected along with the referendum thus became a constituent one, and it did produce a constitution in April 1946. According to the rule of ratification devised by this assembly, the document was submitted to a second popular referendum that, however, rejected this particular constitutional proposal. A second Constituent Assembly was then elected. It too produced a (slightly different) constitution, which was approved in October 1946 in a third referendum, and the Fourth Republic was born.

Though it would have been difficult to imagine a more democratic constituent process from the procedural point of view,[8] one key feature of the process was certainly not arrived at democratically: the electoral law used to elect both assemblies. This law implemented by the provisional government that emerged from the war and the resistance provided for the first time in French history proportional representation. Thus it could be argued subsequently that this choice implied a constellation of parties that could produce a constitution only with an "assembly government," dependent on a plurality of parties, and thus a weak executive power.[9] The argument could not be proved since the Third Republic with its different electoral law also produced a plurality of parties, but it also could not be disproved.[10] While Charles de Gaulle as the head of the provisional government originally accepted proportional representation, his followers never tired of implying that the process was dominated by something close to a conspiracy of the left, or of the "parties." Thus, in spite of its apparently ultrademocratic character, the foundation of the Fourth Republic remained a contested one, especially given the high abstention rate in the final referendum. Again in terms of the referendum rule used the abstention rate should not have mattered, yet it did. The supposedly nondemocratic dimension of the founding came to be more remembered in the end than the tortured attempts to derive the legitimacy of a new beginning only from a democratic procedure.[11]

HISTORICAL TYPES OF CONSTITUTION MAKING

Fully aware of the depth of the problem of "the beginning," Hannah Arendt was one author who thought that this problem, with all its "perplexities" that she brilliantly explored, could be solved. She looked to find "a beginning containing its own principle," and in this search she hardly considered the method of constitution creation irrelevant. She distinguishes three such methods, according to the source of constitutions. Constitutions according to her can be products of a long process of organic evolution, can be acts of already established government, or can be created by revolutionary assemblies in the process of constituting a government.[12] We should add to this list that acts of government can be attributed to legislatures, to executives, or to judiciaries. Moreover, the assemblies she considered revolutionary can take either the form of conventions whose task is only constitution making while other assemblies deal with the daily political business or that of extraordinary bodies that exercise the plenitude of all political powers while producing a constitution. In either case in fact the revolutionary legal form can be used in nonrevolutionary political contexts.[13] Focusing on the legal form alone, we thus have six pure types of constitution making if we disregard the possibility, in fact the likelihood of combinations.

This list can be, however, further reduced. While in theory constitutions can be indeed made by the judiciary, this method is not likely to exist in isolation.[14] Something must be done by other political instances, even if mythological ones, before judges can begin to interpret and thus create through interpretation. In the actual contexts with judges being major actors of constitutional development (in the United States: because of the Common Law tradition of judge-made law and the difficulties of the current amendment rule) either the model of long-term legal evolution or some kind of mixed model was dominant. Indeed in this sense any successful constitution-making process will be a mixture of at least two methods. By whatever method constitutions in the formal sense are originally produced, for unavoidable logical and historical reasons either judicial interpretation and constitutional revision processes, or both, mould all of the constitutions in the material sense, including supposedly unchangeable ones, if they are lucky enough to survive. Since my concern here is the original creation of constitutions, this important point concerning the necessarily mixed nature of constitution making can be left aside, and the idea of constitution making through the judiciary can be bracketed for the time being. Thus the six pure types of constitutional origins can be safely reduced to five.

Arendt has not provided us examples to sufficiently illustrate even her own three types. It is hard to know precisely what exactly she had in mind in describing the post–World War I and post–World War II constitutions in a more or less blanket way as acts of (already constituted) governments. Certainly the formation of the Weimar Republic and the Fourth Republic, to which she makes an oblique reference as "systems," in the eyes of their opponents cannot be understood from the legal point of view as acts of already existing governments. The *Grundgesetz,* of which Arendt was likely thinking,[15] was in a sense the product of already existing provincial governments, which had constitutions and elected political organs that were to fully survive the formation of the new federal state.

But this was equally the case for the making of the U.S. Constitution in 1787, in the case of which Arendt specifically applauds the fact that it arose not from a juridical state of nature, but on the bases of already constituted, "small republics." In fact both the U.S. Constitution and the *Grundgesetz* were, legally speaking, produced by representatives of state legislatures assembled in a body created only for that purpose, but were not produced by those legislatures themselves through the bound mandates of the delegates (as a treaty, like the Articles of Confederation ratified in 1781, still was). In both cases they formed an entirely new government.

Thus, they both contained an element of established legislatures participating in constituting a government, but the body in each case in spite of the different terminologies (Constitutional Convention vs. Parliamentary Council) was a special one called for a single purpose, coexisting with established provincial legislatures that retained all other functions. And while it is true that the leaders of the German *Länder* explicitly rejected the model of calling a constituent assembly, it was the French revolutionary model (practiced also during the making of the Weimar Constitution) that they rejected, and not the model of the U.S. foundation.

Admittedly, the processes of public participation so important to Arendt were very different in the cases of the Philadelphia Convention and the Parliamentary Council, and even the methods of ratification were different since in the United States, specially elected state conventions rather than the regular state legislatures had this task as against the German case. Politically, moreover, one process was the end result of a revolutionary dynamic and the other of military defeat and occupation.

Finally, Arendt is right to reemphasize Karl Loewenstein's judgment that the framers of the *Grundgesetz* exhibited a "deep distrust of the people." But even these special circumstances do not allow the *Grundgesetz,* representing the legal order of a state that came into being as the product of a specially elected body that existed neither before nor after its constituent activity, one that very

234 Chapter 7

much had its own independent dynamics, to be summarily described as an act of government.[16]

If we want an example of constitution making as an act of government, the making of the Fifth French Republic will serve us much better. Here indeed a government, and specifically its executive branch through the Ministry of Justice, produced a constitution tailor made for itself. Legal continuity was to be sure maintained, with Parliament voting (under the great political pressure of that moment) to cede its own constitutional revision role entirely to the executive, with members of the legislature degraded to a merely consultative role.[17] Could such a vote be anything other than implicit response to the threat of force? It may be that under the conditions of the existing crisis, many of the legislators did not wish to be in a position where they would block the road to the only perceivable solution. In either case, the process of the making of the Fifth Republic had the threat of force steering it. This process could have been hardly more different than the classical constituent assembly model of the making of the Fourth Republic, another possible, but (as I already indicated) implausible reference of Arendt's "governmental constitution making."

One may, of course, grant that constitution making through a regular parliament is also an act of government, especially where strong executive dominance reduces the assembly to its instrument. Nevertheless, a parliament is a democratically elected instance and is, under contemporary conditions, far more open to democratic scrutiny than is the executive branch. Thus it makes a certain amount of sense to keep the two forms, parliamentary and executive constitution making, apart, especially because, as I will show, the latter unlike the former is a likely terrain for constitution making under demanding normative principles.

With these considerations in mind, the five types of constitution making can be illustrated, at least in a preliminary way, by focusing on the different agencies that have produced constitutions in the modern world:

1. constitutional convention
   Massachusetts Convention 1780; Philadelphia Convention of 1787; and in the purely formal sense, the German Parliamentary Council 1948 (Russia: failed attempt in summer of 1993)

2. sovereign constituent assembly
   Pennsylvania Convention 1776; the Constituent Assembly 1789–91; the National Convention 1793–95; the Weimar Assembly 1918; the French Constituent Assemblies of 1945; Bulgaria and Romania in 1990

3. normally elected legislature
   a. single chamber model, or two chambers meeting separately: nine American state legislatures 1776–77; Spanish ("constituent") Parliament of 1977; Czech and Slovak Republics 1992

    b. National Assembly model (two chambers meeting together): France 1875; Poland 1992–97; South Africa 1995.

4. executive
Napoleon Bonaparte's governments in 1799, 1802, and 1804;[18] French Ministry of Justice in 1958; Yeltsin's government, fall 1993; Menem's government in Argentina, 1994.

5. evolutionary process
Constitution of the United Kingdom; New Zealand; Israel; constitutions of Connecticut and Rhode Island through the nineteenth century.

Undoubtedly these five types of constitution making (as all typologies) do raise boundary problems.[19] How is one to categorize constitutions like the one produced in 1994 in Argentina when (as traditionally the case in many Latin American countries) the formalities of the U.S. model were followed but where the forms were apparently the cover for governmental, indeed presidential constitution making or at best a bargain for two political leaderships? A point that was lost on no one in Argentina.[20] In such a case, which is fully thinkable only in a setting in which there is little constitutionalism, I would stress the real political process and disregard the rather empty forms. Forms are generally not empty, but they can be, sometimes.

    The first three processes of constitution making on my list presuppose the autonomy of the three types of assembly. But focusing only on such bodies, it remains fair to ask another type of question about boundaries. Why were the two French assemblies of 1945 more extraordinary or less "normal" than the Spanish Parliament of 1977? Indeed, some people do (I believe incorrectly) refer to the body that made the Spanish Constitution as "the constituent assembly." Is this a matter of mere nomenclature? In both 1945 and 1977, after all, the stake was the transition from dictatorship to democracy, also in the legal-constitutional sense. This (as it turns out important) question can be, I believe, answered in spite of the fact that historians refer to neither process as a revolution. The French assemblies became constituent explicitly on the basis of a referendum that decreed the end of the Third Republic and established (or in effect legalized) a provisional government, provisional precisely because it was operating under circumstances when the old constitution existed no longer and the new did not yet exist. These classical unicameral constituent assemblies were each charged to produce a constitution in a limited time (six or seven months) and were to be in session only until they completed voting on a constitutional draft and a referendum on their draft could be held. In Spain, the new 1977 bicameral legislature was elected on the bases of a fully legal "Law for Political Reform" passed by the last Franquist Cortes ("the harakiri Cortes") and was confirmed in a popular referendum in 1976 and for a normal legislative period that lasted beyond the making of the constitution. Moreover, the actors them-

selves were quite aware of the distinction between what they took to be the traditional European route of constitution making, involving a sovereign constituent assembly, and the method that they eventually adopted after serious
disagreement. The option of legal "ruptura," involving the creation of a provisional government for the duration of constitution making, though demanded
by the democratic opposition (similarly to the "left" in many other settings:
from West Germany in 1948 to South Africa in 1992) was in the end explicitly
rejected. So was the idea that the assembly should dissolve itself, along with the
call for new elections once its constituent work was over.[21] In France, the assemblies were producing constitutions for a future in which they themselves (along
with all then-operative powers) would cease to exist, and where they would be
replaced by differently constituted, newly elected bodies. In Spain, Parliament
was producing a constitution under which it and the existing monarchy would
continue to operate.[22] In sum not only the practice, but also the theory of these
two constituent processes was different, with the 1945 French assemblies operating with the classical Sieyèsian theory of the constituent power, while the
Spanish constitution makers explicitly agreed to abandon that model in favor of
a method of legal continuity.

In some of the newly forming democracies today all of these options were
in principle open. In Hungary, for example, there were (unsuccessful) calls in
1989 to elect a national constitutional assembly, though it is unclear to me
whether it was to exist side by side with the last Communist Parliament, or
operate as a traditional European constituent assembly. Probably, the discussion never got far enough to pose this important question. The first freely
elected parliament of 1990 could have been (but was not) elected (as in Bulgaria and Romania) as a sovereign constituent assembly. The new constitution
so far has been produced by a plurality of instances in a variety of settings: the
National Round Table of 1989, the last Communist Parliament, the two major
parties of the first freely elected Parliament acting through that body, the new
Constitutional Court, and the second freely elected Parliament have been the
main constituent actors so far. After the failure in 1996 of comprehensive parliamentary constitution making,[23] this process might perhaps produce a constitution through long-term evolution with the Constitutional Court being
the major protagonist. Some very much advocate this option. But they forget
about the severe potential problems of a republic of judges in an age of democratic legitimacy.

DEMOCRATIC THEORY
AND MODELS OF CONSTITUTION MAKING

Can democratic theory (or theories) help us with such choices wherever they
arise? The question, in other words, is whether the five options of constitution

making can be ranked by the criteria of different democratic theories. Each of the following theories has significantly different consequences for evaluating different paths of constitution making.

Revolutionary Democracy (Sovereign Dictatorship)

The classical European approach of constitution making since "the age of democratic revolutions" is the road of the sovereign constitutional assembly.[24] Left-wing radicalism in particular has pushed for this option wherever possible. On a theoretical level however, it is the doctrine of constituent power from Sieyès to Schmitt that represents the most important justification for this approach. This doctrine assumes not only the well-known distinction between *constituant* and *constitué,* but also that in the transition between two constitutions, that is, two *pouvoirs constitué,* there is a revolutionary hiatus, a condition *ex lex,* in which the only source of legitimate authority is the constituent power, which under democratic conditions is the revolutionary nation or people. Since the nation as such cannot provide a constitution, the task as well as all the power falls to an instance that can legitimately do so in its name.

The Abbé Sieyès provided a democratic argument to sustain this difficult last step through a particular interpretation of Jean Jacques Rousseau's general will that in his view could be formed by a genuinely representative assembly. This synthesis of direct democratic legitimation with a political model that radically excluded all direct democracy could not possibly work, and certainly did not work in 1791–92. Schmitt's particular doctrine of sovereign dictatorship is the only serious attempt to deal with the difficulty on the theoretical level. According to Schmitt, the constituent assembly with whom the constituent power of the people identifies is commissioned only to carry out the task of constitution making. He too believed that for the duration of constitution making the assembly must exercise all powers: constituent as well as legislative, executive, and judicial, since no powers outside the representative assembly can be legally provided for without the constitution that is to be made. This is the meaning of the adjective *sovereign* that Schmitt used to qualify this particular type of revolutionary dictatorship to be distinguished from the more limited commissarial dictatorship that has no constituent powers and whose aim is the protection or restoration of an existing constitution. Though legally unlimited, the constituent assembly can remain in power and accomplish its tasks only if the people as the constituent power identifies with it. Schmitt's theory of democracy assumes not so much the actual, or juridical, identity of the assembly and democratic will as did Sieyès, but a variety of possible sociologically manifested acts of identification, as, for example, the revolutionary insurrections that saved the Constituent Assembly in 1789. Another such act of identification is a national, majoritarian referendum. In Schmitt's view, one that follows the point of view of Jacobin critics of the Constitution of 1791, the legitimacy and viability of the constitution requires popular ratification. It was this view, rather than the original one of Sieyès, that survived as part of the revolutionary tradition of the French revolution.

Evidently Schmitt had important reservations concerning the 1791 Constituent Assembly of which Sieyès was a leading architect and ideologist. His major problem is not with the fact that the commission of this assembly, originally the estates general, came from the king and not the people. Revolutionary popular identification with the assembly changed the commissioning instance of the new Constituent Assembly from king to people. But he considers it a fatal omission that in line with Sieyès's peculiar interpretation of Rousseau, the assembly did not consider it essential to have its constitutional product ratified in a popular referendum (by the mere "will of all" as against the general will). Thus the National Convention of 1793, which openly exercised revolutionary dictatorship but offered its constitutional work for ratification in a popular referendum, acted in a more legitimate manner as a commissioner of the *verfassungsgebende Macht*. Yet even this assembly in terms of Schmitt's theory (he is ambiguous on the actual case) should have immediately dissolved itself when the result of the referendum was positive and the dictatorship of the convention was supposed to be over.

The model of constitution making by a constitutional assembly, which Schmitt considers fully democratic, thus involves five elements: (1) the dissolution of all previously constituted powers; (2) a popularly elected or acclaimed assembly with plenitude of powers; (3) a provisional government rooted entirely in this assembly; (4) a constitution offered for a national, popular referendum; and (5) the dissolution of the constituent assembly upon the ratification of the constitution that establishes a duly constituted government. The legitimacy of this model derives from an origin when a purely factual power establishes itself as the source of all legal validity. Such a legitimacy is a democratic one when the factual power is incontestably that of the united people or nation in the political sense. From this point of view the more previously established or constituted powers that participate in the process, the more the enterprise is interpreted as illegitimate attempts to usurp the place of the constituent power. Schmitt was especially critical of the use of the amendment process (which he interpreted entirely in terms of constituted powers) to change what is essential in constitutions. But even comprehensive constitution making through ordinary parliaments was entirely unacceptable in his eyes. This last judgment of course corresponds to the reigning view in the United States since James Madison and the *Federalist Papers*. Schmitt, however, regarded the U.S. model itself as representing a "mixed" type, incorporating on the level of both the process of the Constitutional Convention and constitutional result two incompatible decisions: one by the people as the *pouvoir constituant* for a unitary national government, and another by a different constituent power, the states, for a (con)federal government.

Finally, and characteristically for Schmitt, presidential constitution making has a very eminent place in his conception. According to him the constituent power cannot be procedurally limited in advance—even the form of constitution making through a sovereign assembly need not be followed by the people. Thus, if ratification in popular referenda can express identification with a constitution in the case of constituent assemblies, given a full rupture with duly constituted powers, the same type of popular acclamation demonstrates the presence of the constituent power and its identification with the constitution irrespective of the method of drafting. In particular the constitutions produced under charismatic Napoleonic leadership meet Schmitt's standard that is ultimately based on his idea of a potential link between democracy and popular dictatorship. To be sure the approval for plebiscitary-charismatic constitution making remains an idiosyncratic one in the tradition of revolutionary democratic thought. In Schmitt's version in any case the revolutionary democratic position implies the following ordering of the possible forms of constitution making:

1. sovereign constituent assembly
2. constitution making through a popular executive power
3. U.S. model seen as a mixed one
4. parliamentary constitution making
5. evolutionary process (absence of a clearly defined "decision" by the constituent power, hence a marginal case of a constitution and of constitution making from Schmitt's point of view)

Dualist Democracy (Republican and Rule of Law Position)

Hannah Arendt subjected the revolutionary democratic position to a withering critique, the intensity of which was undoubtedly linked to the fact that Carl Schmitt became the leading exponent of this position. Implicitly following Schmitt's textual lead, but reversing his evaluation, Arendt focuses on the famous lines of Sieyès according to which the constituent power finds itself "in the state of nature." She variously rejects both the interpretation that the constituent can rest only on atomized individuals and that no legal restrictions of any type can bind it. Using the admittedly exceptional U.S. case, she seeks to show that it is possible both to derive the constituent power from already organized political bodies and the legal authority of the constitution from a different source than the mere identity of the constituent. According to her, when the source of power is the atomized totality of individuals or the imagined totality of the nation, and when legal authority is derived exclusively from this very source the constitution will be "built on quicksand."

Evidently for Arendt public freedom and participation, both as the source of revolutionary constitution making and the dimension to be institutionalized in republican constitutions, represents the major criteria by which revolutions and constitutions should be judged. Less obvious but equally important is the fact that she also believed that republican politics must be based on the rule of law, and not, as "democracy" even, the rule of any group however large. Using the first criterion, that of democratic participation, she placed what she took to be the revolutionary models of the United States and France first on her list of constitutionalist experiments to be admired, even though the latter degenerated according to her to a permanent revolution in the juridical sense, one unable to found free institutions. Only these great revolutions involved, at least in the beginning, the extraordinary commitment of a large number of (admittedly self-selected) people to political debate, discussion, and participation directed toward the creation of free institutions, more prosaically constitution making. Only here could she hope to apply Thomas Paine's dictum: "A constitution is not an act of a government, but of a people constituting a government." Last on her list were the post–World War I and post–World War II efforts in which governments, supposedly, managed to exclude general political participation and discussion and drew up the basic laws they themselves preferred under the cover of the work of their experts and legal advisors. In between the two is her preference for the British path, which produced an unwritten constitution implied in "institutions, customs, and precedents," for which she accepts William Gladstone's claim that it "had proceeded from progressive history." It might, moreover, follow from her conception that constitutions produced by normal legislatures, which generally involve extended discussion at least within the walls of parliament itself, would be still preferable to ones produced within ministries of justice and imposed on the legislature itself through party discipline or offered to the electorate without such detour. She implies as much when she celebrates in general constitution making in the thirteen original colonies, though she elsewhere realizes that most of the state constitutions were indeed the products of the regular legislatures.[25] For presidential or plebiscitary-charismatic constitution making she has nothing but withering scorn.

Finally, using her second criterion, that of the rule of law, as well as that of success in building a constitutional tradition, Arendt staunchly maintained that only the Americans (ever) succeeded at revolutionary constitution making, even if they too failed to create a genuine republican constitution institutionalizing participation. Thus her ordering of the forms of constitution making is more or less the following:

1. U.S. model seen as a republican one
2. sovereign constituent assembly
3. evolutionary process
4. parliamentary constitution making
5. constitution making by the executive branch

Arendt's reasons for preferring the U.S. to the French model are worth exploring. She is certainly more disturbed than Schmitt by the fact the Constitution of 1791 was neither popularly commissioned nor ratified, and that the whole effort between 1789 and 1791 was cut adrift from the people to whom "the resolutions and deliberations" should have been taken back. The criticism is convincing enough, but is unenlightening in relation to all the later efforts (stylized by Schmitt) that followed a democratized model of the sovereign constituent assembly with the plenitude of powers. Indeed in this particular argument Arendt clearly goes much too far when she suggests that the first French effort at popular constitution making was the ancestor of expert and governmental imposition of constitutions, an implausible point she can make only because her category of governmental constitution making is so diffuse. Her second argument, however, cuts to the core of the difference between the U.S. and the French models. Accordingly, the Americans were fortunate enough to be able to avoid their constituent power being thrown back into a legal state of nature Sieyès and his followers (eventually the majority of the *Assemblée Constituante*) could not avoid and postulated as logically unavoidable and even desirable. As in the doctrine of Sieyès, the constituent power of the French revolution was indeed in the state of nature to the extent that no previous forms of organization and legality (e.g., the royal veto) were allowed to limit it. The way was open for the fiction of the "people" or the "nation" to justify in the short term the dictatorship of an assembly. Even worse, in the longer term the constituent power was identified in France with the changing will of the mobilized multitude on which no stable rule of law could be erected, a permanent political reservation and threat in the face of all constituted powers. Such indeed was Carl Schmitt's conception of the *verfassungsgebende Gewalt,* even if not Sieyès notion of the *pouvoir constituant,* and it was the former interpretation that corresponded to the constant overturn of the constituted powers in the French Revolution in Arendt's analysis. Legal authority based on such a notion of constituent power cannot be, according to her, institutionalized with any stability at all.[26] The Americans, according to Arendt, moreover, did not attempt to derive power (a matter of fact) and legal authority (a matter of normative validity) from the same federated source. "No doubt, the laws owed their factual existence to the power of the people and their representatives in the legislatures; but these men could not at the same time represent the higher source from which these laws had to be derived in order to be authoritative and valid for all, the majorities and the minorities, the present and future generations." What Arendt did not believe was that such authority could be derived from the "I will" or the "I decide" of a revolutionary assembly, Sieyès's *pouvoir constituant* or Schmitt's sovereign dictator. Thus her republican theory is formulated emphatically as a dualistic one.

To be sure, Arendt is above all successful in showing the separation of democratic popular sovereignty and the conservation of legal authority under the

constitution, in a civic religion administered by the Supreme Court, an institution capable of preserving the constitution through augmentation.[27] With
this said, the independent origin of the legal authority of the Constitution is
still in some doubt, both in reality and her analysis. She states that the U.S.
constituents were not only legally elected, but exercised their powers "in
accordance with laws and limited by them." Thus on the one hand she seems
to be asserting the legal continuity of the Constitution with previous legal
arrangements like the state constitutions, the Common Law, and perhaps the
Articles of Confederation as well. Because she takes this point for granted,
she does not detect the drama of Madison's efforts to defend the legality of
the actions of the convention in the face of weighty charges of illegality.[28] In
this particular line of reasoning the U.S. search for a deeper foundation of the
new legal authority was a function only of an inherited Judeo-Christian idea
of law as command. I think inconsistently, she also maintains however the
existence of a legal hiatus, that forced the Americans too to search for the
foundation of the legal authority of the future that, unlike the French, they
did not wish to root in popular power alone. According to Arendt, with the
passing of the plausibility of natural law tradition rooted in religion, the U.S.
framers had some difficulty in deriving the legal authority of the Constitution that was eventually sacralized, from an entirely separate source. And this
seems to confirm Schmitt's defense of the radicalism of Sieyès and the French
Revolution.

It is, however, in this context that Arendt's implicit separation of origin and
form, of the "who" and the "how" of constitutional foundations, serves her
well. The subjects of constitution making in the United States were holders of
political power continuous with the past, arising from the states, and eventually the townships. The authority of the Constitution, however, arose from the
way and manner the delegates of this power organized the process as a whole
at the drafting and ratifying conventions. This is what she means by a beginning containing its own principle, saving the act of foundation from "dictat-
ing violence" without any reference to an absolute.[29] The principle of public
discussion involving "mutual promise and common deliberation" is thus the
source of the authority of the new system of power. In this version of her argument, the principle of deliberation and mutual respect contained in the beginning is for Arendt the foundation of both the later legal authority and the
sacralization of the Constitution, which helped to protect its stability even
from the consequences of the failure to institutionalize public freedom in
structures of small-scale participation in politics.[30]

Dualist Democracy (Revolutionary Position)

Arendt was quite conscious of the exceptional nature of the U.S. constitution-
making context, and in particular of the fact that preexisting federal institu-

tions are the presuppositions of a constituent power that does not run into the danger of a legal vacuum. In addition, aside from her little interest in model building another reason why she never attempts to stylize U.S. constitution making as a model is because she believes that the Americans too actually failed to institutionalize public freedom. I am convinced that on this crucial point she was, however, failed by an idea of politics derived from the ancients, one that she thought she rediscovered in the councils of modern revolutions. It is here that Bruce Ackerman has been able, in a highly suggestive analysis, to go beyond Arendt, but at the cost of rather questionable model building. The Americans in the revolutionary epoch according to him have been trying to institutionalize not a purely republican but a dualistic politics, the two-track politics of ordinary legislatures and extraordinary mobilizations linked to constitutional change. Thus on the level of a duly constituted political order, Ackerman manages to suggestively link what in Arendt's republicanism are two entirely separate terms: the politics of participation and the law protecting-augmenting activity of the judicial branch. Moreover, dualism in Ackerman's theory is not merely between law and power, but appears also as two forms of democracy within the system of power itself.

At the root of many of the problems[31] of Ackerman's imaginative conception lies a conception of constitutional origins that is both theoretically and historically problematic, and that nevertheless is elsewhere used both as the measuring rod by which contemporary efforts at constitutional politics are mercilessly judged, as well as a point of view from which concrete recommendations can be made. To Ackerman the making of the 1787 Constitution was an act of revolution, and the people who made it were revolutionaries who liberated themselves from an unusable legality.

Were, however, Madison and his colleagues revolutionaries because they finished the ongoing institutionalization of the American Revolution, or because they carried out a (luckily) peaceful revolution against the Articles of Confederation? The first is evidently the view of Arendt, while Ackerman seems to believe both statements to be true. Following the conception of Kelsen he mistakenly argues that if the Constitution of 1787 were not revolutionary in the legal sense, our fundamental laws would still be based on the Articles of Confederation, which the 1787 Convention would have merely amended. To avoid such a possibility, he therefore wishes to build on and develop the well-known case for the illegality of the actions of the convention. As a result he considers Madison's repeated attempts, intellectual and political, to save a threatened and tenuous legality to be a case of transparent lawyerly pleading.[32] Moreover, he seems to miss the full sense of Madison's point in *Federalist* #49, which implies that the new system of politics must not only be dualistic in outcome, but must also have a dualistic starting point. In 1787 such origins were provided for by the politics of the established legislatures, which in the United States retained all of their previous powers through the period of drafting and ratification, and the politics of the extraordinary convention that was, however, restricted to the making and proposing of a constitution to other instances legally established or to be legally established. Of course the federal dimension (as against the national one) of the U.S. Constitution (nonamendable nature of equal state representation in the Senate, the federalist dimension of Article V) definitely expressed the crucial role of legally constituted powers throughout the process of designing the new regime. Clearly, however, aside from establishing a national dimension of power that was based on the interests of the majority of individuals (rather than states) in the country, the convention also institutionalized another, superior political tract, protecting its own "higher law achievement" by a rigorous amendment structure (the level of difficulty of Article V) and by the creation of a federal judiciary (in its Hamiltonian, later Marshallian interpretation).[33] The text, in other words, can be made sense of only if we recognize the plurality of its sources, that is of the forms of power institutionalized in it.

Ackerman, however, seems to believe that a monistic revolutionary beginning can produce a dualistic outcome. Thus even with respect to Arendt's oscillation between legal continuity and communicative action as the sources of the Constitution's authority, he takes a step toward a more unitary conception based on the a rather mythologized idea of popular sovereignty, a step that actually minimizes the differences between constitution making through a sovereign constituent assembly and a constitutional convention of the U.S. type. Therefore Ackerman would be forced to analyze the very different outcomes in terms of the evidently different choices of design of the constitution makers in the two countries of the United States and France. The easily demonstrable historical link between origins and design is thus lost in his conception. So is Arendt's justifiably critical perspective with respect to the European pattern of revolutionary democratic constitution making.[34]

The most questionable feature of Ackerman's argument, however, is his unabashed transformation of the U.S. pattern into a model. The U.S. model becomes worthy of imitation because of its successful institutionalization of dualistic politics. Ackerman's last book, *The Future of the Liberal Revolution,* frankly asserts this particular implication, as he proposes late in 1992 to the Poles and the Russians that they form special constitutional conventions outside the framework of operation of the existing regular parliaments, under presidential leadership, and supported by mass mobilization.[35]

He is of course aware of most of the other options of constitution making. His order of preference turns out to be largely though not completely similar to that of Arendt, though the dualistic goal might have suggested otherwise. According to Ackerman, a constituent assembly with the plenitude of all powers might do the job as well as a separate convention, since as he says "many plausible texts" have been produced this way. He forgets to consider how few viable and especially dualistic traditions have emerged through the classical European method, and why. As against the largely implicit but severe judgment of Arendt, he considers the German model—which he rightly sees as partially parallel to the original American, but without popular participation—as "half as good" as its forerunner but still potentially usable because of the "thoroughgoing synthetic character" of the *Grundgesetz*. Similarly to Arendt, moreover, he too considers an evolutionary method of achieving constitutional legitimacy potentially viable, but the British pattern rightly strikes him as tailored to unique and unrepeatable circumstances. Instead his example here is that of Spain, disregarding the normal parliamentary character of its constitution-making process, as well as the fact that in this particular sense all durable constitutions achieve their legitimacy and indeed their durability through an evolutionary process in which interpretation, revision, and changes in the political culture interact in the longer term. Surprisingly, therefore, given Spain's obviously parliamentary model, he has only negative comments on parliamentary constitution making, because this method is supposedly incapable of insulating the constitution against normal political decision making.

Let me note that this last argument is neither empirically nor logically convincing. We should keep in mind that parties at any given time capable of producing constitutional legislation under difficult amendment rules will not wish to make future parties to be in an easier position to reverse their original work. But even when operating under easy amendment rules or even voting by simple majority, parties may not know if it will not be their competitors who will be in the future capable of exploiting such rules against them. Thus in either case there are reasons to insulate the constitution against future legislative majorities. Ackerman seems to be saying that it is the monistic institutional interests of Parliament that militate against a future dualistic structure. But the same point would then have to apply to monistic constituent assemblies, which Ackerman does not in fact criticize.[36]

It is interesting to consider why, beyond such arguments that many would consider hopelessly "legalistic," Ackerman so vehemently rejects parliamentary constitution making. First, he is (rightly) concerned with present East Central European versions of this method as leaving the constituent and quasi-revolutionary process indefinitely open and as potentially degenerating to continuous constitutional tinkering that seriously endangers the dualistic structure that differentiates constitutional law from ordinary legislation. I myself have argued in chapter 3 of this text that such a process itself runs the danger of permanent revolution under some imaginable circumstances. Moreover he thinks that piecemeal constitution making in particular, and the parliamentary model in general cannot reliably produce a high level of symbolic commitment to the constitution and constitutional patriotism, which in his view require an extraordinary process. In any case, Ackerman's ranking of different forms of constitution making is the following:

1. U.S. model seen as a presidentially led, revolutionary democratic one
2. sovereign constituent assembly
3. German type of nondemocratic dualism
4. evolutionary process
5. parliamentary constitution making

His recommendations to the Poles and Russians (as well as his critique of the Hungarian pattern dominated by Parliament and Constitutional Court) are based on this hierarchy. I should note that Ackerman's message to the Poles and the Russians, consistent with the dualistic strain in his own thinking but inconsistently in terms of his linkage of revolution and constitution, carries no explicit advice of illegality. As we know of course illegality and provisional government did in the end turn out to be a key feature of the making of the Yeltsin Constitution. Ackerman's own exploration of the problem of the illegality of the Philadelphia Convention, however, should have warned him of the difficulties of staying within the limits of legality when establishing a potential duality of power between legislative and constituent instances. But the revolutionary strain in his thought apparently made him insensitive to the obvious dangers. Unfortunately, perhaps because he has already decided the illegality of the original, he is little concerned about what illegality would mean in the wholly different contexts that he now addresses.[37]

Granted, the quasi-revolutionary mobilization around the making of the constitution Ackerman advocates, would further differentiate between the road of parliamentary constitution making and a special convention, but only as we have seen by bringing the latter procedure close together with revolutionary constituent assemblies. Let us again concede that Ackerman was serious about advocating a legally unimpeachable strategy to Lech Walesa and Boris Yeltsin, at variance with his historical reinterpretation of the origins of the U.S. Constitution. Nevertheless, even without the benefit of hindsight it is worth noting the explosiveness of a situation in which charismatic leaders backed by popular mobilization did succeed in making a constitutional proposal to a sitting legislature that would probably wish to reject the very obvious consequence of such an effort: strong elements of presidentialism in the constitution. Why should we have ever assumed that either the Polish or Russian legislature would sufficiently limit themselves, as did Congress in 1787, or that Walesa or Yeltsin would be able to exhibit the self-restraint of a Washington? But if neither side could show self-restraint, the road would be open to full-fledged constitutional crisis, or worse: civil war. A constitution can emerge from such a setting only if one side manages to impose it on the other, a poor foundation for future legitimacy and stability.

What I am driving at is the following. The revolutionary interpretation of Ackerman's position would lead to very dangerous political outcomes if accepted. He seems to be aware of this and is therefore only recommending it to Poles and Russians in a version that comes close to Arendt's dualistic or legalistic one. But even the dualistic version can have the tendency to turn into the revolutionary one, when adopted under circumstances where the political, social, and cultural preconditions of the U.S. pattern of constitution making are absent. Accordingly, Ackerman's theoretical ambiguity (between dualism and monism) is that of the ambivalence of the U.S. model of constitution making itself, abstractly considered. We must recognize that this ambivalence is difficult to sustain: The model can thus reappear as a revolutionary democratic monistic one or a dualistic, nondemocratic, nonrevolutionary one under historically different circumstances. This serious difficulty throws negative light on the whole idea of the imitation of the American and perhaps any other model.

Liberal Democracy: From Models to Principles

It is surprising that Ackerman, after lamenting that East Europeans have run away from the originality of their "revolution," himself insists on the imitation of the U.S. model of constitution making as the way to recover this originality. But what should such a choice be based upon? Imitation of anything is a poor reason, especially because, as we have seen, concrete models have a way of turning into something quite different when adopted under dramatically different circumstances. Thus, with situated givens, the circumstances must come first. Among them lies the important givens of a country's or a culture's own constitutional experience from which it is possible to learn.[38]

Reflexivity and learning, however, does not in itself deal with the legitimation problem that is Ackerman's main concern. Aside from the slow traditionalization or even sacralization of the constitution that requires fortunate circumstances subsequently, only political principles can produce legitimacy. This was Hannah Arendt's insight. But when it comes to principles rather than rules or models we are inevitably stuck with a plurality of these among which it is impossible to establish a hierarchy.[39] Unfortunately, reflecting on the model character of U.S. constitution making, she found only one such principle, that of public communication, and she turned this into an overly concrete conception of a form of organization.[40] The advantage of focusing on principles, however, is precisely that it allows us when choosing or evaluating an approach today to focus not on the choice of a model or a concrete type of organization but rather the plurality of principles plausibly used to legitimate results produced in a variety of historical experiences.

But what are the principles that pertain to constitution making and how are they to be used? One would expect help here from more formal political theories, rather than approaches (direct democracy, participatory democracy) focusing on concrete models of participation. Unfortunately, most liberal theories of constitutionalism are result oriented (possibly because of the British origins of liberal theory, where only the result can be evaluated).[41]

John Rawls is a liberal who is among those who are interested above all in a substantive outcome: one that institutionalizes the two principles of justice and is capable of guaranteeing their efficacy under specific social, cultural, and political settings. Even when in *Political Liberalism* he comes to accept Ackerman's dualistic conception, he is less interested in constitution making than in the existence of an institutionalized two-track structure, establishing the duality of both law (higher and ordinary) and lawmaking instances (constitutional and legislative).[42] A line of argument in his earlier work, *Theory of Justice*, is, however, an exception to such result orientation, because it explores the legitimacy of results in terms of an idealized procedure in which all participants would assent to such a result. While he would continue to evaluate and criticize existing arrangements in terms of their structure, and not in terms of empirical processes that led to their establishment, the argument nevertheless comes up with a principle-oriented perspective that leaves the back door open for the evaluation of processes as well. In particular his analysis of the "constitutional convention" can be of use to constitution makers and their critics.[43]

According to the Rawlsian perspective, constitutions (and legislation) could be considered just if they incorporate the principles of justice, and are so constructed, as if the actors took into account at the moment of their origins only the circumstances (economic level, political culture, patterns of interaction, and so on) of a given society but not the interests, opinions, and endowments of the goal rational actors engaged in institution building. At the stage of the "constitutional convention" this ideal assumption is understood in terms of a modified "veil of ignorance," or a veil of ignorance "partially lifted." We are still not to think of actual assemblies and discussions. The difference between the "original position" and the "constitutional convention" is only that in the latter actors are allowed to know the concrete society for which they wish to construct rules.

This conception is abstract enough to be applied to settings where "constitutional democracies" are in the process of being established.[44] Moreover, unlike the principle of communicative interaction to which Arendt appeals, it is impossible to confuse the idea of the veil of ignorance with a concrete model of organization. Rawls's conception is potentially suggestive for the makers of constitutions for several reasons. First this is obviously so because he sets out a minimum condition in terms of the outcome without which the process too could not have been legitimate: the incorporation in political institutions of the first principle of justice (the second belongs for him more to the stage of legislation) consisting of civil and political rights (*Theory of Justice*, 197; 221ff). Second, because he suggests not only that the citizen must decide "which constitutional arrangements are just for reconciling conflicting opinions of justice" but also that he or she will regard "some ways of designing this [constitutional] machine more just than others." To be sure he does not apply his concept of democratic participation to this level, perhaps fortunately, because it is not easy to formulate what democracy entails before democratic institutions are established. Third, because he is quite clear about the fact that abstract principles should not be generated into concrete constitutional models, but rather should be applied in such a way that we select among the plurality of possible just arrangements the one most feasible, that is, most suitable in the sense of capable of being established, and effective, as well as being able to guarantee the principles of justice *given the beliefs and interests of people in given society and political tactics that can be effective given these.* And while this point is made in relationship to institutions that are in any case conceived in procedural terms, it perforce applies to procedures creating institutions if they are to be just. Fourth because, he tells us, that there ought to be both a separation of constitution making and legislation (two stages) but also an interaction (a back-and-forth movement) between these two processes, mutual learning as it were, if the best constitution is to be found. Finally, he does give us at least one principle by which the procedures of constitution making could be normatively evaluated: that of the veil of ignorance itself, which importantly is conceived as to allow for degrees to which the participants are not to know specific circumstances. In my view this principle can be made sense of particular historical settings only if it is interpreted in terms of a plurality of other principles.

Since the idea of the "veil of ignorance" is hypothetical and fictional, it allows for empirical translations that do not assume the restrictive conditions to literally apply but only to hold as a regulative principle aiding reflection. In the context of constitution making what we would then ask is not necessarily whether the actors were actually ignorant about their interests in the process of constitution making, but only whether they are willing to suspend, or rather cancel out on, the wishes and arguments of their interlocutors the consequences of their actual knowledge. This second assumption could of course be interpreted merely in terms of the result, whether or not the constitution turned out to be one that could have been the product of people ignorant or for the moment disinterested in their interest. In that case we would have a reason to rationally attribute the "veil of ignorance" to the actors. But it could also refer to the process: Did the participants act in such a way that we could rationally believe what must of course be a fiction, that they did not know or that they distanced themselves from their interests? Such an apparently outlandish claim or belief can be made plausible only if we discover other principles at work in the actual process that led to institutional solutions and that demonstrably reduce the dominant role of some particular interests, of which the actors must, of course, be aware.

PRINCIPLES RELEVANT TO CONSTITUTION MAKING

We must get beyond the idea of using a model or even one specific organiza-tional form to evaluate efforts at constitutional politics. But we must also overcome the liberal tendency to focus, in the case of constitutions, only on the substantive result as against the processes of institutionalization and rein-stitutionalization. One way of doing this is to find principles that would flesh out a counterfactual perspective with institutional solutions that have helped, in order to achieve democratic legitimacy in the history of constitutionalism. In my view the continuing worldwide influence of U.S. constitutionalism is due not only to the historically pioneering position and stability of the U.S. Constitution, but also because it constitutes a series of principles that were taken very seriously at the moment of origin as well as later periods of recon-struction. These principles hold important positions in the narratives that we tell and retell about this constitutional tradition, following the first story told by Madison and his colleagues. While one would not expect to institutional-ize all of these principles in current designs of the procedures of constitutional politics, without paying attention to a sufficient combination of them, consti-tutional construction cannot become democratically legitimate.

Publicity

As is well known, the U.S. Constitution was drafted without any public access to the process, while the French Constitutions of 1791 and 1793 were pro-duced under the gaze of and with the participation of open galleries. In fact two empirical models of the public sphere were involved, one in which con-straint was largely absent (in the United States) and another where all relevant points of view could be heard (in France). The superiority of the U.S. model was attained only by fully opening the process, after the convention did its job, to formal and informal gatherings, to the press and pamphleteering, and the election of assemblies for ratification. This model of communication thus managed to recombine the torn dimensions of a free public sphere in a process of significant consequence. In particular, the Bill of Rights was the product not of the convention, but of the public processes of discussion and criticism (cf. Leonard Levy).[45] Today it is unthinkable that legitimate consti-tution making bypass extended public discussion. Such discussion socializes the main actors who can therefore advance and defend positions for which normatively convincing arguments can be devised. Moreover, it allows under-represented points of view to be expressed and given serious hearing. But con-stitution makers also continue to need the full freedom of deliberation. Thus the two dimensions of publicity, deliberation and openness, should not be connected in a single organizational framework.

Consensus

A U.S. constitution could have been produced by the states having the majority of the population, probably leaving little option for the smallest states than to eventually join on the terms of the majority. The voting rule used by the convention, however, gave each state an equal vote, thus potentially a minority veto over majority decisions. As far as the result was concerned, on the most difficult issues of the day (representation of states versus individuals; Southern representation) consensual formulas were preferred even when a majority could have had its way. Today, aside from issues of federalism, party political representation too is an important area where consensual solutions are possible and desirable. Both the *Grundgesetz* and the Spanish Constitution were devised through consensual arrangements cutting through federalism-centralism and party political cleavages. As these examples show, even before constitution-making bodies meet electoral rules can be devised that incorporate the preference for consensus rather than majoritarian democracy on the level of constitutional politics at least, for example, proportional representation. Under majoritarian electoral and decision rules constitutions turn into those of the victor's only.

Legal Continuity

There were the evident challenges to legality in the process of producing the U.S. Constitution. The convention was commissioned to recommend amendments to the Articles of Confederation; it produced a new Constitution instead. It proposed a method of ratification at variance with the revision rules of the articles (qualified majority versus unanimity, special conventions versus state legislatures). Yet there were good faith attempts to repair a threatened legality. Madison and his colleagues did turn to Congress and the states with their recommendation and did not attempt to bypass them by directly appealing to the people of the country or even the states. Moreover, they attempted to have the new ratification rule accepted as itself an amendment to the articles. While Congress did not formally amend the articles, it did as the convention asked and sent the Constitution to the states for approval. The states in turn did not rule on the procedure but proceeded to organize special conventions as the convention and the Constitution specified. It is undeniable that a very threatened legal continuity was thereby restored, at least partially or arguably. In all recent attempts at parliamentary constitution making from Spain to Hungary and from Poland to South Africa, the method of amendments produced either new ratification rules for completely new constitutions or completely revised constitutions produced in a piecemeal manner. Either way legal continuity was preserved.

Legal continuity is especially important in defending the identity and security of individuals in the midst of a large-scale political transformation. It announces to the population that the rulers themselves are always under law and cannot simply impose their arbitrary will.

Plurality of Democracies

The U.S. Constitution was drafted by delegates of state legislatures and, on their wishes, was ratified by special state conventions elected for this purpose alone. Modern constitutions are generally produced by two democratic instances: the drafting assembly (regular parliament or constituent assembly) and popular (national or federal) referenda. Given the exclusionary implications of any type of formal democratic procedure, combining a plurality of forms has important compensating effect. In fact historically not all referenda ratify constitutions, in effect demonstrating that when those initially excluded have another channel of participation open to them they can use this in more than a merely symbolic way. On the part of the initial actors involved in drafting the constitution the opening to a second, entirely different democratic channel shows their good faith and forces them to think beyond the interests represented in the assembly. Moreover, the temporal gap between two democratic procedures provides special opportunities for a public discussion that now has a complete proposal available, one that can still be changed by those sufficiently active and organized.

In all countries, direct and representative forms of democracy can be combined. In federally organized countries or in countries with strong, independent local government a second axis of plurality is provided on the central and decentralized dimensions. The more these types can be combined in a plausible procedure, the greater the potential democratic legitimacy of the constitution.

Veil of Ignorance as an Empirical Process

The idea of the veil of ignorance brings our attention to the need for a plurality of principles that must be taken seriously if a procedure of constitution making is to be regarded as just. In a much more limited sense, however, this idea can be given some more immediate empirical content. Actors cannot be ignorant about their needs and interests, but there are possible empirical choices that can reduce the knowledge that they could use in a particularistic way. Here I will list only the main such options, with little commentary:

a. *The differentiation of the instance of constitution making from that of legislation.* This is one way that the actors can use to put themselves in a position where they might not fully know the relationship of their interests to specific choices of design. One such mechanism is provided by the U.S. formula, or by traditional constituent assemblies especially with a rule like the one inspired by Maximilien Robespierre (unfortunately disastrous in the given case), banning the constituents from entering the first regular elections. Such formulas to be sure establish a veil of ignorance only for individuals, not for groups, regions, parties, or classes.

b. *The creation of new electoral rules at the time of constitution making.* A great deal of experience shows that the creation of new electoral rules always puts political parties, whatever they may think, less than fully able to anticipate the power relations of the future. Thus unless they are completely satisfied with the existing electoral rule and wish to structure many new dimensions of the constitutional order around it, the designers of constitutions will do well to chose a new electoral rule with uncertain results. Of course such results will seem more uncertain when electoral rules are not achieved by imposition and will in fact be uncertain the more distant the fashioning of the rule is from the next election. The electoral rules of course represented one of the most important and most contentious issues in front of the U.S. framers.

c. *The timing of constitution making.* The problem of the veil of ignorance could be translated into that of finding an optimal time to make constitutions. Relevant actors could choose to act at a time and even deliberately be chosen to act when their knowledge of the link between interest and design was insufficient. Adam Przeworski,[46] for example, whose interest seems to be only the stability of democracy and not questions of justice, uses the category of the veil of ignorance to depict an actual situation in which the actors do not know the balance of forces in their society, and in particular whether they will be strong or weak in democratic contestation, whether they will belong in the end to majorities or minorities. In such a setting, according to Przeworski, actors will opt for an institutional framework involving strong checks and balances, including protection for minorities, and such an institutional framework will have a good chance to manage subsequent conflicts and become stabilized. When actors do actually know the balance of forces, whether these are even or uneven, the chances of future constitutional stability are much weaker. Przeworski goes on to argue that actors can be in position of ignorance with respect to their interests in a future field of forces to the extent that they design their institutions before elections or after an election that turns out to be indecisive. The second of these conditions, however, is not open to design, while the first is an option only for parliamentary constitution making, since special assemblies and conventions cannot legitimately delay their constitution-making functions.

Reflexivity

Learning from the past or constructing a process capable of learning from itself is to begin with a cognitive rather than a normative principle. Nevertheless, electorates have the right to expect that those they elect for the important task of designing their institutions learn from all relevant experience. Moreover, reflexivity can also entail that the process of design and not only its results are made open to reflection and criticism. In fact many constitutional results have been historically prefigured in the methods of constitution making, and even earlier, the methods of choosing delegates. In the United States, for example, the fact that delegates were chosen by the state legislatures in a manner similar to the election of Congress made it more or less inevitable that a voting by states would be chosen at the convention, and this could be used as an argument against representation based on the number of individuals in each state. If voting by size of population were desirable, it was asked, why don't we vote in that manner here? When allowed to consciously engage in and publicly debate the design of a procedure of constitution making, a political community can gain access to outcomes at an all-important stage where in fact many key issues will be decided. To the extent that a procedure is constructed involving a time horizon, it remains open to discussion and critique at its various stages.

Many of the projects of constitution making of the last twenty years have been characterized by increasing reflexivity. All major efforts indicate learning from the repeated failure of revolutionary democratic constitution making and the need to satisfy the demands of democracy and legality in a new way. It proved especially helpful to reflect on the failure of past revolutionary democratic efforts in one's own political community as in Germany in 1848 and in Spain in 1977. Reflexivity in this sense also entailed that many of the principles of constitution making listed here have been consciously debated and integrated. More recently, in the Eastern European "revolutions" against the heritage of "the Revolution" it has been possible to make learning from the past even more conscious and fruitful for constitutionalism. In particular the institutional innovation of Round Tables in Central Europe allowed the formulation of radical change, which inherited parliaments could then proceed to legalize. Poland and Hungary achieved a further level of reflexivity when the constitution-making process was conceived from the beginning (by many perhaps reluctantly) as having to establish an interim constitution and pass through several stages. This already allowed some of the learning stressed by Rawls concerning the interaction of constitutional and legislative processes.

Finally, in South Africa, a temporally extended method of constitution making of several carefully delineated steps was formally organized with the intention of dealing with fundamental problems only when these could be handled consensually, allowing each solution to prepare the political and social psychological foundations for dealing with the next problem. Thus fully using the scarce resource of time, the country is apparently able to manage the difficult journey from consociationalism to constitutionalism.[47]

CONCLUSION

There is of course the possibility of too much learning, as Niklas Luhmann warns us, with respect to the legal domain. Learning can and must also mean learning not to learn.[48] Constitutionalism must imply raising the threshold of possible learning, that is, to try not to immediately learn in the face of empirical disappointments. In constitutions this effect is achieved with relatively difficult amendment rules. With respect to constitution making the same desideratum means that the process should not be left open indefinitely. As the extreme case of Great Britain shows, one of the crucial weaknesses of constitution making by ordinary parliaments is the lack of sufficient legitimacy to close the process, which would mean tying the hands of future parliaments and elevating the present parliament to an illegitimately higher status than all subsequent ones. At the same time we can now see that parliamentary constitution making, as exemplified by the very successful Spanish case, can do justice to many of the principles presented here. Parliamentary constitution making of course can always rely on the principle of legal continuity. This may or may not mean working under a difficult amendment rule.[49] When involving in addition high consensus requirements, and when supplemented by extended public discussion and other (direct or federal) democratic channels, parliamentary constitution making can generate sufficient legitimate authority to definitively close the process by establishing a constitution significantly more difficult to amend.

As the example of the first genuinely democratic constitutional assembly, the French National Convention in 1793 shows, closing the process or making sure that it will remain relatively closed is not, pace Ackerman, easy for such bodies. Here too the issue is that of legitimacy. In the case of most historical examples of sovereign constituent assemblies the difficulties of organizing consensual drafting procedures and processes of public participation were striking. As Hannah Arendt has seen, the radical legal discontinuity such assemblies imply makes it extremely difficult to maintain the authority of their product in the face of changes of democratic opinion. Dependent on a mobilized public, the drafters, moreover, have a great deal of difficulty in integrating losing or minority opinion into a consensus that would also reflect the wishes and interests of nonmobilized or minority parts of the population. Indeed if the procedures are at all moments open to the public, something difficult to avoid at times of revolutionary mobilization, such assemblies may have difficulty in respecting the principle of coherence without which constitutions cannot work.

The point of this argument is to reverse the rank order of forms of constitution making that is characteristic of all the democratic theories of constitutions treated here. Accordingly the U.S. model preserves its pride of place only if we note again how difficult it has been to imitate this model where the underlying political culture, the inherited institutional conditions, and the conditions for consensus have been significantly different. Parliamentary constitution making turns out to be very much the second-best option, as long as it incorporates many of the principles stressed here. The historically exceptional, generally nonimitable, and certainly nondesignable evolutionary pattern comes next, followed by revolutionary democratic constitution making. Finally, only constitutions produced by the executive really merit Arendt's strictures concerning governmental constitution making. We must continue to criticize this road recently adopted in Russia, in spite of the apparent success of the Fifth Republic in France, and the attractive character of some of its institutions. While the last word on the debate between parliamentary and presidential government has surely not been said, presidential constitution making is a difficult to legitimate, potentially authoritarian road both for constitution making and large-scale revisions of the constitution.

Notes

PREFACE

1. See J. Cohen and A. Arato, *Civil Society and Political Theory* (Cambridge, Mass.: MIT Press, 1992). Our distinction between civil society as a movement and as institution was influenced by Cornelius Castoriadis and Alain Touraine.

2. A. Stepan and J. Linz, *Problems of Democratic Transition and Consolidation* (Baltimore: Johns Hopkins University Press, 1996).

3. Hannah Arendt, *On Revolution* (New York: Viking, 1965).

4. János Kis, "Between Reform and Revolution: Three Hypotheses about the Nature of Regime Change," *Constellations* 1, 3 (1995): 399–419.

5. Steven Holmes and Cass Surstein, "The Politics of Constitutional Revision in Eastern Europe," in S. Levinson, ed., *Responding to Imperfection. The Theory and Practice of Constitutional Amendment* (Princeton, N.J.: Princeton University Press, 1995), 275–306. I consider the complementary strengths and weaknesses of this conception and that of Ackerman in "Constitutional Learning," in A. Arato, *Civil Társadalom, Forradalom és Alkotmány* (Budapest: Uj Mandátum, 1999), 333–55.

6. Bruce Ackerman, *The Future of the Liberal Revolution* (New Haven, Conn.: Yale University Press, 1992).

7. Given my mixed track record, I will desist from predicting it. It seems I am very good at foretelling elections, but less successful in foretelling the actions of elected officials.

8. See my articles in *East European Constitutional Review:* "Elections, Coalitions and Constitutionalism in Hungary" (Summer–Fall 1994): 3, 3–4; 26–32; "Parliamentary Constitution Making in Hungary" (Fall 1995): 4, 4: 45–51; and "The Constitution-Making Endgame in Hungary" (Fall 1996): 5, 4: 31–39; and especially the Hungarian essay volume *Civil Társadalom, Forradalom és Alkotmány.*

9. See A. Arato, "Constitutional Learning," 333–55.

10. I consider the successful ending of parliamentary constitution making in Poland to have been entirely contingent, in other words. The bifurcation of the process into a learning period and final synthesis was achieved in Poland as in the United States between 1781 and 1787 in a more or less ad hoc way. In South Africa a similar double structure was institutionalized by the interim constitution achieved in roundtable negotiations.

11. See Frank Michelman, "Can Constitutional Democrats Be Legal Positivists?" *Constellations* 2, 3 (1996): 293–308.

CHAPTER 1. INTERPRETING 1989

1. I have in mind works like János Kornai's *The Economics of Shortage* and his articles from the 1980s; Iván Szelenyi and György Konrad's *Intellectuals on the Road to Class Power;* János Kis and György Bence's *Toward an East European Marxism* as well as Kis's editorials in *Beszélő;* Tamás Bauer's *Planned Economy, Investment, Cycles* as well as his various articles in the early 1980s, and Ferenc Feher, Agnes Heller, and György Markus's *Dictatorship over Needs.*
2. See J. Habermas's "Die nachholende Revolution," in *Die nachholende Revolution* (Frankfurt/M: Suhrkamp Verlag, 1990), 179–204; "The Rectifying Revolution," *New Left Review* 183 (September-October 1990). To be sure some like E. P. Thompson also occupy this space, even if without the intellectual substance of Habermas's argument. Thompson, in an incomprehensibly contemptuous and resentful review of Ralf Dahrendorf, charges that the revolutions of 1989, after a promising beginning, were hijacked or betrayed by elements open to "Western advice and more blatant interventions." Thus, in a sense already crying Thermidor, he plays the role not of Marx but of Leon Trotsky. See "Liberal Complacence," *Dissent* (Summer 1991).
3. Of these I have so far taken two, seeing little need to distinguish (in the present context) Stalinist and Marxist-Leninist positions. I add Habermas's as the third relevant type of left position.
4. Ernst Nolte, "Die unvollständige Revolution. Die Rehabilitierung des Bürgertums und der defensive Nationalismus," *Frankfurter Allgemeine Zeitung* (January 24, 1991): 27.
5. See A. Arato, "Revolution, Civil Society and Democracy," in *From Neo-Marxism to Democratic Theory: Essays in the Critical Theory of Soviet-Type Societies* (Armonk, N.Y.: M. Sharpe, 1993), 296–312.
6. I leave to the side that this view is mistaken for the great French Revolution, in spite of the reference to François Furet supporting it. After all, Furet has tirelessly battled in his major work *Interpreting the French Revolution* (Cambridge: Cambridge University Press, 1981) precisely against its interpretation as bourgeois. Moreover, the radical phase of the revolution surely involved a partially successful battle to violently dispossess the clergy and the aristocracy as ownership classes. Of course if we identify all European forms of sub- and superordination as bourgeois, as does Nolte (strikingly following Theodore Adorno and Max Horkheimer's genealogy), the false argument can be saved, if by an even falser one.
7. See the outstanding article "Maistre" by M. Boffa in F. Furet and M. Ozouf, eds., *A Dictionary of the French Revolution* (Cambridge, Mass.: Harvard University Press, 1990).
8. It is noteworthy that despite his somewhat high-handed treatment of liberal positions, Habermas has for the first time been forced to admit in this context the relative relevance at least of the totalitarianism thesis stressing the elements of identity between the National Socialist and Soviet type regimes. "Die nachholende Revolution," 186; "The Rectifying Revolution," 8–9.
9. Daniel Chirot, "After Socialism, What? (Ideological Implications of the Events of 1989 in Eastern Europe for the Rest of the World)," ms. delivered at a conference on civil society and the end of authoritarian regimes, University of California at Los Angeles, December 1990.

10. Chirot has no difficulty in accepting the Japanese system as liberal, in spite of its de facto one party nature that he notes; nor does he challenge the popular identification of American "liberalism" as "socialism" or social democracy (ibid., p. 9).

11. Indeed he is ready to pronounce social democracy of the Western European type as another experiment that has failed (ibid., p. 8).

12. In spite of Chirot's repeated mention of the category of civil society, he sees in it only the terms of a strategy against Communist rule, and not the way beyond the cycle of liberalism and dictatorship.

13. Ralf Dahrendorf, *Reflections on the Revolution in Europe* (New York: Random House, 1990).

14. See in particular Carl Schmitt, *Die Diktatur* (Berlin: Dunker & Humblot, 1923); Hannah Arendt, *On Revolution* (New York: Viking Press, 1965 [1963]); and Cornelius Castoriadis, *L'institution imaginaire de la societé* (Paris: Seuil, 1975). The distinction can be derived also from *The Federalist.* See the article by Bruce Ackerman, "Neo-Federalism," in Jon Elster and Rune Slagstad, eds., *Constitutionalism and Democracy* (Cambridge: Cambridge University Press, 1988) Interestingly, in spite of her respect for *The Federalist,* Arendt derived the distinction from Sieyès directly.

15. *Reflections,* 42; 76–77.

16. To be sure at times Dahrendorf somewhat conflates the two levels, and it becomes unclear in which sense he thinks there can be third or fourth ways. This does not, however, justify Thompson's complete misreading of him on this point.

17. *Reflections,* 63–65; 90–91.

18. While, for example, he considers social democracy, weakened by its very victories, to be on the decline in the West, it is not clear whether he would recommend social democratic solutions in the East, for a while, after the transition to a market economy is fully completed. Ibid., 54–58.

19. Ibid., 86. The claim also cannot be sustained in reference to the making of the U.S. Constitution. Evidently many of the American framers were political philosophers, and all of them were politicians. Moreover, there was much to disagree about, as the debates of the Federalists and anti-Federalists were to show even beyond the obvious issue a degree of centralism. There were conflicts between the adherents of democracy and republican elitism, and those of republican activism and civil privatism. The debate between Thomas Jefferson and James Madison concerning an extensive vs. a limited role of the constituent power in settled constitutions was perhaps the most interesting of these disagreements, involving very different constitutional choices.

20. This is shown by the long delays and hesitations caused in economic policy in all the countries by the inability of the various governments to resolve the question of privatization and reprivatization. In Hungary, the only functioning constitutional court in the region has rightly insisted on the constitutional nature of the initial decisions.

21. See Ackerman, "Neo-Federalism." Cornelius Castoriadis's idea of a modern autonomous society keeping open the option of questioning its most fundamental institutions points in the same direction. To be sure neither he nor Arendt could see a way of doing this within a constitution, without putting all of it into question, without revolution, in other words.

22. Ibid., 27–28.

23. In this context he simply does not see what Manfred Riedel has first masterfully demonstrated, namely, that the concept of civil society has undergone dramatic historical

transformation since the eighteenth century. A concept that simply identifies the civil and the political (Burke, Madison) is not the same as one that involves their differentiation (G. W. F. Hegel, Tocqueville). Nor is the matter of identification with (Hegel, Marx) and distinction from (Antonio Gramsci, Talcott Parsons) the bourgeois irrelevant. Finally, it is also a distinct innovation when thinkers like Jacek Kuron, Adam Michnik, Claude Lefort, and Alain Touraine begin to include social movements in the concept. On all this, see Jean Cohen and Andrew Arato, *Civil Society and Political Theory* (Cambridge, Mass.: MIT Press, 1992).

24. See N. Luhmann, *Grundrechte als Institution* (Berlin: Duncker & Humblot, 1965).

25. Arendt has most forcefully stressed this point in *On Revolution,* insisting on the two dimensions of liberation and the establishment of freedom as linked yet distinct. Under established constitutions, the former is embodied in constitutional rights that establish "constitutionalism." But according to her, a democratic constitution is more than constitutionalism; it is also the establishment of a new system of power.

26. On this issue see the debate between Gyula Tellér and János Kis in *Beszélö* II 6 and 7 (February 2 and 9, 1991). In my view both positions, the one insisting on the support for independent initiatives from below and the other insisting on the need for legal institutionalization from above, are right and complementary.

27. This is my translation of the real thrust of Habermas's "Die nachholende Revolution," literally "the overtaking revolution," translated as "The Rectifying Revolution" in *New Left Review.*

28. To Habermas, along the lines of his theory of communicative action, modernity is not exhausted by the liberal themes of differentiation and pluralism as it is to Dahrendorf, but it includes the democratic moment of the institutionalization of discourse. Nevertheless, the two concepts of modernity are compatible; one completes the other. Democracy and communication are not as such modern ideals; to become modern they require the autonomization and self-distantiation of actors not possible without the liberal dimension, which, however, is generically modern.

29. See *Le Débat* (November-December 1990). Hungarian translation: *Népszabadság* (March 15, 1991).

30. "Die nachholende Revolution," 184–85.

31. Ibid., 180.

32. Ibid., 181. There is nothing in the lines quoted from Joachim Fest to justify this interpretation, but all the more in Habermas's own argument.

33. Ibid., 202–3.

34. While it is entirely unclear with whom Habermas is debating in this context, it is curious nevertheless that he identifies this position in his typology as an extreme antisocialist, or right wing one.

35. Heller, given her definition, amazingly enough seeks to disqualify October 1917 as a revolution. See "Eastern Europe's Glorious Revolutions," ms. p. 9. Hungarian trans. in *Holmi* II 12 (December 1990).

36. February 21, 1991.

37. For the right he was too liberal and antistatist. For the liberals he was too close to visions of a "third Road."

38. Ferenc Feher, "The Fourth Wave: The Place of the Revolutions of 1989 in History," unpublished ms.

39. See chapter 4, this volume.

40. For the best theoretical location of these cases see János Kis, "Between Reform and Revolution: Three Hypotheses about the Nature of Regime Change," *Constellations* 1, 3 (1995): 399–419.

41. This idea that the comparativist must know at least one case thoroughly and from within (i.e., a participatory perspective) is of extreme importance at a time when political science is increasingly rejecting a case- and even area-study approach as mere "journalism." The one case need not be, however, a regionally specific one. Juan Linz and Alfred Stepan, with their outstanding knowledge of some of the Latin American and South European cases, almost instinctively know what is really at stake in East and Central Europe. Knowing one case means that one also knows what one does not (yet) know about another one and leads to the right kind of humility in the face of the new.

42. Robert Dahl, *Polyarchy* (New Haven, Conn.: Yale University Press: 1972), 34–40.

43. Arend Lijphart, "Democratization and Constitutional Choices in Czecho-Slovakia, Hungary and Poland 1989–1991," in Gy. Szoboszlai, ed., *Flying Blind: Emerging Democracies in East-Central Europe* (Budapest: Hungarian Political Science Association, 1992), yearbook of the association; Friedbert W. Rübb, *Designing Political Systems in East European Transitions: A Comparative Study of Bulgaria; Czecho-Slovakia and Hungary* (Bremen: ZERP, 1993); *Disskussionspapier* 3/93 (Papers on East European Constitution Building, 3); and Jon Elster, "Miscalculation in the Design of East European Presidencies," *East European Constitutional Review* (Chicago: Fall 1993 and Winter 1994): 95–98.

44. This analysis cannot be a fully consistent use of the rational choice paradigm, because in the coming epoch the working-class parties stood to benefit from majoritarian systems that would make them one of the largest parties gaining from built-in disproportionality as long as they retained their unity. If the parties in the first countries moving to universal suffrage were still too pessimistic about their electoral chances, the new parties in the subsequent countries had to learn that their interests would be better served by plurality elections. However, they were emphatically ideological parties that strongly identified democracy with proportional representation on the ideological level. A more recent example of such ideologically based choice was the decision of the SPD (Social Democratic Party, Germany) the Parliamentary Council of Chiemsee for PR. The SPD could have had no doubt that it was allying itself with small parties on this issue only because of reasons of principle.

45. See Murray Faure, "The Electoral System," in M. Faure and J.-E. Lane, *South Africa: Designing Democratic Institutions* (London: Sage, 1996), 89–104; Claire Robertson, "Contesting the Contest: Negotiating the Election Machinery," in S. Friedman and D. Atkinson, *The Small Miracle: South Africa's Negotiated Settlement* (Johannesburg: Ravan Press, 1994), 44–67.

46. Lijphart, "Democratization and Constitutional Choices," 100–1; Rübb, "Designing Political Systems," 8, 21, 23.

47. Lijphart is forced to admit, for example, that of the three countries he considers, Hungary did not adopt presidentialism, bicameralism, or PR; the Czecho-Slovak Republic too remained parliamentarian; and only Poland adopted all three institutions expected by the hypothesis (op. cit., 104). But in fact the results of the original negotiations in Poland established guaranteed seats for two-thirds of the lower house, while the rest of the seats (one-third of the lower house, all of the Senate) were elected through plurality voting. The additional criteria brought in by Lijphart, though highly relevant empirically, almost completely eliminate the explanatory power of the original hypothesis. Interestingly, Rübb considers the Czech and Slovak Republic the one country out of four (now including Bulgaria)

that initially opted for PR as the best case for the Rokkan hypothesis, and, he rightly adds, that fit between theory and the cases depends on the mode of extrication (op. cit., 21). But amazingly enough he considers the Czecho-Slovak case extrication by capitulation and then, completely at variance with this diagnosis, goes on to explain why the Communists (whose claims no longer could matter) here had reason to accept PR. He forgets, in other words, that the hypothesis refers to two, more or less equally strong and equally cautious sides engaged in genuine negotiation and that in a model of "extrication by capitulation" he must explain why the (in this case overwhelmingly) stronger side opts for PR. This cannot be done by the use of the Rokkan hypothesis. Interestingly, Jon Elster, who quite rightly notices why the Czech and Slovak case cannot be used to confirm the "Rokkan hypothesis," considers Hungary, Poland, and Bulgaria to have more or less satisfied predictions based on it. This he can do because he considers negotiated outcomes to be equivalent to power-sharing arrangements even when the initially chosen electoral rules are different than the PR "predicted" by Rokkan. Moreover he inexplicably disregards the fact that the Hungarian outcome is parliamentarian and unicameral and the Bulgarian outcome is unicameral as well. According to Elster, the three cases for which the argument "works quite well" confirm only three of the nine predictions. Elster is, however, right to insist on the irrelevance of the "Rokkan hypothesis" for a case like Romania, where the institutional design was imposed even though here all three of the Rokkan predictions were confirmed (PR, bicameralism, presidentialism). Yet it obviously won't do to reduce the Rokkan hypothesis, as he seems to do, to the entirely tautological idea that where the results emerge from genuine negotiations they are negotiated. See "Rebuilding the Boat in the Open Sea. Constitution-Making in Eastern Europe," unpublished ms., 41–43.

48. Lijphart, op. cit., 105. In fact if one removed this restriction, and looked at a larger number of cases than did Lijphart, Rübb, and Elster, the facts would superficially seem to fit the theory better. Many of the East and Central European democracies (ten out of twelve in the survey of EECR) did eventually chose some kind of proportional representation for the chamber in which government originates the choice seems to have some plausibility. To be sure, the result in the several countries is less impressive if we treat mixed rules as not identical to PR (four out of twelve are mixed, and a fifth was originally mixed as well). Following this approach, the prediction with respect to the choice of presidential or semi-presidential regimes is born out even more impressively. Only Hungary, the Czech Republic and Slovakia wound up with pure parliamentary regimes in the region, if we make parliamentary election of the head of state a key criterion, which may of course occasionally (as in the case of Austria) mislead. But in fact all that this approach would prove upon closer examination is that non-Rokkanian models of imposition in East Europe often produced, superficially, power sharing outcomes, while Rokkanian processes of negotiation produced Rokkanian outcomes relatively seldom.

49. They could have insisted on strengthening constitutional protections of private property, of course, but apparently did not. But even this would have led only to constitutional or judicial review, not to a presidential form of the separation of powers.

50. See Lijphart's simple statement. "Democratization and Constitutinal Choices," 101.

51. We should not worry about the fact that they were initially mistaken and were badly defeated in Hungary and Poland at least in the first free elections in the plurality or majority races. In Croatia, even more dramatically, it was the nationalist opposition that was to benefit from both conversion strategies of majoritarianism and presidentialism. The institutional designs emerging from the Round Tables (or in Croatia from reform Communist

imposition) were a function of what the hegemonic parties of the old regime believed to be in their interest. And this in no case corresponded to the similar judgments of leaders of Rokkan's turn-of-the-century oligarchic bourgeois parties. The fact that the bourgeois parties' choice would have been the right one for the Communists tends to disguise the fact that the latter were much more ambitious and aimed at the democratic conversion of power and not just power-sharing guarantees.

52. The Polish Senate, to be sure, was first proposed by Aleksander Kwasniewski at the Round Table. But he did so in order to offer a carrot to the other side, which was reluctant, of course, to accept unfree elections for the Sejm.

53. Claus Offe, "Capitalism by Democratic Design? Democratic Theory Facing the Triple Transition in Eastern Europe," in *Varieties of Transition. The East European and East German Experience* (Cambridge, Mass.: MIT Press, 1997), 29–49. The triple transition is to an effective territorial state structure capable of dealing with significant centrifugal aspirations when these exist, to a market economy, and to political democracy. We should note, however, that with the exception of the three previously federal countries the first transition is not a difficult task in the ex-Communist countries, while it was indeed a challenge in Spain, which did not face an economic transition. Thus transitions in Spain, Hungary, Poland, Bulgaria, and Romania were all double transitions. Moreover, while I do see the structural economic problems in East Central Europe to be greater than in Latin America, even if some of the politically most difficult tasks like macroeconomic stabilization are the same (as Przeworski rightly argues), I am not sure whether the greater structural challenge is a disadvantage (as Offe always automatically assumes) or an advantage (as I tend to think at least with respect to Central Europe) from the point of view of the patience of the population that is asked to sacrifice.

54. Arend Lijphart and Carlos Waisman, "Institutional Design and Democratization," in Arend Lijphart and Carlos Waisman, *Institutional Design in the New Democracies. Eastern Europe and Latin America* (Boulder, Colo.: Westview Press, 1996), 3–6.

55. Adam Przeworski, *Democracy and the Market* (Cambridge: Cambridge University Press, 1991), 139ff.

56. In the actual developments they were helped by the difficulties of establishing new social democratic parties during transitions in which all new parties had to support economic liberalization. But even where a new or old Social Democratic Party has been successful, in the Czech Republic and Germany, Communist parties remain effective political competitors.

57. It presents a further though not insuperable difficulty, however, that these three regimes, Portugal, Spain, and Mexico, have had three very different transition paths.

58. See János Kis, "Between Reform and Revolution," and Andras Bozoki, "A magyar átmenet összehasonlító nézöpontból," and (with Bill Lomax) "Történelmi reváns," the last two in Bozoki, *Konfrontáció és konszenzus* (Szombathely: Savaria Press, 1995), 131–75; 293–337.

59. As pioneered by the four-volume study *Transitions from Authoritarian Rule,* ed. Guillermo O'Donnell, Philippe Schmitter, and Laurence Whitehead (Baltimore: Johns Hopkins University Press, 1986).

60. See in particular Przeworski's *Democracy and the Market.*

61. See Przeworski, *Democracy and the Market.*

62. Juan Linz and Alfred Stepan, *Problems of Democratic Transition and Consolidation* (Baltimore: Johns Hopkins University Press, 1996).

63. See *Transitions from Authoritarian Rule*, v. IV, p. 39; in the third volume there is a more elaborate typology by Alfred Stepan, whose difficulty is simply having too many types. With such a typology the comparative approach turns into one of concurrent case studies, and it is difficult to see how the study of one set of cases could become useful for the analysis of a second set.

64. Scott Mainwaring, an expert on Brazil, describes, for example, the category of top-down reform as more or less a zero set. See Scott Mainwaring, "Transition to Democracy and Democratic Consolidation: Theoretical and Comparative Issues," in Mainwaring et al., eds., *Issues in Democratic Consolidation* (South Bend, Ind.: University of Notre Dame Press, 1992), 321. Mainwaring (pp. 321ff.) as well as J. Samuel Valenzuela, "Democratic Consolidation in Post-Transitional Settings," in *Issues in Democratic Consolidation*, 57–104, seem to be working with a three-part scheme of collapse-extrication-transaction. But it is clear that by extrication and transaction they have in mind two subtypes of negotiated transition, depending on different constellations of power. This becomes clear if we examine the countries listed under transaction (or "reform") by Valenzuela: the main negotiated cases (Spain, Hungary, and Poland) and some marginal cases of pacted transition (Brazil and Chile) are included under the heading. (Mainwaring, who does not try his hand at Eastern Europe, mentions Spain and Brazil.) The evolution of the Brazilian case may lie behind this classification that leaves no room for Mexican type of reform. In 1986 it still seemed possible that the Brazilian regime would continue indefinitely as some kind of liberalized, and only partially democratized, authoritarian form of rule. This made Brazil, at that time, more similar to Mexico than the Southern European cases, or to Argentina and Uruguay, where the bureaucratic authoritarian regimes either collapsed or were negotiated out of existence. The cases of Mexico and Brazil together had to seem sufficiently important to be seen as constituting one possible path of transition. See Luciano Martins, "The 'Liberalization' of Authoritarian Rule in Brazil," and Kevin J. Middlebrook, "Political Liberalization in an Authoritarian Regime: The Case of Mexico," in v. II of *Transitions from Authoritarian Rule* (Baltimore: Johns Hopkins University Press, 1986). After the democratization of the Brazilian regime, the case of Mexico was apparently forgotten, and Brazil was now linked to the very different and indeed classical negotiated case of Spain, opening up a great puzzle concerning why their results were so different.

65. *Transitions from Authoritarian Rule*, 40, 41, and 48ff.

66. In the case of O'Donnell's later analysis for example. Subsequently, Adam Przeworski, who systematized the dichotomous conception of extrication and collapse in a rational choice, game theoretical model, reduced the possible outcomes even further. He came to the surprising conclusion that the modalities of transition do not seem to matter after all for the type of democratic institutions that are in the end adopted (94, 98–99). If true, this could not be so for the reason that he states, namely, that "our cultural repertoire of institutions is limited." Indeed the choices that he mentions (presidential vs. parliamentary government; electoral system; forms of organization of interests) could be supplemented by many others (constitutionalism vs. majoritarianism is the most important) and together these choices allow for a large variety of possible democratic outcomes. While the common international discourse of democracy that Przeworski specifically mentions (rational choice criterion?) and even more common cultural and political heritage do cause a convergence toward one democratic model, even for the southern cases important differences in outcome must be registered. This is all the more true for the East and Central European new democracies, where in the context of very different political traditions dem-

ocratic institutions come in quite different sizes and shapes. If the modalities of transition do not seem to matter for the different outcomes, it is either because some other factor counts for more. It is also possible, however, that these modalities themselves were reconstructed in an inadequate manner.

67. See Bolivar Lamounier, "*Authoritarian Brazil* Revisited: The Impact of Elections on the Abertura," in A. Stepan, ed., *Democratizing Brazil* (Oxford: Oxford University Press, 1989), 43–79. Analogous predictions concerning "Mexicanization" were once made for Eastern Europe and were later abandoned.

68. Przeworski gave this idea a characteristically deterministic formulation in *Democracy and the Market,* 58–66. But the same idea is still implicit in the much more careful analysis of Scott Mainwaring, "Transitions to Democracy and Democratic Consolidation," in *Issues in Democratic Consolidation,* 302, 321.

69. This terrain was stressed, however, by Lamounier, "*Authoritarian Brazil* Revisited," and is noticed, but without due attention, by Mainwaring, op. cit., 302. Not surprisingly, both are analysts of Brazil, the case that came closest to the Mexican model.

70. This sharp differentiation is characteristic of all works of the transition literature. As usual, O'Donnell and Schmitter are the most cautious and assert only that "liberalization can exist without democratization" (*Transitions from Authoritarian Rule* v. IV, 9–11). The positions of Przeworski, op. cit., 54–6, Mainwaring, op. cit., 298–302, and even Stepan, "Introduction," *Democratizing Brazil,* ix, are more schematic, though on page xi, the later, inconsistently but rightly, says that "democratizing pressures from below in civil society added new weight and greater depth to the initial liberalization efforts." Linz and Stepan are even less consistent, because they maintain the sharp differentiation, op. cit., 3, while they consider the civil society, certainly crucial in the period of liberalization, a key arena for the consolidation of democracy. They can do this only by defining democratization in a way that applies only to an already established democracy or at best to a democratic revolution: "democratization requires open contestation over the right to win control over government, and this [?] in turn requires free competitive elections." According to this view, even the establishment of the Round Table negotiations and, in Poland, the immediate, bargained result of such negotiations, would not constitute democratization.

71. See Linz and Stepan, 4. The idea of an electoralist nontransition is an important one, even if elections do, ceteris paribus, democratize.

72. See Juan Molinar Horcasitas, "Changing the Balance of Power in a Hegemonic Party System," in *Institutional Design in the New Democracies,* and Ann L. Craig and Wayne A. Cornelius, "Houses Divided: Parties and Political Reform in Mexico," in S. Mainwaring and T. Scully, *Building Democratic Institutions* (Stanford, Calif.: Stanford University Press, 1995). Even at the moment of this writing it is of course not yet clear if successive waves of Mexican reform accomplished a transition "to" democracy. But it is safe to say that they have accomplished (if there are no radical reversions) a transition "from" authoritarian rule, establishing a much more liberal and a more democratic political order in the process. Ultimately, if (a big if!) the PRI (Institutional Revolutionary Party) manages to continue winning elections, we may still consider, from a functional point of view, the liberalization and democratization of Mexico as survival strategies of a (previously) authoritarian power elite. From an institutional point of view, however, this consideration becomes relatively unimportant.

73. During a lecture in December 1997 at the Graduate Faculty of the New School for Social Research, Castañeda argued that the common legitimation reserves of the originally

revolutionary dictatorships help to bottle up change and lead to an unstructured political development when change does erupt.

74. See note 66.

75. Juan Linz and Alfred Stepan (*Problems of Democratic Transition and Consolidation: Southern Europe, South America and Post-Communist Europe* [Baltimore: Johns Hopkins University Press, 1996]), who have managed to demonstrate the very real applicability of a comparative conception originally derived from the southern cases to East and Central Europe, operate with much broader typologies. But they produce a descriptive conception of paths that gives us almost as many possibilities as empirical cases and that are only loosely related to the regime types (totalitarianism, posttotalitarianism, authoritarianism, and sultanism) they consider central for determining transition paths, 54ff. Even more seriously, they do not manage to find a place for the Mexican type at all, in either of their two approaches, although in one context (295ff.) Bulgaria appears as a case of "controlled" transition as against cases of collapse and negotiation. While this is the best of their many typologies, Bulgaria's inclusion under regime-controlled transition is doubtful especially because of the importance of the negotiations, of which they are of course aware. Three-part typologies, superficially including a reformist type, appear in the works of S. Valenzuela and S. Mainwaring. This I believe is the right approach. Yet, upon closer examination, these leave no room for genuine top-down reformist cases. While Valenzuela includes under the heading of reform many classically negotiated cases like Spain, Poland, and Hungary, we look for the case of Mexico in vain.

76. The only Central European case Przeworski can claim to be familiar with.

77. *Democracy and the Market*, 94; also see the more differentiated account in O'Donnell's "Transitions, Continuities and Paradoxes," op. cit., which nevertheless seems to affirm the uniqueness of Spanish success with the negotiated path, as well as the essay by J. Samuel Valenzuela ("Democratic Consolidation in Post-Transitional Settings," 76), who, in spite of the Chilean case that concerns him above all, partially reverses the evaluation between negotiated cases and cases of collapse to the benefit of the former and calls attention to the hazards of the collapse of authoritarian regime. The strong prejudice against negotiated transitions is reaffirmed for the case of South Africa, which to me shows just the opposite, by Courtney Jung and Ian Shapiro, "South Africa's Negotiated Transition: Democracy, Opposition, and the New Constitutional Order," *Politics and Society* 23, 3 (1995).

78. In the first statement of the case, the precariousness for democracy of the violent overthrow of dictatorships was stressed (11) and the advantages of pacts (where possible) was insisted on (39). O'Donnell and Schmitter, *Tentative Conclusions about Uncertain Democracies*, v. IV of *Transitions from Authoritarian Rule*.

79. See *Transitions from Authoritarian Rule*, v. IV, 41–44. They do not tell us what are the likely consequences of a nonnegotiated model steered primarily from above. Qualitatively higher levels of democracy emerge in their analysis as a result of protest and reform under limited democracies, a point that will be reaffirmed by Valenzuela, op. cit.

80. Op. cit., 67–70. Operating with extremely complex typologies, and with at least seven different transition paths, some of their key insights are vitiated by such a serious concession to a historical case study approach. Moreover, while their approach is distinguished by their stress of the preferability of negotiated transitions to models of collapse, their typology neglects—in spite of its pluralism—cases of top-down electorally driven cases of reform. Thus they overestimate the likelihood that civilian regimes will opt for negotiated transitions and miss the opportunity to analyze the option between reform and

negotiated transition in terms of legitimation resources, even though they do stress in other contexts the "political economy of legitimacy and coercion" (76ff).

81. Ibid., 87ff and 205ff.

82. A crucial variable here is the timing of new constitution making, and the ease or difficulty of transforming an authoritarian constitution by the method of internal amendments. The Chilean constitution making occurred early (1980–81) with respect to the actual transition, *and* (or rather *because*) it was constructed as a constitution extremely difficult to amend. Indeed, authoritarian reservations were built into the very method of amendment. In Poland, constitution making occurred at several junctures, but in any case relatively late, and under very easy amendment rules.

83. Note that self-limitation worked in relationship to the electoral rule chosen by the Civic Forum leadership, namely, proportional representation rather than first-past-the-post voting. It did not work in relationship to constitutionalist restraints. The Czechoslovak Constitutional Court was made considerably weaker than the Hungarian Court.

84. Op. cit., chapter 2.

85. Some analysts like Offe are extremely skeptical concerning the possibility that (in their view) theoretically and normatively disoriented and (in their view) disorganized actors would be capable of self-limitation. I cannot understand this view given the fact that the history of every Central European transition is replete with such instances.

86. See my 1990 article, "Revolution, Civil Society and Democracy," 296–312.

87. Claus Offe, *Der Tunnel am Ende des Lichts* (Frankfurt/M: Campus, 1993).

88. When comparing West Germany after the war with East Germany currently, and when comparing all the current cases with East Germany, Offe is of course right to note the disadvantages of the current and especially the non-German cases. His basic argument is something like this: "If it is so difficult in the case(s) with such advantages, what are we to think of the chances of the much less advantaged ones." In making this argument he disregards the evidence of his eyes, namely, that the democratization of East Germany is at least as fast as that of the West four decades before and that democratic institutions are at least as viable in most of the Central European countries as in the "neue Bundesländer."

89. Jon Elster, "When Communism Dissolves," *London Review of Books* 12, 2 (1990). The argument is repeated and clarified in "The Necessity and Impossibility of Simultaneous Economic and Political Reform," a working paper for the ACLS (American Council of Learned Societies) conference on Constitutionalism and the Transition to Democracy in Eastern Europe, June 18–20, 1990.

90. "Privatisierung der Oekonomie als demokratisches Projekt? Paradoxien des 'politischen Kapitalismus' in Osteuropa," ms. 1991. See the English translation, "Capitalism by Democratic Design? Democratic Theory Facing the Triple Transition in Eastern Europe," in *Varieties of Transition* (Cambridge, Mass.: MIT Press, 1997), 29–45

91. "Capitalism by Democratic Design," op. cit.

To be sure Offe vastly exaggerates the difficulties by postulating that majorities presumably (according to him in all countries) share political cultures opposed to both market and democracy. His fear that conservative forces left over from the old regime may capitalize on this political culture is mistaken as well (see pages 12 and 16).

92. An important advisor of former Prime Minister Tadeusz Mazowiecki told me that the Hungarian politicians were lucky not to have to operate in such a strongly democratizing context as the Poles, and in particular not to have such strong links with social movements. I should note that this was an opinion coming from the democratic opposition and

not from the authoritarian liberals, whom this very source has strongly criticized. I wonder if it was not precisely the new isolation of the Mazowiecki-Geremek group from "society" that produced Walesa's victory, and even Stanislas Tyminski's placing ahead of the prime minister in the subsequent presidential campaign.

93. See in particular L. Lengyel, "Reformdiktatura vagy bürokratikus autoritarianizmus," *Valóság* 5 (1989).

94. "Economic Reforms, Public opinion, and Political institutions: Poland in the East European Perspective," in L. C. Bresser Pereira, A. Przeworski, and J. M. Maravall, *Economic Reforms in New Democracies: A Social Democratic Approach* (Cambridge: Cambridge University Press, 1993), 132–98.

95. Indeed these phenomena lead interpreters to ask whether it is not Latin Americanization, rather than integration into Europe, that is in the cards for the countries of East Central Europe. Even in Europe after all there are some poor capitalisms like Greece, Turkey, and perhaps Portugal; the Spanish success story seems to be unique. See "Spiel mit Einsatz: Demokratisierungsprozesse in Lateinamerika, Osteuropa und anderswo," *Transit* I, 1. (1990): 201–4.

96. The turn to civil society would furthermore help to solve or at least lessen another problem up till now assumed insoluble. By this route the enrichment of the very few through privatization could be moderated and legitimated. Let me stress that I never did believe that universal distribution of state property through coupons could produce a people's capitalism. While there may be possible safeguards especially if the formula were used together with other options, this road, if made the primary one, could easily lead to the rich acquiring more and for less than through direct sales. But as Erzsebet Szalai has shown, genuine pluralism in the forms of privatization (including sales and giveaways, foreign and domestic owners, small- and large-scale, manager and employee participation, as well as ownership by both persons and institutions) could certainly produce a wider circle of owners than Elster fears. Equally important, consultations regarding the specific method of privatization in each case with employee councils, unions, local self-governments, and other interested parties would make the whole process more broadly acceptable than the current extremes of spontaneous and state-controlled privatization.

97. I am not suggesting of course that there not be an all-out effort to support the living standards of those most in need. But such an effort could not make it materially worthwhile for most strata to delay their demands.

98. Offe's conclusions are supported by Przeworski ("Spiel mit Einsatz," 201–4). According to him while in developed countries with strong unions and parties, the poorer parts of the population have been willing to defer their material aspirations for the sake of investments because of their confidence in being able to participate in the products of growth, in underdeveloped countries, because of the closeness of the poor to the material threshold of existence, and because of uncertainties in development one is less ready to wait. In these countries, including East Central Europe, Przeworski predicts oscillation between trying to achieve austerity through governmental decrees and social pacts, neither able to achieve the desired results. The second of these options is related to the civil society-oriented strategy proposed here. Przeworski considers it problematic because of the unwillingness of state actors to accept them, the weakness of the unions that cannot bind their members, and the exclusive nature of pacts that exposes them to challenges by those not included. I don't, however, see why state actors will not be willing to follow such policy if they have no other way, or why a corporatist model of exclusiveness based on absence of publicity and restriction of

relevant partners has to be followed. Presently, the weakness of unionism represents the most important similarity of the East European countries to Latin America, but one must ask whether this is a cause or an effect of underdevelopment. I am fairly optimistic that a strong unionism can emerge in Hungary, Poland, and Czechoslovakia precisely if both sides are willing to accept trading in material demands for organizational rights. One precondition of this, however, remains either the total displacement of the old official unions, or, if this is not possible, its full acceptance as a partner in defending worker interests.

99. For Latin American parallels see A. Stepan, *Rethinking Military Politics: Brazil and the Southern Cone* (Princeton, N.J.: Princeton University Press, 1988).

100. Preuss's point could be continued by stressing the absence of the semantics of the great revolution in 1989. He himself notes two features of this: the absence of the discourse of friend-enemy and the fact that these were "revolutions without revolutionaries." See "The Influence of Carl Schmitt on the Legal Discourse of the Federal Republic of Germany," 1990, unpublished ms., 29–30, and *Revolution, Fortschritt und Verfassung* (Berlin: Wagenbach Verlag, 1990), 62–63.

101. *Revolution, Fortschritt und Verfassung*, 59–62.

102. Hence revelations concerning the self-aggrandizement of leading figures represented an important turning point in East Germany, where uniquely there was previously little cynical insight into the corruption of the ruling elite. For the politics of the Round Table, see especially Preuss, "The Round Table Talks in the Former German Democratic Republic," 1991, in J. Elster, ed., *The Round Table Talks and the Breakdown of Communism* (Chicago: University of Chicago Press, 1996).

103. See A. Arato, "Revolution, Civil Society and Democracy." Today I would somewhat expand my framework to include the legal-constitutional dimension as a fourth level on which we can ask the question concerning the relevance of the concept of revolution to a given set of events. The article in question mentions only systemic, phenomenological, and hermeneutic levels. On this, see chapter 3, this text.

104. The distinction corresponds to the more usual one between political and social revolution, also at times used by Preuss. (See "The Influence of Carl Schmitt on the Legal Discourse of the Federal Republic of Germany," paper delivered at the conference, "Carl Schmitt and the Challenge to Democratic Theory," Graduate Faculty, New School for Social Research, Spring 1990.) It seems to me that going back to Preuss's own intellectual source, Carl Schmitt, the distinction he has in mind can be made more precise. Schmitt recognized four possible levels of constitutional change: 1. the change in the identity of the state, as in an act of federation; 2. the change of the identity of the *pouvoir constituant*, as from monarchical to popular sovereignty; 3. the change of constitution, given the persistence of the constituent power; and finally, 4. changes in constitutional law, given the persistence of "essentially" the same constitution (*Verfassungslehre* [1928] seventh and unchanged edition [Berlin: Duncker & Humblot, 1989]). Evidently, only 2 and 3 are properly considered revolutions, in distinction to state formation and (structural) reform.

105. *Revolution, Fortschritt und Verfassung*, 59; "Constitutionalism and Constitutional Change in the GDR," ms., 64.

106. In *Verfassunglehre* Schmitt depicts the dictatorship of the proletariat as a full-fledged model of sovereignty, next to the models of monarchical and popular sovereignty (p. 121, for example). Unlike Heller, he would have most likely considered the councils or the party as different forms of identification made possible by the same model whose constituent is the working class.

107. It may be that when arguing this point Preuss has stayed close to the Marxian model in which modern revolutions are proletarian revolutions that indeed battle over the meaning of popular sovereignty with their bourgeois revolutionary forerunners. Actually, there are a few, if examples of revolutions that are exclusively from one form of (unitary) popular sovereignty to another, and all of these come from areas with rather peculiar forms of popular sovereignty: China and Cuba in particular, and perhaps Iran.

108. Indeed, even the monarch's body was redoubled, at least in the Western Christian tradition. See E. Kantorowicz, *The King's Two Bodies* (Princeton, N.J.: Princeton University Press, 1957).

109. Technically this was facilitated by the fact that special references to the powers of the party were almost everywhere late additions to the constitutions in the East.

110. This interpretation, moreover, can be supported in Carl Schmitt's understanding of the classical doctrine of popular sovereignty. The party would accordingly become the sovereign dictator, the constituent assembly, of the popular constituent power, which would have the right, as did the Convention Nationale in 1793, to more or less permanently suspend the constitution it itself creates, even before enacting it. Until such a constitution were actually enacted, the constituent assembly (the central committee) would preserve its dictatorial powers, without violating popular sovereignty. Only revolutionary overthrow could prove that popular sovereignty was no longer being exercised, but usurped. Accordingly, the 1989 revolutions could defend the constitution, and the *pouvoir constituant* against a usurper, all constitutional reference to whom could be removed by mere change in constitutional law, by mere amendment.

111. One might even argue that the first device was needed to avoid overloading the revolutionary process with the two simultaneous tasks of replacing the existing sovereign by a new one and changing the very form of sovereignty. Such overloading could easily lead to stopping on the first of these levels, in the process creating a unitary sovereignty linked to the destructive dialectic of identification. Even if fictional, the device of assuming no change in the identity of the sovereign focuses actors on the second problem, changing the very character of sovereignty, which if successful would allow the completion of the revolution.

112. *On Revolution* (New York: Viking Press, 1965), 152. The American framers to be sure did not formally drop the notion of sovereignty. Arendt's claim should therefore be rephrased to indicate only that when the American revolutionaries used the term *popular sovereignty*, they referred to a plurality of already constituted bodies and not to the unity of the otherwise atomized population.

113. This interpretation of the American process of constitution making is not accurate, unfortunately. Although the constitutional convention was elected by already constituted bodies, the thirteen states, it did not follow any existing rules for its procedures and violated its actual mandate, which was to amend the Articles of Confederation but not to replace it and write an entirely new constitution. Nor did it follow the existing requirements for ratification, which involved unanimity, rather than a qualified majority (three-quarter) of the member states. See the articles by Bruce Ackerman and Stephen Holmes ("Precommitment and the Paradox of Democracy") in Elster and Slagstad, op. cit. Thus of the two aspects of Sieyès's thesis about the *pouvoir constituant* being in the state of nature, the U.S. Constitutional Convention contradicted only one, by referring to already constituted bodies that were preserved in federalism. The East European constitution makers contradicted in effect both aspects, to the extent that they referred to civil society (an

uncertain thesis in some countries to be sure) and by adhering to already existing constitutional legality.

114. The first of these has no parallel in the United States. Neither the Continental Congress nor the Constitutional Convention assumed the rules of its predecessor, though the latter was instructed to do so by the Congress. Even the method of ratification used by the Congress was abandoned. On this point see Ackerman, "Neo Federalism."

115. Of course the internal structure of these constitutions, their technically low level and many obvious contradictions express the deep tension between party rule and even paper constitutionalism. This does not change the fact that the constitutions were written constitutions having amendment rules that allowed them to be changed from within. Their normative status was moreover reinforced by the immanent critique of the post-Helsinki accords oppositions, that often took their stand on the basis of current constitutional realities.

116. "Constitutionalism and Constitutional Change in the GDR," 4–5, 8. According to Preuss the stress on civil society brings the East European revolutions closer to the American than the French model after all.

117. Schmitt did not opt for a constitutionalism embodying permanent revolution as Preuss claims, but sought to work out a dualistic conception ("The influence of Carl Schmitt," 14). In the *Verfassungslehre* even the *rechtsstaatliche* part of modern constitutions, the opposite of its political part to Schmitt, belongs to the essential part of the constitution, even if ambiguously. It is another matter that the political dimension, the latent *pouvoir constituant,* Schmitt hopes to maintain within settled constitutions is conceived in a most unattractive and, indeed as Preuss says, threatening manner. It is from this conception that the ambiguities regarding the Rechtsstaat follow. Ernst Fraenkel derived his notion of the dual state, still so important for our understanding of modern "totalitarianisms," from just this Schmittian conception.

118. "Speculation about the Interrelation of Politics and Constitution Making," unpublished ms., 1991.

119. This is a mistake that Jadwiga Staniszkis seems to make when she argues for a statist process of transition. I believe moreover that Laszlo Bruszt ("Transformative Politics in East Central Europe," *Working Papers on Transitions from State Socialism* [Ithaca, N.Y.: Cornell University Press, 1991)] considers her views and mine to be polar opposites only because he too seems to have a zero-sum conception of the relationship of state and civil society. My view, however, is a positive-sum one, and I have for this reason argued for a strong government in Hungary that only a great coalition between SZDSZ and MDF could have provided. But even such a government could remain strong only if it helped to expand civil society, as well as the channels of communication between social organizations, initiatives, and movements with Parliament and government.

CHAPTER 2. CIVIL SOCIETY, TRANSITION, AND THE PROBLEM OF INSTITUTIONALIZATION

1. Well, not quite beyond dispute. Claus Offe has repeatedly argued that the East and Central European transformations (unlike other revolutions, supposedly!) had no proper theory or conceptual frameworks to guide them. He does not say what the model for such a

theory or framework would be (*State and Revolution? What Is the Third Estate?* or some imagined piece of social science?), but in any case his claim reduces the orientation to the reconstruction of civil society (whose existence he neither confirms nor denies) to the *false consciousness* of the epoch at best. Of course the same thing could be said about the relevant works of Lenin or Sieyès. See *Varieties of Transition* (Cambridge, Mass.: MIT Press, 1996).

2. Andrew Arato, "Social Movements and Civil Society in the Soviet Union," in *From Neo-Marxism to Democratic Theory* (Armonk, N.Y.: M. E. Sharpe, 1993), 313–30; as well as J. Butterfield and J. Sedaitis, *Perestroika from Below* (Boulder, Colo.: Westview Press, 1991).

3. Adam Przeworski has even formalized this idea in *Democracy and the Market* (Cambridge: Cambridge University Press, 1991). It is part of his conception that liberalization from above cannot succeed in stabilizing an authoritarian regime. If success, however, is to be defined in terms of lengths of time that are meaningful to the actors undertaking such reform, the histories of post-Stalinism and the case of Mexico prove that he is wrong.

4. A. Przeworski, *Democracy and the Market.*

5. See Timothy Garton-Ash, *The Uses of Adversity* (New York: Random House, 1989), which is a sustained demonstration of this claim, even if his focus is slightly different than mine.

6. L. Kolakowski, "Thèses sur l'espoir et le désespoir" [1971], in Z. Erard and G. M. Zygier, *La pologne: une société en dissidence* (Paris: Maspero, 1978).

7. See A. Michnik, "The New Evolutionism" [1976], in *Letters from Prison* (Berkeley: University of California Press, 1988), as well as A. Michnik, *L'Église et la gauche, le dialogue polonais* (Paris: Seuil, 1979).

8. Michnik, *L'église et la gauche.*

9. "Thèses sur l'espoir," op. cit.

10. K. Wojcicki, *Telos* (Spring 1981): 47.

11. Jacek Kuron, "Pour une platforme unique de l'opposition," in Z. Erard and G. M. Zygier, *La Pologne: une société en dissidence* (Paris: Maspero, 1978).

12. The editors of *Beszélő*, "Társadalmi Szerződés" [*Social Contract*] (Budapest, 1987). The same point has been made in many of János Kis's earlier editorials in this underground journal.

13. A. Arato, "Critical Sociology and Authoritarian State Socialism," in J. Thompson and D. Held, *Habermas: Critical Debates* (Cambridge, Mass.: MIT Press, 1982), 196–218; 309–11, and now in *From Neo Marxism to Democratic Theory* (Armonk, N.Y.: M. E. Sharpe, 1993), 59–83.

14. J. Staniszkis, *Poland's Self-Limiting Revolution* (Princeton: Princeton University Press, 1984).

15. Alain Touraine et al., *Solidarity. Poland 1980–1981* (Cambridge: Cambridge University Press, 1983).

16. Coming from KOR as well as the clubs of democratic Catholic intellectuals (KIK), Experience and Future (DiP), as well as the Flying University.

17. I do not believe for a minute the story repeated by Przeworski that the authorities were seeking a political deal, but could not find an electoral formula under which democratic legitimacy could be attained for their continued hegemony. While the Solidarity leadership (and the Episcopate) would have accepted even an authoritarian *Rechtsstaat* without any element of democratic elections, it is not likely that even such a solution was at that time acceptable to the Leonid Brezhnev government, without whose consent no deal was possible.

18. I do not believe, however, that it was possible to stop the politization of the movement, to restrict Solidarity to either a narrow trade union identity or to a cultural one. The continual pressure of the regime, and its tendency to use its prerogative to violate or restrict earlier agreements, continually drove the movement forward even if it merely wanted to preserve its earlier accomplishments.

19. This crucial idea of "society's fear of itself" was developed by J. Corradi and his collaborators in their project on the culture of fear in Latin America.

20. For this argument see chapter 1 of Cohen and Arato, *Civil Society and Political Theory* (Cambridge, Mass.: MIT Press, 1992).

21. Elemér Hankiss has given us a pioneering analysis of the "second society" in Hungary under late Kádárism. Using the model of the relationship of the first, official, and state-controlled economy with a second, semilegal, partially private economy, Hankiss depicts in several writings of the mid-1980s a society with "first" and "second" publics, cultures, legalities, forms of association, and consciousness, in short everything except two politics (*Diagnózisok* 2. [Budapest: Magvető, 1986]). While he does not have a thesis concerning the origins of this "duplication of the social paradigm," evidently he does give the second economy, an unintended consequence of the economic reform of 1968, pride of place in the whole process. Evidently, the phenomena Hankiss describes depended both on the regime's desire not to disturb the domestic and international environments of the partially reformed two-sector economy and on its search for legitimation that depended on social demobilization and the de facto freeing of the private sphere. My greatest reservation about Hankiss's thesis is that he does not sufficiently differentiate between unofficial mechanisms on which the reproduction of all Soviet type societies depend (e.g., horizontal contacts among managers), structures, and processes that are independent of the regime but are not consciously organized and have no political dimension, and organized activities, a few of which are directly political (e.g., the second public of the samizdat).

22. "Gondolatok a közeljövöröl," in *Beszélö* 3 (Budapest, 1982).

23. T. Bauer, "A második gazdasági reform és a tulajdonviszonyok," in *Mozgó Világ* 8, 11 (Budapest, 1982). The editorial board of the journal was purged after this issue. After 1989 social scientists of all kinds cried, "Mea culpa, we did not predict it," implying that no one had. Bauer, however, spoke of the beginning of the general crisis of the Soviet imperium in 1982, and so he did predict "it." Was he lucky? Yes. Was he *merely* lucky? As his unpublished ms. "From Cycles to Crisis" indicates, he had a well-grounded economic argument based on his earlier sophisticated work on economic cycles under state socialism. But of course his perspective was also that of a participant, and his optimism, using Gramsci's distinction, was as much the optimism of will as that of intellect. Note, however, that a person never known for his optimism, George Márkus, made an analogous argument, independently of Bauer in late 1981. See "Planning the Crisis," *Praxis International* 1(1)(1981).

24. This and the following draw on republished issues of *Beszélö*, in three volumes (Budapest: AB Beszélö kiadó, 1992).

25. Speech at Monor meeting.

26. Samizdat publication, Budapest 1987.

27. *Fordulat és reform* (1987 final text), *Medvetánc* 2 (Budapest, 1987).

28. The events too quickly surpassed the programs in their radicalness. By 1989, in fact, the democratic opposition and its new organizations completely abandoned the idea of a compromise that would leave some definite powers (e.g., the presidency) in the hands of the ruling party. Paradoxically the reformers of the ruling party and some of the more

moderate opposition tried as late as September 1989 to produce such a solution, with an argument that explicitly referred to the Polish compromise, that a far more powerful movement than the Hungarian was forced to accept. The November 1989 referendum, organized by the democratic opposition, put an end to such an effort for good. Does this outcome show the irrelevance of the *Social Contract* as a proposal? The answer is a negative one for five reasons: (1) Having been developed from a Polish model, the proposal came to very much anticipate the lines around which agreement in Poland itself was to be possible. (2) Even more importantly, the proposal provided a clear picture of how a negotiated solution had to work in *the first* country where the ruling party and the Soviet Union could disengage, without bloody and anarchic consequences. Once this happened the way was open in other countries, first Hungary, to expand the realm of the possible, eventually beyond all strategic self-limitation. (3) In Hungary itself the presence of several programs with elements of built-in self-limitation were crucial in generating a reform discussion, which would have been *initially* too threatening to both reformers and the public without the hope in some kind of structural compromise. Indeed it was important in September 1989 for reformers in the party leadership to believe in the possibility of such a compromise, and for their belief to be confirmed by the perhaps self-interested action of some of the opposition. (4) The stress of the *Social Contract* on self-limitation lost its strategic, but not its normative, sense. We see this as we are witnessing the revival of self-destructive revolutionary postures and semantics in several East European countries, mainly on the political right. (5) The stress of the proposal on a three-part structural change, involving the state, the economy, *and civil society* has not lost its meaning (as this chapter tries to show) even as the major political parties lost sight of the third component. In my view, in face of criticism by their allies, the radical economists, the leaders of the democratic opposition were perhaps too quick and too thorough to give up their stress on an active civil society and elements of industrial democracy.

29. I am combining, reducing, and slightly altering the typologies presented in two excellent articles by I. Stumpf: "Rendszerkritika, alternativitás generációs köntösben," in *Magyarország politikai évkönyve 1988* (Budapest: R-Forma kiadó, 1989) and "Pártosodás 89," in S. Kurtán, P. Sándor, and L. Vass, eds., *Magyarország politikai évkönyve* (Budapest: Aula-Omikk, 1990), 386–98.

30. Istvan Stumpf, "Rendszerkritika, alternativitás generációs köntösben," in *Magyarország politikai évkönyve 1988*.

31. Istvan Stumpf, "Political Socialization of New Generation—Alliance of Young Democrats," in *How to Be a Democrat in a Post-Communist Society* (Budapest: Institute for Political Science, Hungarian Academy of Science, 1991).

32. E. Bilecz, "Szárszó '88,'" in *Magyarország politikai évkönyve 1988*, 342–50.

33. Ibid.

34. Ibid., 334.

35. For ecology, see László Sólyom, "A társadalom részvétele a környezetvédelemben," *Medvetánc* (Budapest, 1988); interview with János Vargha, in K. Bossányi, *Szólampróba: Beszélgetések az alternativ mozgalmakról* (Budapest: Láng kiadó, 1989); and G. Lányi, "A kuvik éve—környezetvédelmi jelzések," in *Magyarország politikai évkönyve 1988*, 144–61.

36. See two articles by Istvan Stumpf, op. cit., as well as an interview with Laszlo Kövér in A. Richter, ed., *Ellenzéki kerekasztal* (Budapest: Ötlet kft., 1990).

37. For some of its documents, see "Duna Kör," in *Magyarország politikai évkönyve 1988*, 704–12.

38. Laszlo Bruszt, "Az érdekképviseleti monopóliumok alkonya," in *Magyarország politikai évkönyve 1988,* 189–96.

39. For the founding documents, see TDDSZ, in *Magyarország politikai évkönyve 1988,* 770–9; FSZDL (The Democratic League of Independent Unions) and MOSZ (National Alliance of Workers Councils), in *Magyarország politikai évkönyve* (1991) (Budapest: Ökonomia Alapitvány, 1992), 712ff and 727ff.

The key difference between the latter two organizations is the stress on the defense of interests of employees and relatively small sharing in ownership and management by the FSZDL or LIGA that on the whole seeks to differentiate these functions, and MOSZ that seeks more classical forms of worker ownership and self-management. In effect, however, both organizations are independent trade unions.

See also the interview with L. Bruszt in A. Richter, ed., *Ellenzéki kerekasztal* (Budapest: Ötlet kft., 1990).

40. For documents, see "Nyilvánosság Club," in *Magyarország politikai évkönyve 1988,* 752–55; as well as G. Bányai and J. Bercsi, eds., *Lel-Tàr* (Budapest: Tudósitások kiadó, 1989), 133–41.

41. "Független Jogász Fórum," in *Lel-Tár,* 49–53.

42. The founding document foresaw its self-dissolution on the day when press and communication were perfectly free and guaranteed in a new constitutional state and when the pluralism of opinions was fully established. See *Magyarország politikai évkönyve 1988,* 753. That time has not yet apparently come in the view of the club!

43. See the vivid description in the interview with M. Haraszti, in *Uncaptive Minds* 2, 1 (January-February 1989).

44. Interestingly, the three organizations were to receive 55 percent of the first round vote for party lists, as against the 43 percent of the nationalist parties that were to form the governmental coalition, and 30.3 percent for the two liberal parties. All the historical parties together were to receive 22 percent of the vote, while all Communist successor parties and organizations received 19.7 percent.

45. See the interviews with L. Kövér and especially V. Orbán, in A. Richter, ed., *Ellenzéki Kerekasztal portrévázlutok* (Budapest: Ötlet kft, 1990).

46. L. Bruszt, "1989: The Negotiated Revolution in Hungary," *Social Research* 57, 2 (Summer 1990): 372–74; G. Halmai, *Az egyesülés szabadsága* (Budapest: Atlantisz, 1990), 97–107.

47. On this problem of "societal debate," see Bruszt, "1989: The Negotiated Revolution in Hungary," 373–74.

48. Istvan Kukorelli, "The Birth, Testing and Results of the 1989 Hungarian Election Law," *Soviet Studies* 43, 1 (1991): 138.

49. D. Ost, *Solidarity and the Politics of Anti-Politics* (Philadelphia: Temple University Press, 1990).

50. For a useful summary of these activities, see *Reinventing Civil Society: Poland's Quiet Revolution 1981–1986* (New York: The U.S. Helsinki Watch Committee, 1986).

51. For excellent presentations of these criticisms, from two different sides, see the articles by Alexander Smolar and Andrzej Walicki, in F. Fehér and A. Arato, eds., *Crisis and Reform in Eastern Europe* (New Brunswick, N.J.: Transaction Press, 1991), 175–252; 335–92.

52. Conversation with J. Kuron, Warsaw, February 1987.

53. See David Ost's excellent *Solidarity,* chapters 7 and 8. I am in full agreement with this analysis, from which I learned a lot, except for the hypothesis of a neocorporatist bargain

intended by the Solidarity leadership and actually consummated by the Round Table agreements of early 1989. Only in 1981, when Solidarity was primarily a workers' organization, was the neocorporatism analogy usable, even then only partially. In 1988–89, Solidarity was a political organization primarily, as Ost himself shows; thus its pact with the authorities belongs to a different species than any "social pact" or "social partnership."

54. Thus it is misleading, and prejudicial, to refer to the Polish Round Table agreements, as does Przeworski, as "the Magdalenka agreement." For the best analysis available to me, see Wiktor Osiatynski, "The Roundtable Talks in Poland," in Jon Elster, ed., *The Roundtable Talks and the Breakdown of Communism* (Chicago: University of Chicago Press, 1996), 21–68.

55. Claus Offe, *Varieties of Transition* (Cambridge, Mass.: MIT Press, 1996), needs to explain why he does not consider the *Social Contract* or the reform economists' *Fordulat és reform* (turning point and reform) adequate theoretical programs of change. Is it because he has never heard of them? Several of us have referred to these texts (the first of which was available in English translation) in our writings of the late 1980s as well as early 1990s.

56. FKGP, the Small Holders; SZDP, the Social Democrats; KDNP, the Christian Democrats; and MNP, the Peasant Party. The eighth group was a satellite of the MDF.

57. Note that this last position is now refuted by Juan Linz and Alfred Stepan (*Problems of Democratic Transition and Consolidation* [Baltimore: Johns Hopkins University Press, 1996], who are the only ones among their colleagues who have taken up this aspect of my argument in *Civil Society and Political Theory* (Cambridge, Mass.: MIT Press, 1992) and especially in "Revolution, Civil Society and Democracy," in *From Neo-Marxism to Democratic Theory.*

58. Guillermo O'Donnell and Phillip C. Schmitter, in *Transitions from Authoritarian Rule* (Baltimore: Johns Hopkins University Press, 1987), and Alfred Stepan, *Rethinking Military Politics: Brazil in the Southern Cone* (Princeton, N.J.: Princeton University Press, 1988).

59. For an interpreter who sees the so-called liberalization process as democratization on the microlevel, see Manuel Antonio Garreton, "Popular Mobilization and the Military Regime in Chile: the Complexities of the Invisible Transition," in Susan Eckstein, ed., *Power and Popular Protest: Latin American Social Movements* (Berkeley: University of California Press, 1988). The invisible transition to democracy is the "recomposition and reorganization of civil society."

60. *Polyarchy* (New Haven, Conn.: Yale University Press, 1971), 33ff.

61. See A. Przeworski, *Democracy and the Market* (Cambridge: Cambridge University Press, 1991); J. Kis, "Between Reform and Revolution. Three Hypotheses about the Nature of Regime Change," *Constellations* 1, 3 (January 1995): 399–421.

62. Note that in Latin America and Southern Europe, where the devastation of the civil sphere never equaled that under Communist regimes, civil society did not to the same extent have to be created before the transitions.

63. Elster, ed., *The Roundtable Talks.* On the Hungarian Round Table, see especially Andras Bozóki, in Béla Király and András Bozóki, eds., *Hungary in Transition?*

64. A. Bozóki, "Ut a rendszerváltáshoz: az Ellenzéki Kerekasztal," in *Mozgó világ* 8, 35 (1990); for a contrary position, see the interview with L. Sólyom, in A. Richter, ed., *Ellenzéki kerekasztal*, 140, whose recollections, however, tend to support the view expressed by Bozóki and most of the FIDESZ and SZDSZ delegates, as well as by I. Kónya, one of the key organizers on behalf of the Independent Forum of Jurists, later parliamentary fraction leader of MDF. For the latter, see the interview in *Ellenzéki kerekasztal*, 21. Evidently, the

MDF at the time was not unhappy with the exclusion of the public, as the remarks of Sólyom, then a key MDF negotiator, indicate.

65. See Adam Przeworski, "Economic Reform, Public Opinion and Political Institutions: Poland in the Eastern European Perspective," in L. C. B. Pereira, J. M. Maravall, and A. Przeworski, *Economic Reforms in the New Democracies: A Social Democratic Approach* (Cambridge: Cambridge University Press, 1993), 132–98.

This argument of Przeworski should be taken seriously, even if his critique of the Polish reform (and his positive appraisal of the more moderate "social democratic" approach of the right of center government in Hungary 1990–94), at variance with his own earlier analysis, turned out to be entirely wrong.

66. Laszlo Kemeny, "Civil érdek-képviseleti szervek 1995–ben," in *Magyarország politikai évkönyve* (Budapest: Demokrácia Kutatásole Alap., 1996), 304–10.

67. Jean Cohen and Andrew Arato, *Civil Society and Political Theory.*

68. See Alain Touraine, *The Voice and the Eye: An Analysis of Social Movements* (New York: Cambridge University Press, 1981).

69. Maria Lado and Ferenc Toth, "Az Erdekegyezteto Tanacs 1995-ben: a hadviselés éve," in *Magyarország politikai évkönyve*, 293–303.

70. On this, see my three essays in *East European Constitutional Review* (Fall 1994), (Fall 1995), and (Fall 1996), cited in chapter 1. Subsequent installments did not have to be written because of the collapse of the project as described by the last of these articles.

71. I leave to the side whether it is logical or not (it is not) for an ordinary law, or even a two-thirds law, to regulate constitutional revision or amendment or ratification.

72. See the brilliant little pamphlet (available in eight or so languages) *You and the Constitution,* published by the South African Constitutional Assembly (the two houses of Parliament deliberating together).

73. For the distinction, see the last three chapters of *Civil Society and Political Theory.*

74. The court did this while also protecting referenda, most recently (in 1997, in the case of the referendum proposal concerning ownership of arable land by foreigners) against parliamentary encroachment and manipulation as well.

CHAPTER 3. REVOLUTION, RESTORATION, AND LEGITIMATION

1. Quoted by Mona Ozouf in "Revolution," in F. Furet and M. Ozouf, eds., *A Critical Dictionary of the French Revolution* (Cambridge, Mass.: Harvard University Press, 1989), 806–17.

2. Reinhart Koselleck, "Historical Criteria of the Modern Concept of Revolution," in *Futures Past* (Cambridge, Mass.: MIT Press, 1985), 54.

3. On this concept, invented by Jacek Kuron, popularized by Jadwiga Staniszkis who never understood its normative meaning, see A. Arato, "Revolution, Civil Society and Democracy," in *From Neo-Marxism to Democratic Theory* (Armonk, N.Y.: M. E. Sharpe, 1993), 296–312. This essay, written in March 1989, still very much underestimated the potentialities of radical revolutionary ideologies in the region.

4. I am writing this line in August 1998. Other versions of the chapter (originally written between 1990 and 1992) have been published, first in Hungarian, by *Politikatudományi Szemle* in 1993, and in English, in Michael Kennedy, ed., *Envisioning East Europe* (Ann Arbor: Uni-

versity of Michigan Press, 1995). Aside from unavoidably changing the tense, I restricted myself to a few cosmetic changes. Only the few paragraphs dealing with the reprivatization of property are new. As a result, the piece is now more a document of its original time than a historical reconstruction five years later when the outcome of the conflicts is clear.

5. See, e.g., L. Bruszt, "1989: The Negotiated Revolution in Hungary," *Social Research* 57, 2 (1990); and F. Miszlivetz, "The Unfinished Revolutions of 1989: The Decline of the Nation State," *Social Research* 58, 4 (1991).

6. See *Csendes? Forradalom? Volt?* (Budapest: Twins Publishers, 1991). In this volume my good friend Miklós Sükösd ("Ki beszél itt forradalomról? Az átmentés mint erkölcsi probléma") classes me with those who wish for a second revolution after the post-Communist system change. He unfortunately misunderstood my position. Not only did I reject and fear any kind of second revolution but I don't think that *átmentés*, i.e., the conversion of former powers into new ones, was the central problem for the present, that Kádárist Hungary was totalitarian, and that the element of civil society was absent from the transition. I believe the system change was a self-limiting revolution and does not require to be complemented by a new one. To be sure, the term may decompose into the radical revolution of the right or the self-limiting liberalism of the center. As chapter 4 in this volume clearly indicates, my idea of preserving the spirit of the self-limiting revolution always referred to the legal and constitutional institutionalization of the elements of participation and public influence already present in the system change.

7. Charles Tilly, for example, uses the reappearance of revolutions understood in the broadest possible sense against French scholars who have claimed the end of revolutions in the sense of "great revolutions," i.e., in the narrow sense. See "Europe's Changing Revolutions, 1492–1992," *Working Paper of the Center for Studies of Social Change* (New School for Social Research, October 1991) 130, 1–2. In order to do this, and to define the East European events as revolutions, Tilly, however, changes his criteria of just two years earlier for revolutions in the broad sense and omits the characteristic of "armed struggle." Cf. "Changing Forms of Revolution," *Working Paper of the Center for Studies of Social Change* (New School for Social Research, January 1989) 803. He thus inadvertently demonstrates the role of political rhetorics in the construction of the concepts of "revolution," "revolutions," a point passed over by the designation of "idealism" ("Europe's Changing Revolutions," 17). As I see it Keith Baker, Tilly's target, does not reduce revolutions to "nothing but the alteration of ideas," but merely demonstrates the role of revolutionary discourse in the cultural unification of a diverse set of events and discourses, in the formation of the identity of the broader European cultural phenomenon of the French Revolution. I don't see any reason why Baker should deny, for example, that sovereign power was divided during the events leading to the formation of the Estates General and that the transformation of that body and the acts of the National Assembly meant or led to the replacement of one group in power by another. (By this criterion, however, there were many revolutions between 1789 and 1795, at least four in my rough count!) See from this point of view, Keith Baker, "Inventing the French Revolution," in *Inventing the French Revolution* (Cambridge: Cambridge University Press, 1990), 203–23. It may be of course that Tilly and Baker are quite right in their criticisms of one another and that we need a broader view encompassing both of theirs.

8. *From Mobilization to Revolution* (Reading, Mass.: Addison and Wesley, 1978), 190–96.

9. Tilly has, for example, not yet furnished a demonstration of the usefulness of a broad concept of revolution, by giving us a nomological theory revealing something essential

about great revolutions by exploring the causal relations governing all "revolutions." This may be one of the tasks of his forthcoming book, *European Revolutions, 1492–1992.*

10. *State and Social Revolutions* (Cambridge: Cambridge University Press, 1979).

11. Skocpol's book has a single reference to the American Revolution under the heading of "War for American Independence" (p. 63). Her example of political revolutions are the Glorious Revolution and the Meiji Restoration (note 4, p. 294).

12. See Hannah Arendt, *On Revolution* (New York: Viking, 1965).

13. *Revolution and the Transformation of Societies* (New York: Free Press, 1978).

14. Eisenstadt almost admits this when he claims that no set of events fully satisfies these criteria, but the "great revolutions" do to a greater extent than other versions of change. Ibid., 9.

15. "Social Movements, Revolution and Democracy," in *Graduate Faculty Philosophy Journal* 10, 2 (1985): 129.

16. On this, see F. Furet, *Interpreting the French Revolution* (Cambridge: Cambridge University Press, 1981.

17. "Social Movements, Revolution and Democracy," 136.

18. Ibid., 140; see also A. Touraine, "La nascita delle società post-communiste," *Problemi del socialismo* 4 (1990): 27–28.

19. Touraine has now abandoned the stress on the abolition of an *old* regime and seems to imply that the *forceful* abolition of a *previous* regime by a *revolutionary* movement would suffice to satisfy the relevant criteria for revolution. But in his view *revolutionary* movements remain obsolete. See "La nascita delle società post-communiste," 27–28.

20. R. Koselleck et al., *Geschichtliche Grundbegriffe* (Stuttgart: Kolta Verlag, 1975); F. Furet, *Interpreting the French Revolution* (Cambridge: Cambridge University Press, 1981); Lynn Hunt, *Politics, Culture and Class in the French Revolution* (Berkeley: University of California Press, 1984); Keith Baker, *Inventing the French Revolution* (Cambridge: Cambridge University Press, 1990), chapter 9; F. Furet and M. Ozouf, *Critical Dictionary of the French Revolution* (Cambridge, Mass.: Harvard University Press, 1989).

21. Jürgen Habermas, *Legitimation Crisis* (Boston: Beacon Press, 1975).

22. Keith Baker, *Inventing the French Revolution,* 203. According to Baker, our century is a century of revolutions because "men and women throughout the world have not ceased to play out and elaborate . . . [the] script for politics invented in 1789."

23. I am revising my schema presented in A. Arato, "Revolution, Civil Society and Democracy."

24. Eisenstadt, op. cit., 175–76; Koselleck, op. cit., 46–52.

25. Lynn Hunt, *Politics, Culture and Class in the French Revolution* (Berkeley: University of California Press, 1984), 27.

26. Ibid., 20.

27. Ibid., 32, 38–39.

28. F. Furet, "Terror," in *Critical Dictionary of the French Revolution,* 138.

29. Hannah Arendt, *On Revolution.* (New York: Viking, 1965).

30. Hans Kelsen, *General Theory of Law and State* (Cambridge, Mass.: Harvard University Press, 1945), 117.

31. For Kelsen such a change of identity follows ruptures because they vitiate the link of a legal order to the "original historical constitution," which is the basis of its validity. Cf. the interesting article (whose conclusions I cannot share) by J. M. Finnis, "Revolutions and the Continuity of Law," in A. W. B. Simpson, ed., *Oxford Essays in Jurisprudence* (Second Series) (Oxford: Clarendon Press, 1973).

32. Carl Schmitt, *Verfassungslehre* (Berlin: Duncker & Humblot, 1928), 92–96. For Schmitt the key distinction is between changing: 1. the constituent power (*Verfassungsver-nichtung*, or annihilation of a constitution); 2. the constitution (or replacement of a con-stitution); and 3. constitutional laws (*Verfassungsrevision*). According to him 1. and 2. are both revolutions whether or not the change occurs through utilizing the order's own rules for change, a point that I contest. Furthermore, while at times Schmitt seems to identify the changing of the constituent power with the replacement of a given state (and their respec-tive continuity as well) in other, more persuasive contexts (e.g., op. cit., 50) it becomes clear that the state, especially as an entity of international law, should be differentiated from the constituent power, which may be altered within a given state. France remained France (in spite of the Jacobin government's repudiation of debts) even as it moved from monarchi-cal to popular sovereignty. To be sure this distinction leads to four types of change refer-ring to the state, the constituent power or principle of sovereignty, constitutions, and con-stitutional laws. While for my present purposes I am collapsing constituent power or principle of sovereignty and constitutions, I tend to think (with Schmitt) that replacing or changing a whole constitution extralegally, i.e., in a couplike fashion, is already a revolution in the legal sense, even if the principle of sovereignty (monarchy or democracy for exam-ple) is preserved, unlike (pace Schmitt) the two cases of extralegal changing of "some" con-stitutional laws and the legal replacement of a whole constitution as in the case of the move from the Fourth to the Fifth Republic in France. I recognize of course that these last dis-tinctions are quite contestable.

33. See H. L. A. Hart, "Self-referring Laws," in *Essays in Jurisprudence and Philosophy* (Oxford: Clarendon Press, 1983), 173–78.

34. So is the legal restoration of property arrangements interrupted by a regime with whom legal continuity is claimed. See the interesting analysis of Ethan Klingsberg in "Judi-cial Review and the Hungarian Transition from Communism to Democracy: The Consti-tutional Court, the Continuity of Law, and the Redefinition of Property Rights," *Brigham Young Law Review* 1 (1992): 92ff.

35. Only in permanent revolutions is a constituent power fully unbound a permanent feature of "legal" reality. Given the theoretical possibility of such a case, however, the legal definition of revolution should in any case be slightly modified, referring to the abolition of a legal order "or" (instead of "and") replacement by another.

36. Nationalist programs indeed often are used by authoritarians of the old Communist regimes seeking to preserve dimensions of their power. While in some countries nationalism has not been an important force politically (Hungary, Poland, the Czech Republic), right-wing revolutionary authoritarianism is found everywhere, with different impact to be sure.

37. SZDSZ, *A rendszerváltás programja* (Budapest: SZDSZ pamphlet, 1989).

38. For the sake of more convenient English usage, I will render *rendszerváltás* most of the time as change (rather than the more correct exchange) of systems.

39. Note that the following paragraphs are word for word the ones I wrote in 1992. In 1998 of course what it claims is far more obviously true, and the thesis could have been rad-icalized: A political system allowing smooth alternation in power is in place, and the threshold to a private market economy has been definitely passed. I prefer to leave the orig-inal wording in order not to appear to be optimistic with the help of hindsight.

40. Amazingly enough many countries in the region, especially the ex-Soviet republics, have only now established the hybrid system based on informal regulation and a "neither plan nor market" form of coordination that characterized the Kádár era in Hungary after 1968.

41. Unfortunately the trends since late 1991 have involved a slowdown not only in the area of the privatization of state enterprise but also for the creation of new private firms. See Maria Zita Petschnig, *Jelentések az alagútból* (Budapest: Pénzügykutató Rts. 1992), 26–7, 101ff. Petschnig convincingly argues that Hungary's road from a statized economy has been halfhearted, and she notes the continued dependence of even new firms on the state sector as well as state tax policy.

42. On this point I disagree with János Kis, who seems to argue that the more popular and bloodier a revolution, the less likely is there to be a continuity in the state administration. See "Az elit megmaradásának elvéröl," *Beszélö* (February 9, 1991).

43. A. Arato, "Critical Sociology and Authoritarian State Socialism," in D. Held and J. Thompson, eds., *Habermas: Critical Debates* (Oxford: Blackwell Publishers, 1982), 196–218.

44. See the remark by P. Szalai in "1989-ben még megvolt (We still had it in 1989)," in András Bozóki et al., eds., *Csendes? Forradalom? Volt?* (Quiet? Revolution? Did It Happen?) (Budapest: Twins kiadó, 1992).

45. Z. Zsille, "Békés ellenforradalom? Reklamáció az elmaradt rendszerváltozás ügyében (Peaceful counterrevolution? Complaints in the cause of a system change that did not take place)," in *Csendes? Forradalom? Volt?*, 197.

46. Miklós Szabó, "Akadozó rendszerváltás," in *A váltás rendszere* (Budapest: Politikai tanulmányok intézete, 1992).

47. See, e.g., Gyula Tellér, "Az elit nem vész el, csak," in *Beszélö* (February 2, 1992). In spite of my disagreement on this point, I do agree with Tellér's main argument, which, instead of quasi-revolutionary attacks against surviving elites, promotes the self-organization of civil society, in the form of countervailing powers. Unfortunately his oversimplified sociological diagnosis, focusing on persons and elites, gives ammunition to those who opt for the former strategy; it tends to drum up support in SZDSZ (of which Tellér is a politician) for the various plans of the coalition to promote political purges and trials. In his reply, János Kis, while conceding the thesis of the survival of elites, focuses on the structure-forming consequences of the statist policies and attitudes of the governing coalition (''Az elit megmaradásának elvéröl," *Beszélö* (February 16, 1992), 5). The two positions have different strategic consequences. That of Tellér leads to an alliance of all new forces, including MDF and SZDSZ, against survivals from the old regime, perhaps including the MSZP, the ex-state party now seeking to redefine itself as social democratic. Kis's position, to the alliance of all modern and antistatist forces, most of the opposition in other words, possibly including elements of the MSZP, against the ruling coalition.

48. Miklós Sükösd is right in focusing on the conversion of power (*átmentés*) as the target of those who wish for a revolution after the exchange of systems, in effect a "second revolution." It may even be that some radical democrats who speak for this position present their own perspective by stressing civil society. But it is certainly wrong to link the idea of the democratization of civil society in general to the struggle against conversion and to the desire for a second revolution. The program of the self-limiting revolution, as I show, is an interpretation of the exchange of systems, and not some kind of future addition to it. It is another question that one might wish to preserve something of the spirit of the self-limiting revolution in future institutions. This would require not a revolution but a particular constitutional design for an evolving liberal democratic rule of law state. "Ki beszél if forradalomról? Az átmentés mint erkölcsi probléma (Who Is Speaking Here of Revolution? Conversion as a Moral Problem)," in *Csendes*, 95ff.

49. For a very different interpretation of these demonstrations, see Tamás Hofer, "Harc a rendszerváltásért szimbólikus mezöben. 1989. március 15-e Budapesten," *Politikatudományi Szemle* 1 (Budapest 1992). I do not doubt the significance of demonstrations in Budapest and their role in helping to delegitimate the existing system. I also believe that the demonstrations provided ritualized forms for carrying out symbolic conflicts or affirming (in the case of March 15, 1989) the short-lived unity of the opposition. I even accept the idea of demonstrations as "revolution play" playfully confronting authorities with the possibilities of violent conflict. And yet the legal demonstrations of 1989 and 1990 remained what illegal and semilegal ones were in Hofer's own words: "possibilities for the expression of pressure that were calmer and safer than frontal oppositional attacks would have been" (35). They remain then the typical public forms of a peaceful change of systems that is not experienced as revolutionary change.

50. Compare his governmental speech (in *Magyar Nemzet*, May 23, 1990) where he speaks of "a revolution in Hungary . . . that still demands renunciation and patience . . . a peaceful revolution" with a quotation, reproduced by I. Kónya, the leader of the MDF fraction in parliament: "[I]f you [they?] are demanding quick changes, you [they?] should have made a revolution; now the transition must proceed on a slow, legal road" (*Magyar Nemzet*, October 11, 1990). The reason why the passage is difficult to interpret is because Antall seemingly directs the line at members of his own party who would wish to use a strong state machinery to produce quicker changes, while the Imre Konya quotation is directed against liberals objecting to the continuity of that state machinery. Neither J. Böröcz, op. cit., nor E. Csizmadia, *Magyar Hirlap*, December 7, 1991, who comment on this passage, really clarify to whom and about whom Antall was speaking. Csizmadia does convince me that at least at that time the passage meant that since there was no revolution, don't bother me if my politics relies on some inherited institutions. The passage becomes meaningless, or a mere provocation-manipulation of populist sentiment in his own party, once this sentiment becomes an important factor. I cannot tell to what extent that was the case when the remark was first uttered.

51. Compare his speech to the congress of SZDSZ in spring 1989 where he argues that reform from below is revolution and promotes a popular if "bloodless and legal" revolution in *Szabad Demokraták* 4-5 (1989), and his article "Tájkép a csata elött," in *Elet és irodalom*, August 4,1989, where he contrasts "social revolution" merely with "political freedom." This second article notably rejects any campaign against Communist jobholders.

52. *A rendszerváltás programja*, 67–69. To be sure, some leaders of the democratic opposition may now believe that the absence of large-scale popular involvement and enthusiasm has negatively affected the Hungarian change of systems. This they do, however, without wishing for either a second revolution, this time from below, or state purification and purges from above. Either would endanger the achievement of the first "bloodless" "revolution," the constitutional democratic order. See Kis, "Az elit megmaradásának elvéröl."

53. See especially András Bozóki, "Forradalom vagy átmenet," in *Csendes? Forradalom? Volt?* László Bruszt is the only major scientist who seemed to use the (strongly qualified) term *revolution*, as in "Hungary's Negotiated Revolution," op. cit.

54. See his discussion in *Csendes? Forradalom? Volt?*, 61–63, 77–78, and 81–83, which fits into the interpretive model I described under the heading "postmodern revolution," in chapter 1 this text.

55. *Magyar Nemzet* (August 6, 1990).

56. See, for example, *Magyar Nemzet* (October 4, 1990), 4, as well as *Magyar Nemzet* (March 26, 1991).

57. See I. Csurka, "Meg nem történt forradalom," in *Csendes? Forradalom? Volt?*; Gy Fekete, *Magyar Fórum* (January 1, 1992).

58. See the remark by one leader of the MDF quoted in *Magyar Hirlap*, July 13, 1992, 3, "[W]e need not property reform but a revolution in Hungary." On the revival of the ideology of a second revolution, see Szabó, "Akadozó rendszerváltás," 13. Szabó focuses on a controversial treatise by Imre Kónya (written in August 1992), the parliamentary leader of the MDF, calling for determined measures to purge officeholders from the old regime and especially the media. It is a characteristic of Kónya's "Jacobinism" that he longs for a purification that he knows is not desired by the population, the merely "empirical people," as it were. For excerpts from his paper, see *Magyar Hirlap*, September 5, 1992. For a reply from Kata Beke, a "liberal" member of MDF who since then has left the party, see *Magyar Hirlap*, September 27, 1991.

59. Fekete, op. cit., 9. It is not the point that our revolution is the most pessimistic, the author says, but that it was betrayed.

60. The name of their once active party was revealingly "Magyar October Párt," Party of the Hungarian October, a direct reference to 1956, but also a sly one to the Russian October. The founder of this party was the late György Krassó, a veteran of 1956, who as a dissident never hid his openly revolutionary convictions. His views are now represented by others, in particular, Zoltán Zsille and Jenö Nagy.

61. Zsille, "Békés ellenforradalom?" 199, 200.

62. See T. Hofer, "Harc a rendszeváltásért szimbólikus mezöben," 30–34.

63. See Béla Pomogáts, "Ezerkilencszázötvenhat halotti leple" (The Shroud of 1956), *Magyar Hirlap* (June 16, 1992).

64. Hofer, op. cit., 38.

65. János Kis, "The Restoration of 1956–1957 in a Thirty Year Perspective," in *Politics in Hungary: For a Democratic Alternative* (Boulder, Colo.: Social Science Monographs, 1989).

66. István Deák, "A belsö ellenség alkonya," *Magyar Nemzet* (May 17, 1990); L. Bruszt, "Hungary's Negotiated Revolution," as well as the pieces by Akos Szilagyi and József Böröcz, in *Csendes? Forradalom? Volt?*

67. See the essays by Csurka and Zsille in *Csendes? Forradalom? Volt?*

68. For the views of the latter, see the interviews and reports concerning their March 15, 1992, demonstration in *168 óra* (March 24, 1992), and *Magyar Hirlap* (March 16, 1992). The confusion of many of the 1956 veterans is obvious. Some concentrate on the lack of an important role for them, others more on punishing those guilty of past crimes. Most want to continue the revolution, but it is unclear who they define as their enemies, the government, the Constitutional Court, or the opposition. Of course they hate the surviving elements of the old regime and especially the few hard-line Communists active in the MSZMP the most, yet many of their complaints concerning the collapse of a social safety net, and privatization without the participation of worker constituencies resemble the criticism of just these "left" forces.

69. Conservative with respect to the halfhearted Kádárist modernization. See G. M. Tamás, "Gondolatok a rendszerváltásról," in *Csendes? Forradalom? Volt?* This thesis is not weakened by those (e.g., G. Schöpflin) who point out the ambiguities of this modernization.

70. See also Sólyom's paper for the June 1990 conference of the ACLS at Pécs.

71. "First Year of the Constitutional Court" (Budapest, February 1991), unpublished ms., 21.

72. Decision 2086/A/1991/14 of the Hungarian Constitutional Court, on March 3, 1992, in *Az Alkotmánybíróság Határozatai* (Budapest: UNIO, 1992), 81. The decision is now available in English: "Constitutional Court of Hungary Resolution No. 11/1992," *Journal of Constitutional Law in Eastern and Central Europe* (n.d.) 1(1): 129–57.

73. Ibid., 80.

74. Ibid., 82–83.

75. Ibid., 82. Not even legitimate claims of substantive justice or injustice can be the grounds for violating rule of law principles, in particular the principle of legal security.

76. P. Hack and I. Kukorelli give good descriptions of this train of thought in *Magyar Hírlap* (May 14, 1992): 7, and (June 6, 1992): 7.

77. I. Csurka, "Az alkotmánybíróság döntéséhez," *Magyar Fórum* (March 12, 1992).

78. Zs. Zétényi, *Magyar Fórum* (April 2, 1992).

79. When he became the first president of SZDSZ in late 1989, János Kis gave up his leadership of *Beszélő*.

80. See *Beszélő* (March 14, 1992), where one editorialist, with some self-irony but still reluctantly, accepts the verdict of the Court on the Zétényi-Takács bill. The editor in chief's remarks in the March 7 and 14 issues are also plagued by some ambiguity. Unlike most of his colleagues from the earlier democratic opposition, Ferenc Köszeg does not think it shameful that their party, SZDSZ (unlike FIDESZ), was forced to abstain from voting on the law by its own "radicals." See the exchange of letters with M. Laki in *Beszélő*, March 14.

81. Kukorelli, op. cit.

82. While stressing the principle of legal security, P. Hack is critical of the continued validity and especially the use of regulations inherited from the past. See "A jogbiztonság ígérete," *Beszélő* (July 4, 1992). While a wholesale elimination of old regulations is obviously impractical, in many cases waiting for Constitutional Court decisions is also dangerous, as is shown by the case of a 1974 governmental order concerning the media, only recently declared unconstitutional but temporarily left in effect by the Court.

83. To be sure the Court does seem to assume that the old constitution was a genuine constitution and thus usable to initiate a process of its own transformation. But this assumption is based on the double nature of Communist constitutions, fictional on the level of application yet formally like other constitutions, even if technically of a low quality and full of contradictions that did not matter since the document was not meant to be applied. See A. Arato, "The Dilemmas of the Power to Make Constitutions in East Europe," chapter 4 this text.

84. On the last point, that a legal revolution is not a revolution, politicians of radically opposed ideologies can agree: Cf., for example, the article of Fekete, op. cit., with that of M. Eörsi, "Hol húzódnak az erövonalak," *Beszélő* (August 15, 1992). Eörsi, unlike Fekete, does not consider it a betrayal, or even lament that a revolution did not occur in Hungary.

85. The first charge seems to be a rhetorical device on the right from which leading figures have partially distanced themselves. See, for example, Zétényi, op. cit., and I. Csurka, "Több hét összefüggései," *Magyar Fórum* (Special Olympic Edition, May-June 1992): 2. Csurka and Zétényi, however, did make the completely incorrect charge about the membership of the Court, a charge that the Court, whose president is a former leading member of MDF, felt constrained to rebuke in the daily press. See Csurka, "Az alkotmánybíróság döntéséhez," op. cit., and the report in *Magyar Nemzet* (November 16,1991): 1.

86. See Csurka, "Az alkotmánybíróság döntéséhez." This argument was also subsequently toned down (see "Több hét összefüggései"), possibly because the author was told

that the minister of justice and perhaps the prime minister did not feel the need for a new constitution, for which in any case they did not have a two-thirds majority in Parliament. See the report in *Magyar Hirlap* (April 23, 1992).

87. See the report on a statement by László Sólyom in *Magyar Hirlap* (March 30, 1992): V.

88. See, for example, G. Halmai, "A jogállamiság zöld gyepe," *Magyar Nemzet* (Október 4, 1990), and T. Sárközy, "Allamszervezetünk fejlesztéséröl," *Beszélö* (July 25,1992). András Sajó has even produced a new constitution to make the same point.

89. On this point I am in disagreement with the several articles of Béla Pokol on this subject. See, e.g., "Aktivizmus és az Alkotmánybiróság," in S. Kurtán et al., eds., *Magyarország Politikai Evkönyve* 1992 (Budapest: Economix Rt., 1993), 150–56. See the debate between Pokol and Halmai in *Magyar Hirlap* (March 25, 1992). Pokol represents the point of view of legal postivism and what could be called "strict constructionism." For a complementary debate between advocates of parliamentary majoritarianism and constitutionalism (T. Bauer, A. Sajó, G. Halmai, G. M. Tamás, and myself), cf. *Beszélö* (May 4, 11, 18, and 25, 1991.

90. See A. Arato, "Dilemmas of the Power to Create Constitutions in East Europe," chapter 4 in this volume.

91. Ibid.

92. See P Szalai, op. cit., 191–92, 215. The strategic arguments of Kis against calling such an assembly seem still cogent in retrospect especially in light of the evidence of other countries, such as Bulgaria and Serbia. See *Szabad Demokraták* 4–5 (1989). The SZDSZ could not anticipate that the Round Table will be forced into rewriting most of the old constitutional document and submitting this new text to the new parliament. On this cf. A. Bozóki, "Hungary's Road to Systemic Change: The Opposition Roundtable," unpublished ms.

93. I. Csurka in *Csendes? Forradalom? Volt?*, 151. We should note that the freely elected parliaments of East Germany and Poland and the Czech and Slovak Republic were not sovereign assemblies in this sense. They all adhered to the amendment rule of the previous constitution, which was considered valid until legitimate replacement. Of course such a procedure had disastrous consequences in the case of the Czech and Slovak constitution, whose confederal or federal provisions were never meant to work and were indeed entirely unworkable.

94. The latter is more or less the suggestion of M. Eörsi (op. cit., 11–12), who of course considers the next step possible only after the elections of 1994.

95. The original version of this chapter was largely completed before Istvan Csurka had published his most aggressive and controversial study, "Néhány gondolat a rendszerváltozás két esztendeje és az MDF új programja kapcsán," *Magyar Forum* (August 20, 1992). This "study" was evidently motivated by recent by-election defeats and the low popularity of the MDF and the government. Evidently Csurka came to believe that only a conscious and determined mobilization toward a right-wing second revolution could save his party. In preparation for this he went as far as to challenge Antall's position as the party's leader. Nevertheless, little of substance in the long article was entirely new, neither its blatant anti-Semitism nor its wild rewriting of history and certainly not the idea of a global conspiracy of liberals, cosmopolitans, communists, and Jews against Hungary. The kind of "unmasking" of the parliamentary opposition he proposes has been practiced in every single issue of *Magyar Fórum* from its inception; it is difficult to see why he thinks this tactic that has been more or less a failure so far would now help the MDF to mobilize anyone. His reading of the second electoral round in 1990, attributing victory in part to such unmasking, is

clearly fallacious: MDF owed much more to voters of the Socialist party that considered it less radical and systematically denied the SZDSZ their vote whenever the MSZP candidate was eliminated in the first round. Let us recall that Csurka did not win his own individual constituency. Actually, what is new in the "study" is that now Csurka for the first time proposes concrete, extraconstitutional measures, relying on the use of force, for the MDF government to eliminate all consequences of its April 1990 pact with SZDSZ. He suggests simply that constitutional scruples should be forgotten and the police be used to resolve the conflicts with the media presidents and the president of the republic. For the moment the government has neither repudiated nor followed these proposals, condemned by a few national liberal members of MDF. The debate concerning the article has been raging for over a month now (note October 1992).

96. It is interesting to ask why a coalition and its leading party, elected because of its promise to work for slower, less-disruptive change, should eventually commit itself to a project of populist quasi-revolutionary radicalism. As in all East European countries, the greater influence of activists than simple members and members than potential voters is part of the explanation. The militants were driven to the right in electoral and parliamentary confrontations. But the choices of the government also played a role. The avoidance of a great coalition or even a "minimal winning" coalition with the liberal and secular FIDESZ has led to splitting the population according to issues of worldview, a split exacerbated by subsequent attempts to impose the worldview of the coalition by simple majorities. The abrogation of the spirit of the compromise with SZDSZ pointed in the same direction. Since religious traditional older voters represent a minority in Hungary, the majoritarian choices of the coalition (despite its apparently "over large" character) led to dramatic shrinkage of its base, loss in popularity, and losses in by-elections. This infuriated the militants of the MDF, already smarting from defeats at the hands of the Constitutional Court and the president, the country's two countermajoritarian institutions. Their acceptance of Csurka's program could mean a further disaster for the party, which in order to do well in elections would have to occupy the center of the political field. Thus the logic of the development of the MDF points more to the use of extraconstitutional means than to preparation for a normal election.

97. G. M. Tamás, "A Pohárnok-ügy," *Magyar Hirlap* (May 4, 1992).

98. Several pamphlets and essays by members of the SZDSZ have also emphasized this theme. See G. M. Tamás, "Gondolatok a rendszerváltásról," and M. Szabó "Akadozó rendszerváltás."

99. G. M. Tamás has also made this point. See "Gondolatok a rendszerváltásról," in *Csendes? Forradalom? Volt?*

100. *Le Débat* (November-December 1990). Hungarian translation: *Népszabadság* (March 15,1991).

101. Consider the revival of traditional terms like *vàrmegye* and *föispàn* in the first draft of the law on local self-government, indicating the regional administrative units on the one hand and their prefect like, government-appointed administrators on the other. Since the legislation involved two-thirds parliamentary majorities, under the pressure of the opposition, the powers of these entities and officials were reduced. The governments representative in the counties are now called "representative of the republic." Recently, in spite of agreements, the government has been trying to increase their power at the expense of elected mayors and councils.

102. Note the distinction of the Czech Republic with its very different history, whose economic liberals are indeed violent restorers with respect to property (reprivatization),

and who have in other respects too jumped on the restorationist-revolutionary bandwagon (political justice, purges).

103. See Eric Vogelin, *From Enlightenment to Revolution* (Durham, N.C.: Duke University Press, 1975), 175ff.

104. Indeed this strategy has the hope of convincing some of the adherents of the idea of "overtaking Europe" by focusing on the prior need for not only a radical break but also the rolling back of the film, as it were, to a rather unspecified place representing a proper national starting point of development. For so-called national liberals, in Hungary all found in the MDF or near it, this might be more attractive in principle as a starting point, in spite or even because of its vagueness, than nineteenth-century liberal England, suggested by some others, which is evidently unattractive to the population. That "catching up" and "rolling the film back" can be made to appear compatible is indicated by Habermas's uncritical linking of these terms: "Die nachholende Revolution," in *Die nachholende Revolution* (Frankfurt/M: Suhrkamp, 1990). To be fair, in the single case of the Czech Republic, one might be able to justify such linkage. But what was East Germany before Communist rule? Simply a capitalist country?

105. In *Csendes? Forradalom? Volt?*, 217.

106. On this see C. Sunstein, *The Partial Constitution* (Cambridge, Mass.: Harvard University Press, 1993).

107. Massimo Boffa, "Counterrevolution," in F. Furet and M. Ozouf, eds., *A Critical Dictionary of the French Revolution* (Cambridge, Mass.: Harvard University Press, 1989), 640–47.

108. Even reprivatization of land or of church real estate may not achieve their goals in the face of determine opposition on all levels of life as well as the unpracticality of the proposals once concretized.

109. (Note 1998). In retrospect, however, it is more likely that the obsolete ideology, however attractive to small groups, might have rather *delegitimated* projects that could have been supported by much wider groups on other grounds: self-interest or retributive justice. Given, however, the empirically well-documented limits of nationalist ideology in the given context, it is not clear what the option of the radical rights could have been. They were, I think, successful in pointing to the legitimation problems of the new regime but unable to solve their own.

110. In Bulgaria and the Czech Republic the character of this right is different: economic liberal rather than populist-authoritarian. Interestingly enough they have been more successful in passing relevant legislation, the so-called lustration laws. Poland was a close call in terms of antiagent revelations that were narrowly defeated by Lech Walesa and the parliamentary opposition and, after the fact, the Constitutional Court. Only in the ex-GDR have quasi-revolutionary projects of justice been taken up by primarily other than right-wing groups, in this case some of the ex-civil rights activists who experienced their revolution as "stolen" by the Western parties and government.

111. Sensing the paradox, Csurka has now partially relocated his anger concerning the Round Table agreements to the SZDSZ-MDF pact. But he is still in paradoxical situation because his leader, József Antall, was an architect of both agreements, and the second gave MDF precisely those majoritarian instruments (constructive no-confidence vote, abolition of most two-thirds laws) that Csurka would wish to exploit against all opponents, or rather enemies. What he laments of course is that the MDF had to give something for this that turned out to be significant, the presidency to Arpád Göncz of SZDSZ.

112. For the meaning of this distinction, see Szabó, "Akadozó rendszerváltás."

113. See G. M. Tamás, "A Pohárnok-ügy," *Magyar Hirlap* (May 4, 1992).

114. The two best-known targets, the presidents of radio and television, Csaba Gombár and Elemér Hankiss, were moderate dissidents, active above all among reformist social scientists. Gombár was present at the founding of MDF at Lakitelek in 1987, the only one to clearly mention the program of a multiparty democracy. Hankiss, a prisoner after the events of 1956, had the special misfortune to become the target of a demonstration of '56ers on March 15, 1992. The two are attacked by the government not because of their pasts, but because of their refusal to fully deliver their medium to the governing coalition and its ecclesiastical allies. But significantly, they became targeted by radical revolutionary groups and organizations.

115. On this, see Csurka, "Néhány gondolat," 2.

116. See, e.g., Mona Ozouf, "Public Spirit," in *Critical Dictionary of the French Revolution*, 771–80.

117. I do not see how Bruce Ackerman can miss this important linkage in his important little book, *The Future of the Liberal Revolution* (New Haven, Conn.: Yale University Press, 1992). He recommends burning the files (on which retroactive justice would supposedly be based) but firing the people. On what grounds? If it is mere membership in a given class (say party members), the number involved may be too large, and in any case the results would be unjust if individual guilt or innocence is not explored. Why is firing in many cases not punishment, comparable to many criminal verdicts? He may be too much under the influence of the case of East German universities were the issue was generally that of competence, and where replacements were in fact available. But even that case resulted in much injustice toward past and future generations of East Germans.

118. See J. Eörsi, "A gyöztesek törvénye," which reports the relevant remarks of I. Csurka in the parliamentary debate, *Beszélö* (November 16, 1991). Csurka's point seems absurd in relation to the statute in question that would not touch the economic managers at all, and makes sense only because he sees the law as merely a part of a comprehensive revolutionary strategy.

119. Unless they are protected by constitutional safeguards, as the requirement of the president of the republic to countersign some appointments and dismissals as in the case of the presidents of radio and TV, colleagues Gombár and Hankiss.

120. Subsequently the Constitutional Court affirmed a piece of political legislation of the first freely elected Parliament, the so-called agent statute that provided for the lustration of several categories of people holding political office after the second parliamentary elections (giving them the choice of leaving office or being unmasked as former agents or receiving information from agents). It has moreover sustained the decision of the government to initiate trials against perpetrators of mass shootings in 1956, under International Human Rights conventions ratified by Hungary. The result of these decisions, without much popular support, has been extremely meager.

121. Theda Skocpol, *State and Social Revolutions*.

122. See the debate in *The Journal of Democracy* 1 and 4 (1990) between Juan Linz and Donald L. Horowitz.

123. See, e.g., Habermas, *Structural Transformation of the Public Sphere* (Cambridge, Mass.: MIT Press, 1991).

124. One might claim that abstention in the Hungarian Parliament is actually a weak "no," since 51 percent plus 1 refers to all those voting. But in the above cases each faction

abstained because it wanted to hide internal disagreements; several members in each case wanted to vote "yes" with the coalition.

125. President Sólyom would have liked such power, which the Court's majority would probably have used to support the prime minister against the president.

126. Csurka later, however, actually recommended, or rather demanded, government actions self-admittedly anticonstitutional, justified supposedly by the president's, in his opinion but not the Court's, unconstitutional actions. See "Néhány gondolat," op. cit.

127. In defending the former police chiefs and shielding the secret agents of the old regime, the same Mr. Horvath frankly asserted the principle of the continuity of the state under new top management. To be sure, following the example of Prime Minister Antall, he also took an argument from the storehouse of the opposition and pointed to repressive and authoritarian aspects of many Western states that supposedly also lent unquestioned legitimacy to his own practices.

128. *Magyar Hirlap* (April 1, 1992): 5.

129. The danger was not therefore a choice between Csurka and Boross as the strong man of MDF, as a recent issue of *Beszélö* implies, but their combination, which operated for a long time.

130. He spoke of the degeneration of public opinion, and its nonidentity with the people's final opinion, which of course corresponds, by definition, with his own. See "Néhány gondolat," op. cit.

131. One and only decision of the empirical people must of course be accepted as authentic: the second round vote of about 40 percent of the population in April 1990 that led to the coalition government of 1990–94. Too bad, however, that in that vote the main populist intellectuals were defeated in their respective constituencies. That was presumably again only because of the empirical people!

132. Kis treats these two concepts as two possibilities, while I am inclined to think that they merge as a single option. See "Az elit megmaradásának elvéröl," 5.

133. This weakening of Parliament does not make the government strong. It becomes exclusively dependent on its apparatus and is forced into concession after concession that allows the rebuilding of the Kádárist administration in nationalist colors. Moreover, the reinforcement of the existing state apparatus only preserves and reproduces the clientelistic networks and elite bargaining processes that have led to the economic failure of the Kádárist regime. In this sense too the strengthening of the state apparatus cannot and has not led to a strong government. On the contrary, its weakness and inconsistency in the recent two years has been striking. When these become evident, the search for enemies in Parliament, press, and society as a whole in the name of national unity is resumed. This search has now become almost delirious in the writings of Csurka. See "Néhány gondolat," op. cit.

134. I was not convinced in 1992, and I am not convinced in 1998. The participation of the SZDSZ in the government between 1994 and 1998, and FIDESZ leadership of the coalition of 1998, show the weakening of liberal ideology in each case, to the benefit of pragmatic adjustment in the first case and a shift to nationalist rhetoric in the other.

135. See *Csendes? Forradalom? Volt?*, 22–25, and especially 214.

136. See the contributions of G. Fodor and Akos Szilágyi to *Csendes? Forradalom? Volt?*, 77–80.

137. See the report in *Magyar Hirlap* (May 14, 1994).

138. Hack believed that the Court's decision identified the *Rechtsstaat* with the *rendsz-erváltás* from the point of view of constitutional law ("Mit jelent a jogállamiság," *Magyar Hirlap* [May 14, 1992]). In reality the Court identified the exchange of systems *with the creation of the* Rechtsstaat, which was revolutionary in the political sense but on the basis of procedural continuity in the legal sense (2086/A/1991/14: 5–6) collected in *Az alkotmány-bíróság határozatai, 1992* (Budapest: Unió, 1992), 77–94. To be sure, the idea of revolution in the political sense does not (as we have seen) adequately represent the Hungarian change of systems even if we go beyond the dimension of legality. Nor is the idea of a second revolution from above excluded from the Court's definition, as long as it stayed within the limits of legality, in the case of the Hungarian constitution and its guardian, an admittedly difficult task.

139. "Gondolatok a rendszerváltásról," 120–22.

140. "A szabadelvü üzenet," *Beszélö* (July 4, 1992).

141. "Kimaradni a rossz spirálból," *Beszélö* (February 1, 1992).

142. "A szabadelvü üzenet," *Beszélö* (July 4, 1992). The extensive published excerpts unfortunately omit the sections of Kis's speech in which he returns to this second reason for popular dissatisfaction. He tells me that what he argued was that the second problem, the absence of noticeable signs of system change in everyday life, cannot be corrected without making the popular sense of insecurity even worse. This way of putting the issue, however, merely gives two symmetrical bases of potential popular appeal to the radical revolutionaries and the liberals. For my taste at least, this is a rather weak position for the side that represents modern liberal and democratic values.

143. Gy Tellér was the first to reintroduce this emphasis in "Az elit nem vész el, csak." While originally the leaders of SZDSZ were uncomfortable with such reminders of their own earlier ideology, the appeals to and for an independent civil society have been since then too numerous to reproduce here. See, however, Kis, "Az elit megmaradásának elvéröl," and Köszeg, "Most vagy soha," *Beszélö* (March 14, 1992): 6.

144. See the already cited discussion in *Csendes? Forradalom? Volt?*

145. See Arendt, *On Revolution.*

146. Which, following Weber, I do not consider, strictly speaking, related to the complex of legitimation, but to that of economic interest. It is when economic interests of a group suffer that the compensating effects of legitimation in the sociological sense come into play!

147. See Claus Offe, "Capitalism by Democratic Design? Democratic Theory Facing the Triple Transition in Eastern Europe," in *Varieties of Transition* (Cambridge, Mass.: MIT Press, 1997), 29–49.

148. See chapter 2, this text.

149. I am not claiming that using the old amendment rule to change the old regime completely preserves the old legal identity (Kelsen), or that it is necessarily invalid (Alf Ross), or that it is a mere cover, without consequence, for legal revolution (Schmitt), but only that the constitution so produced starts out with a legitimation deficit. This is exacerbated if the procedure in question involves a limited parliamentary procedure only.

150. Sólyom, op. cit.; Eörsi, op. cit. On this concept, and its contrast with democratic constitutionalism, see chapter 4, this text.

151. In the case of the president of the Court the issue is all the more serious, because gaps in constitutional legitimacy undermine the democratic justification of constitutional review.

CHAPTER 4. DILEMMAS OF THE POWER
TO MAKE CONSTITUTIONS IN EAST EUROPE

A version of this essay was originally prepared for the conference "Comparative Constitutionalism: Theoretical Perspectives" at the Cardozo School of Law, October 13–14, 1991. More or less that version was published in *Cardozo Law Review*, January 1993. The current chapter is completely rewritten, not only to take advantage of hindsight, but also because of serious problems with the original.

1. Hannah Arendt *On Revolution* (New York: Viking Press, 1965).

2. As a possible improvement on the Jeffersonian formula, she does not consider the Madisonian option (*Federalist #49*) that occasionally (rather than in every generation) there will be a need to have a recourse, through the Constitution itself, to the constituent activity of "the people." And from her point of view she was right, because Article V of the U.S. Constitution, of which Madison was thinking, in the form used historically, worked more as an instrument of government than (as its unused convention formula might have been) a vehicle for a people constituting a government.

3. Bruce Ackerman, "Neo-federalism?" in J. Elster and R. Slagstad, eds., *Constitutionalism and Democracy* (Cambridge: Cambridge University Press, 1988), 153–93. The same author's *We the People* (Cambridge, Mass.; Harvard University Press, 1991) continues this train of thought, which Ackerman sees as the expansion of Madison's insight concerning the constitutional possibility of occasionally calling upon the constituent activity of the people. Since Madison was obviously referring to Article V, I originally misunderstood Ackerman's argument as having also to do with the Constitution's formal amendment rule. It is now clear, however, that he has in mind extralegal, non-Article V revisions modeled above all on the activity of the Philadelphia Convention itself. While the ambiguity is in the Constitution itself, and thus Madison is also not free of it, nevertheless in my view Ackerman's perspective is more neo-Jeffersonian than neo-Federalist. At the time of the original composition of this chapter, Ackerman has not yet developed his own analysis of the constitutional changes in East Europe, *The Future of Liberal Revolution* (New Haven, Conn.: Yale University Press, 1992). I hope that my reconstruction of the perspective that he *might* take on East European constitution making is not too far off the mark. I should note that on a lot of important though more peripheral issues I am only in partial agreement with him. I do not accept wholesale purges of officials and jobholders, and I do not think that the questionable legitimacy of the process of Hungarian constitution making—indeed a serious matter—justifies his criticism of the activism of the Hungarian Constitutional Court. Cf. "Revolution, Restoration, and Legitimation," chapter 3, this text. In both cases it seems to me that Ackerman unnecessarily compromises the defense of liberal institutions that does not merely depend on the acceptance of a plausible scenario for constitution making.

4. Ulrich Preuss, "The Influence of Carl Schmitt on the Legal Discourse of the Federal Republic of Germany," paper delivered at the conference "Carl Schmitt and the Challenge to Democratic Theory," Graduate Faculty, New School for Social Research, February 15–17, 1990; U. Preuss, *Revolution, Fortschritt und Verfassung* (Berlin: Wagenbach Verlag, 1990); U. Preuss, "The Roundtable in the German Democratic Republic" [1991], in Jon Elster, ed., *The Roundtable Talks and the Breakdown of Communism* (Chicago: University of Chicago Press, 1996).

5. Gordon S. Wood, *The Creation of the American Republic 1776–1787* (New York: Norton, 1972).

6. S. Holmes ("Precommitment and the Paradox of Democracy," in *Constitutionalism and Democracy*), 195–240, rightly distinguishes between enabling and disabling limits, but tends to argue that both represent an increase in democratic power to do things in the present. I accept the distinction, but not the automatic reference to democratic power. Moreover, some limits, e.g., to constitutional rights involve an increase in power for an entity (the political system or the state) that is limited only in the broad sociological sense and not in any specifically legal-political sense. See Niklas Luhmann, *Grudrechte als Institution* (Berlin: Duncker & Humblot, 1965).

7. See Luhmann, *Grundrechte als Institution* (Berlin: Duncker & Humblot, 1965) on the "fuction" of fundamental rights, and *Legitimation durch Verfahren* (Berlin: Luchterhand, 1975), on the two narratives in terms of which we describe democratic politics, official and informal.

8. Jon Elster, "Introduction" to *Constitutionalism and Democracy*, 1–17.

9. Whatever the possible conflicts between the opinion and will of majorities and individual rights, and there are many, I am convinced that liberal and democratic constitutionalism are mutually reinforcing.

10. Cambridge, Mass.: Harvard University Press, 1980.

11. Cass Sunstein, "Constitutions and Democracies: An Epilogue," in *Constitutionalism and Democracy*, 327–53.

12. Ackerman, "Neo-federalism?," 172, 197ff. A defense of rights by the Court cannot ordinarily be identified with a challenge to abolish that right through constitutional amendment. Such a view tends to sacrifice liberal constitutionalism to the democratic one!

13. See papers 40, 53 (James Madison), and 78 (Alexander Hamilton), in C. Rossiter, ed., *The Federalist Papers* (New York: Mentor, 1961).

14. "Neo-federalism?," 157; Wood, *The Creation of the American Republic*, chapters 8 and 13. In light of Wood's evidence and a dispassionate reading of *The Federalist Papers*, it is certainly wrong to dismiss Ackerman's reading of this text as "imaginative," but not supported by his source (Holmes, "Precommitment and the Paradox of Democracy," n. 79) even if the relevant citations (not the only ones possible) are assembled somewhat carelessly. What Holmes's discussion amply proves, however, is the presence of a very different, in my view, neotraditional interpretation of constitutions in *The Federalist* (recall Madison's Platonism in #49 [Madison], which states that one would not have to stimulate the future unreflective veneration of the constitution in a nation of philosophers, which, however, is obviously not possible). Similarly, Sunstein's critique establishes only the presence of a strong republican strain in Madison's view of normal politics, not the absence of the pluralist strain. In effect, then, the conceptions of both normal and constitutional politics are internally ambiguous in the document, a fact that can lead to four distinct interpretations (democratic-pluralist; democratic-republican; neotraditional-pluralist; and neotraditional-republican). A more complex interpretation would then insist on the importance of dualistic politics precisely for reinforcing republican elements with respect to pluralistic normal politics. This interpretation might accommodate the tension between democratic and neotraditional constitutional politics by distinguishing (unlike Holmes) between the democratic character of constitutional revision and its level of difficulty and by considering the possibility of identity formation and reference to tradition without quasi-religious veneration.

15. See *Federalist* #49 (Hamilton).

16. This seems to be Woods's final verdict in chapter 15 of *The Creation of the American Republic*.

17. The point is fudged by Hamilton in *Federalist* #85.

18. Ackerman indeed has made revolutionary refoundings of the republic—the Reconstruction and the New Deal—the two major instances of the return of constitutional politics within his dualistic model. This interpretation of the theory in fact weakens it and tends to concede that with these extraordinary exceptions American politics has been monistic.

19. Several attitudes in fact are possible with respect to a dualistic politics in American society: One can take a normatively positive attitude that is empirically skeptical (Arendt), one that is normatively positive and empirically optimistic (Ackerman), one that is skeptical empirically and negative normatively (Holmes), and finally one that is optimistic about the possibility of a republican correction of normal politics, but on a purely republican rather than dualistic basis (Sunstein). The most serious objection to the argument as presented here would come from Holmes, who would insist on the importance of vastly limiting the channel of constitutional politics for the sake of both democracy and political efficiency. These two objectives do not amount to the same thing as he seems to think. In my view, great limits on the use of the power to revise constitutions empower the state rather than any democratic constituency. At best effectiveness is purchased at the cost of democratic legitimacy. But in conflict or crisis situations, a relatively low level of democratic legitimacy would diminish the ability of the state to act, hence to be effective.

20. This does not mean that "normal politics" cannot be democratically corrected on the level of its procedures, or even that extraordinary political mobilization as well as long-term trends in the political culture cannot introduce greater democratic responsiveness and accountability.

21. Jean Cohen and Andrew Arato, *Civil Society and Political Theory* (Cambridge, Mass.: MIT Press, 1992), chapter 8.

22. See *Federalist* #53 (Madison), and the more grudging acceptance of this point by Hamilton in #85. The negative example Americans had in mind was the Septennial Act, by which the British Parliament extended its own tenure in office. The possibility of such acts of self-aggrandizement is not only conceded by defenders of parliamentary sovereignty, but is considered a good expression of the meaning of the British constitution. See A. V. Dicey, *Introduction to The Study of the Law of the Constitution* [1885, 1915] (Indianapolis, Ind.: Liberty Classics, 1982).

23. This is true even if the limits do empower. Disabling (as against enabling) limits do not empower in the specific respect under discussion.

24. See Ackerman "Neo-federalism?," 153–54. While I think Ackerman's phrase "democratically inferior" (163–64) is well chosen, I do not see the reason for his total denial of democratic justification for electoral-representative party politics whether or not we introduce the idea of its republican correction (Sunstein "Constitutions and Democracies"). While normal politics in the American sense is important from the point of view of the search for private happiness, it also provides a form of political participation for those who do not choose a public, political life. Nor do I believe that Ackerman's one passage critical of the element of populist justification for constitutional politics (n.60, 186) provides an adequate replacement for it. The interesting idea of vastly enriching the vocabulary of Americans through the availability of higher law-making politics does not prove the democratic superiority of this political channel.

25. *The Structural Transformation of the Public Sphere* (Cambridge, Mass.: MIT Press, 1991).

26. On the latter of these see Holmes "Gag Rules or the Politics of Omission" in *Constitutionalism and Democracy*

27. In my view it is the stress on open, extended, and multileveled public discussion that shifts the final principle of constitution making from the people abstractly considered to civil society, rather than the representations of the institutions of civil society in a constitution making body (cf. Preuss, "The Roundtable of the GDR"). The "people" as a whole can participate in the framing of a constitution only by electing delegates, voting in ratification, or by forms of more immediate identification, for example, acclamation, demonstration, and the like. The principle of extended public discussion, though not dispensing with elections and voting, puts the stress on deliberation by individuals organized in "publics" and associations. While not excluding the participation of the unorganized, this approach multiplies the influence of organized and associated individuals.

28. See especially, Holmes, "Precommitment and the Paradox of Democracy."

29. Which is not the case in the United States despite appearances. The never-tried road of a new constitutional convention provided for in Article V is not per se more difficult procedurally. It is perhaps avoided in part because it is relatively easy. More likely of course, as it has been often said, the danger of wholesale revision prohibits the use of this potentially revolutionary option.

30. It is logically possible, but politically not very likely, that one could change the essence of a constitution through a single amendment. Carl Schmitt, e.g., *Verfassungslehre* (Berlin: Duncker & Humblot, 1928, 102–6), sought to portray such a change as invalid and even impossible, but it is not entirely clear in what sense. One of his examples, the "impossibility" to simply amend the power to amend itself, is an interesting example for his thesis. Nevertheless, even changing the power to amend might make a democratic constitution more consistent internally, in Schmitt's own terms more consistent with its own spirit, especially if the original draft incorporated fundamental inconsistencies. Technically of course one can change the power to amend, without a revolution.

31. See Sanford Levinson, ed., *Responding to Imperfection* (Princeton, N.J.: Princeton University Press, 1995) and my article "Slouching Toward Philadelphia," in *Constellations* (1996) 3(2).

32. Again, for political reasons, and not for legal ones as Schmitt seems to imply!

33. I am not at all proposing that appeals to imitation and tradition should be simply abandoned. There is much that is worth imitating in the West, as well as to affirm in specific national histories. I stay within the Weberian theory to the extent that I believe that an empirical framework of legitimation will be inevitably a composite. But I do believe that a legitimation complex needs to have a core of principles, which, given the East European struggle for the liberation and democratization of civil society (as well as independent normative considerations), point to a combination of liberal and democratic constitutionalism. The current chapter focuses only on the democratic dimension of this project.

34. This contrast resembles, but is not identical with, the distinction between "acts of government" and "acts of the people" that Arendt derives from Paine, and Ackerman from Madison. In fact arguing from popular sovereignty one can derive two different types: a sovereign assembly à la Sieyès and a nonsovereign convention à la Madison. Constitution making by "government" can take other forms than constitution making by ordinary parliament. See "Forms of Constitution Making and Theories of Democracy," in chapter 7 this text. Here I operate with a simpler contrast, both to sharpen the contrast and because only this is relevant to the Central European cases I am discussing.

35. In my view they will do the latter, only if their partners are not sufficiently strong or popularly accepted, and, if (a big if) they have a good chance of dominating such an assembly. Aside from the Bulgarian Communists, to my knowledge, it was only the allies of Pozsgay in Hungary who thought of this solution *relatively early* in the process.

36. Sieyès and his followers, contrasting the will of all with the General Will, obviously believed that even popular ratification would diminish their sovereign claims. Later, plebiscitary ratification has come to be seen as a needed confirmation of having acted in the name of the sovereign.

37. The U.S. example seems to speak for this as well, because, although not fully sovereign because it had only constitution-making powers, the Philadelphia Convention appealed to "We the people." Nevertheless, as the extreme case of the previous Articles of Confederation show, federal or confederal constitutions are difficult to change because of the plurality of original sovereigns to which they refer. This may have played a role in the making of the *Grundgesetz* too, with its many entirely unchangeable provisions.

38. They were abrogated to be sure legally by the transitions of 1989. But this was done on the basis of the formal, hitherto paper, constitutions that had to be treated suddenly as the actually operative basic law.

39. A constitution may of course provide a formula, like the Convention model of Article V that can turn, when used, into revolutionary abrogation of the whole. By including this formula as an amendment rule, and through the wording of the Article, it is obvious that what is meant is only a second possible procedure for revision. The revolutionary deed of leaving such a commission and the original constitution behind can be neither provided for nor, however, blocked if the revolutionaries have sufficient force at their disposal. To go a step further, a constitution may decree its existence for only a limited time and make this provision self-referentially unchangeable. But what would stop a decidedly nonrevolutionary legislature from reenacting the same constitution with or without the provision of further time limitations? Even by the very lax Kelsenian standards (according to which a revolution is when a constitution is altered not according to its valid rules of change) that would not be a revolution.

40. The same may not be equally true for a convention model, which can claim absence of legal break and illegality, as even Madison tried to do. As the next chapter will argue there are reasons to take these at times lawyerly claims in the *Federalist* seriously. On the basis of a dualistic foundation, such as the one stressed by Arendt, of both legal continuity and extraordinary public involvement, we can entertain the legitimacy of even significant or large-scale constitutional change within the Constitution as long as the change satisfies the demands of democratic justification to a similar degree as the origins.

41. The last point will be rigorously true, as Alexis de Tocqueville and Dicey recognized, only if there is a tribunal capable of pronouncing acts of the legislature unconstitutional. Otherwise, an unchangeable constitution will only invite what legislatures in any case would do from time to time, namely, to enact hidden constitutional amendments under the guise of ordinary legislation.

42. H. L. A. Hart, *The Concept of Law* (Oxford: Oxford University Press, 1961) and H. L. A. Hart, "Self Referring Laws," in *Essays in Jurisprudence and Philosophy* (Oxford: Oxford University Press, 1983), 170–78. See also Peter Suber, *The Paradox of Self-Amendment* (New York: Peter Lang, 1990).

43. Dicey, *The Law of the Constitution,* 285–86.

44. Strictly speaking, as Tocqueville, and following him Dicey, realized, they can do this only when there is a constitutional court (or I should add, an executive with a strong veto

power, as the king in 1791–92) to reject supposedly ordinary legislation masking constitutional revision. Interestingly, when there is no such possibility, the differences between an unchangeable constitution and a fully "flexible" one disappear.

45. Even the legislatures (Poland, Hungary) and the one constitutional assembly that emerged from a roundtable (Bulgaria) that were subsequently elected in free elections maintained a procedural continuity with the old order symbolized especially by the procedure of amendment (on which there is more below). Depending on the case, this continuity could lead to amendment-happy parliaments as well as conditions in which constitution making was totally subverted. The most fateful example of the latter was the Czech and Slovak Republic, where the utilization of the old procedure (which made absolutely no difference under monolithic Communist rule) led to complete constitutional impasse and contributed to the breakdown of the federation.

46. The idea of legal and constitutional revolution is of course far more paradoxical than those of "gentle" and even "negotiated" as the Czechoslovak example, a far more classical revolution than the others, shows. *Gentle,* i.e., nonviolent, can mean simply that the other side, in this case suddenly minus Soviet military support, was unable to fight a rapid change of power. *Negotiated* in this case meant not that immense and one-sided pressure was not used, but only that two unequal sides used negotiation to disengage without violence, which they rejected for very different reasons. Neither term represents a break with the revolutionary idea of rupture, even if in the Czechoslovak case the forms of legality were adhered to. These forms, e.g., parliamentary deliberations, operated under tremendous outside pressure and, unlike the GDR, actually extraconstitutional interference (packing of the Parliament). Legal or constitutional revolution meant, above all in Poland and Hungary, that the old legal forms and procedures were to an extent allowed to operate under their own logic, producing some consequences unintended by the main parties in the negotiations. To be sure the terms *negotiated* and *nonviolent* are entailed by legal and constitutional. The opposite is not true.

47. *Verfassungslehre,* 102ff.

48. In a note (p. 104) that reveals a contemptuous attitude for the actual (rather than ideal) German people, "whose desire for legal appearances is stronger than its political sense," Schmitt asserts that this people might more readily accept the restoration of the hereditary monarchy of the Hohenzollerns and the implied abrogation of the Weimar constitution, if this was done by a constitutional amendment (Article 76). He turned out to be more or less right, unfortunately.

49. The highly important decision of the Hungarian Constitutional Court on March 3, 1992 (that declared the unconstitutionality of an act of Parliament seeking to bypass an already expired statute of limitations and to pursue retroactive justice), is the best example of the legal fiction of continuity turning into legal reality. The Court defined the very meaning, and normative force, of the Hungarian change of systems from the legal point of view by the state of affairs that "the Constitution and the organic laws that introduced revolutionary changes from the political point of view were established through adhering to the rules of the earlier legal order with regard to law making, in a formally unimpeachable manner." This argument is deeply connected to the East European idea of a self-limiting revolution. The justification for turning fictions into realities lies in the single sentence: "[O]ne cannot establish a state resting on the rule of law in spite of the rule of law." Thus if we seek to establish the rule of law we must act *as if* we were already operating under it. See Magyar Köztársaság, Alkotmánybírósága 2086/A/1991/14. English version: Constitu-

tional Court of Hungary: Resolution No. 11/1992, in *Journal of Constitutional Law in East and Central Europe* (n.d.) 1(1): 129–57. For more on this decision, see chapter 3, this text.

50. Referenda, mentioned in the 1972 Constitution, legally regulated in Act. XVII of February 1989, became a method of constitutional amendment probably through oversight. A. Sajó tells me that a 1987 statute on the sources of law (Act. XI) has formally mentioned this possibility.

51. The conversion of fictions into operative law could have legally absurd consequences where the legal provisions were haphazardly put together. The most obvious instance was the fate of a directly elected presidency. This *constitutional* provision (in my view potentially authoritarian) was (1) agreed to by the National Round Table as a one-time device, (2) passed by two-thirds of the old Parliament, (3) narrowly defeated in a referendum of November 1989, (4) passed by the old Parliament once again as an amendment, a decision whose validity (5) was upheld by the Constitutional Court. After free elections the law was (6) given up in an agreement of the two largest, now opposing parties, and (7) replaced by Parliament by a two-thirds vote by the parliamentary election of the president. Finally, (8) an attempt to restore direct presidential elections (in spite of the majority of votes) failed in a referendum because of a level of participation way below the required 50 percent.

52. Czechoslovakia being only an apparent exception to this rule because of its move to what was supposed to be a more genuine federalism. Even here the procedure of constitution making involved a surviving, strongly federalist amendment rule from the Constitution of 1968, one whose efficacy could never be tested before. The actual exception is Poland, whose roundtable established a bicameral parliament for the first time.

53. *Verfassungslehre*, 103.

54. This point is valid even if we do not accept Kelsen's idea that using a regime's own rule of change implies the survival of the old legal identity. Continuity does not mean identity. The constitution of 1989–90 is not merely an amended version of the Constitution of 1949, as its enemies have charged.

55. It is another matter that by the time the constitution was formulated, the issue of unification vastly overshadowed that of constitution making. As Preuss argues, even in context of the drive for unity there were good reasons to formulate a GDR constitution. My point is that those interested, the makers of the revolution, had not the power to push it through, and the procedures of the Round Table, otherwise attractive, were partially responsible. Of course it was the election of March 1990 that decided the issue. Its outcome also shows, however, that the dissidents went too far in an antipolitical direction and not far enough in involving a nascent political society in the process of constitution making and fighting for a constitution.

56. The latter was actually considered and discussed in late 1988 and early 1989.

57. That does not include me. See the debate in *Beszélő*, May 4, 11, 18, and 25, 1991, between T. Bauer, G. Halmai, A. Sajó, G. M. Tamás, and myself.

58. Nevertheless I do not share the view of those who maintain in Hungary today that the cleanest solution would have been the establishment of a constituent assembly in 1989, instead of the Round Table negotiations. At that time, this would have implied both a revolutionary posing of the question of power that the Hungarian population clearly did not want as well as a very likely exploitation of an election called too early by the reform Communists around Pozsgay, Bulgarian style. What was needed subsequently was not a constitutional assembly, threatening a fusion of all political powers and violating the element of self-limitation so crucial to the Hungarian transition, but new decision rules

for making and ratifying the final version of the new constitution. On this, see chapter 7, this volume.

59. A case in point is the Bulgarian Constitution passed in July 1991, which as a document might have been acceptable to many members of the opposition who reject it only because of its origins. Madison's advice (*Federalist* #40) to overlook the origins and focus on the constitution itself is apparently not easy to follow. Granted, the argument used by the opposition is that there was still a Communist majority in the Grand National Assembly. Since this was the result of a free election, the argument is not particularly convincing. It seems that everyone notices the dangers of parliamentary majoritarianism when someone else has the majority. The trick would be to take the next logical step. Finally, lack of legitimacy on the level of enactment can easily be transferred to elements of the document itself. In Bulgaria, for example, many charge that the constitution interferes with the power of government and is almost unchangeable simply in order to protect the interests of a party (BSP) having a majority in the constituent body, but expecting to be defeated in the subsequent election. (Communication from Rumyana Kolarova.)

60. A. Bozóki, "Hungary's Road to Systemic Change: The Opposition Roundtable," unpublished ms. June 1991; Preuss, "Roundtable in the GDR," op. cit.

61. It was striking that as late as June 1990, unlike their Hungarian colleagues, the Polish participants in an ACLS conference on Comparative Constitutionalism in Pécs, Hungary, still laughed at the suggestion that their Round Table had any legitimation problem whatsoever. By this time, however, the new group around Walesa had already made the charge of a red-pink bargain. This opened up a legitimation problem for the Mazowiecki regime more clearly than the loss of support for economic reasons. The point, however, is not that Solidarity lacked legitimacy at the time of the agreements. At that time, as the elections showed, Solidarity still maintained an overwhelming support as the representative of society, based not only on votes but on the history of the '80s.

62. See Preuss, "Roundtable in the GDR," op. cit. Hence revelations concerning the self-aggrandizement of leading figures represented an important turning point in East Germany, where uniquely there was previously little cynical insight into the corruption of the ruling elite.

63. *Verfassungsentwurf für die DDR* (Berlin: Basis, 1990), art. 135.

64. Three out of the six major parties were clearly wrong about what electoral system favored them; the two most bitter antagonists, the Free Democrats and the Communists, both favored individual mandates that turned out to favor neither. In particular the MSZMP, which contained the only leaders with extensive political experience, would have been totally wiped out if either a first past the post–individual-mandate system or a two-round majority-plurality system were followed.

65. One could say of course that such a system would increase the mandates of the largest parties and eliminate those of the smallest. Yet no party could know for sure which they would be, and indeed two signers of the accords failed to make the 4 percent threshold.

66. See: "Forms of Constitution Making and Theories of Democracy," chapter 7, this text.

67. Note, March 1993: It is on this point that this article turned out to be fundamentally at odds with Ackerman's thesis in *The Future of Liberal Revolution*. Ackerman refers to my article, but does not note this important difference between our related conceptions. My analysis in any case is supported by a close reading of the vicissitudes of Hungarian politics since the national elections of 1990.

68. It would be best to examine the evolving relation of rule and practice in each case. This I can do only in the Hungarian case, which I can study directly, since there is no secondary literature on the practice of any of the countries.

69. Judicial review is not entirely foreign to the British tradition, indeed a coherent case can be made by Dicey (*The Law of the Constitution* [46ff, 51ff]) for the presence of judicial review in the ability of litigants to appeal to mother country courts over the legislatures of the dominions. In this train of argument there cannot be judicial review of the statutes of the Parliament in Westminster because that body is simultaneously a constituent assembly. Dicey also presents a good case when he argues that the British constitution, including even the principle of parliamentary sovereignty, is judge-made [pp. 116ff]. There is nevertheless a fundamental contradiction between parliamentary sovereignty, whatever its origins, and judicial review of statutes, one that he does not deny.

70. The Constitutional Court in October 1990 affirmed the obligation to hold a ratificatory referendum if a new constitution were adopted (894/B/1990) (*Az Alkotmánybíróság Határozatai* 1990 [Budapest: Unió, 1990], 247–49).

71. Though its rule of change implies that two-thirds of the votes of all deputies is a requirement of amendments. But since this discussion is under National Assembly, we could interpret the requirement as referring only to efforts to change the Constitution by a parliamentary vote alone.

72. This move was, strictly speaking, not an amendment of the Constitution. The constitutional amendment that provided for the direct election of the first president of the republic began with the phrase "*If* the occupation of the office of . . . the president takes place *before* the election of the new parliament" (my emphases), 1989, XXXI, par. 40. The Round Table agreed, however, that the president would be elected in 1989, i.e., before the parliamentary elections of 1990. See the text of the agreement as well as the complete constitutional amendment in *A Magyar Országgyülés Jogalkoátsa*, 1990, appendix, 271–22 and 272ff.

73. The very first (January 1990) decision of the Constitutional Court (1/1990 [II.12]) examined the constitutionality of yet another 1990 amendment, one that restored the direct election of the president *after* the parliamentary elections. The Court, implicitly assuming the right to review amendments, permitted this particular amendment because the referendum dealt formally only with the timing of the presidential elections, though in the appended explanation it asked the population to support or reject parliamentary elections for this office. While rejecting a particular interpretation of the referendum, the Court did not contest the right of referenda to deal with constitutional questions and to bind even the constitutional legislator (i.e., Parliament by a two-thirds majority). The 1990 July referendum, organized because the freely elected Parliament once again restored indirect elections of the president, was not reviewed by the Court. Only in 1993 did the Court rule that a referendum cannot carry out a "veiled amendment of the Constitution" and that the amendment of the Constitution can follow only the procedure prescribed by the Constitution (2/1993 [I. 22]).

74. In the end, a variation of the referendum formula was favored by default by the Constitution Drafting Committee in its Draft of 1998. This draft proposed holding referenda to nullify amendments on the request of one-fifth of the deputies or 300,000 citizens. It would of course be comparatively easy to get the required number of MPs to so move. But, because of turnout threshold requirements, it would be difficult to get the required participation to annul an amendment.

75. Andrzej Rapaczynski, "Constitutional Politics in Poland: A Report on the Constitutional Committee of the Polish Parliament," *The University of Chicago Law Review* (1991) 58(2): 604, points out, however, that the Senate was in effect a one party body with ninety-nine out of a hundred seats controlled by Solidarity, and thus it was less representative than the "Round Table Sejm," with its guaranteed seats for the "left" and its two allied parties. The same Rapaczynski polemicizes against proportional representation elsewhere in the same article. On the other hand, Wiktor Osiatinsky, who in a later context considered only a genuinely proportional representation adequate for a constitutional assembly, arguing that the loss of representation of one-third of the electorate in the election of 1993 made the legitimacy of the parliament to make a constitution questionable in "Poland's Constitutional Ordeal," *East European Constitutional Review* 3(2) (Spring 1994): 31–32, always affirmed the superior legitimacy of the Senate in 1989 compared with the contractual Sejm. I would not wish to dismiss these interesting arguments simply by pointing out that Rapaczynski advised the Sejm, Osiatinsky, the Senate in 1990–91. In fact both by normative criteria (free vs. unfree elections) and interims of popular belief in validity, the Senate was an institution of greater legitimacy. It seems also true, however, that in part because of its ideological homogeneity, the Senate was less suited to make a constitution for a complex society, aside from not having the legal authority to do so. Walesa was to use this disjunction between legality and legitimacy to bring down the whole project of constitution making during the first parliamentary session.

76. See A. Rapaczynski, "Constitutional Politics in Poland," and W. Osiatynski, "Poland's Constitutional Ordeal," 30.

77. Leszek Lech Garlicki, "The Presidency in the New Polish Constitution," *EECR* (Spring/Summer 1997): 81–89.

78. The place of the presidency was a key issue that already divided the separate constitutional projects of the Sejm and the Senate. See Rett R. Ludwikowski, *Constitution-Making in the Region of Former Soviet Dominance* (Durham, N.C.: Duke University Press, 1992), 155.

79. I call it "dualistic" rather than "antinomic" because the two procedures in question were not concerning the same process and were not contradictory, without a clear decision rule between them, as against Hungary, where referenda and parliamentary revision coexisted for a while. The dualistic structure in Poland has misled interpreters. S. Holmes and C. Sunstein, "The Politics of Constitutional Revision in Eastern Europe," in S. Levinson, *Responding to Imperfection*, take literally (p. 292) the formula of a two-thirds vote of the Sejm found in article 106 of the Little Constitution as meaning the lower house alone (while in practice at least—even in case of the passing of the Little Constitution itself—the rule included, in a subsidiary way, the Senate and even the president), while their own appendix states the National Assembly formula as the amendment rule, when it was really the constitution-making rule (320–21). In general the two authors do not adequately distinguish between amendment as the vehicle of constitution making and the new amendment structure of the constitutions that are made. Only in Hungary was this line completely blurred, and this was probably one of the reasons why that country alone was not able to produce a completely new constitution.

80. I am quoting from the Little Constitution, into which Article 106 was incorporated, unchanged. See the document in Ludwikowski, op. cit., 528.

81. I cannot tell whether this was done merely through interpretation, or if there was a constitutional amendment or constitutional law that explicitly mandated the interpreta-

tion. I also cannot pinpoint the time when this interpretation or redefinition originated, and if, after the Amendments of April 1989, the formula of amendments without consulting the Senate was ever used. I am inclined to guess that it was done through interpretation, and because of the greater legitimacy of the Senate, and its own ties to it, the Solidarity government or its minister of justice reinterpreted the law from the moment the Senate first convened. But I stand to be corrected by those who know better.

82. It would be easier for the Senate to amend than to reject, because two-thirds of the Senate, which would certainly support a bill that they have passed as a whole, might not be ready to reject each and every amendment to it.

83. See Ludwikowski, op. cit., 155ff.

84. In May 1994 it seems clear that the rule was still used to amend the method of creating a new constitution ("Constitutional Ordeal," 36). The next important amendment, in March 1995, which diminished the powers of the president after parliamentary dissolution, to the benefit of the outgoing Parliament, is said by two sources to have been passed by the National Assembly (i.e., the joint session of Sejm and Senate) overriding Walesa's veto. See EECR's "Constitution Watch," *East European Constitutional Review* (Spring 1995): 20, and Ludwikowski, op. cit., 159. The former source also adds that this was the first time the Little Constitution was amended. The two statements both cannot be true, because the Little Constitution's amendment rule was the same Article 106, which guaranteed the Sejm's primary role and made no mention of the National Assembly. Thus it would have to have been amended to produce an amendment procedure in which the National Assembly plays the main role. But when? Perhaps, and I am speculating, this was done by a constitutional law (and was not called what it would have been, namely, an amendment). If this took place, it is possible that the May 1994 revision of the rules of constitution making, logically enough, transferred amending powers to the National Assembly. But I cannot exclude the possibility that the Sejm, to overcome Walesa's opposition, referred final passage to the National Assembly already in session, to consider drafts for the new constitution. Here too I am ready to be corrected by Polish friends.

85. According to Rapaczynski, a similar rule was already enacted in the "Fall of 1990" in the form of a statute (op. cit., 605. fn. 19). Whatever that statute may have provided for, it was not an elaborate set of rules for constitution making as in the case of the Constitutional Act of April 23, 1992. For the origins of the latter, cf. *EECR* (Spring 1992): 9ff.

86. I have only the Hungarian text: "A Lengyel Köztársaság Alkotmánya Megalkotásáról es Elfogadásáról (On the Creation and Ratification of the Constitution of the Polish Republic)," in K. Toth, ed., *Kelet-Europa Uj Alkotmányai* (Szeged: JATE University of Szeged, 1997), 183–85.

87. See Osiatynski, "Constitutional Ordeal," 36.

88. On the making of the Constitution of 1997, see chapter 6, this text.

89. Because of internal divisions, the committee agreed to produce no draft of its own, but to receive drafts from other legally specified sources that would later be unified or integrated. It was a miracle, given the many submitted drafts, that the job could be accomplished in this manner.

90. I am relying in this context on Osiatynski's convincing presentation in "Constitutional Ordeal," 32–36.

91. The Constitution of the Republic of Poland in *Constitution Making Process* (Warsaw: Institute of Public Affairs, 1998).

92. I can still hear the laughter of members of the Socialist delegation during 1994 coalition negotiations, when (as a guest expert of the SZDSZ) I dared to suggest that we may

learn something from the Bulgarian amendment arrangements. They were wrong to laugh, and the outcome in Hungary shows why. On this, see chapter 6, this text.

93. To be sure, verbally, the Constitution of 1965 was not abrogated, as would have been expected in the pure type of revolutionary constitution making, only its organization of political power was. See Toth, op. cit., 41. But, with respect to this latter dimension, the provisional government abolished the old law and established interim regulation through its own "Constitutional Acts" that were of course not produced, and in the absence of a legislature could not be produced according to the law of change of the 1965 Constitution. Thus indeed the legal order of that constitution was gone and was replaced according to a new, revolutionary rule of change. The legal definition of revolution (see chapter 3, this text) was thus completely satisfied.

94. To be sure by reading only Article 106 of the Little Constitution and not observing how the Constitution was actually amended in Poland between April 1994 and 1997, Holmes and Sunstein think that the Polish rule was a two-thirds rule focusing on the Sejm alone. But even then the Polish procedure is not much more flexible than the Bulgarian one, if we for the moment discount the fact that in the second case some matters are excluded from this procedure.

95. Despite the large number of amendments in Hungary and Poland against, it seems none in Bulgaria are strong empirical arguments against my case. But a two-thirds parliamentary revision rule requires that parties capable of cooperating have two-thirds of the votes. This was not the case in Bulgaria in the period after 1991. Thus there were not only no amendments, there were also very few efforts to amend. (In the United States when we speak of the difficulty of our amendment rule in the empirical sense, we have in mind the failure of innumerable efforts to amend.) However, the existence of a more difficult path of amendment and the uncertainty of the sphere of operation of each rule does potentially yield a much more rigid amendment regime in Bulgaria than in Poland and Hungary. On this, see directly below.

96. Not a convention in the American sense, as Holmes and Sunstein imply, because it would not coexist with the regular assembly and can play the role of the legislative assembly temporarily, if it wishes.

97. My English text (Ludwikowski, 371) says "changes in the form of state structure and state administration." My Hungarian text (*Kelet-Europa Uj Alkotmanyai*, 83), however, has "changing the state structure and form of government."

98. Holmes and Sunstein themselves suggest a three-level amendment regime, entailing (1) the enshrining of fundamental civil and political rights up to the point of a German type of unchangeability (in Bulgaria such level of insulation is avoided); (2) heavily insulating "the broad outlines of constitutional arrangements"; and (3) weakly protecting all else including social rights. This whole arrangement comes close to the Bulgarian one, except for the greater rigidity implied in the first level. The Bulgarians to be sure enshrine the rule providing for the whole arrangement, but that move is a measure of their greater consistency, for the obvious reason that if the amendment rule could be changed according to the least demanding method, the levels could be eliminated from it altogether, and the easiest path of amendment could become the only path.

It may very well be the case that Holmes and Sunstein propose this particular amendment scheme as what should be finally included in constitutions, once a more easy amendment rule has done its work. They cannot clearly do so, because they have not distinguished the two contexts in which constitutional amendments appear in new democracies: method of transition vs. instrument of constitutionalism and constitutional politics in settled constitutions.

99. Needless to say, I am unconvinced that because of the relatively well-functioning government of spring 1997, the need for such an amendment, which would have implied only a minimal strengthening of the president, has disappeared (*EECR* [Spring/Summer 1997]: 7). However, the chances of a parliamentary process of amendment-strengthening presidential prerogatives against itself is in any case small. The strengthening of parliamentary prerogatives, however, should have had a better chance. Around January 1994 the major parliamentary parties (i.e., both the BSP and the UDF) pushed for an amendment to extend parliamentary control to include caretaker governments, currently responsible only to the president (*EECR* [Spring 1994]: 5). Which was the pertinent procedure in this case? Quite evidently, parliamentary representatives assumed that the ordinary National Assembly was fully competent, and submitted drafts to its Legislative Commission (*EECR* [Summer and Fall, 1994]: 5). But we don't know what would have happened if the amendment had been adopted in the normal parliamentary way, whether for example it would have been challenged in court, because the government fell and Parliament was dissolved. It is hard to find many other examples of efforts to amend the Constitution, because subsequently governing parties lacked the two-thirds majority. The 1994 effort, however, represented an institutional interest of Parliament against the president. Note that a similar amendment was passed in Poland over Walesa's veto, in 1995.

100. Even the United States might, in spite of the strangeness of this notion to our ears, if an amendment to reduce equal representation in the Senate were passed.

101. But the power of the Court depends on a relatively inflexible constitution. The Court has already shown its power by invalidating many unconstitutional statutes. (See the issues of *EECR* especially in 1995 and 1996.) Does it wish to weaken itself by assenting to an easier amendment regime? Note that the issue will come up only at a time when the parliamentary votes for amendments are available.

102. I have been educated on this topic by the unpublished dissertation of my student Dinu Pietraru, "Constitution Making in Romania: 1989–1990." See also Lutwikowski, op. cit., 122ff and 529ff, for the text of the Constitution.

103. As Elster and Holmes shrewdly noticed, this power to override court decisions gives Parliament the power to revise the Constitution without having to use referenda. See "New Constitutions Adopted in Bulgaria and Romania," *EECR* (Spring 1992): 12. I doubt, however, the constitution makers intended the loophole as such a hidden amendment rule. It is not at all unusual, as Tocqueville first noticed, for supposedly inflexible constitutions to be in fact vulnerable to hidden constitutional revision through statute. Only a strong constitutional court can stop such an abuse. The Romanian court is, however, weak!

104. I am relying on the reports of the *EECR*, which reveal no serious effort to undertake constitutional revision. In the electoral campaign of 1996, the major contenders promised constitutional change (*EECR* [Fall 1996]: 21). I am waiting to see if the promises of President Constantinescu to reduce the powers of the presidency will be introduced. Coming from him, such a badly needed amendment could indeed pass. But the strongest institutional reason speaks against his initiating it at a time when he may wish to preserve his ability to influence the political process.

105. See Lutwikowski, 129, who frames the option a little differently.

106. Osiatynski, who has always strongly recommended a participatory process of constitution making with an emphasis on civil education, is quite skeptical whether the Polish

constitution-making process satisfied the legitimation requirements I would insist on: consensus and publicity. See his "Constitutional Ordeal" and his "A Brief History of the Constitution," *EECR* (Spring/Summer 1997): 66–76. I see the matter more comparatively, and especially in relation to Hungarian constituition making. When the legitimation problems of the effort in Poland emerged after the elections of 1994, there were attempts to open up the process and address them. The Hungarian procedure, where consensus requirements were fulfilled at least with respect to parties, the process had no public character at all. Finally, the fact that the Polish Constitution was ratified in a referendum also has its symbolic importance.

107. For both countries, see chapter 6, this text.

CHAPTER 5. CONSTITUTION AND CONTINUITY IN THE EAST EUROPEAN TRANSITIONS

1. To footnote this paragraph would require a library. In my view, the special issue of *Cardozo Law Review* 3 and 4, on "Comparative Constitutionalism" (January 1993): 3–4 represents the most advanced thinking on most of the relevant topics. This is also now available as Michel Rosenfeld, ed., *Constitutionalism, Identity, Difference and Legitimacy* (Durham, N.C.: Duke University Press, 1994). I would only add Bruce Ackerman's *We the People* (Cambridge, Mass.: Harvard University Press, 1991) and Jürgen Habermas's, *Faktizität und Geltung* (Frankfurt/M: Suhrkamp, 1992), as indispensable sources for a theory of liberal and democratic constitutionalism.

2. Jon Elster, "The Necessity and Impossibility of Simultaneous Political and Economic Reform," in Greenberg et al., eds., *Constitutionalism and Democracy* (New York: Oxford, 1993), 267–74.

3. See Cass Sunstein "On Property and Constitutionalism," in *Constitutionalism, Identity, Difference*, 383–411. While I agree with Sunstein that "initial allocation" of property is the task of the democratic process, and not of constitutions, a constitution may very well regulate the type of process by which such allocation is to be made. It can protect certain types of existing property (e.g., cooperative property) against takings, it can limit discrimination with regard to state action (e.g., between owners and nonowners who may have suffered in the past), and it can provide for qualified majorities in relationship to all privatization and reprivatization decisions of Parliament.

4. A. Arato, "Revolution, Restoration and Legitimation," in chapter 3, this text.

5. Recently this thesis has been challenged by Stephen Holmes ("Back to the Drawing Board," *East European Constitutional Review* 2, 1 [1993], 21–24). I will return to his arguments.

6. Jacques Derrida seems to identify violence, beginning and a condition before law ("The Force of Law: The Mystical Foundation of Authority," in D. Cornell et al., eds., *Deconstruction and the Possibility of Justice* [New York: Routledge, 1992]). Thus he has little difficulty in proving that all law must originate in violence. For a more differentiated conception of violence, see Hannah Arendt, *On Violence* (New York: Harcourt Brace 1969).

7. *Philosophy of Right*, paragraph 273 and addition (T. M. Knox translation [Oxford: Oxford University Press, 1952], 178).

8. *Philosophy of Right* paragraph 274 and addition (Knox translation: 179 and 286–87).

9. Hannah Arendt, *On Revolution* (New York: Viking Press, 1965), 143–45.

10. Alexis de Tocqueville, *Democracy in America,* trans. George Lawrence (New York, 1969), 165; *Recollections,* trans. A. T. de Mattos (New York: Columbia University Press, 1949). The latter text is less consistent on this issue. On the one hand, Tocqueville demonstrates that in France some American-type solutions, such as two chambers and an independently elected presidency, would have the opposite consequence than in America: a powerful, and unchecked executive (194). On the other hand, as a constitution maker he engaged in some attempts (quite reasonable) at borrowing from the U.S. constitution (200–1 and elsewhere more implicitly).

11. Alexis de Tocqueville, *Democracy in America,* trans. George Lawrence (New York, 1969), 113; Arendt, *On Revolution,* 141ff.

12. David A. J. Richards, "Revolution and Constitutionalism in America," in *Constitutionalism, Identity, Difference,* 85–142.

13. See Carl Schmitt, *Verfassungslehre* [1928] seventh ed. (Berlin: Duncker & Humblot, 1989), 374ff, also 86. Victory in the war for the unionist side meant, according to Schmitt, only that the federation ceased to exist and the United States became a unitary state (375). He does not, however, fully accept John C. Calhoun's argument and maintains only that the federal constitution represented an antinomic combination of a unified state ("federal" sovereignty) and treaty ("states rights").

14. Jon Elster, "Constitutional Bootstrapping in Philadelphia and Paris," in *Constitutionalism, Identity, Difference,* 57–83. Elster deals with a whole range of issues having to do with the procedures of constituent assemblies, of which only that of ratification is relevant to cases where sitting parliaments formally retained the tasks of constitution making. It was in this context, however, that the legal-constitutional breaks in the United States and France were the most explicit.

15. I do not mean to de-emphasize the continuity of state constitutions and the common law as important dimensions of the conservative aspect of the American Revolution. These features of the U.S. legal order do not affect the relationship between revolution and (federal) constitution, where there was an arguably clear break in legality. Yet, sociologically of course, the success of the U.S. founding did rest on a double continuity on legal and organizational levels. It is possible that neither dimension of continuity fully works in practice without at least an element of the other.

16. Cf. Ulrich Preuss, "Constitutional Powermaking for the New Polity," in *Constitutionalism, Identity, Difference,* 143–64, where he seems to argue that there is no third alternative to the French model of citizenship rooted in the constitution (thus self-constitution ex nihilo) and a German model of a constitution rooted in a preexisting prepolitical entity, specifically the nation. Against this view both Hegel and Arendt have stressed different (English and American) versions of a model in which the constitution is the work of preexisting political entities. It is this latter conception that reemerged in Central European practice, as Preuss himself once stressed, focusing on the role of civil society. See "The Influence of Carl Schmitt on the Legal Discourse of the Federal Republic of Germany," 1990, unpublished ms., as well as *Revolution, Fortschritt und Verfassung* (Berlin: Wagenbach Verlag, 1990).

17. The second of these problems could not be solved in Arendt's view in the modern world by reference to natural law premises or to nature's God, as the American revolutionaries variously tried to do. Her own attempted solution is, however, ambiguous. She maintains on the one hand that only the emergence of a civic religion of the constitution, from

almost the first moment producing a form of quasi-traditional authority, could ground the authority of law in America (*On Revolution*, 199–200). On the other hand, she argues that the act of beginning in the United States was saved from its own arbitrariness by the communicative principle that was incorporated in the events and discussions surrounding the making of the Federal Constitution (ibid., 214–215). In the first interpretation the Supreme Court plays the major role, as the stand-in for the Roman senate, an authoritative body without power, whose conservative task is to creatively augment the written document, thereby nurturing its authority amidst the vicissitudes of change. In the second interpretation the emphasis is on the amendment process that creates democratic opportunities for acts of refounding within the original foundations. Try as she might, Arendt does not succeed in linking the two interpretations by identifying the amending process itself with conservative care for the constitution (ibid., 203). Ackerman has been somewhat more successful in *We the People*, but in his case the gap between a normative prescription for and an empirical interpretation of American reality is never overcome.

18. Arguably, the Parliamentary Council that produced the Grundgesetz and was rooted in the governments of the Laender had similar foundations as the U.S. constitution-making effort.

19. This point has been challenged in relation to the so-called social rights. See Herman Schwartz's response to Sunstein, "In Defense of Aiming High," in *East European Constitutional Review* 1, 3 (1992): 25–28. I do not want to enter into the thorny problem of whether the countries of the East should constitutionalize social rights as rights. My view is that since at present such rights cannot be enforced, they might indeed tend to devalue constitutionalism in general and should therefore be declared as something structurally different than civil and political rights, e.g., parts of the long-term policy aims of the state. More importantly in the present context, the so-called social rights of the Communist systems were not rights at all on the level of the real, operative, unwritten constitution, but only benefits paternalistically disposed over. Thus they cannot be preserved as social rights. Indeed, paternalistic benefits as aspects of state prerogative should not be saved at all.

20. Thus the contrast between the forms of continuity in the American Revolution and the East Central European system change was not simply that between continuity of political bodies (United States) and legal continuity (East Europe). In the United States legal continuity played an important secondary role on the level of the states, while in East Europe so did the continuity of preexisting organizations of civil society. Indeed, as far as the latter context is concerned, the degree to which civil society was preorganized very much affected (when other things were equal) the viability of the strategy of legal-constitutional continuity.

21. Hans Kelsen, *General Theory of Law and the State* (Cambridge, Mass.: Harvard University Press, 1945).

22. H. L. A. Hart, "Self-Referring Laws," *Essays in Jurisprudence and Philosophy* (Oxford: Clarendon Press, 1983), 173–78.

23. This process was seen in two steps, originally: first the creation of a few organic laws absolutely necessary for organizing democratic elections, and second the creation of a new constitution by the freely elected parliament. In Poland exactly this road was followed. Interestingly, the rule of revision itself has been changed to accomplish the first result. In Hungary the first stage was expanded, and a more or less new constitutional draft emerged, one that contained, however, the old rule of revision. It was assumed, however, that a sec-

ond stage, the production of a brand new constitution would follow and the "provisional" constitution would be replaced. On the outcome, see chapter 6 of this text.

24. For this notion, see H. L. A. Hart, *The Concept of Law* (Oxford: Oxford University Press, 1961), 86–88, and elsewhere.

25. Here I will refer to this as the method of (radical) continuity. In Spain the same method was called "ruptura pactada." See Jose Maria Maraval and Julian Santamaria, "Political Change in Spain and the Prospects of Democracy," in G. O'Donnell and P. Schmitter, eds., *Transitions from Authoritarian Rule* (Baltimore: Johns Hopkins University Press, 1986), v. 3.

26. In Hungary this last step took a referendum in November 1989, which the radical opposition won. The majority of the opposition parties at the Round Table conceded to the Communists their preferred time table and method of choosing a president, a provision that was assumed on all sides to have been tailored to elect Imre Pozsgay of the then-ruling party. In Poland more formally elaborate concessions did lead to the election of Jaruzelski to a strengthened presidency by Parliament. In Hungary the office was designed to be weaker, but popular election would have secured the president greater legitimacy.

27. From a purely political point of view it is obvious that outgoing Communist parties could still interpret legal continuity as a guarantee of some kind. Specifically, staying within the framework of old rules of revision meant that any attempt to change the constitutional framework as to exclude them from politics or to persecute their members as a class could be resisted much more effectively. On the other hand, the immense majority of the population and at that time the important opposition parties considered peaceful disengagement of the old regime and a nonviolent transition to be amply worth the price of such formal concessions. For a thorough analysis of this process and its logic see János Kis, "Between Reform and Revolution," *Constellations* (1995) 1: 399–421.

28. Here I am relying on the dissertation of Dinu Pietraru, Department of Sociology, Graduate Faculty, New School for Social Research, New York, New York.

29. See A. Arato, chapter 4, this text.

30. On this see the nice exchange reproduced by Tamás Bán, "The Establishment of the Hungarian Constitutional Court" (in Hungarian), in *Világosság* 32 (1993). For a detailed description of the constitutional structure of Hungarian state socialism, see György Szoboszlai, "Constitutional Transformation in Hungary," in György Szoboszlai, ed., *Flying Blind* (Yearbook of the Hungarian Political Science Association, 1992), 315–30.

31. Bruce Ackerman, *The Future of the Liberal Revolution* (New Haven, Conn.: Yale University Press, 1992), 60–68.

32. Compare the various earlier and later essays of Preuss already cited. He has come back to stressing the positive implications of the method of continuity only once, when reintroducing an earlier work of 1990. See "Constitution Making and the Foundation of a New Polity," in ZERP-Diskussionspapier 2/1993, a text that is to serve as a new introduction to the forthcoming English edition of *Revolution, Fortschritt und Verfassung*. Preuss's oscillation, which also seems to be between a theory of civil society and a conception of the *pouvoir constituant* derived from Carl Schmitt, is apparently very much conditioned by German experience. However things may be in the "new" *Bundesländer* [the former GDR], a Hungarian, e.g., will find it hard, after the last five years of movements, initiatives, forms of interest representation, and voluntary association building, to accept the idea implicit in much of the recent work of Preuss (as well as Claus Offe) that there is no civil society in

"the East" and that it is at best being created from above (an inevitably contradictory exercise). See, e.g., "Patterns of Constitutional Evolution and Change in Eastern Europe," ZERP-Diskussionspapier 2/1993, 9–23 and 36–37.

33. Both images are Jon Elster's, though he does not polemicize against the method of continuity.

34. For the best analysis, see Allison K. Stanger, "Czechoslovakia's Dissolution as an Unintended Consequence of the Velvet Constitutional Revolution," *EECR* (Fall 1996), 40ff.

35. The fact that the federal assembly voted for the dissolution of the federation as proposed by all three governments does not change the state of affairs that without a referendum legal continuity was abandoned. Significantly, the new method of dissolution itself was not and could not have been adopted as a constitutional amendment. In fact the vote for dissolution on the federal level passed only narrowly. On this, cf. *EECR* 1, 3 (1992): 4, 10, and 14–17; and 2, 1 (1993): 4 and 10.

36. No wonder Preuss, one of the architects of the new GDR constitutional draft, would rather not hear any more about this method.

37. Ackerman seems to accept such a claim (*Future of Liberal Revolution,* 60), made by the right wing of the UDF in Bulgaria. The fact is that the two-thirds requirement and the balance of mandates in the Grand National Assembly allowed only constitution making through consensus. The bringing together of Bulgaria and Romania (in spite of the key differences in their respective elections, forms of rule, constitutions and bargaining processes, roles of the opposition, and so on) under the heading of former apparatchiks "manipulating the symbols of liberal democracy" is altogether inappropriate. I am not convinced that this description applies to Romania, but it certainly does not to Bulgaria especially in view of processes that took place after the ratification of the constitution.

38. On this, see the report of Dwight Semmler in *EECR,* (1993) 2(3): 20.

39. Preuss rightly considers this option a unique attempt to combine revolutionary constitution making (since Article 146 would have imposed no limits whatsoever on the makers of the new constitution) and continuity (since Article 146, though no amendment rule, was nevertheless a part of the old constitution). Admittedly this formula on its own would have represented the most extreme limit of the strategy of continuity, and precisely its nearness to a revolutionary rupture with the *Grundgesetz* could have been a reason why even on the left it received insufficient support. (Analogously, the second method of revision provided for by Article V of the U.S. Constitution, the calling of a constitutional convention for making amendments, has never been resorted to.) And yet it is hard to accept Preuss's conclusion, derived directly from Carl Schmitt and Hans Kelsen, that a constitution cannot contain rules that allow its abolition altogether ("Constitutional Powermaking," 653). The simple amendment rule that can be used even to completely transform itself is such a rule, as Hart has shown against Kelsen (see Hart, "Self-referring Laws," op. cit.). Carl Schmitt admitted the possibility of such total self-revision, but considered it only so much playacting that masked a political revolution. See *Verfassungslehre,* 102–6. Yet a "revolution" masked in this way may have a very different logic than classical revolutions. Thus, here too there is a third option neglected by Preuss: Aside from rupture and continuity, there can indeed be a complete replacement of a constitution without a gap between constitutions. On choosing the wrong option, see especially the two articles by Dieter Grimm in the outstanding volume edited by B. Guggenberger and T. Stein, *Die Verfassungsdiskussion im Jahr der deutschen Einheit* (Munich: Hanser Verlag, 1991), 119–29; 261–69. Grimm argues con-

vincingly for a two-step method involving entry according to Article 23 and for drafting a new constitution according to Article 146.

40. Since in the Czech and Slovak cases the sitting federal Parliament continued to function through the process of republican constitution making, a timetable of the replacement of one constitutional reality by another could be agreed upon and a legal vacuum could be avoided in a way analogous to the U.S. pattern of 1787–90. But for this to work, and to avoid a situation of dual power, full cooperation of all the relevant legislative bodies and executives was required. In my view this could happen only in states (the United States or the Czech and Slovak Republic) where republican-provincial governments controlled decisive blocs of deputies in all the legislatures, especially the one being asked to dissolve itself.

41. The Czech and Slovak constitution, originally of 1968, and as amended according to the old rules of revision in 1989–90, retained for constitutional revisions the votes of three-fifths of the lower house elected in national proportional voting and the votes of three-fifths of *each of* the Czech and Slovak sections in the federally elected upper house, giving veto power in effect to three-tenths plus one (or thirty-one) of the deputies of the latter house if the nations vote as blocks. (See Lloyd Cutler and Herman Schwartz, "Constitutional Reform in Czechoslovakia: E Duobus Unum?" *The University of Chicago Law Review* (1991) 58(2): 519 and 549.) This model obviously combined two types of democracy, centralistic and federal, but maintains nevertheless a version of the purely parliamentary process of amendment that also makes constitutional revisions (and indeed also the making of an entirely new federal constitution!) extremely difficult. While this method gave little chance to democratic revisions of the operation of the two legislatures, at least it also made it difficult for the legislatures to further restrict democracy, an idea not particularly foreign to the minds of many Czech and Slovak deputies. Apparently, however, as in Hungary, here too referenda (federally organized) could alter the constitution, leading to an antinomic structure as well.

42. The republics of the former Yugoslavia and the former Soviet Union (except for Russia) followed the Czech and Slovak model of constitution making through nationally legitimated republican parliament. Only in some of the cases did this project succeed. Where there was violence it was due not to internal crises of constitution making as in Russia, but to various combinations of war between republics and interethnic strife within some of them.

43. In the Parliament elected in October 1993 the new post-Communist led coalition had the two-thirds votes to enact a constitution. It would have been a grave mistake, one that they did not make, to enact a constitution by imposition in a society where they received only 35 percent of the actual votes.

44. It, however, has no authoritarian elements, does not have a communitarian definition of citizenship, and does not, in a self-contradictory way, hope to create civil society and democracy from above. Nor has it been a document unable to play a role in the normalization and limitation of state power, because of the efforts of a Constitutional Court made uncommonly strong *by the constitution itself.* U. Preuss considers these negative features to be likely components of the emerging East European constitutions. (See "Constitutional Aspects of the Making of Democracy in the Post-Communist Societies of Eastern Europe," ZERP-Diskussionspapier 2/93, University of Bremen.) The whole train of argument applies poorly to Slovenia, the Czech Republic, and probably Poland as well. Finally, the notion that the constitutional definition of pluralism, parties, and associational life imply that these do not now exist and must be created from above is simply mistaken. More promising was Preuss's earlier attempt (in *Revolution, Verfassung und Fortschritt*) to argue that reg-

ulation and even limitation of civil society in constitutions can be enabling as well as disabling and can represent the emergence of constitutions that are not only of the state, but of civil society as well.

45. See A. Arato, chapter 4, this text. In Hungary this point has been repeatedly stressed by András Sajó and Gábor Halmai.

46. A. Arato, "Revolution, Restoration, and Legitimation," chapter 3, this text, and János Kis, "Between Reform and Revolution," 405.

47. "Between Reform and Revolution," 417–18.

48. Aleksander Smolar, "Prises de vue d'une bataille: Les dernières elections en Pologne," *Esprit* (November 1993).

49. "Prise de vue d'une bataille."

50. Miklós Haraszti made this interesting point in a public lecture and discussion at the Graduate Faculty, New School, in November 1993. Even though the point can be contested logically, its empirical implications do not thereby disappear.

51. "Between Reform and Revolution," 418.

52. Ibid.

53. Arato, chapter 3, this text.

54. For more detailed arguments concerning this issue, see Arato, ibid., and especially Ackerman, *The Future of Liberal Revolution,* chapter 5. It is inexplicable, however, why Ackerman accepts purges of officeholders, after brilliantly arguing against the "mirage" of retroactive justice. Legally organized purges like "lustration" do involve retroaction, as well as punishment, aside from other potential violations of rights. In the end it becomes unclear what policies his passionate argument is directed against besides the holding of political trials. If the files were burned as he suggests, a significant part of "lustration" too would become impossible. Should former party members above a certain rank and lower officials be fired, i.e., "punished," when former agents can continue to serve in any position they wish?

55. See Arendt, *On Revolution,* 143–145, who, following Paine, compares constitution making as an act of government on the one hand, and as an act constituting a government on the other.

56. Ibid. Curiously her argument did not turn out to be right for the country she most intended it, the Federal Republic, until 1989 at least.

57. The last minister of justice of the old regime proudly claims an important part in the process leading to the new constitution well before the National Round Table ever met, and to some extent also afterward. (See Kálmán Kulcsár, "A 'jog uralma' és a magyar alkotmánybíráskodás," in *Politikatudományi Szemle* 1 (1993): 33, note 3.) If he is right, and he is certainly right to some extent (I don't have sufficient documentation to precisely evaluate the respective roles of the Round Table and the ministry of justice), he is justly proud of his role. Nevertheless, from the point of view of those contesting the legitimacy of the document, this argument would be merely an admission of what they charged all along. Certainly, the role of the last (formally speaking) Kádárist ministry of justice cannot add to the legitimation of a document that is to represent a completely new type of constitutional reality.

58. See Derrida, "The Force of Law," op. cit., 35, on the future-oriented, anticipatory-retrospective structure of revolutionary legitimacy.

59. The second part of this chapter will attempt to answer these questions through a study of the Hungarian experience in constitutionalism and a consideration of several proposals concerning the refurbishing of the legitimacy of the constitution.

60. Evidently if the constitution were not rigorously enforced, the whole method of continuity would amount to not only a formal matter, which it always is, but also to a mere formality. In the Polish case too, such interpretation would be out of place, but here constitutional continuity was achieved through a difficult political struggle and not through legal means.

61. On its origins, see the article by T. Bán, op. cit.

62. For a critique, see Béla Pokol, *Pénz és politika* (Budapest: Aula, 1993).

63. On the distinction of liberal vs. democratic constitutionalism, see A. Arato, chapter 4, this text. From a somewhat different but related perspective, the same contrast is developed in the deep and sophisticated article by the late Carlos Santiago Nino, "A Philosophical Reconstruction of Judicial Review," *Cardozo Law Review* (January 1993).

64. Decision 2086/A/1991/14 of the Hungarian Constitutional Court, typescript, 7.

65. For an analysis, see chapter 3, this text.

66. The abortion decision of the Court, that in the name of the protection of the value of life prohibits the full freedom of abortion in any period of the pregnancy, seems to be the only exception to their rights-based jurisprudence. Not having declared (or definitively disallowed) the full legal personhood of the fetus, the Court did not limit the rights of women in terms of another right. To be sure, in the name of the rights of women, the Court also prohibited the making of a law that would completely forbid abortion. Nevertheless, it is a fact that in principle the decision does allow (even if it does not require) the trumping of a fundamental right by a substantive value. The Parliament in fact could have made a more restrictive law than the compromise the right wing coalition accepted, for political rather than constitutional reasons.

67. See Ethan Klingsberg, "Hungary: Safeguarding the Transition," *East European Constitutional Review* 2, 2 (1993): 44–48.

68. See, e.g., István Csurka, in *Vasárnapi Jegyzetek* (Budapest: Püski kiadó, 1991), 84–89.

69. Thus fears for the very existence of the Court, given its countermajoritarian practice in context of a "soft" constitution always, were exaggerated (Ackerman, *The Future of the Liberal Revolution*, 108–10). Undoubtedly part of the parliamentary majority might have wished to sweep aside the Court and the constitution. But József Antall, who, given his own priorities, had little interest in doing so, always knew better: There never was popular support for such a move. The Court's crisis management, described below, has been quite successful all along in splitting the right-wing opposition to its decisions. Not that all its other effects were of equal benefit to the tradition of constitutionalism.

70. See John Hart Ely, *Democracy and Distrust* (Cambridge, Mass.: Harvard University Press, 1980) as well as the article by Carlos Santiago Nino, op. cit.

71. On the relevant decisions, see A. Arato, "The Hungarian Constitutional Court in the Media War: Interpretations of the Separation of Powers and Model of Democracy" (in Hungarian) in *Civil Társadalom, Forradalom és Alkotmány* (Budapest: Uj Mandátum, 1999), 217–41.

72. One may take the view that the Court has done this in order to reinforce its own role as the only countermajoritarian institution. Indeed, this argument has been affirmed also outside the Court. Kálmán Kulcsár, e.g., sees no alternative to such a role, given the strengthening of the executive and the elimination of many legislative areas requiring two-thirds majorities (see Kulcsár, op. cit., 14–15). Nevertheless, important constitutional provisions with consensus requirements do survive, above all the remaining areas where two-

thirds votes are required. The specification of new contexts where presidential agreement
to appointments was necessary, during the pacted constitutional revisions of 1990 (that
specifically established this requirement for the presidents of radio and television), would
have been senseless if the president had no right to weigh and consider. Why give the president a new prerogative if it is not to have any substance whatsoever? In the case of a
national integrating figure, such a prerogative is always consensus reinforcing, even if the
president is not originally a member of an opposition party, as is presently the case, simply
by the nature of his office, above the parties. It is another matter, that the consensus-
demanding features of a constitution, as all of its other features, can in the end be defended,
in the legal sense, only by the constitutional court. This need not diminish the political
ability of other instances like the president to defend the constitution in other ways and
other contexts. See also Arato, "The Hungarian Constitutional Court in the Media War."

73. For the distinctions between "democratic constitutionalism" and liberal constitutionalism on the one hand and democratic majoritarianism on the other, see chapter 4, this
text, which relies in this respect on the works of J. H. Ely and Bruce Ackerman.

74. Compare the two decisions of the Constitutional Court—962/B/1997 and
13/D/1996/4—which appeared in *Magyar Közlöny,* February 1996 and October 1997.

75. Thus the view of Ethan Klingsberg (op. cit., 45–46), that the privatization decisions
of the Court allowed a minority member of the coalition (the FKGP, the Small Holders) to
bargain effectively within the government and Parliament, cannot be taken as the "justification" of the Court's decision. It may be possible to argue that the decision saved the coalition, though we will never know if this was actually the case. Nevertheless, even saving a
particular coalition is not a normative argument (and perhaps not even a pragmatic one),
and saving the influence of this particular, blackmailing minority (Klingsberg's own point)
is even less so. It should be noted, moreover, that (1) the claims of the Small Holders were
never supported by the population, either electorally or in the polls (a point Klingsberg
admits, but claims, strangely enough, that not supporting contrary referenda against any
reprivatization is a proof of legitimacy); (2) that some members of the Court (in particular Justice Imre Vörös) were right to predict that the decision would help create legal insecurity over land and thereby seriously harm agriculture (would this pragmatic consideration not outweigh the ones mentioned by Klingsberg?); and (3) that the two decisions of
the Court, rejecting the actual Small Holder formula, but allowing a watered down replacement, led to actually an important reason for the splitting of this party. (So much for preserving their ability to bargain, actually nonexistent after this decision.) On the last two
points, cf. Kulcsár, op. cit., 24.

76. Sólyom, "Az Alkotmánybiróság soha sem esett ki a semleges szerepéböl," *Magyar
Nemzet* (May 12, 1993).

77. Conceded, but somehow made a virtue of by Klingsberg, op. cit.

78. See A. Sajó, "Preferred Generations: The Paradox of Restoration Constitutions,"
Constitutionalism, Identity, Difference, 335–52, as well as Klingsberg, "Hungary: Safeguarding the Transition."

79. The Court is obviously aware that declaring the 1974 decree unconstitutional but
leaving it in effect has already allowed governmental spokesmen to claim that this means
that the decree can be used in a version allowing the government operational control and
not just legal supervision. After all, if the decree is unconstitutional it must be so, according to them, for "a good reason." The Court has been careless in not providing an interpretation of a decree that it was leaving in effect, at least to lessen the potential for its

authoritarian use. Nevertheless its reasons for declaring the measure unconstitutional were different than what Ferenc Kulin and Tamás Katona, members of the ruling coalition, have implied. According to the Court, the very fact of regulating the media through a decree and not a law is unconstitutional in itself. Furthermore, the absence of guarantees for free access to the media make the law unconstitutional also in substance. The Court neither mentions that direct governmental control is a necessary implication of the original decree, nor adequately guards against this interpretation. In later decisions (on the appointment of heads of tribunals of judges) the Court distinguished between constitutional and unconstitutional interpretations of a law. To the extent that it was leaving the disputed decree in effect it should have specified its acceptable interpretation as well. On this, see Arato, "The Hungarian Constitutional Court in the Media War."

80. It is certainly an absurd exaggeration (cf. Klingsberg, who quotes an unnamed advisor to the Court to this effect, p. 45) that the Court faced a potential "revolution" in either of these instances. In fact the claims of the parliamentary majority did not have popular support, or even large-scale social movements behind them.

81. András Sajó, "How the Rule of Law Killed Hungarian Welfare Reform," *EECR* (1996) 5(1): 31–41.

82. See Pokol, *Pénz és politika,* chapters V and VI.

83. Holmes's argument on this score is hardly consistent. ("Back to the Drawing Board," in *EECR* 2, 1 [1993]). On the one hand he applauds the temporary nature of the constitution, while on the other he attacks the activism of the Court that is inevitable given the interpretive problems of such a hastily amended document. If the Court were to simply defer to the popularly elected legislature as Holmes apparently wishes, then Hungary would be ruled by a constituent legislature, and not under the interim constitution. Again, the Hungarian right frankly draws this latter implication, which Holmes's plea for interim or transitional constitutions simply obfuscates. The only consistent constitutionalist critique of the Court's activist jurisprudence must argue for early and clear-cut constitutional synthesis. Cf. Bruce Ackerman, *The Future of the Liberal Revolution,* op. cit. Finally, genuine acceptance of the amended, interim constitution with all its unavoidable gaps and ambiguities implies a creative model of judicial interpretation. Not surprisingly, such is the position of Justice Sólyom, the president of the Court (*Magyar Nemzet* interview, op. cit.).

84. Kulcsár, op. cit., 14–15.

85. Arato, "Dilemmas," 679–80; Ackerman, *The Future of the Liberal Revolution,* 99ff.

86. These had to do with foreign ownership of land, to which the opposition cleverly attached a question having to do with Hungary's plan to join NATO. In the end, only the question concerning NATO was asked, and it is now highly doubtful that FIDESZ, the leading party of the new government, wishes to jeopardize Hungary's OECD (and future EU) membership by denying foreigners to own arable land.

87. In general I see three such mechanisms that make judicial review compatible with democracy: (1) a democratic process of constitution making; (2) the requirement of keeping the democratic process open; and (3) a democratically accessible revision or amendment rule.

88. It may be that the Court, knowing full well whom it faced for the between 1990 and 1993, had no alternative than to crisis-manage in the way represented here. Not only its role, but perhaps that of the constitution in the transition, was at stake. But such political crisis management, continuing to whittle down the legitimacy of the constitution it seeks

to protect, cannot be an option for very long. Thus the Court should have recognized the need for the democratic relegitimation of the constitutional document, assuming of course that the elections of spring 1994 would have provided a viable political constellation (need not be "coalition") behind such a process.

89. Or at least let off some steam and get some (supposed) popular support on behalf of acts of corrective justice that the president, the Court, and the lower courts won't allow anyway. On this point Holmes's text is inexcusably vague, because he does not tell us what desirable "compromise" solutions would look like. See "Back to the Drawing Board," 25.

90. Ibid., 22.

91. Ibid., 23. This argument of Holmes, comparing the Court to the old politburo, is clearly wrong. For a non-Hungarian audience it should be pointed out that "unelected" here means elected by Parliament by a two-thirds majority, for nine years, rather than life! The judges are thus indirectly elected, on the basis of demanding consensus requirements. It is hard to know if Holmes realizes that his rhetoric simply continues that of the most extreme right.

92. This is the thrust of his argument the first time he mentions the issue of property. See "Back to the Drawing Board," 21ff.

93. See Holmes's contribution to "Forum on Restitution," in *EECR* 2, 3 (1993): 32–34.

94. For a careful and judicious discussion of the options, see Frank Bönker, Claus Offe, and Ulrich Preuss, "Efficiency and Justice of Property Restitution in East Europe," ZERP-Diskussionspapier 6/1993. See also S. Avineri's contribution to "Forum on Restitution," in *EECR* (Summer 1993): 34–37.

95. In Hungary a sector of society, dissatisfied with the existing trend of privatization and the absence of political retribution, does use an overall diagnosis and argument almost identical to that of Holmes as a springboard from which to attack mere human rights squeamishness. Unlike Holmes, however, the relevant figures of the authoritarian right like Csurka clearly understand that such a project is that of a revolutionary regime capable of eliminating its political and social antagonists, who are by no means confined to Communist holdovers and include the independent press as well as liberal politicians (see A. Arato, "Revolution, Restoration and Legitimation," chapter 3, this text). If such a solution, the project of a second revolution, is not what Holmes has in mind his proposal falls apart. It is beyond me, for example, how strong governments are imaginable in Poland or Hungary without a constitutional resolution of the conflicts pertaining to the powers of government, and especially the separation of powers. Hungary's interim constitution leaves just these issues unresolved. Disregarding the constitution would, however, not settle the issue between already established centers of power. As far as learning from past (i.e., current) failure and designing a more appropriate (i.e., statist) constitution is concerned, Holmes leaves out one essential detail: Who is to design this more authoritarian constitution and how? Could anyone guarantee two-thirds of the parliamentary seats to the Hungarian right in the 1994 election, the only legal avenue for instituting the kind of constitutionalist program he seems to prefer? Note that in his survey of parliamentary sentiment he conveniently leaves out the opposition, again in the manner of the right-wing authoritarians of governing coalitions. This was a rather large mistake in view of the polls of the last three years.

96. "The Necessity and Impossibility of Simultaneous Political and Economic Reform," op. cit.

97. S. Holmes, "Precommitment and the Paradox of Democracy," in J. Elster and R. Slagstad, eds., *Constitutionalism and Democracy* (Cambridge: Cambridge University Press, 1988), 194–240.

98. Niklas Luhmann, *Grudrechte als Institution* (Berlin: Duncker & Humblot, 1965). As Luhmann has shown, rights and the government's ability to act are a zero-sum game in relationship to specific issues, and hardly in terms of the whole nexus of the political system and society.

99. How are we to understand the point that a policy can be unjust morally, inefficient economically, but be "politically correct"? ("A Forum on Restitution," 33.) The issue of land reprivatization in Hungary to which Holmes refers proves exactly the opposite of what he hopes to prove. It was popular neither among the population at large nor even among the activists of the largest governmental party. Conceding reprivatization to a small coalition member, the Independent Small Holders, did perhaps keep the MDF-led government together but eventually at the price of the disorganization of agriculture and further erosion of governmental popularity. Just look at the polls starting six short months after the 1990 general elections! Pace Ellen Comisso, to whom Holmes refers, no one in the MDF, not Antall or Csurka, and especially not the few national liberals, ever considered the Small Holders to be an "extraordinarily attractive coalition partner." A little knowledge of the history of parties during the last few years might have helped in this context. More importantly, had the Court been more consistent in blocking reprivatization, the MDF might have been forced into a different coalition with far more social support, one that could have produced a more consistent and rational economic policy. It is such option, and not a "national-Christian coalition" appealing to perhaps 20 percent of the population that should have been both "rational" and even "extraordinarily attractive" for the MDF, as many of us said all along.

100. Logically, other options are imaginable but they are not serious in our context. After an undemocratic, aliberal form of rule that claimed revolutionary legitimacy this particular mixture cannot be proposed seriously. While Stephen Holmes seems to propose a democratic, nonrevolutionary and nonliberal option, his model in fact either presupposes a quasi-revolutionary constituent assembly, or a statist-authoritarian government with few legal limitations. Finally, a liberal and revolutionary but nondemocratic option, though imaginable perhaps, has not been seriously proposed. At one point rather early in the change of systems, G. M. Tamás came close to such an option. Today, however, he is flirting with an Arendtian republican notion of politics.

101. In this context Holmes's empirically plausible though normatively dubious thesis is that future constitution makers have learned from the human rights-oriented "negative constitutionalism" of the Court that they should stress in the future a "positive constitutionalism" that focuses on establishing the powers of Parliament and government ("Back to the Drawing Board," 23). Undoubtedly nationalist-authoritarian democrats have learned this very lesson that represents a tendentious and mangled restatement of some theses of Hannah Arendt who, however, knew very well that it was precisely negative constitutionalism that guaranteed the success of the American version of constitution making. Thus she never advocated a choice between negative and positive constitutionalism. Nor did she identify the latter with mere majoritarianism.

102. See the interview "Az alkotmánybíróság," op. cit.

103. Mr. Sólyom and his colleagues have had at one time a more ambitious meaning of coherence than mere consistency. Their earlier references to an "invisible constitution"

indicated the claim that they are able to make decisions (even perhaps specific parts of the constitution) on the basis of a theoretically reconstructed logic of the document as a whole, derived more from its underlying philosophy than from the text itself (cf. Kulcsár, op. cit., 28). But what is the philosophy underlying this patchwork document? No one ever has made it clear. Not surprisingly Sólyom now backs away from such an argument and claims only that the "invisible constitution" is the consistent structure of case (i.e., precedent) law.

104. This point is in effect conceded by Kulcsár, a strong defender of the Court's actual practice. According to him, only where European norms give the Court guidance is activism justified. Otherwise, especially when political conflicts are at stake, the Court should practice self-limitation (op. cit. 31). But self-limitation in effect means conceding the point of view of the governmental coalition, generally one of the sides in political conflicts. Given the fact that it can be often in the interest of ruling majorities to interfere with the democratic process, such a self-limitation can lead precisely to conceding governmental interference with the democratic process. Exactly this has happened in Hungary in the case of the struggle over the media.

105. This point of view is consistently more sophisticated, more aware of actual problems, than that of authoritarian statists like Antall. It is quite another matter that Antall, a superior tactician, understood, unlike Csurka, that both in the country in 1990 and in MDF one can win only by occupying the center. Unfortunately, by 1993, the MDF as a whole had moved so far to the right that while Antall could defeat Csurka by occupying the party's center, he could thereby not regain his command of the country's center. He thus already lost the general election of 1994 before his death.

106. Although once in the same party, the MDF, the positions of Sólyom and Csurka are polar opposites.

107. I. Csurka, "Föld, alkotmány, rendszerváltozás," in *Vasárnapi Jegyzetek* (Budapest: Püski kiadó, 1991), 87–89. Holmes makes the same point with respect to property at least (21).

108. Ibid., 88.

109. The only trouble with this argument is that the very Parliament he wishes to liberate from all legal shackles was the last instance carrying out full-scale constitutional revisions, which, along other things, vastly strengthened the power of the prime ministership in the hands of his own party. Csurka's lament is only that something had to be given in exchange for this, namely, the presidency to the candidate of the SZDSZ. Crudely put, he wants to go back on both deals his party made. Hence his mythology of Western pressure at the time of the two constitutional negotiations.

110. Though unfortunately he is willing to accept the related idea of a large-scale replacement of jobholders and administrative officials. See *The Future of the Liberal Revolution*, 95–97.

111. See *We the People*.

112. See *The Future of the Liberal Revolution*, 52–60.

113. One that I, like Ackerman, once thought not only attractive but potentially applicable in Central Europe at least. See "Dilemmas," op. cit.

114. And whose Round Table he advised as a constitutional lawyer. In that context, Preuss advocated and helped to design a completely new constitution replacing the old one.

115. See Arato, "Dilemmas," 678–79 and 682–83.

116. With the one time extraordinary exception of the referendum of November 1989 dealing with a single disputed feature of the Constitution, the election of the president.

117. To the extent that some parts of democratic procedure are today enshrined in European and international agreements concerning rights, a semiauthoritarian, i.e., formal deformation of the democratic process is unlikely to be fully accepted by the Court. The same is not true for a variety of possible policies, accomplishing authoritarian goals through means not specifically banned by European agreements, and indeed practiced by various existing European governments. While such practices point more to oligarchy than to authoritarian rule, one could indeed put together an authoritarian order by choosing the appropriate features of various European polities.

118. While it would be unlikely that any future constitutional convention would approve (by 50 percent plus 1 of the votes) a strong court and judicial review, it would be difficult to generate two-thirds votes of an elected Parliament to eliminate these features from the present Constitution. If final ratification would involve popular participation, and public discussion followed by referendum, the point would be all the more true. The Court today may not be very popular, but it is certainly more so than the parties and Parliament.

119. M. Eörsi, "Hol húzódnak az erővonalak," *Beszélö* (August 15, 1992).

120. The only real change Justice Sólyom would like to see is one making constitutional change more difficult in the future (see *Magyar Nemzet* interview, op. cit.). He does not see that this cannot be legitimately done by a form of constitutional tinkering that does not mobilize additional sources of democratic legitimacy.

121. See Arato, chapter 4, this text, and especially Ackerman, *We the People* and *The Future of the Liberal Revolution*, 111–12.

122. See chapter 7, this text.

123. *On Revolution*, 199, and 214–15.

CHAPTER 6. REFURBISHING
THE LEGITIMACY OF THE NEW REGIME

In possession of all the relevant documentation and linguistic requirements, I have thoroughly studied and written on the Hungarian case. I cannot say this in the Polish case, where I have to rely on the excellent secondary literature and above all the articles of Wiktor Osiatynski in *EECR*. I hope the comparison proposed here will not be based on too many errors with respect to Polish developments, and that scholars interested in either country can find it useful.

1. Thus I cannot agree with the classification found in Juan Linz and Alfred Stepan's *Problems of Democratic Transition and Consolidation* (Baltimore: Johns Hopkins University Press, 1996), according to which Poland in the 1980s represented a sui generis case of a Soviet-type society having become an authoritarian formation, while Hungary is grouped with Bulgaria and Czechoslovakia as alternative options within a "posttotalitarian" regime type. The mistake is linked to both a relative neglect of the economy in designing the classification scheme and the inability to establish clear thresholds for regime types. If we look at the economy as a whole (and not just agriculture) the Hungarian system was more reformed than the one in Poland. If we understand a Soviet type formation to be defined by a constitutional setup (the primacy of prerogative power inherent in a single central institution) plus the dominance of a specific ideology with clear economic consequences, neither Poland nor Hungary have passed these thresholds clearly enough to be reclassified, along with the South European and Latin American dictatorships, as authoritarian.

2. Endre Babus, in *Heti Világgazdaság* (July 6, 1995); see my article, "Parliamentary Constitution Making in Hungary," *EECR* 4(4) (Fall 1995): 45–51. The phrase "invisible constitution," coined by presiding Justice Sólyom of the Hungarian Constitutional Court, had
several meanings. At first he seemed to imply the existence of a set of principles (á la the
early Ronald Dworkin), which the Court can refer to in "hard cases" of interpretation.
Later, however, he seemed to shift to an emphasis on the structure of precedents established
by the Court itself, as an interpretive reference point equal in importance to the existing
constitutional statutes. Both interpretations can justify the leading role of the Court in
fashioning the actually valid meaning of an evolving set of constitutional rules.

3. I owe this example to Carl Schmitt who was making the opposite point, namely, that
such a use of an amendment rule would be *illegitimate* within the given regime and therefore express a secret or bashful revolution. *Verfassungslehre* [1928] (Berlin: Duncker &
Humblot, 7th, ed. 1989), 104. He is right, but I maintain nevertheless that such amendment
would be *legally valid*.

4. See Preamble, *A Magyar Köztársaság Alkotmánya* (Budapest, 1990).

5. "The Constitutional Act of Poland," in Rett Ludwikowski, *Constitution Making in the
Region of Former Soviet Dominance* (Durham, N.C.: Duke University Press, 1996), 510.

6. Compare Article 146 with the 1994 foreword of President Herzog to the current version. *Basic Law for the Federal Republic of Germany* (Press and Information Office of the
Federal Government, 1994). Article 146 was amended after unification by adding the
phrase, "which is valid for the entire German Nation following the achievement of the
unity and freedom of Germany," between the original "this Basic Law" and "shall cease to
have effect . . ."

7. See Mark F. Brzezinski, "Constitutionalism within Limits," *EECR* 2(2) (1993): 38–43.

8. The Constitutional Court too, hitherto a defender of the old constitution, faced a new
situation in 1994. Even if constitutional review was not going to be severely restricted on
the formal level, its practice, as in the well-known Austrian case, could be put under
extreme pressure if the new government chose to reverse court decisions through constitutional amendments, something that happened only once in the previous period. Though
opposed to any kind of constitution making not by itself, the Court and its friends had to
be careful not to push the coalition into a pattern of the repeated use of amendments.
Indeed, both the Court and the parties now had to face the possibility of destructive constitutional conflicts based on the most important feature of constitutional incoherence in
the new regime: the deep and unresolved tension between a purely parliamentary and relatively easy revision rule and a Constitutional Court with extraordinarily wide competence
to review legislation. These two powers are in effect constituent ones; any of the existing
ambiguities of the text, perhaps even gaps and omissions, can in principle be resolved
either through amendment or though judgments by the Court. Indeed a clash between the
two instances, more dangerous than any so far, could not be excluded. It could not be
excluded even that the formal powers of the Court itself would be challenged, especially to
the extent these were provided for not by the Constitution, but by the Law on the Constitutional Court, a two-thirds law that can be altered with the vote of two-thirds of those
present. After the conflict with the Court over its economic program, members of the governmental coalition raised the possibility of modifying this law with the intention of trim-
ming the overblown powers of the justices. The president of the Court immediately
pointed out that the body has the right to review such two-thirds laws. But a simple constitutional amendment (impossible only in the current constitution drafting period),

which would require a little more than the same qualified majority (two-thirds of all members), could of course overrule or even forbid such review, or require that in such cases the Court itself vote by qualified majority. If the Court then proceeded to review the amendment (a possibility that is neither affirmed nor denied by the constitution) the country would be thrown into open constitutional crisis.

9. I do not have the expertise to evaluate and compare the variety of problems of codification and legal inconsistencies present in both constitutions. I maintain that these could have been dealt with in general by the ordinary amendment process. It is otherwise with the problem of legitimacy, as well as great structural problems that require a broader framework of consensus and public support than ordinary amendments of primarily a technical character.

10. According to Kelsen's concepts a constitution is not new in the material sense if it preserves the fundamental institutions of legislation in the broadest sense of its predecessor. Admittedly, for him a constitution would also not be new in the formal sense if it was produced according to the amendment rule of this predecessor, or even if its rules of constitution making were produced according to this amendment rule. Most of contemporary scholarship considers this latter view of Kelsen mistaken. See his *General Theory of State and Law* (Cambridge, Mass.: Harvard University Press, 1945) as well as Peter Suber, *The Paradox of Self Amendment* (New York: Peter Lang, 1990).

11. See Pawel Spiewak, "The Battle for a Constitution," *EECR* 6 2(3)(1997): 89. I should admit that Spiewak cannot make this point consistently, because he also criticizes the new Constitution for having decisively weakened the power of the presidency as well as the Senate. Yet others who emphasize the transformation of the presidency, like Leszek Lech Garlicki, consider parliamentarianism to be a return to normalcy ("The Presidency in the New Constitution," *EECR* 6 2(3): 88) probably because they consider the presidency created in April 1989 "abnormal."

12. Meaning just over two-thirds (375 out of 560) of the seats of the National Assembly in Poland, representing the combined sessions of Sejm and Senate that now had the task of constitution making. In Hungary the socialist liberal coalition had 72 percent of the seats of the unicameral legislature.

13. See Arato, "Elections, Coalition and Constitutionalism in Hungary," *EECR* 3, 3(4) (1994): 26–32; Wiktor Osiatynski, "After Walesa," *EECR* 4, 4 (1995): 35–44.

14. I do not mean of course proposals by Osiatynski or outside observers like Bruce Ackerman, both of whom wished to promote liberal constitutions and constitution making freed from the imperatives of ordinary politics. The proposals for independent constituent assemblies of party politicians had a very different function. When this idea first emerged in 1989, it tended to be promoted by Communists or their partners who hoped to dominate the process, as they in fact could to an extent in Bulgaria. When a figure like József Torgyán of the Small Holders revived the notion, he had in mind canceling out the results of the 1994 elections. Finally, when President Kwasniewski temporarily flirted with the idea of an independent constituent assembly, he did so to force the parliamentary Constitutional Committee to act more quickly and decisively on behalf of a proposal that he supported.

15. Cf. Osiatynski, "A Brief History of the Constitution," *EECR* (Spring-Summer 1997): 66–67. As the reader of chapters 4 and 5 will notice, I too try to advocate a high level of public involvement in constitutional discussions and have done so for years, even if no more successfully than Osiatynski. That such a proposal is not entirely unrealistic is shown

by the remarkable little pamphlet, published in several languages in South Africa, called *You and the Constitution* (Constitutional Assembly: n.d., probably 1995).

16. I do not of course think that legality and legitimacy are necessarily bifurcated and in conflict, only that they were in the given situation of a transition within legal continuity, where only the Senate was elected in a fully free election. The clash between the bodies has been reduplicated by their advisors, Andrzej Rapaczynski and Wiktor Osiatynski, on whom the non-Polish reader must depend. For their most comprehensive statements in English, see Rapaczynski, "Constitutional Politics in Poland," *University of Chicago Law Review* (Spring 1991): 595–631, and Osiatynski, "Poland's Constitutional Ordeal," *EECR* (Spring 1994): 29–32.

17. According to Rapaczynski, a similar rule was already enacted in the "fall of 1990" in the form of a statute (op. cit., 605, fn. 19). Whatever that statute may have provided for, it was not an elaborate set of rules for constitution making as in the case of the Constitutional Act of April 23, 1992. For the origins of the latter, cf. *EECR* (Spring 1992), 9ff.

18. I have only the Hungarian text: "A Lengyel Köztársaság Alkotmánya Megalkotásáról és Elfogadásáról (On the Creation and Ratification of the Constitution of the Polish Republic)," in K. Tóth, ed., *Kelet-Európa Uj Alkotmányai* (Szeged: JATE Press, 1997), 183–85. The new, 1997 Polish Constitution is available in English in Institute of Public Affairs *Constitution Making Process* (Warsaw: IPA, 1998): 255–326.

19. See reports on Poland in *EECR* 1, 1 (1992): 2; and *EECR* 1, 2 (1992): 12–14.

20. See report in *EECR* 4, 3 (1995): 17.

21. "After Walesa," *EECR* 4, 4 (1995): 10. Osiatynski goes on to argue that under the threat of an authoritarian reversion Kwasniewski could put the opposition in an impossible situation: either to except the constitution prepared by the coalition along with the legitimacy bonus to the government or to accept responsibility for the new elites' later authoritarian acts, which could have been constrained by a new constitution. It soon became obvious that Osiatinsky was not right on several points. (1) Kwasniewski wished to accelerate the process, even against the will of his own partisans, as his bluff concerning an independent constituent assembly was to show (report, *EECR* [Winter 1996]). (2) He tried to guarantee the development of Constitutionalism even if the project failed, as it is shown by his proposal to strengthen the Constitutional Tribunal through apparently using the amendment rule (report, *EECR* [Spring-Summer 1996]). (3) The Constitutional Committee remained open to inputs from a variety of sources, and it cannot be said that it produced merely the constitution of the governing coalition. Thus the choice offered to the opposition was not really the one Osiatinsky feared. Finally, (4) success in constitution making did little to relegitimate the governing coalition that went on to lose the 1997 elections shortly after the new basic law went into effect.

22. Because of internal divisions, the committee agreed to produce no draft of its own, but to receive drafts from other legally specified sources that would later be unified or integrated It was a miracle, given the many submitted drafts, that the job could be accomplished in this manner.

23. See report, *EECR* (Summer 1995): 17–23; Osiatynski, "After Walesa," 37.

24. The change was passed by the Sejm that for the first time made popular ratification compulsory rather than merely possible. Osiatynski, "Poland's Constitutional Ordeal," 36. The lower chamber could still apparently use the ordinary amendment route for constitutional change.

25. I am relying in this context on Osiatynski's convincing presentation in "Poland's Constitutional Ordeal," 32–36.

26. The agreements do not refer to ratification by popular referendum but do not exclude it. Such a referendum is currently required by the law on referenda—1989 [XVII]—and was included in all three draft proposals submitted to Parliament: András Bragyova, *Az új Alkotmány egy Koncepciója* (Budapest: Hungarian Academy of Science, 1995) and Ágnes Maczó Nagy, *Új Magyar Alkotmány* (Budapest: Inter Leones, 1995), and Hungarian Ministry of Justice, "A Magyar Köztársaság Alkotmányának Szabályozási Koncepciója," draft (Budapest, February 1995).

27. A Magyar, "Szocialista Párt és a Szabad Demokraták Szövetsége." *Koaliciós Megállapodása,* Budapest, June 24, 1994, unpublished ms.

28. See J. Kis, "A rendszerváltást lezáró alkotmány," *Népszabadság* (August 19, 1994), Bragyova, *Az új alkotmány egy koncepciója,* 19.

29. "Megállapodás az új alkotmány megalkotásáról," Budapest, May 4, 1995 (originally signed by leaders of the parliamentary fractions of five out of six parties).

30. The prime minister was less protected in the Little Constitution than his Hungarian counterpart, because that document established a constructive vote of no-confidence merely as one possibility (and therefore an irrelevancy) alongside a traditional vote of no-confidence that could still remove a prime minister even when his successor was not simultaneously nominated (Article 66). There was also individual responsibility for ministers, which would have made it difficult for a Polish minister of justice to preempt parliamentary discussion by producing his own draft, something that indeed happened in Hungary (Article 67). For a contrast, see paragraphs 33(4) and 39/A(1) of the Hungarian Constitution.

31. See reports in *EECR* 2, 1(2) (1993): 8–9; 2(2) (1993):10–11.

32. See report in *EECR* 4, 2 (1995): 20.

33. See report in *EECR* 5, 2 and 3 (1996): 17.

34. *EECR* 5, 1 (1996): 18.

35. "A Magyar Köztársaság Alkotmányának Szabályozási Koncepciója."

36. "Megállapodás az új alkotmány megalkotásáról," Budapest, May 4, 1995 (signed by leaders of the parliamentary fractions of five out of six parties). The part of the agreement concerning an amendment moratorium did not find its way into law or into the House Rules.

37. See A. Sajó, "How the Rule of Law Killed Hungarian Welfare Reform," *EECR* 5(1) (1996): 31–41. Forgetting for the moment that reform was only slowed down and not "killed" even in the author's own presentation, and that in his view it was not the rule of law but the quest for material justice that did the harm, I agree with the basic thrust of this article.

38. It is of course hermeneutically absurd to claim that the Court "only" interprets but does not or should not change the Constitution.

39. "Megmarad-e a fekete gólya," interview in *Népszabadság* (August 19, 1995). Three years before, in the famous "Zétényi" decision on retroactive justice, the Court postulated a rather different role for itself: the defense of the continuity of the rule of law against all calls for a second revolution. From a legal point of view at that time the Court refused to recognize that what occurred in Hungary was a revolution at all. On this, see Arato, "Revolution, Restoration, and Legitimation," chapter 3, this text.

40. Those who think that the Court is currently rather close to the positions of the three center right opposition parties obviously think that these two options are only one. It is hard to believe that the opposition parties, so elated by the reversals suffered by a govern-

ment so strong in mandates at the hand of the Court, would have voted in the last parliamentary session to reverse one of its decisions.

41. At one time the president of the Court entertained the idea that the Court may be able to review constitutional amendments. He never claimed, however, that amendments could be judged unconstitutional merely because they contradicted court decisions, and certainly not because following the existing amendment rule could be construed as unconstitutional. The whole idea of reviewing constitutional amendments was, it seems, eventually abandoned. Thus the constituent activity of the Court cannot extend to transforming the existing revision rule.

42. Judges need to be nominated by the majority of a parliamentary committee in which all parties with a recognized caucus get one vote. They are to be elected through the two-thirds vote of Parliament (*A Magyar Köztársaság Alkotmánya*, 32/A pars. 5 and 6). Between 1990 and 1994 the center right governmental coalition could neither nominate nor elect on its own. Between 1994 and 1998 the center left coalition could elect but could not nominate. Since 1998 the new center right government can nominate if it has the support of a small right-wing party outside of it, but cannot elect. The few candidates who have made it through this process are not among the country's more distinguished jurists. Responding to this situation, Chief Justice Sólyom began to promote the extraconstitutional solution of prolongation of judges already in office by a procedure that could evade the high consensus requirements for appointment. As far as I can tell, this effort has failed.

43. The Court denied the right of Parliament to interpose its own referendum, with rather different questions, when the necessary number of signatures for the calling of a compulsory popular referendum was already authenticated (962/B/1997). This was, in my view, a sound piece of judicial interpretation in defense of direct democratic rights clearly established by the Constitution, even if the Court violated an earlier precedent (3/1996 II. 23) to reach this correct decision. To be sure, in the United States, at least, it would have been customary to state the fact of the reversal of an early precedent, "wrongly decided." The Hungarian Constitutional Court tried instead, in my view unsuccessfully, to make the two relevant cases entirely different. This mistaken strategy of argumentation does not change to soundness and the constitutional conservatism of the 1997 decision that was made in the face of unattractive attempt by Parliament to deny popular rights that were to be sure themselves manipulated by the political right.

44. In my view it was unfortunate that the committee adopted a two-step approach and offered only guidelines for the first plenary discussion instead of a draft constitution.

45. This draft was produced by the committee after incorporating all possible objections to its guidelines in 1996. Because of the objections of two right-wing parties to continued constitution making without consultative referenda and the one-sided abrogation of the coalition of a moratorium on amendments under current rules, this draft never had a chance to be submitted to Parliament. I refer to it [1998 draft] only to indicate the direction the project was likely to move under the guidelines (1996 Guidelines A [May], B [June] or C [October]). I also refer to the Ministry of Justice proposal from 1994 as MJ Proposal.

46. The 1998 draft returned to the 1989 formulation that in legally defined cases (popular sovereignty) is exercised also through referenda. This draft leaves open the possibility of keeping the law as it currently is: Referenda can be called on the basis of petitions by 100,000 people and must be called if supported by 200,000 people. There is, however, a list of issues, including constitutional change, on which referenda cannot be held (pars. 94 and 95).

47. I am relying here on the proposal of the Ministry of Justice (hereafter MJ Proposal) produced in February 1995 that presented three variants to replace the current regulation (32–34). The first two involved direct elections and election by a chamber expanded with delegates chosen for this purpose. These options were bound to fail. The third option invoked the Greek example—the only European one where a single chamber elects the president. It involved dissolution of Parliament if the president could not be elected in three rounds by (successively fewer) qualified majorities. The new Parliament would get three chances as well, and only in the very last (sixth) round would the president be chosen by a simple majority. This procedure would have of course a far better chance than the current Hungarian regulation to achieve the latter's stated purpose: the election of a president by consensus rather than governmental fiat.

48. Guidelines A IV.8d. This limitation was taken out of subsequent drafts, but instead it was added that the Constitutional Court generally does not have the right of review over decisions of the courts. Guidelines B VI. 1a; Guidelines C VI. 1–4; C also proposes that the current list of those with standing be reduced. Both of these limits are abandoned by the 1997 draft, which gives standing either to a vast list (variant A) or (variant B) to all (par. 173c) and restores the ability to review ordinary court decisions if an unconstitutional rule is implicated in the decision (par. 173 d). Note that the various proposals to limit the Constitutional Court came from representatives of almost all the parties but also from the progressive inability of the drafting committee to continue to agree on any provisions that would limit the Court.

49. The distinction between rights of citizens and state goals is gone in the 1998 draft. But the relevant social rights tend to be defined within the limits of the government's budgetary capacities [pars. 40–47].

50. I had the opportunity to submit to the drafting committee a recommendation concerning the advantages and disadvantages of these and other options and the possibility of combining options.

51. The Bulgarian constitution makers were able to do just this. I called this fact to the rather amused attention of the subcommittee dealing with public law issues at the time of the 1994 coalition negotiations. The inability of East Europeans to take one another seriously is rather striking. I should have perhaps referred to the dual amendment structure of the *Grundgesetz,* but I thought and still think that a mechanism that makes parts of the constitution unchangeable gives too much power to a Constitutional Court that could very well interpret such a structure in an expansive manner.

52. It was to be sure not a good idea to even slightly open the door to an interpretation according to which the Court could not review the procedures followed in the case of amendments [governmental draft p. 81 seeks to make the distinction between "formal criteria" and control of contents]. It seems to me true in any case a court could review a piece of legislation called an amendment, if it does not, according to its view, procedurally qualify as an amendment under the amendment rule.

53. Garlicki, "The Presidency in the New Constitution," *EECR* (Spring-Summer 1997): 81–89.

54. Ibid.

55. Osiatynski, "A Brief History of the Constitution," 7.

56. Pawel Spiewak, "The Battle for a Constitution," *EECR* 6, 2(3) (1997): 94.

57. Ewa Letowska, "A Constitution of Possibilities," *EECR* 6, 2(3) (1997): 80.

58. "The Battle for a Constitution," 94.

59. "A Constitution of Possibilities," 80–81.
60. Ibid., 78.
61. Osiatynski, "A Brief History of the Constitution," 75.
62. Osiatynski (op. cit., 76) makes this claim that does not fully convince me.
63. This is especially true after the 1997 election when the Solidarity government came to power with the goal of amending a constitution they disliked. For this effort they had neither the necessary two-thirds majority nor even the support of the coalition partner Freedom Union, one of the architects of the new Constitution.
64. Spiewak, op. cit., 91–92.
65. See report, *EECR* 6 2(3) (1997): 26.

CHAPTER 7. FORMS OF CONSTITUTION MAKING AND THEORIES OF DEMOCRACY

1. To Carl Schmitt, form really does not matter; all forms are problematic. No procedure can be defined in advance. Only the "who" of the *pouvoir constituant* matters, not the how, and not even the specific agent of the *pouvoir constituant.* The presence of *pouvoir constituant* identification with form legitimates a variety of possible forms of "sovereign dictatorship," e.g., all efforts in France from 1791 to Napoleon's three plebiscites. See *Verfassungslehre* [1928] seventh and unchanged edition (Berlin: Duncker & Humblot, 1989).

2. Kelsen to be sure restricts the "legal" concept of constitution in the material sense to "the rules that regulate the creation of general norms" or "legislation" (*General Theory of Law and State* [Cambridge, Mass.: Harvard University Press, 1945], 124), and only on the level of political theory does he concede the inclusion of those "norms that regulate the creation and competence of the highest executive and judicial organs" (ibid., 258–59). The more restricted legal usage he argues for has little purpose and is in fact hardly tenable given Kelsen's own argument that legislative, executive, and judicial functions cannot be neatly differentiated among three entirely separate branches of government.

3. Ibid., 125. While Schmitt rejects understanding the constitution primarily in terms of its "formal" character, his own distinction of constitution and constitutional law makes sense only on the basis of something like the material and formal distinction (*Verfassungslehre* [1928], 11–20). Otherwise the idea of the core, or essence, or spirit of the constitution that he considers solely within the "competence" of the constituent power (and not of any revision rule) would have no content. The constitutional laws that can be legitimately altered in his conception through amendment are evidently parts of the constitution in the formal but not in the material sense. In fact it is a key part of Kelsen's conception that a constitution in the formal sense may include laws that are not part of the constitution in the material sense. The reverse is also true, according to him. As the example of U.S. judicial review and the resulting multitude of precedents show, it is possible for a practice or a rule to be part of the material constitution that is not provided for by the written constitution or any of its amendments. Finally both Kelsen (124) and Schmitt (18) agree that the special forms of the constitution providing for stability exist for the sake of the material constitution, and not the other way around. It is because a material constitution is worth protecting that we establish and insulate it with the devices of a constitution in the formal sense.

4. See H. L. A. Hart's, *Concept of Law* (Oxford: Oxford University Press, 1961).

5. See Friedrich Hayek, *The Constitution of Liberty* (Chicago: University of Chicago Press, 1960).

6. In particular the legal positivists: Austin, Kelsen, and Hart.

7. Most recently: Jacques Derrida; but it was Hannah Arendt who wrestled with this question most dramatically. Cf *On Revolution* (New York: Viking, 1965).

8. See Jean Foyer, "The Drafting of the French Constitution of 1958," in R. A. Goldwin and A. Kaufman, eds., *Constitution Makers on Constitution Making: The Experience of Eight Nations* (Washington, D.C.: American Enterprise Institute for Public Policy Research, 1983), 9–10; David Thompson, *Democracy in France Since 1870,* 5th ed. (Oxford: Oxford University Press, 1969), 232–37.

9. See Foyer, op. cit., 9, and especially Michel Debré, "The Constitution of 1958," in W. G. Andrews and S. Hoffman, *The Impact of the Fifth Republic in France* (Albany: SUNY Press, 1981), 4–5. Debré's claim that Charles de Gaulle convened a constituent assembly is technically incorrect. His claim that in France the proportional electoral system produced a plurality of parties is not borne out by the history of the Third Republic, which he also accuses of representing assembly and party government, in spite of its majoritarian two-round electoral system. Debré's reference to that electoral rule is hard to understand (p. 2) especially given the ability of the same system to produce "cohesive majorities" in the Fifth Republic. According to Debré, it was out "concern for democracy" that General de Gaulle did not, erroneously, present his own draft constitution in 1945, at a time when he "seemed omnipotent" (4).

10. A majoritarian, two-round electoral system as that of the Third and Fifth Republics may produce greater disproportionality than even plurality systems because it keeps parties in the race that will get votes but in the end few seats. Thus the same system may not produce as a great a reduction of the number of parties as a plurality, first-past-the-post system. In a plurality system those parties survive that are capable of taking first place in single-member districts. In a relatively homogenous society only a few parties have this ability, hence the tendency of plurality elections toward two-party systems. In a two-round electoral system those parties survive that are capable of forming potentially successful coalitions for the second round. This means that parties that do not lead or even take second place in any district can manage to survive and play an important role. According to this line of reasoning, PR did not create the multiparty structure of the Fourth Republic, but only allowed it to survive from the time of the Third. Only the introduction of English-type plurality voting that a circle of jurists around Michel Debré apparently wanted could have reduced the number of parties.

11. W. Osiatynski rightly argues ("Poland's Constitutional Ordeal," *EECR* 3[2] [1994]: 29–38) that proportional representation has special relevance to constituent assemblies where the issue is not governability, but the inclusion of all important forces in the process. He does neglect the likelihood, however, that an assembly elected by PR is likely to preserve it.

12. *On Revolution* (New York: Viking, 1965), 144ff.

13. For the various levels of the concept of revolution, systemic, phenomenological, hermeneutic, and legal, see A. Arato, "Revolution, Restoration, and Legitimacy," chapter 3, this text.

14. A. V. Dicey considers the English Constitution to be judge-made. While the point is historically plausible, it conflicts with the idea of Parliament being simultaneously a con-

stituent assembly within the model of sovereignty. See the introduction to *The Law of the Constitution* [1885, 1915] (Indianapolis, Ind.: Liberty Classics, 1982).

15. See her sole reference in this context to Karl Loewenstein's "Verfassungsrecht und Verfassungsrealität," in *On Revolution*, fn. 7, chapter 4, page 300.

16. The role of the Western Allies can be safely disregarded in this context. They wished to have a constituent assembly and popular referenda and failed to impose these. They wished to establish Federalism, but the German Länder themselves wanted the very same kind of system, and the specific brand of center and federal relations was developed by the German participants themselves. Thus it seems Peter Merkl is right to conclude that "the Allied influence was more ostentatious than real" (in *The Origin of the West German Republic* [New York: Oxford University Press, 1963], 114–15), even if the negative public response to their behavior is not to be neglected.

17. See David Thomson, *Democracy in France since 1870*, 5th ed. (Oxford: Oxford University Press, 1969), 265. His negative and summary description is more or less confirmed by the details presented by participant Jean Foyer (op. cit., 15–17), who apparently thinks that because of the exclusively parliamentary rule of constitutional revision of the Fourth Republic that stymied genuine constitutional change, there was no other way than to more or less bypass Parliament altogether. The fact, however, that Parliament voted for a revision rule eliminating its own role, or reducing it to a merely advisory one, indicates that it was not at that historical moment at least impossible for a process including Parliament to structurally revise the rest of the constitutional rules. A procedure could have been devised that gave the president an important though not totally dominant role. Since Parliament voted for the latter type of revision rule, it also could have voted for the former.

18. The famous lines "je suis le pouvoir constituant" were apparently actually uttered. See R. R. Palmer, *The Age of Democratic Revolution* (Princeton, N.J.: Princeton University Press, 1959), I, 214.

19. For the differentiation of four types of constituent processes among the states of the period of the American Revolution, see Palmer's subtle analysis in *The Age of Democratic Revolutions*, 217–28.

Evidently, a taxonomy based on the agency of (or in the case of unwritten constitutions, historical process of) constitution making is not the only one possible. Disregarding the different juridical statuses of constitution-making instances even in the case of the Philadelphia Convention 1787 and the *Assemblée Constitutante* of 1789–91, which he specifically compares, Jon Elster, for example, proposes that we examine constitution-making assemblies from the point of view of a more differentiated analytical framework ("Constitution Making in Eastern Europe: Rebuilding the Boat in the Open Sea," *Public Administration*, 71, 1–2). He stresses the following issues: (1) who convenes the assembly, and does it remain dependent on the convener; (2) what internal rules does the assembly adopt and in particular whether the process is a public one; and (3) what process of ratification is adopted. Elster, moreover, treats these three issues in terms of an important distinction among upstream, midstream, and downstream political legitimacy. None of these criteria of course applies to the case of unwritten constitutions, but my own criterion of agency or source is obviously strained in those cases as well.

More importantly, in the case of my other four types many of the issues that interest Elster automatically follow from type of constitution-making agency involved. Only in the case of the second model can the assembly become fully free from its convener; by the Sieyèsian theory this type of assembly indeed must become free in this sense even if in

1791, in the battle over the possibility of a royal veto of the constitutional draft, it took Sieyès and his side a lot of effort to assert this conception successfully. To my knowledge the issue was never subsequently in doubt in the legal sense for the model in question.

In the case of a model like that of Philadelphia on the other hand, the relationship between convener and assembly remains in doubt to the end, and only self-limitation on at least one of the sides can avoid a fateful conflict of relationship of convener and constitution-making instance, a situation of dual power. In 1787 it was Congress that practiced such self-limitation when it forwarded, in contradistinction to its own rules, the Constitution for ratification by the states in a process in which nine yeses would amount to approval.

On the other hand, in Germany during of the making of the *Grundgesetz,* where the constitution makers had to settle for a lower status to begin with, it was they who practiced self-limitation, and in the case of the one conflict they had with the prime ministers of the Länder, they lost (P. Merkl, *The Origin of the West German Republic* [New York: Oxford University Press, 1963], 65–66). But in 1948–49, of course, the same political parties dominating both the Länder and the council mediated most potential conflicts. In the cases of constitution making by normal legislatures the constitution-making instance is in any case not emancipated from previous legal limits. The issue of internal rules is in fact highly variable and unsuitable for the purposes of classification.

The all-important procedural issue of the publicity of proceedings can, however, be resolved by reference to my types. Executive constitution making is never public; the normal parliamentary method always must be, at least in the formal sense. In reality of course the actual decisions here too, as in all cases, will tend to gravitate to secret informal sessions, which, however, as the recent Spanish case shows are exposed to leaks and revelations to the press. Constituent assemblies and conventions finally are in theory free to follow the original U.S. (secret sessions) or French (public) models. But under contemporary conditions the demand of publicity is very hard to evade, and it is hard to see how any national assembly could avoid the combination of formal publicity and informal, secret decision-making characteristic of normal parliaments.

For these reasons there is either no need or no opportunity to use Elster's first two distinctions for taxonomic purposes. His final one, the method of ratification, however, could be used to add five subtypes to each of my first four types: no ratification, ratification by national referendum, ratification by provincial electorates, by provincial assemblies, and by special provincial conventions. In the case of a federal state all five are in theory possible, while in the case of centralized states only the first two are possible. It is, moreover, all-important in the case of referenda whether they are preceded by significant public discussions or not. But these differences and the large number of subtypes they yield in principle do not require that the simpler set of five types be replaced by a set of twenty-five or fifty types, of which many were never historically realized.

20. On this point, I rely on the report of my student Fiorenza Möring as well as conversations with another student, Carlos Enrique Peruzzotti.

21. See F. Rubio-Llorente, "The Writing of the Constitution of Spain" (with commentary by J. P. Perez-Llorca), in *Constitution Makers on Constitution Making,* as well as Andrea Bonime-Blanc, *Spain's Transition to Democracy. The Politics of Constitution-Making* (Boulder, Colo.: Westview Press, n.d.).

22. I would not, however, refer to it as a predemocratic parliament, since it was evidently elected under a transitional constitution (or organic law) that was already a democratic one

(cf. A. Bonime-Blanc, op. cit., 35). Granted some institutions sometimes survive even in the midst of constitutional ruptures. In France in 1791 the monarchy existed through the whole constituent process and survived; something analogous was true for state legislatures under the U.S. Constitution. But in these rather different cases the constituent body at least was annihilated with the success of its enterprise.

23. See chapter 6, this text.

24. See, e.g., Kelsen, op. cit.

25. *On Revolution*, 141 and fn. 9, 300–1.

26. One could criticize Arendt for both an element of inconsistency as well as a lack of realism for making a virtue of the fortunate but entirely contingent state of affairs that the U.S. Constitution could be more the product of already constituted governments than the French Constitution of 1791. Of course the difference in starting points made all the difference in the world. The governments, or as she prefers to treat them, the "political bodies," of the states already rested on republican rather than hierarchical estate principles. Even before Edmund Burke's critique, but relying on the U.S. example, the followers of J. J. Mounier sought in France to build the new constitutional monarchy on at least some of the constituted powers, like the inherited monarchy, and they decisively failed in this attempt both because of the nature of the inherited institutions and the politics of their incumbents. (See especially R. R. Palmer, *The Age of Democratic Revolutions I*, 489–502.) Sieyès of course tried to make a virtue of this state of affairs, which gave him an opportunity to solve, supposedly for once and for all, the problem of founding a new political society. But in the given situation it was almost impossible to refute the case that he made for the Constituent Assembly to become the embodiment of the nation as the constituent power and the sole source of power and legal authority.

While there is no point in denying the difficulty of the French following the U.S. road, it is nonetheless well worth emphasizing the negative outcome of their particular solution that was to inspire so many subsequent constitution makers. Arendt's point is not so much that the French could have acted otherwise than they did, a point made by Edmund Burke, who believed that the estate institutions of the past could have been preserved and built upon. Her point is much more that the Americans too could have, but did not, make two errors: losing their constituent power by sacrificing the constituted powers of the states, and deriving both the new system of power and the authority of the constitution from the same source. According to Arendt, the Americans were of course in an advantageous position since their preestablished powers were small republics and thus embodied precisely the political form they wished to establish for the new federation that represented among other things the solution of a new constitution built upon constituted powers. In particular the political institutions and constitutions of the states who elected the delegates to the Constitutional Convention, and to whom the work of ratification was to be entrusted remained in full force during and after the constituent process (165–66). In fact preserving a federally organized constituent was a difficult struggle at the Philadelphia Convention. But both the voting rules initially adopted as well as the ratification procedure emerging from the convention implied that the states would survive at the very least as important elements of the union whose constituent power, and later amending power, would not be based merely on the collection of individuals in the country as a whole.

27. She does not realize that Woodrow Wilson's idea of the court as "a kind of constitutional assembly in permanent session" is inconsistent with her argument, since such an assembly would have power as well as authority.

28. See *Federalist* #49, as well as analyses by Ackerman in "Neo Federalism," in *Constitutionalism and Democracy* (Cambridge: Cambridge University Press, 1988), Forrest McDonald, *Novus Ordo Seclorum* (Lawrence: Kansas University Press, 1985), 279–80, and John P. Roche, "The Convention as a Case Study in Democratic Politics," in Levy, ed., *Essays on the Making of the Constitution,* 175–212. Ackerman too misses the drama by assuming extra-legality and missing the desperate effort to remain "always under law."

29. Note that she thus departs from her earlier notion in the *Human Condition* according to which the foundation of republics is production and not action, useful for creating a wall around public freedom, which is thereby institutionalized as public space. *On Revolution* links the notion of the architect of a new city to violence, and indeed crime.

30. Arendt's enthusiasm for the U.S. effort at constitution making was and is well known to be tempered with criticisms. She believed that the Americans turned too quickly to limiting the powers of government and missed institutionalizing that public freedom the exercise of which created the constitution itself. Nevertheless, this point is not made consistently, because as a somewhat reluctant liberal Arendt also supports the establishment of civil liberties as one of the mechanisms protecting the private sphere without which public participation is not possible. They help to guard politics from the impasse of a permanent revolution, which makes it impossible to produce a stable constitution, in her view the true "end" of revolution itself. Thus Arendt's criticism of the U.S. constitution reduces to the point that the Americans did not establish public freedom in the form of something like Thomas Jefferson's proposal for a ward system, a kind of "federalism within federalism," or elements of direct democracy as schools of citizenship and participation. This issue, however, is one of constitutional contents and does not relate to the method of constitution making directly. Arendt is very skeptical in relation to two earlier "proposals" of Jefferson that focused on constitutional politics, one concerning the desirability of periodic revolutions and the other involving a project of holding a constitutional convention in each generation. According to Arendt, the first idea confuses liberation and revolution, while the second disregards the importance of a stable system of legal authority for the institutionalization of republican government.

31. For example, the extremely problematic idea that the U.S. Constitution can be, has been, and should again if need be amended entirely outside the limits of Article V.

32. I myself tended to accept the argument idea for legal discontinuity in "Constitution and Continuity in the Transitions." But now it strikes me that a "revolution" against the Confederation Congress would have anticipated in form, though probably not in its political violence, the second French revolution of 1792 against the Legislative Assembly rather than the revolution of 1789 against the "old regime." No wonder that Madison spent so much effort at attempting to demonstrate the legality of the actions of the convention; it is a mistake to qualify these efforts as merely "legalistic." With the exception of his justifying the shift to a form of ratification by only nine states, where he indeed uses a lawyerly trick, and in the end concedes that the convention "exceeded its powers," Madison's arguments for legality in the narrow sense are in fact serious and worthy of consideration (*Federalist* #40). Evidently the convention did exceed its very real authority in more than the one admitted sense: its actions were "informal," its privileges were "assumed," its propositions were "unauthorized" (ibid.). But it was not a vain hope that these irregularities could still be made consistent with legality, i.e., be blotted out afterward as long as such an effort included not only the action of the voters and delegates to the state conventions, but first the actions of the duly elected authorities as well, that maintained their status from 1787 to

1791. Madison unmistakably argues in other words that the convention did not have "real and final powers for the establishment of the Constitution of the United States . . . [its] powers were merely advisory and recommendatory; that they were so meant by the States and so understood by the convention" and the Constitution proposed would be "no more consequence than the paper on which it is written, unless it be stamped with approbation by those to whom it is addressed." Ackerman undoubtedly would interpret the addressees as "We the people," as suggested by later sections of *Federalist* #40, which he understandably stresses, but the given context indicates Congress and the states as well, at the very least as the only *legal* channel through which the people could be addressed. Madison himself, moreover, spent considerable effort trying to lobby the Confederation Congress, to vote favorably on the Constitution and to follow the convention's recommendations on ratification (Roche, op. cit.). Missing the reasons why he did so, and the fact that he was in significant part successful in this effort, leads to the postulate of a revolutionary rupture in the legal sense where there could not be one on the level of politics precisely because political authority in America in the late eighteenth century, before and after the making of the Constitution, was mainly in the hands of unchallenged state governments under state constitutions. If therefore the principle of the Constitutional Convention deriving its authority ultimately from the people was a revolutionary one, this revolutionary principle was already institutionalized and as we might say today a self-limiting one (R. R. Palmer, I. 231). That means, however, that the revolutionary principle was circumscribed by law, a law that represented the principle of continuity amidst of constitutional change.

But if it were a better interpretation to postulate the dominant position of "the revolutionaries" in the period of constitution making, and to reduce their efforts to stay within the law to "mere show" (Carl Schmitt); if we are to insist on the convention's real, and final power to establish a constitution for the United States and to sweep aside all established powers, a power limited only by the needs of final ratification, the dualistic formula would become in effect a monistic one. What becomes difficult to explain in that case is how the constituted authorities managed to gain so much influence over the design, indeed enshrining their position through the unamendable rule concerning the equal representation of the states in the Senate, how in the end the Federalists were forced to concede a Bill of Rights aimed at that time only against the new Congress but not the states, and so on. It would be far better in my view to see the making of the U.S. Constitution as a special combination of break and continuity, revolution and legality, that is, as a revolution within continuity and in a tenuous and contestable sense within legality as well. It would be better to affirm, less ambiguously than Ackerman, that the dualistic outcome in America was coupled with a dualistic process.

33. I must admit that this is the meaning I originally gave to Ackerman's dualistic conception. He himself, however, prefers another interpretation, one emphasizing revolution and legal discontinuity.

34. Of course Ackerman too can appeal to Arendt's authority, by reaffirming her stress on the generic link between revolution and constitution creation, and her insistence that the process of constitution making is fundamentally a revolutionary process. This, however, is not the same as to stress the dualistic character of such a process, which in one version of her thesis Arendt also stressed. Here lies the source of Ackerman's methodological ambivalence with respect to dualistic politics, and expressed by his uncritical and unreflective (though hardly enthusiastic) acceptance even of the option of constitution making through a sovereign constituent assembly, and his apparent lack of awareness of the full

distance between the classical U.S. and European formulas. Of course, it was the European model that has been most often associated with the revolutionary tradition. But the distance between this and the procedure of the Philadelphia Convention is significantly reduced to the extent that Ackerman puts too much emphasis on the illegality of the way of the second. Evidently, the delegates of the Estates General acted illegally when they resolved to merge the three estates and to stay in session whatever their convener, the monarch, desired until they gave France an entirely new constitution. The argument for the illegality of the Philadelphia Convention is superficially similar. Congress authorized the convention to amend the Articles of Confederation. They unilaterally produced an entirely new one. The amendment rule of the articles required unanimous ratification by all the states. The convention again unilaterally opted for ratification by nine out of thirteen states as sufficient. Moreover they moved the site of ratification from the state legislatures to specially elected state conventions, resembling their own irregular, quasi-revolutionary form ("Neofederalism," in *Constitutionalism and Democracy,* 157–62). Against all this, however, the differences between the two assemblies remain significant as well. The Philadelphia Convention assumed only constitution-making powers. Moreover it did not fully assume them, as did the French assembly that eliminated the royal veto and permitted no popular ratification of their work, the Constitution of 1791. The U.S. Constitution on the other hand, which contained the new rules of ratification (Article VII) was submitted to Congress, which arguably approved them at least tacitly by further submitting the document to the states. It was given the opportunity to insist and indeed could have insisted on the illegality of the acts of the convention and refused to follow Article VII, insisting on adhering to the legality of the Articles of Confederation instead. Moreover, the state legislatures could have refused to call for the election of special ratificatory conventions that bypassed them, but also did not do so. A full rupture with the old regime would have become possible only after such refusal, if the supporters of the convention attempted and succeeded to ratify the Constitution in spite of the resistance of the constituted powers. But this scenario would have implied a revolution not against an authority deemed tyrannical (as the Revolutions of 1776, and 1789), but a revolution against an admittedly poorly working, but nevertheless republican government. What, however, is a second revolution against a democratic authority if not a step toward permanent revolution or counterrevolution?

35. New Haven, Conn.: Yale University Press, 1992. Most strikingly he misses the extremely unusual nature of the figure of George Washington, who was the one presidential aspirant in history until Nelson Mandela who did not use his great potential influence at the constitutional assembly to try to build a strong, presidential institution.

36. It may be useful to recall here a precedent that Ackerman may be under the shadow of, though without mentioning it. The British model of parliamentary sovereignty never represented in itself a method of constitution making and has often been used in Britain to deny the legitimacy of a written constitution that would establish a second, entrenched or "insulated" dimension of lawmaking (cf. H. L. A. Hart, *The Concept of Law* [Oxford: Oxford University Press, 1961], 145–47). According to the dominant interpretation, the only thing Parliament logically cannot do is to bind the hands of its successor by entrenching constitutional legislation. No matter how many times over such legislation would be entrenched, at the beginning lies a vote that needed only a simple majority. The future Parliament can then dismantle even a whole scaffolding of entrenchment by repealing the original simple majority vote to entrench and then to remove all successive entrenchments. This case points, beyond the question of interest, to the issue of validity and even legiti-

macy in a broader sense. Hart, however, seems to be right, both choices can claim validity because on the bases of the ultimate rule of recognition of the British Constitution ("whatever Parliament decides is law") one can equally deny that present Parliament can be stopped from entrenching fundamental laws of its choice, or that future parliaments can be limited by such entrenched laws. What decides the issue in favor of the second position is probably tradition and therefore traditional legitimacy, but there is a modern principle of legitimacy involved as well. By what right, the courts may very well ask, would a parliament very much like its predecessors (who claimed no such right) as well as its successors drastically limit the freedom of future parliaments, and decide a whole range of issues that they will not be able to ordinarily decide? It is difficult to answer such a question. The argument applies to a purely parliamentary model of constitution making in general, and especially one that would in any way make future constitutional revision more difficult.

What I am driving at is that parliamentary constitution making may very well have the motivation to insulate its constitutional product, but may run into legitimacy problems when attempting to do so.

37. In the Polish case at least he advocates what is in effect the model of Massachusetts in 1780, the only instance of the dualistic method producing a constitution in a nonfederal state, namely, a special Constitutional Convention that would submit its document for approval to the sitting Parliament, before popular ratification in a referendum. His advice in Russia is less clear, and it is here that he entertains the possibility of electing a constituent assembly of the European type, though he still seems to prefer a convention focusing on constitutional matters while the normal legislature remains in charge of the economy and economic reform. It is worth noting that his preference is suddenly justified only pragmatically. The case for a separate constitutional convention against all other options is now said to be the following: (1) the isolation of the problem of constitutional order from many short-term issues also on the agenda, and (2) the creation of special incentives for a group to succeed at drafting a ratifiable constitution, a group whose future prestige would heavily depend on the success of this one enterprise (51, 52, 56). The argument is plausible, except for the fact that a high-visibility constitution-drafting committee of a regular parliament, a party deeply committed to the making of a new constitution or even a constituent assembly, could be similarly situated.

38. It was such a reflexive relation to the country's history, and not the desire to imitate the Americans, that led the framers of the *Grundgesetz,* or rather the governments of the Länder that chose the design of the constitution-making process itself that came to reflect the formal aspects of U.S. constitution making. Granted this method did not at first produce what the U.S. Constitution always had since the ratification of the Bill of Rights at the latest, itself a fruit of passionate public discussion, a high level of political legitimacy and identification.

39. Why principles, and why in the plural? When a particular practice will have to be derived from complex constellations of interests, traditions, learning, and temporal sequence, a principle rather than concrete models or sharply delineated rules may be the most normative theory on which we can or should insist. In this context I understand principles as normative standards at the porous borderlines between morals and law, and between universalist morals and situated ethics, which gain their validity in moral and ethical discourses in which we take various levels of situated givens (political culture, needs, and interests of participants, political history, and so on) into account (R. Dworkin, *Taking Rights Seriously* [Cambridge, Mass.: Harvard University Press, 1978], 22ff and 40ff, and J.

Habermas's interpretation of Dworkin in *Faktizität und Geltung* [Frankfurt/M: Suhrkamp Verlag, 1993]. A principle unlike a rule or a legal model is not generally derived from pre-existing legal norm, like a fundamental rule of recognition (Dworkin vs. Hart). Thus they have the advantage of being able to draw on moral resources that have not been formalized and that are available when appeal to legal resources would inevitably turn circular at moments of foundation. Principles can break this circle without resort to violence or arbitrary threats of force. It is for this reason that Arendt's appeal to a beginning that contains its own principle makes so much sense. But the use of principles need not be restricted to moments of rupture and we should not seek an organizational form in which a single principle of legitimacy is fully established. Principles can also help achieve political legitimacy when legal continuity can provide only conditions of security and predictability. Moreover, they are potentially plural and can help establish the authority of a beginning even where empirical political processes, based on strategic competition and pragmatic bargaining, play an important role.

In the case of principles, as Dworkin showed, there is no master principle of recognition that decides which principle has a priority to all others in processes of justification. This is why the appeal to principles inevitably commits us to consider a plurality, an advantage in practice even if it is a disadvantage in theory. In fact, only a plurality of principles can allow us to respect circumstances sufficiently, since a single principle may be too difficult to follow in any given case. A single principle, if insisted on too strongly, may turn out to be straitjacket similar to that of a concrete model. Only reference to a plurality of principles finally has the chance of plausibly canceling out the overly great role of situated interests and opinions, in the sense of the demanding conditions of the "veil of ignorance." From another point of view, only when a plurality of principles is taken seriously can one claim, in a complex society, that all relevant minorities and points of view have been accommodated in a dialogue based on mutual recognition and respect.

40. I believe that this is the point at which Arendt's idea of a beginning that contains its own principle misled her. For her such a beginning would have to be organized in line with her rather counterfactual normative model of politics. For a critique of confusing principles of legitimation and forms of organization, see Habermas, "Legitimation Problems in the Modern State," *Communication and the Evolution of Society* (Boston: Beacon, 1975), 178–205. Unfortunately many of Habermas's followers who speak of "deliberative democracy" have missed this insight. Of course Habermas's disinterest in forms of organization that could plausibly claim their legitimacy under democratic principles has at times been the source of the opposite error, the reduction of his theory to one without an institutional dimension.

41. But here too one can appeal to Madison. In his all-purpose argument in *Federalist* #40 the convention did not exceed its authority (except in one point where the rules were totally irrational); but if it did so, the framers acted in an unauthorized way for reasons of civic duty; and if this were not convincing, the critics should look at the result, which they would not want to reject merely because of its problematic origins. If a constitution according to him fully satisfied the difficult demands of republican (i.e., representative) government (and federalism) it would be a grave mistake to continue to look for an equally good or better outcome produced by a better process (at that time a second constitutional convention advocated by the anti-Federalists). The post–Bill of Rights liberal of course would add the institutionalized protection of fundamental rights to the marks of a normatively adequate constitution, justifying such a document without regard to specific origins.

42. Moreover, Rawl is definitely interested in the process by which a set of rules, originally accepted for pragmatic and perhaps strategic reasons, can gradually become tied up with an emerging civic identity, thus acquire "internal" powers of motivation. But even in this argument the way the rules initially are arrived at is not posed in any depth.

43. Quite evidently the Rawlsian discussion of the original position, more self-consciously than historically older contract theories, constructs an ideal and definitely not a historical context. He tells us that we are not to imagine the original position in terms of an actual assembly with bargaining and coalitions. The purpose of the ideal and hypothetical construct is to allow individuals to reflect on what institutions they would find just if they could assume a genuinely universal perspective. Rawls is above all interested in deducing, and even more justifying, his two principles of justice and in advocating forms of institutionalization compatible with them under specific historical circumstances. Thus, he too is first and foremost result-oriented when it comes to constitutions and brings in an idealized understanding of the origin of constitutions in his "four-stage sequence" in order to consider what should be taken into account when we consider the relationship of his principles of justice to institutionalization under concrete historical circumstances. The concept of the "veil of ignorance" is central in his construction because it gives him a way of imagining the nullification of "the effects of specific contingencies which put men at odds and tempt them to exploit social and natural circumstances to their own advantage," and the setting up of "a fair procedure so that the principles agreed to will be just." Most generally then, the veil of ignorance refers to a condition under which the actors "do not know how the various alternatives will affect their own particular case and they are obliged to evaluate principles solely on the basis of general considerations." *Theory of Justice* (Cambridge, Mass.: Harvard University Press, 1971), 136–37.

44. It is again important to note that in spite of the fact that in a footnote Rawls claims (I think implausibly) that his four-stage model reflects the history of the U.S. Constitution (196, fn. 1), what he produces is a set of critical instrument by which that (or any) constitution could be judged at any of its historical stages. Moreover, as Habermas rightly notices the political process to which Rawls's analysis was meant to apply, given the fact that he is writing under conditions where constitutional democracies already exist, is social reform. To the extent in other words that existing constitutions are found deficient in light of his principles, his model suggests liberal or social democratic reformism that would have to take historical givens into account.

45. "Bill of Rights," L. Levy, ed., *Essay, on the Making of the Constitution* (Oxford: Oxford University Press, 1969), 258–306.

46. *Democracy and the Market* (Cambridge: Cambridge University Press, 1991).

47. For more on the relationship of these principles, and on South Africa, see my essay "Constitutional Learning," (in English) in *Civil Társadalom, Forradalom és Alkotmány* (Budapest: Uj Mandátum, 1999), 333–55.

48. Niklas Luhmann, *A Sociological Theory of Law* (London: Routledge, 1985).

49. When not, it may be advisable to establish a ratification rule of some difficulty.

Index

Ackerman, Bruce, xii, xiii, xiv, 134, 140, 192, 193, 196, 255; Arendt and, 330n34; on constitution making, 131, 132, 191, 244, 245, 246; dualistic conception of, 248, 330n33; extralegality and, 329n28; on *Grundgesetz,* 245; legitimation and, 141; model by, 194–95, 243, 298n67; neo-federalism and, 133; on Philadelphia Convention, 246; on reprivatization/political justice, 191; revolutionary interpretation of, 131, 244, 247, 293n18; on U.S. Constitution, 243

actors, 88, 149–50, 229; civil society and, 67; ruling parties and, 67; self-limitation of, 65

Act XVII (1989). *See* two-thirds laws

Adorno, Theodore, 258n6

alkotmányozási kényszer, 201

Alliance of Free Democrats (SZDSZ), 33, 57, 62, 66, 98, 121, 122, 222, 223; civil society and, 124; constitution making and, 216, 221; judicial appointment and, 227; MDF and, 105, 110, 116, 146; pamphlet by, 107; petition campaign by, 63; stabilization program and, 186; transformation and, 93, 97, 101; Zétényi-Takács bill and, 103, 117

Alliance of Workers Councils, 56

Alliance of Young Democrats (FIDESZ), 33, 55, 57, 62, 63, 66, 121, 122, 222; civil society and, 124; coalition with, 226;

constitution making and, 204, 221; habeas corpus and, 220; reprivatization and, 117; system change and, 101

amendment process, 138, 143, 144, 238; in Bulgaria, 161; in Poland, 157, 225; U.S., 134

amendment rules, xii, 90, 91, 103, 140, 142, 151, 172, 177, 196, 197, 212, 217, 218, 221, 230, 245; amending, 155; in Hungary, 152, 154; parliamentarian, 105; in Poland, 161, 226; problems with, 232; purpose of, 229; Sejm-centered, 157

amendments, 137, 155, 161, 173, 177, 213, 251; ad hoc, 221; constitutional, 39, 162; frivolous use of, 135; in Hungary, 117, 203; model of, 159; multileveled structures of, 162; parliamentary, 227; in Poland, 203; referenda and, 225; unconstitutional, 162

American Revolution, 83, 84, 86, 279n11; constitutionalism and, 89; institutionalization of, 243; revolutionary tradition and, 91; system change and, 306n20

Andrásfalvy, Bertalan, 120

Antall, József, 97, 120, 184, 222, 223; Csurka and, 316n105; cynical Tocquevillianism and, 119; peaceful revolution and, 96; political legitimacy and, 33; reprivatization and, 109; transformation and, 93

276n59; as socialism, 259n10. *See also* economic liberalism
liberal oligarchies, 16–21, 22
Lijphart, Arend, 18, 19
Linz, Juan, x, 24, 28, 30, 261n44; on civilian-led authoritarian regimes, 27; on civil society/democratization, 29; on military dictatorships, 26
Little Constitution (1992), 203, 208, 210, 213, 214, 224; Article 106 of, 300nn79, 80, 301n84, 302n93; changing, 228, 301n84; prime minister and, 321n30; role of, 157; validity of, 202; Walesa and, 215
Loewenstein, Karl: on *Grundgesetz* framers, 233
Long Parliament, 135
Luhmann, Niklas, 189, 255; on rights/government ability, 315n98
lustration laws, 95, 113, 287n110, 310n54

Madison, James, xiv, 135, 136, 137, 238, 250, 251; Article V and, 291nn2, 3; conventions and, 242; revolution and, 243; U.S. Constitution and, 330n32. See also *Federalist Papers, The*
Magdalenka arrangements, 60
Magyar, Bálint: civil society and, 123
Magyar Forum, 105, 118, 285n95
Magyar Narancs, 221
Magyar Nemzet, 58
Maistre, Joseph de, 1, 2, 4, 6, 110
majoritarianism, 115, 206, 251, 286n96, 325n10; constitutionalism and, 264n66, 285n89; individual rights and, 292n9; parliamentary, 298n59
market economy, 31, 32, 95, 263n53; social democracy and, 259n18; transformation to, 4, 95
martial law, 51, 59, 60
Marx, Karl, 44, 89, 260n23; civil society and, 43; on revolutions, 1, 4, 5
mass movements: democratization and, 9; electoral participation by, 34; fundamentalist wings of, 67
Mazowiecki, Tadeusz, 34, 267–68n92; political legitimacy and, 33, 298n61

MDF. *See* Hungarian Democratic Forum
MDNP, 223; constitution making and, 221, 222
media, 73, 111, 187; control of, 75, 77, 94, 181, 184, 185, 186, 189; independence of, 76, 116, 152; institutionalization of, 75–76; parliamentizing, 116; politicizing, 116; popular culture and, 110
Michelet, Jules, 1
Michnik, Adam, 15, 17, 47, 62; civil society and, 43; new evolutionism of, 148; on radical reform, 46; on self-limiting revolution, 48; social movements and, 260n23; on social transformation, 45–46; totalitarianism theory of, 46
Mlynar, Zdenek: civil society and, 43
modernity, 9, 16, 122, 260n28, 283n69; completion of, 10; modernization and, 13
monism: in Hungary, 152–55; in Poland, 155–59
movements, 172; civil-society-based, 65; in Hungary, 54–58
MPP. *See* Hungarian Civic Party
MSZMP, 62, 110, 283n68, 298n64
MSZP. *See* Hungarian Socialist Party
Münchhausen, Baron, 175

nachholende Revolution, 11, 260n27
Nagy, Agnes Maczo, 223
Nagy, Imre, 14, 66, 99
Nagy, W. András, 103
Napoleon Bonaparte, 176, 192, 235
National Party, 18
National Revolutionary Front, xi
National Round Table (NKA), 14, 62, 67, 111, 117, 146; Communist Parliament and, 236
National Salvation Front (NSF), 159, 160, 163
neo-federalism, 133, 292n14
Network of Free Initiatives, 57
new *constitué,* 147–51
new evolutionism, x, 48, 61, 148, 173
NKA. *See* National Round Table
Nolte, Ernst, 4, 10, 258n6; analysis by, 6; incomplete revolution and, 5

About the Author

Dr. Andrew Arato was born in Budapest in 1944 and has lived in New York City since 1957. He earned his doctorate at the University of Chicago and has taught in Budapest, Montevideo, and Paris. He has participated in Hungarian politics since 1990, serving as a journalist for several periodicals and daily newspapers and as an informal political advisor to the SZDSZ. He is the author of *From Neo-Marxism to Democratic Theory,* co-author of *Civil Society and Political Theory,* and co-editor (since 1994) of *Constellations: An International Journal of Critical and Democratic Theory.*

Arato currently serves as the Dorothy Hirshon Professor in Political and Social Theory at the Graduate Faculty of Political and Social Science, New School University. He teaches constitutional theory, political sociology, and comparative politics focusing on the transitions to democracy.

In his spare time, Arato enjoys spending time with his wife, two children, and one grandchild.